Shojo Beat

Demon Love Spell

2

**STORY AND
ART BY
MAYU
SHINJO**

Story Thus Far

Miko Tsubaki is the daughter of the head priest of the Otsubaki Shrine, and she is destined to follow in his footsteps. She works hard day and night to become a great priestess, but it seems she inherited none of her father's powers...

One day Miko goes to help out her friend Shino, who says her boyfriend Kagura has been possessed by an evil spirit. As soon as Miko chants a random spell to banish the spirit, Kagura disappears! Then a little Kagura appears before Miko and tells her he is an incubus who gains his powers from women. He says he's the strongest demon in existence.

Because she is able to seal Kagura's powers, evil demons start to target Miko, so Kagura agrees to protect her...

Miko heads to Izumo on a school trip. She is attacked by a demon, but Kagura saves her in time. Miko discovers the true identity of her attacker is a mischievous fox spirit! Miko treats the fox's wounds, and later that night a cute boy with fox ears appears before her...

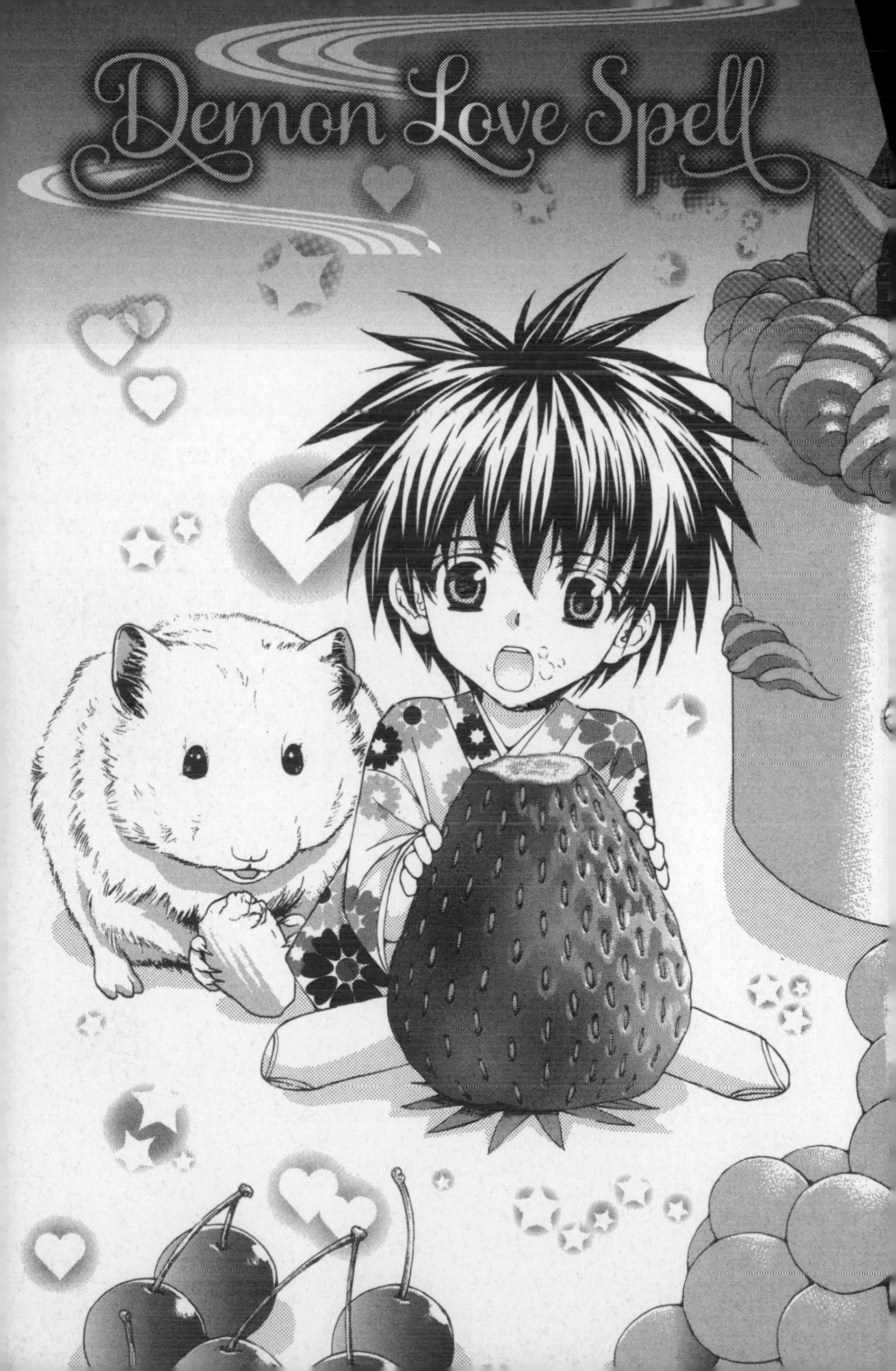
Demon Love Spell

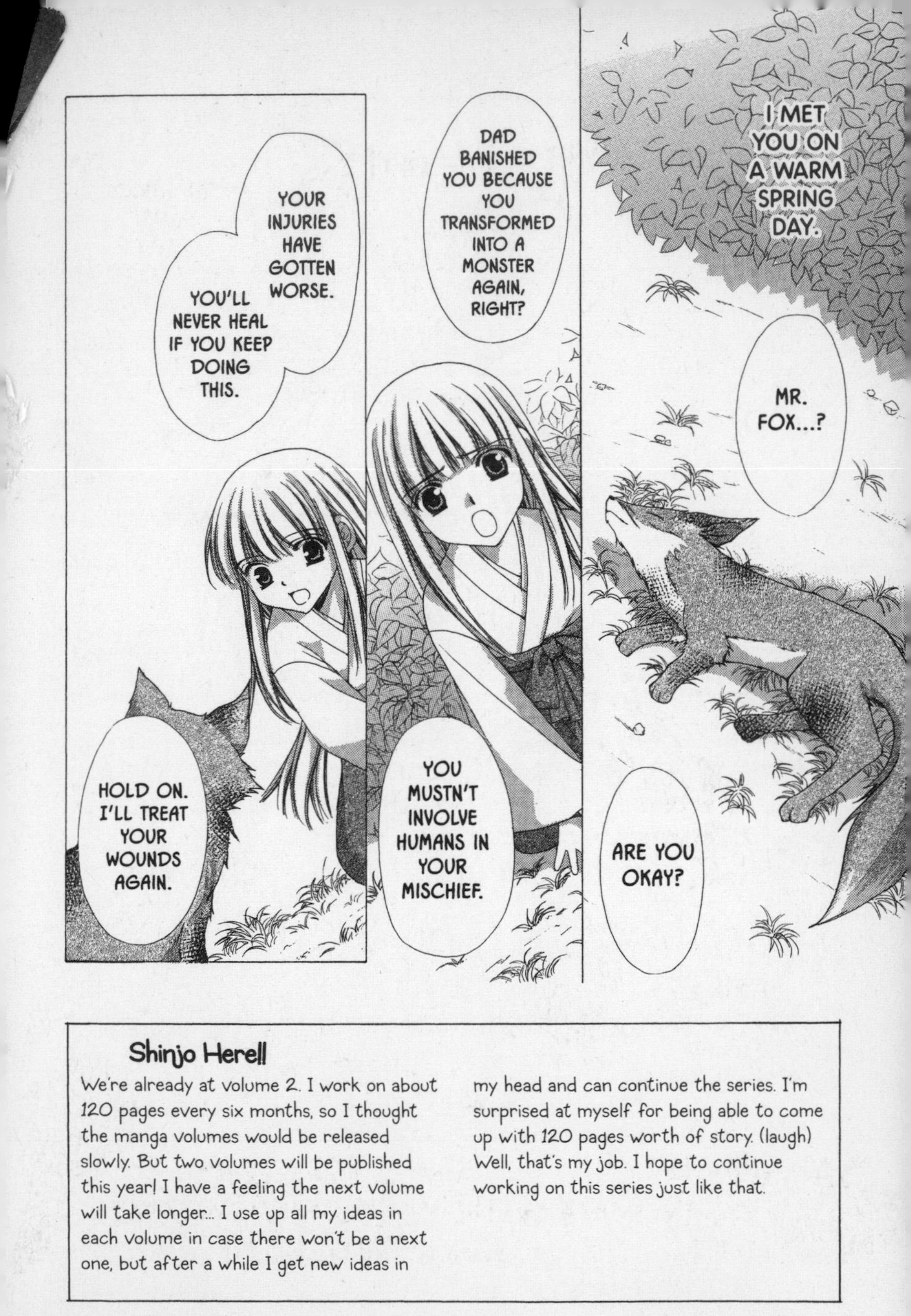
I MET YOU ON A WARM SPRING DAY.
MR. FOX...?
ARE YOU OKAY?
DAD BANISHED YOU BECAUSE YOU TRANSFORMED INTO A MONSTER AGAIN, RIGHT?
YOU MUSTN'T INVOLVE HUMANS IN YOUR MISCHIEF.
YOUR INJURIES HAVE GOTTEN WORSE.
YOU'LL NEVER HEAL IF YOU KEEP DOING THIS.
HOLD ON. I'LL TREAT YOUR WOUNDS AGAIN.

Shinjo Here!!

We're already at volume 2. I work on about 120 pages every six months, so I thought the manga volumes would be released slowly. But two volumes will be published this year! I have a feeling the next volume will take longer... I use up all my ideas in each volume in case there won't be a next one, but after a while I get new ideas in my head and can continue the series. I'm surprised at myself for being able to come up with 120 pages worth of story. (laugh) Well, that's my job. I hope to continue working on this series just like that.

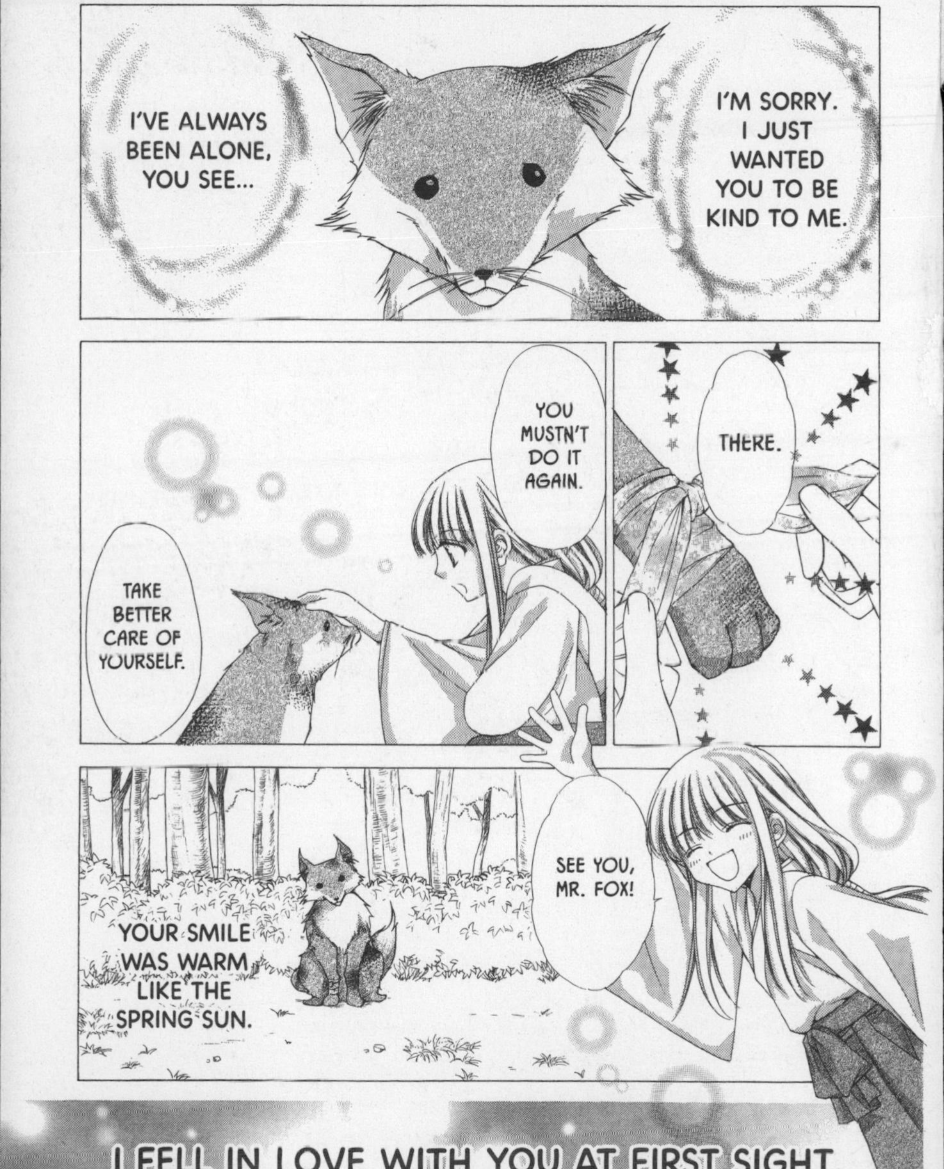
I'M SORRY. I JUST WANTED YOU TO BE KIND TO ME.
I'VE ALWAYS BEEN ALONE, YOU SEE...
THERE.
YOU MUSTN'T DO IT AGAIN.
TAKE BETTER CARE OF YOURSELF.
SEE YOU, MR. FOX!
YOUR SMILE WAS WARM LIKE THE SPRING SUN.
I FELL IN LOVE WITH YOU AT FIRST SIGHT.

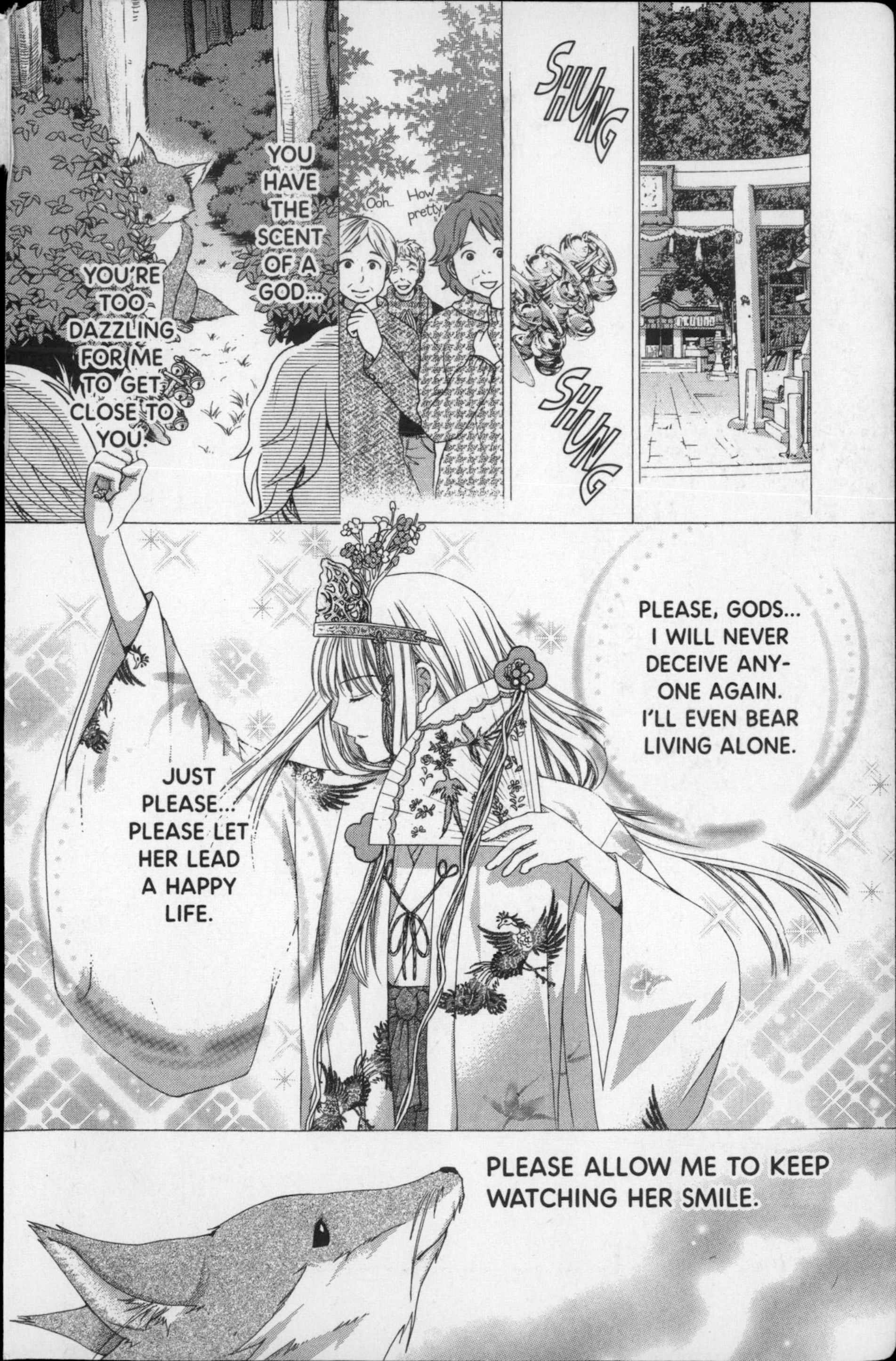
SHUNG
SHUNG
Ooh..
How pretty..
YOU HAVE THE SCENT OF A GOD...
YOU'RE TOO DAZZLING FOR ME TO GET CLOSE TO YOU.
PLEASE, GODS... I WILL NEVER DECEIVE ANY-ONE AGAIN. I'LL EVEN BEAR LIVING ALONE.
JUST PLEASE... PLEASE LET HER LEAD A HAPPY LIFE.
PLEASE ALLOW ME TO KEEP WATCHING HER SMILE.

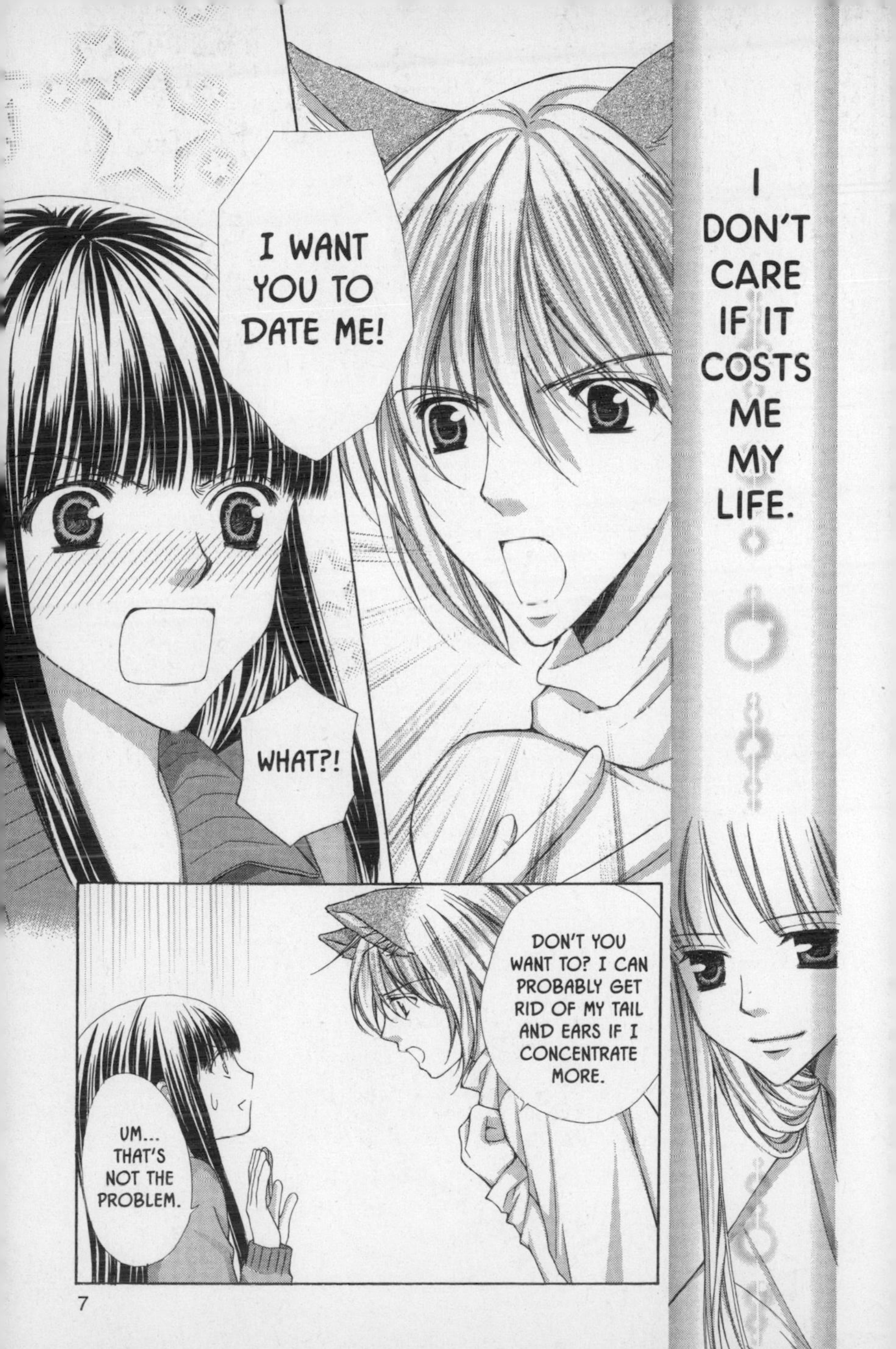
I DON'T CARE IF IT COSTS ME MY LIFE.
I WANT YOU TO DATE ME!
WHAT?!
DON'T YOU WANT TO? I CAN PROBABLY GET RID OF MY TAIL AND EARS IF I CONCENTRATE MORE.
UM... THAT'S NOT THE PROBLEM.

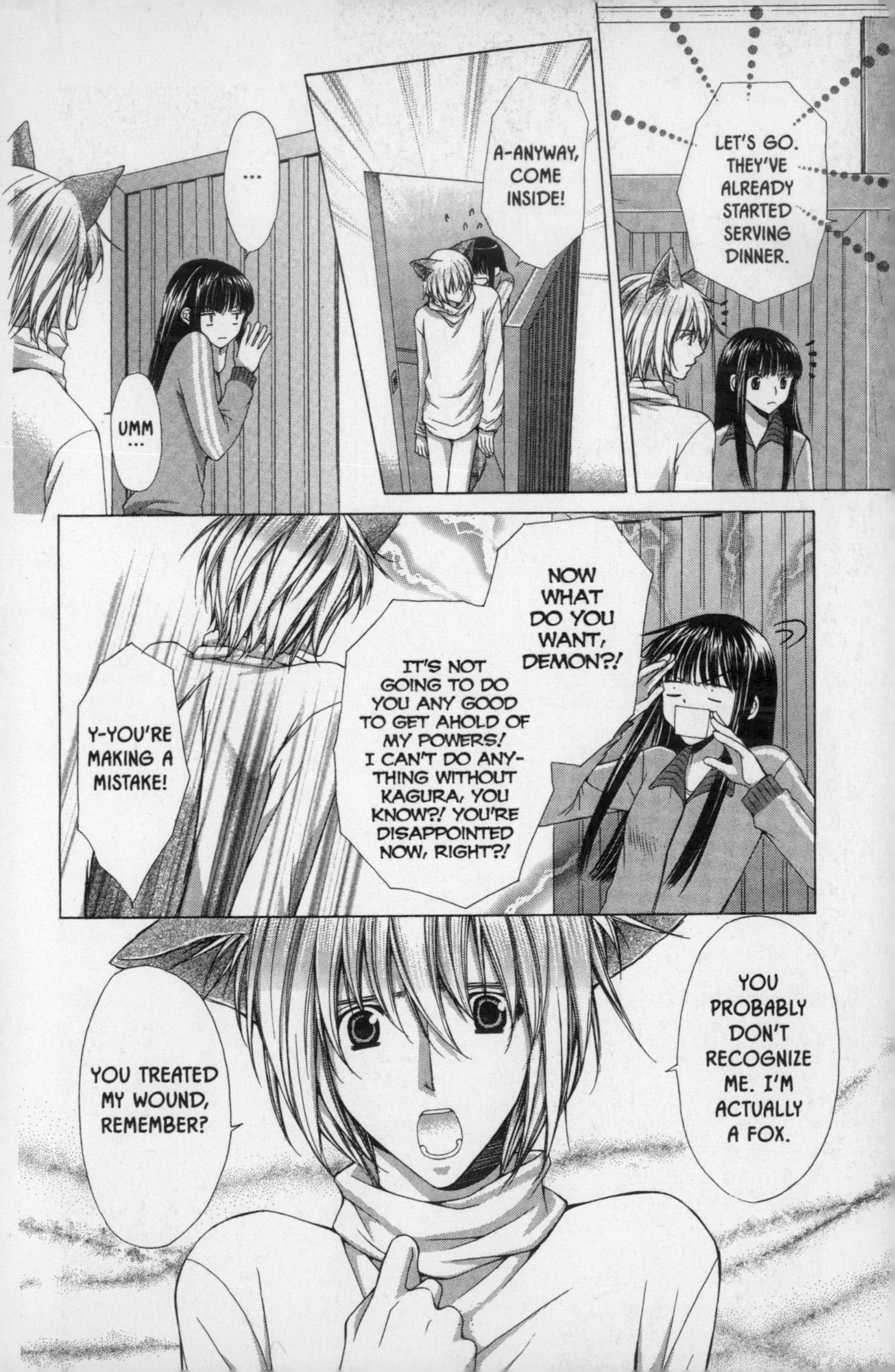
LET'S GO. THEY'VE ALREADY STARTED SERVING DINNER.
A-ANYWAY, COME INSIDE!
...
UMM ...
NOW WHAT DO YOU WANT, DEMON?!
IT'S NOT GOING TO DO YOU ANY GOOD TO GET AHOLD OF MY POWERS! I CAN'T DO ANY-THING WITHOUT KAGURA, YOU KNOW?! YOU'RE DISAPPOINTED NOW, RIGHT?!
Y-YOU'RE MAKING A MISTAKE!
YOU PROBABLY DON'T RECOGNIZE ME. I'M ACTUALLY A FOX.
YOU TREATED MY WOUND, REMEMBER?

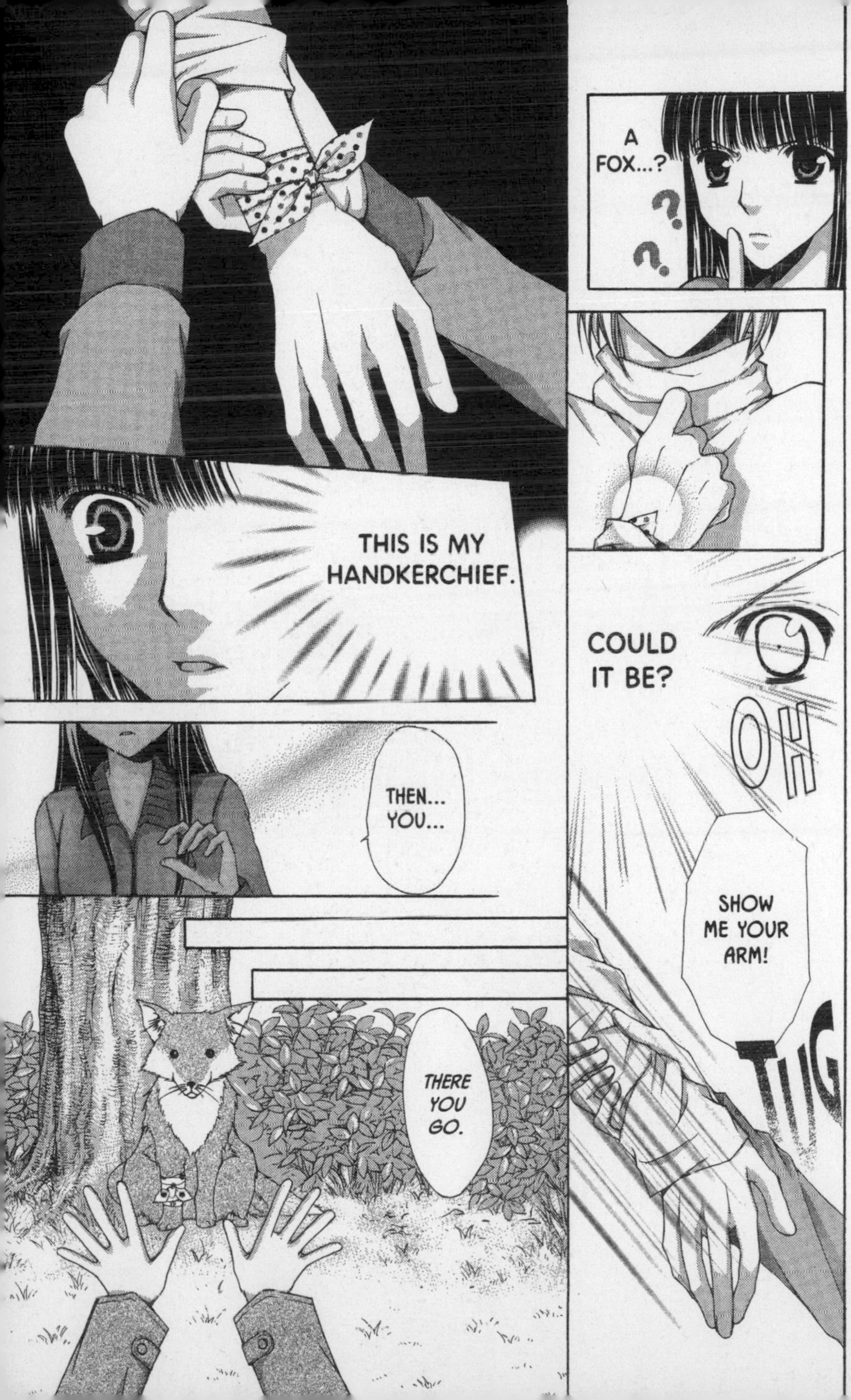
A FOX...?
COULD IT BE?
OH
SHOW ME YOUR ARM!
TUG
THIS IS MY HANDKERCHIEF.
THEN... YOU...
THERE YOU GO.

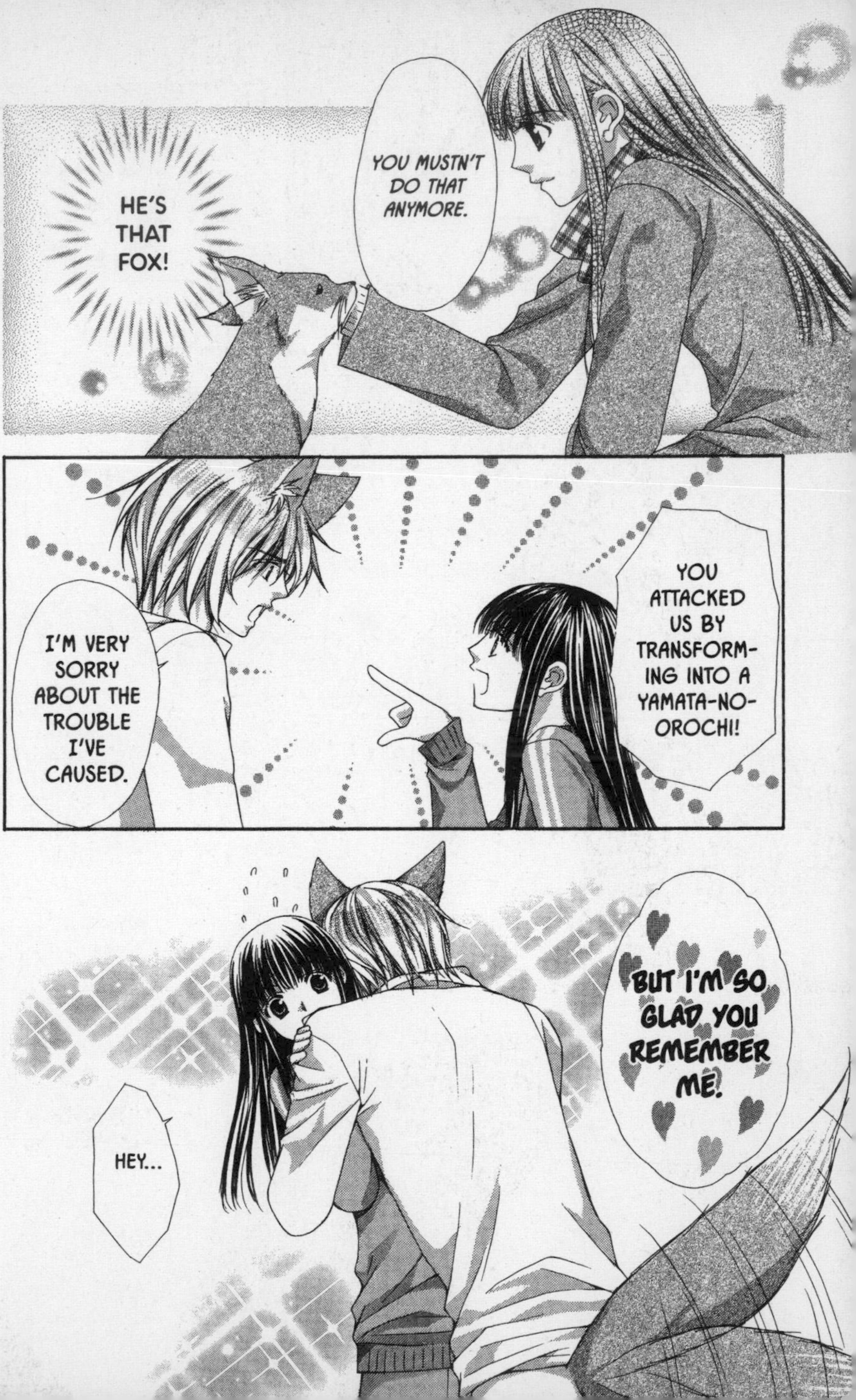
YOU MUSTN'T DO THAT ANYMORE.
HE'S THAT FOX!
YOU ATTACKED US BY TRANSFORMING INTO A YAMATA-NO-OROCHI!
I'M VERY SORRY ABOUT THE TROUBLE I'VE CAUSED.
BUT I'M SO GLAD YOU REMEMBER ME!
HEY...

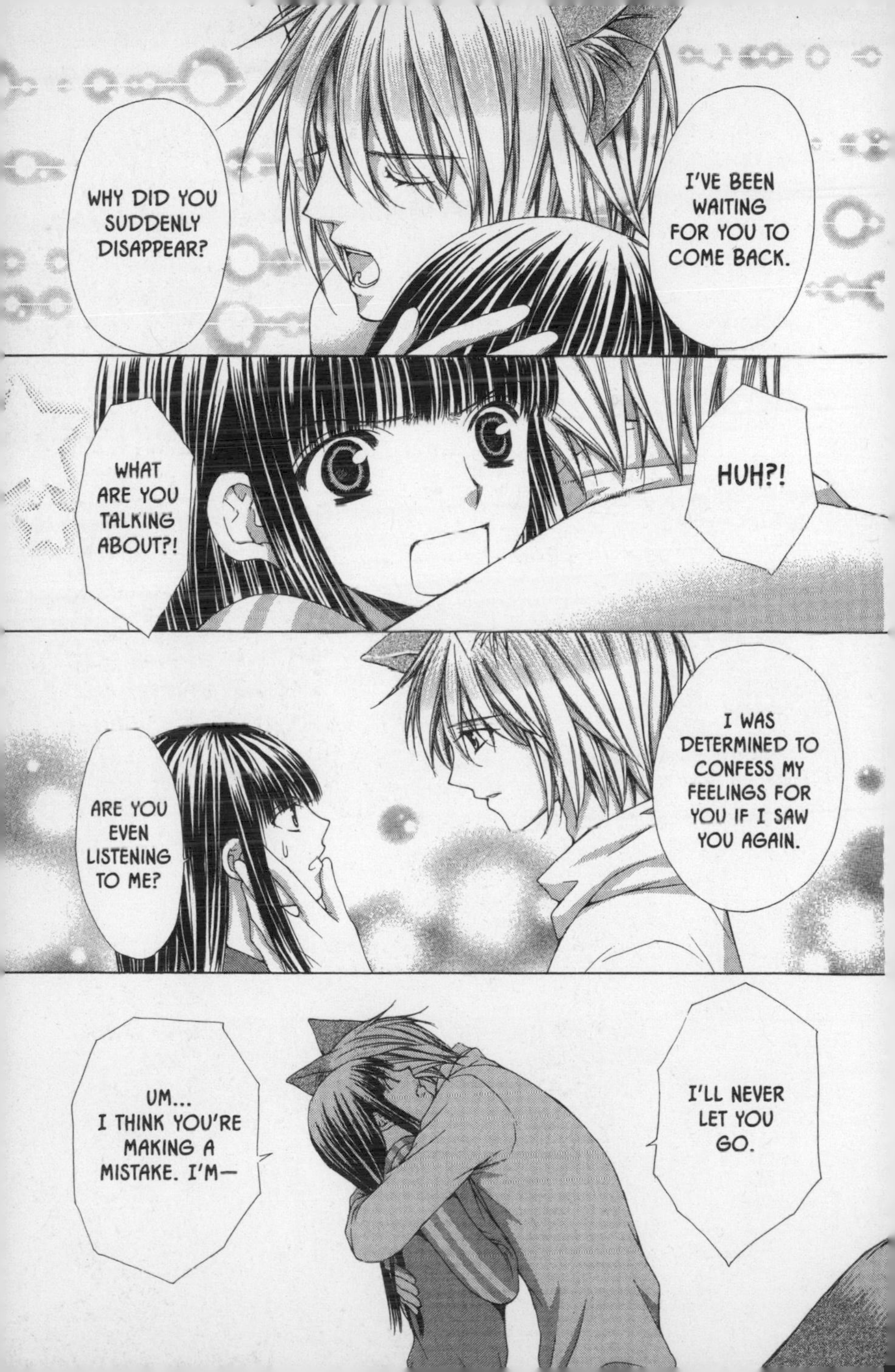
I'VE BEEN WAITING FOR YOU TO COME BACK.
WHY DID YOU SUDDENLY DISAPPEAR?
HUH?!
WHAT ARE YOU TALKING ABOUT?!
I WAS DETERMINED TO CONFESS MY FEELINGS FOR YOU IF I SAW YOU AGAIN.
ARE YOU EVEN LISTENING TO ME?
I'LL NEVER LET YOU GO.
UM... I THINK YOU'RE MAKING A MISTAKE. I'M—

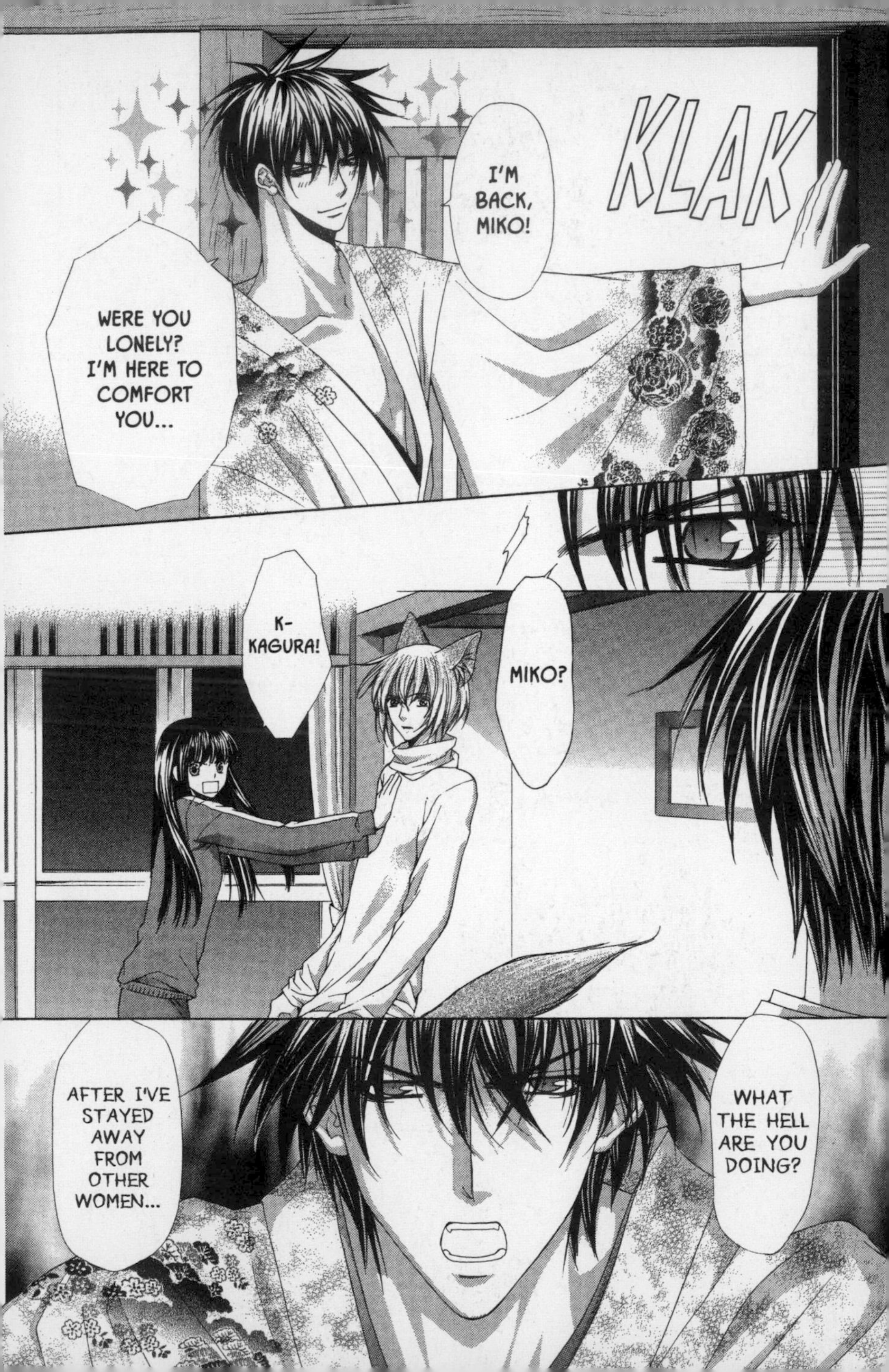
KLAK
I'M BACK, MIKO!
WERE YOU LONELY? I'M HERE TO COMFORT YOU...
MIKO?
K-KAGURA!
WHAT THE HELL ARE YOU DOING?
AFTER I'VE STAYED AWAY FROM OTHER WOMEN...

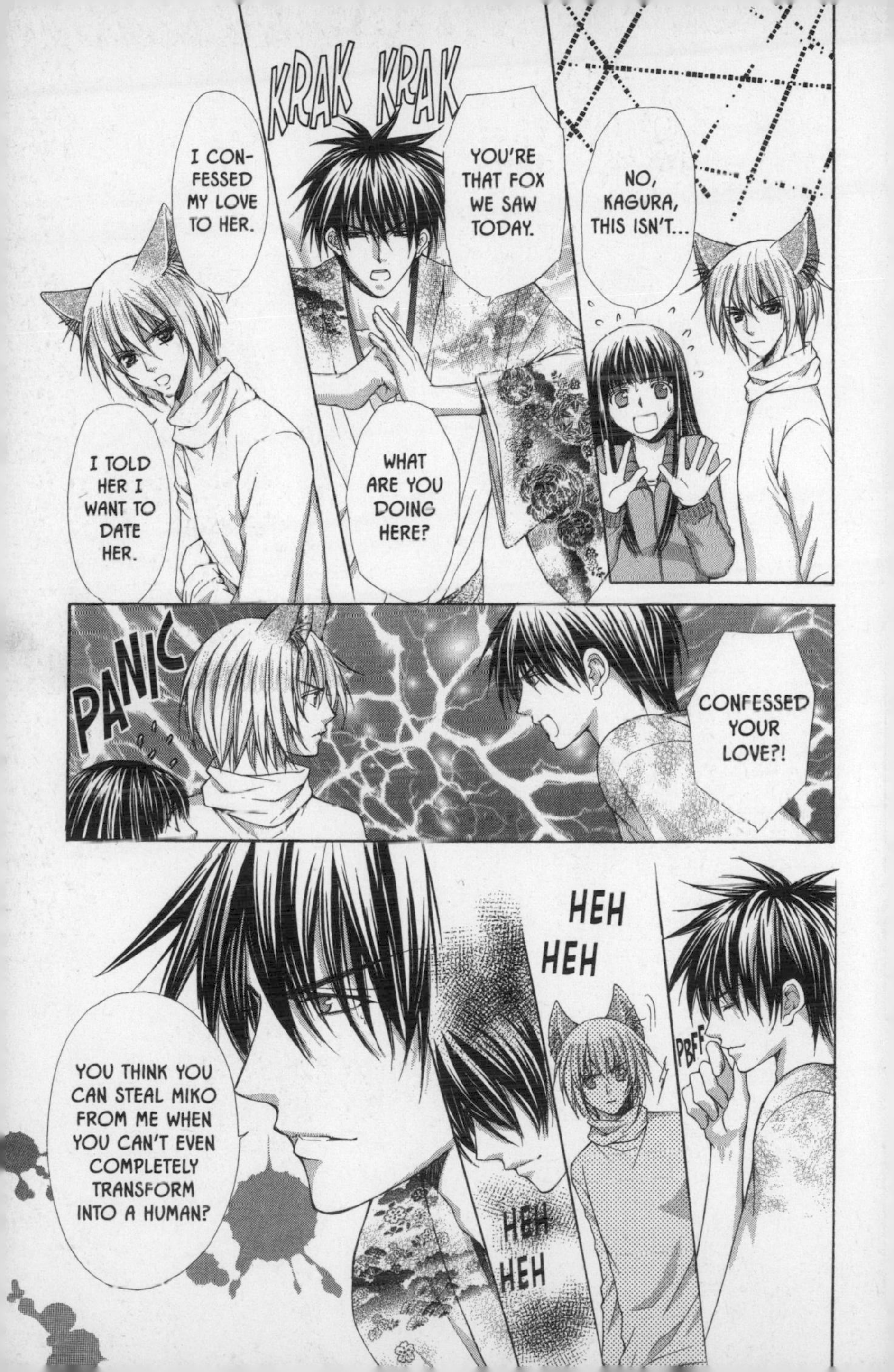

NO, KAGURA, THIS ISN'T...
KRAK KRAK
YOU'RE THAT FOX WE SAW TODAY.
WHAT ARE YOU DOING HERE?
I CON-FESSED MY LOVE TO HER.
I TOLD HER I WANT TO DATE HER.
CONFESSED YOUR LOVE?!
PANIC
HEH HEH
PBFF
HEH HEH
YOU THINK YOU CAN STEAL MIKO FROM ME WHEN YOU CAN'T EVEN COMPLETELY TRANSFORM INTO A HUMAN?

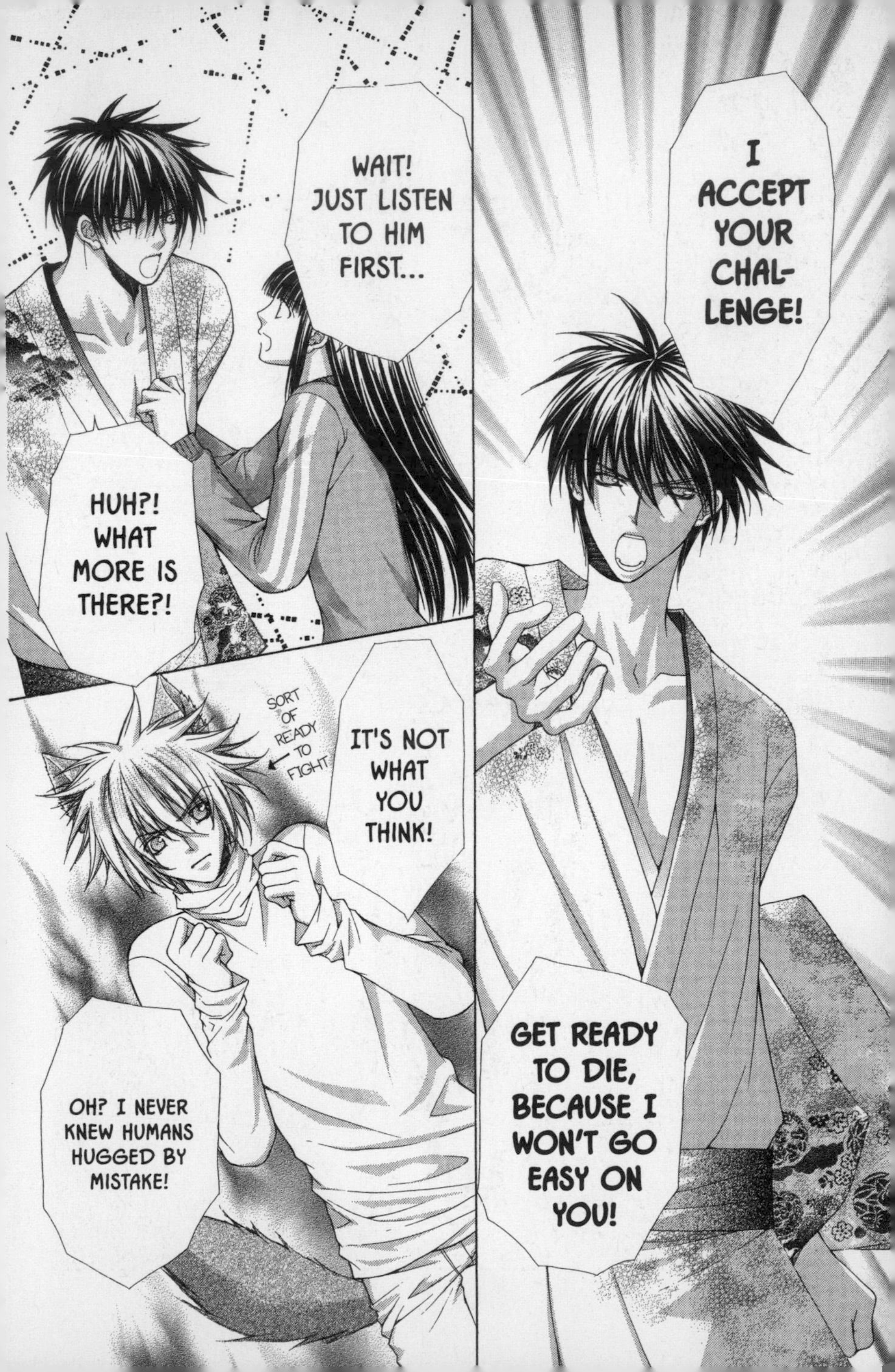
I ACCEPT YOUR CHAL-LENGE!
GET READY TO DIE, BECAUSE I WON'T GO EASY ON YOU!
WAIT! JUST LISTEN TO HIM FIRST...
HUH?! WHAT MORE IS THERE?!
IT'S NOT WHAT YOU THINK!
SORT OF READY TO FIGHT
OH? I NEVER KNEW HUMANS HUGGED BY MISTAKE!

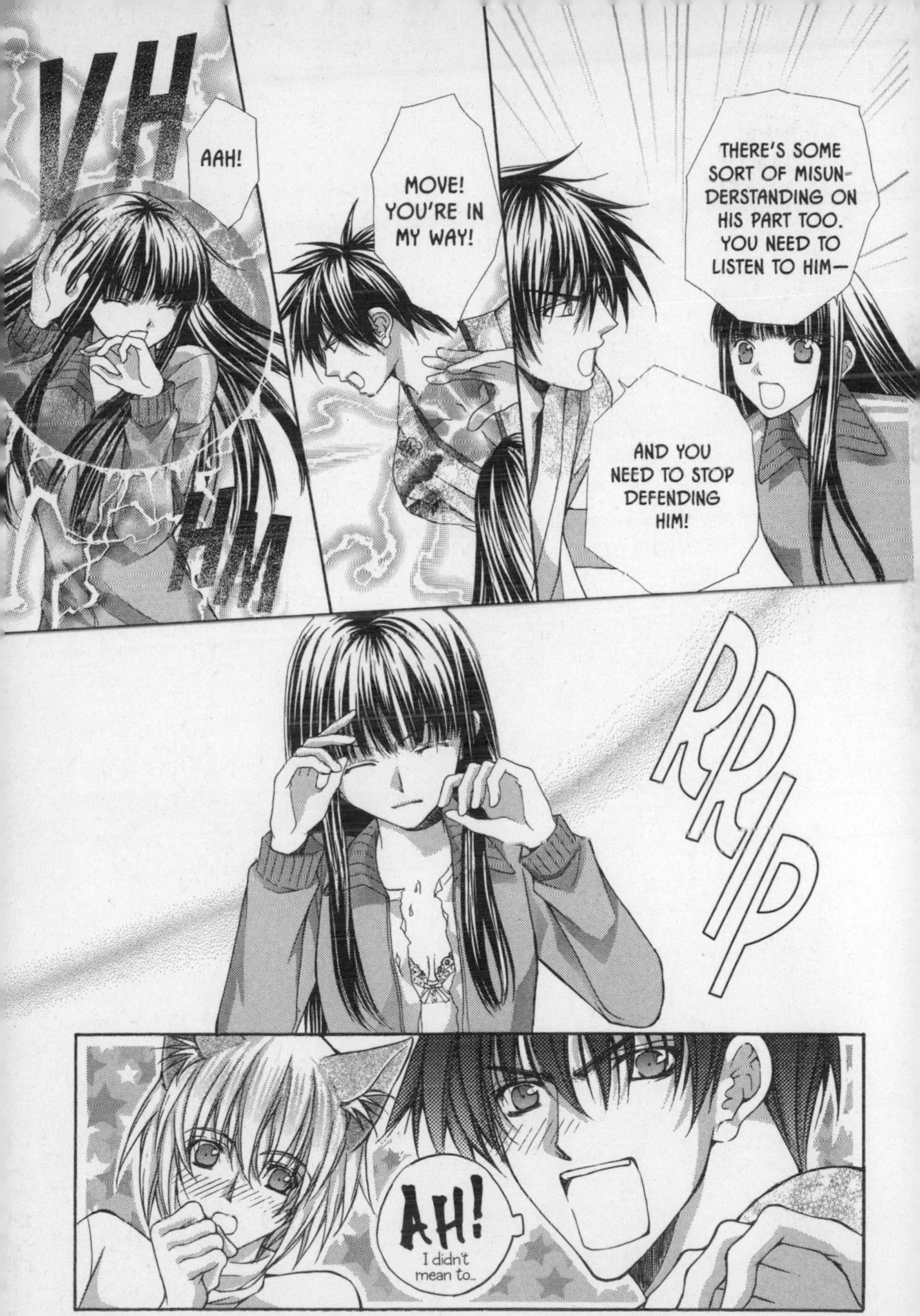
THERE'S SOME SORT OF MISUNDERSTANDING ON HIS PART TOO. YOU NEED TO LISTEN TO HIM—
AND YOU NEED TO STOP DEFENDING HIM!
MOVE! YOU'RE IN MY WAY!
AAH!
VH
HM
RRIP
AH!
I didn't mean to...

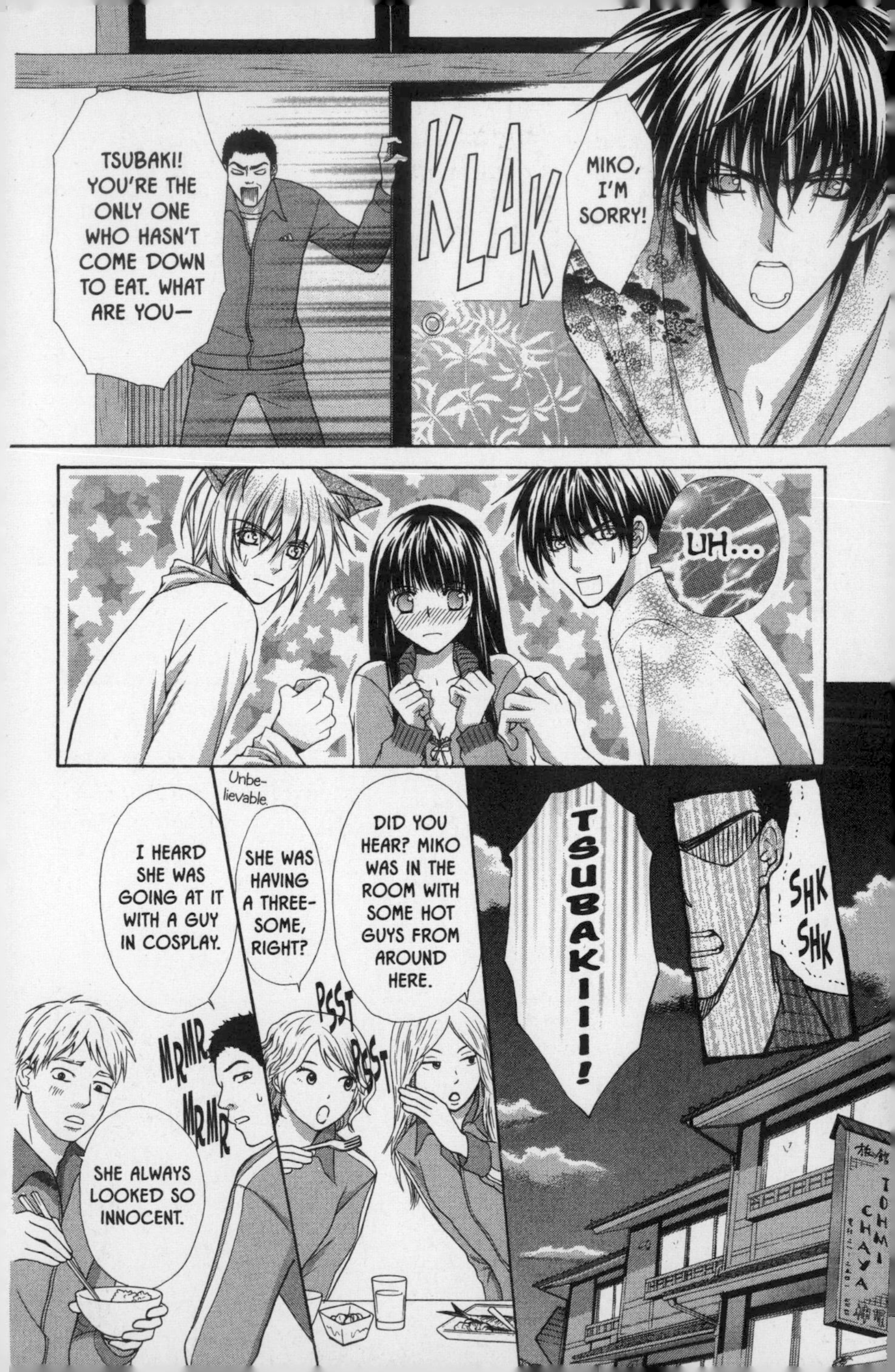
MIKO, I'M SORRY!
KLAK
TSUBAKI! YOU'RE THE ONLY ONE WHO HASN'T COME DOWN TO EAT. WHAT ARE YOU—
UH...
SHK SHK
TSUBAKIIII!
DID YOU HEAR? MIKO WAS IN THE ROOM WITH SOME HOT GUYS FROM AROUND HERE.
Unbe-lievable.
SHE WAS HAVING A THREE-SOME, RIGHT?
I HEARD SHE WAS GOING AT IT WITH A GUY IN COSPLAY.
PSST PSST
MRMR MRMR
SHE ALWAYS LOOKED SO INNOCENT.

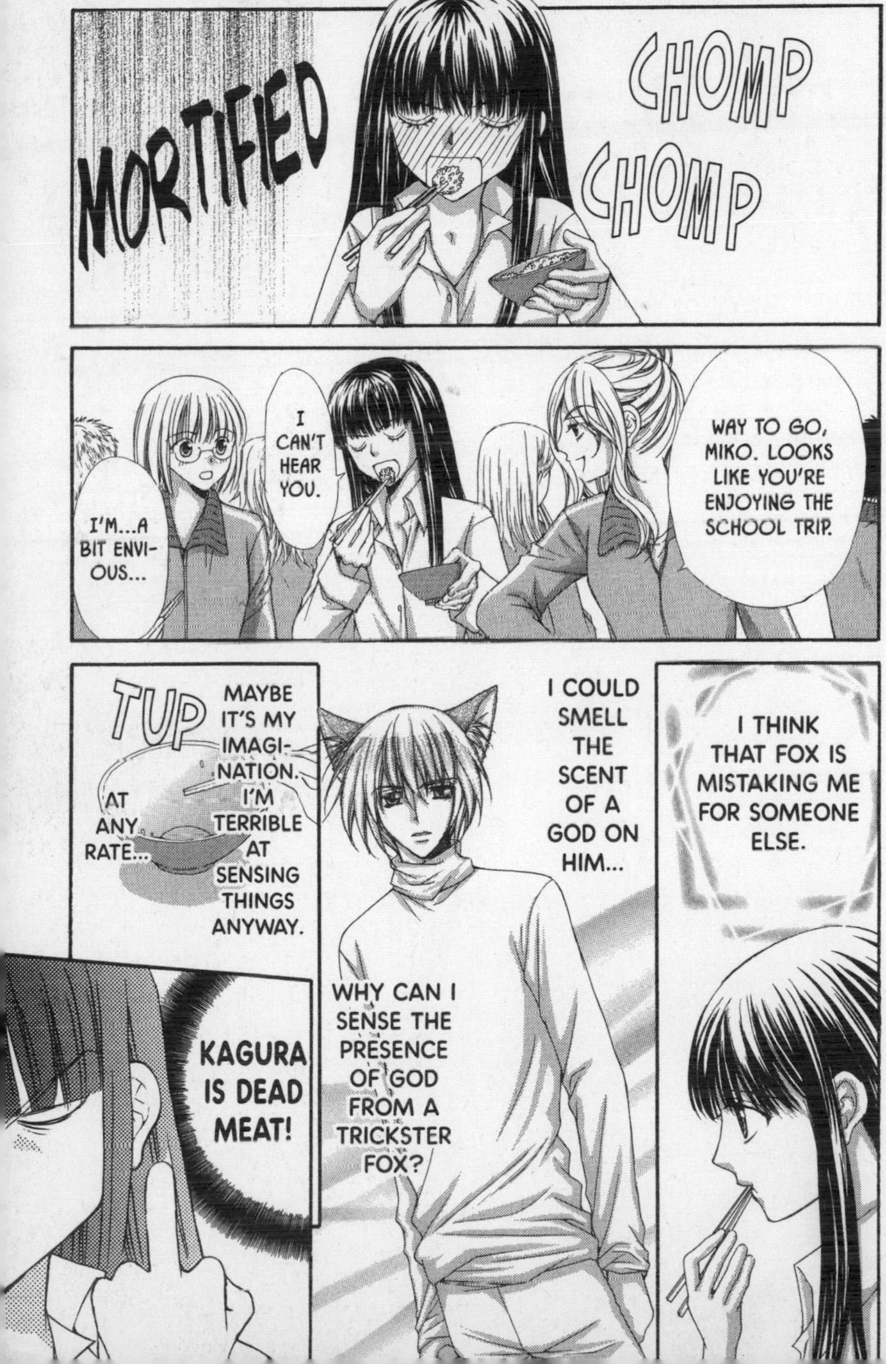
CHOMP
CHOMP
MORTIFIED
WAY TO GO, MIKO. LOOKS LIKE YOU'RE ENJOYING THE SCHOOL TRIP.
I CAN'T HEAR YOU.
I'M...A BIT ENVIOUS...
I THINK THAT FOX IS MISTAKING ME FOR SOMEONE ELSE.
I COULD SMELL THE SCENT OF A GOD ON HIM...
MAYBE IT'S MY IMAGINATION.
I'M TERRIBLE AT SENSING THINGS ANYWAY.
TUP
AT ANY RATE...
WHY CAN I SENSE THE PRESENCE OF GOD FROM A TRICKSTER FOX?
KAGURA IS DEAD MEAT!

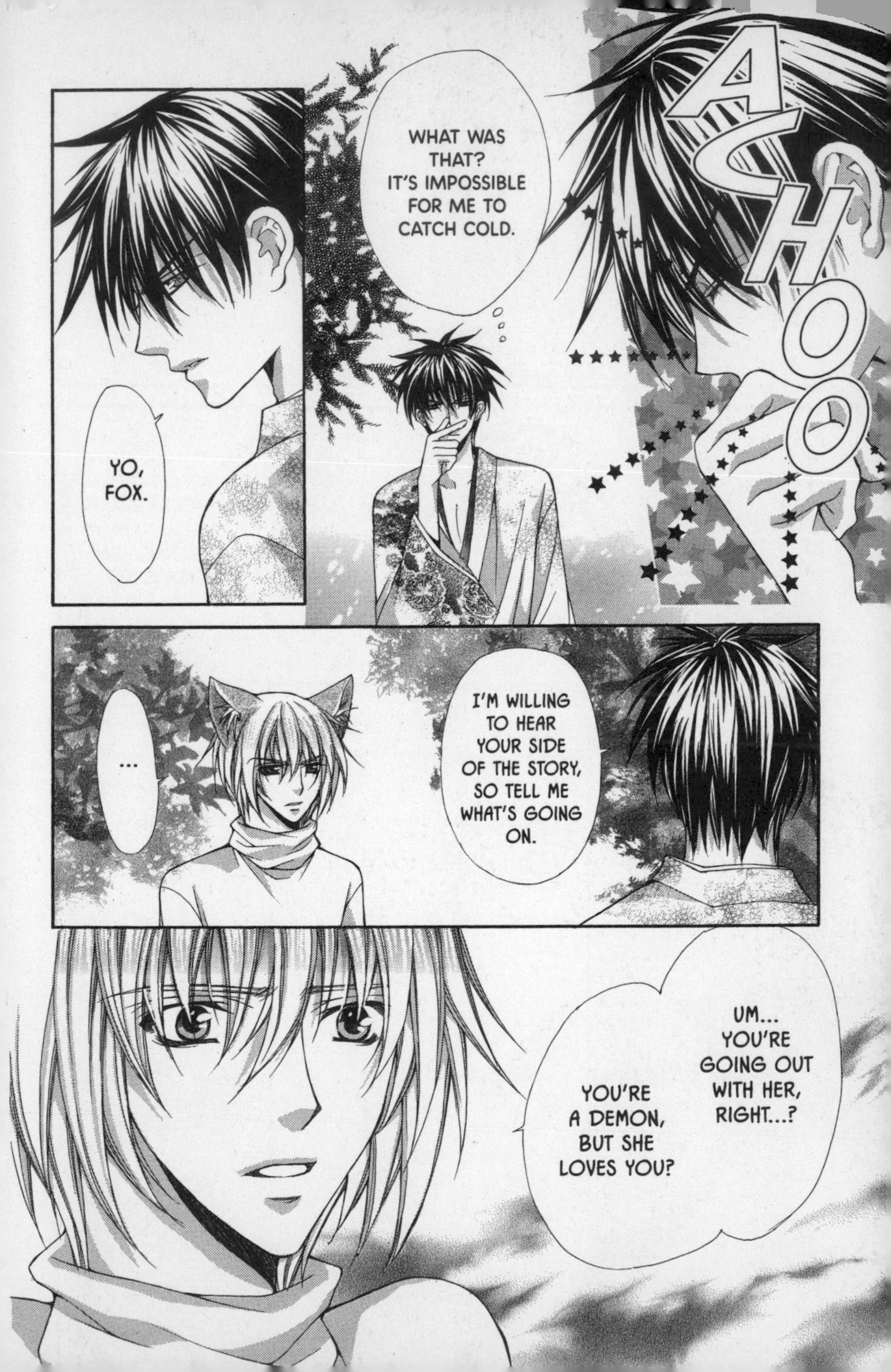
ACHOO
WHAT WAS THAT? IT'S IMPOSSIBLE FOR ME TO CATCH COLD.
YO, FOX.
I'M WILLING TO HEAR YOUR SIDE OF THE STORY, SO TELL ME WHAT'S GOING ON.
...
UM... YOU'RE GOING OUT WITH HER, RIGHT...?
YOU'RE A DEMON, BUT SHE LOVES YOU?

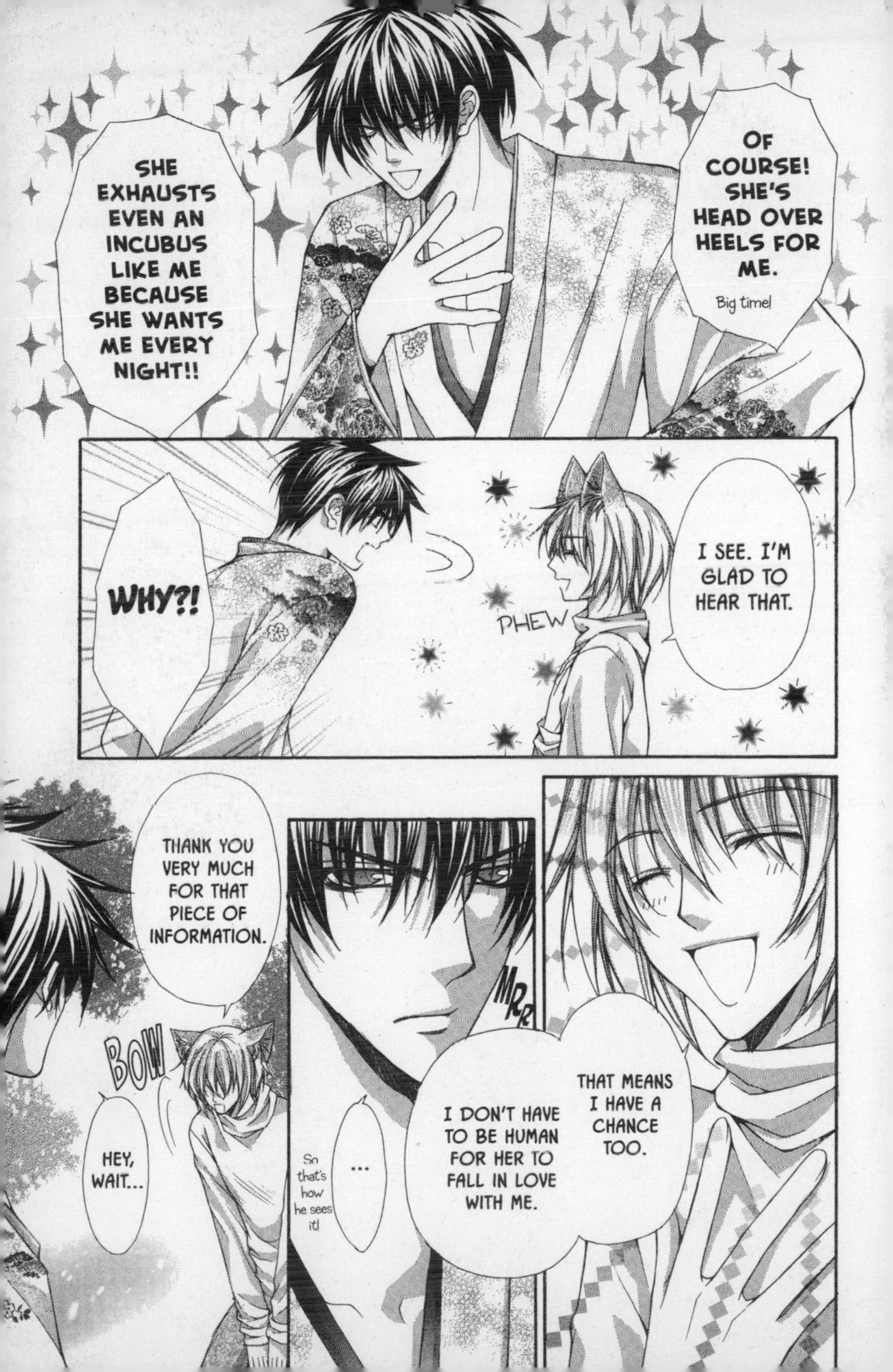

OF COURSE! SHE'S HEAD OVER HEELS FOR ME.
Big time!
SHE EXHAUSTS EVEN AN INCUBUS LIKE ME BECAUSE SHE WANTS ME EVERY NIGHT!!
I SEE. I'M GLAD TO HEAR THAT.
PHEW
WHY?!
THAT MEANS I HAVE A CHANCE TOO.
I DON'T HAVE TO BE HUMAN FOR HER TO FALL IN LOVE WITH ME.
MRR
...
So that's how he sees it!
THANK YOU VERY MUCH FOR THAT PIECE OF INFORMATION.
BOW
HEY, WAIT...

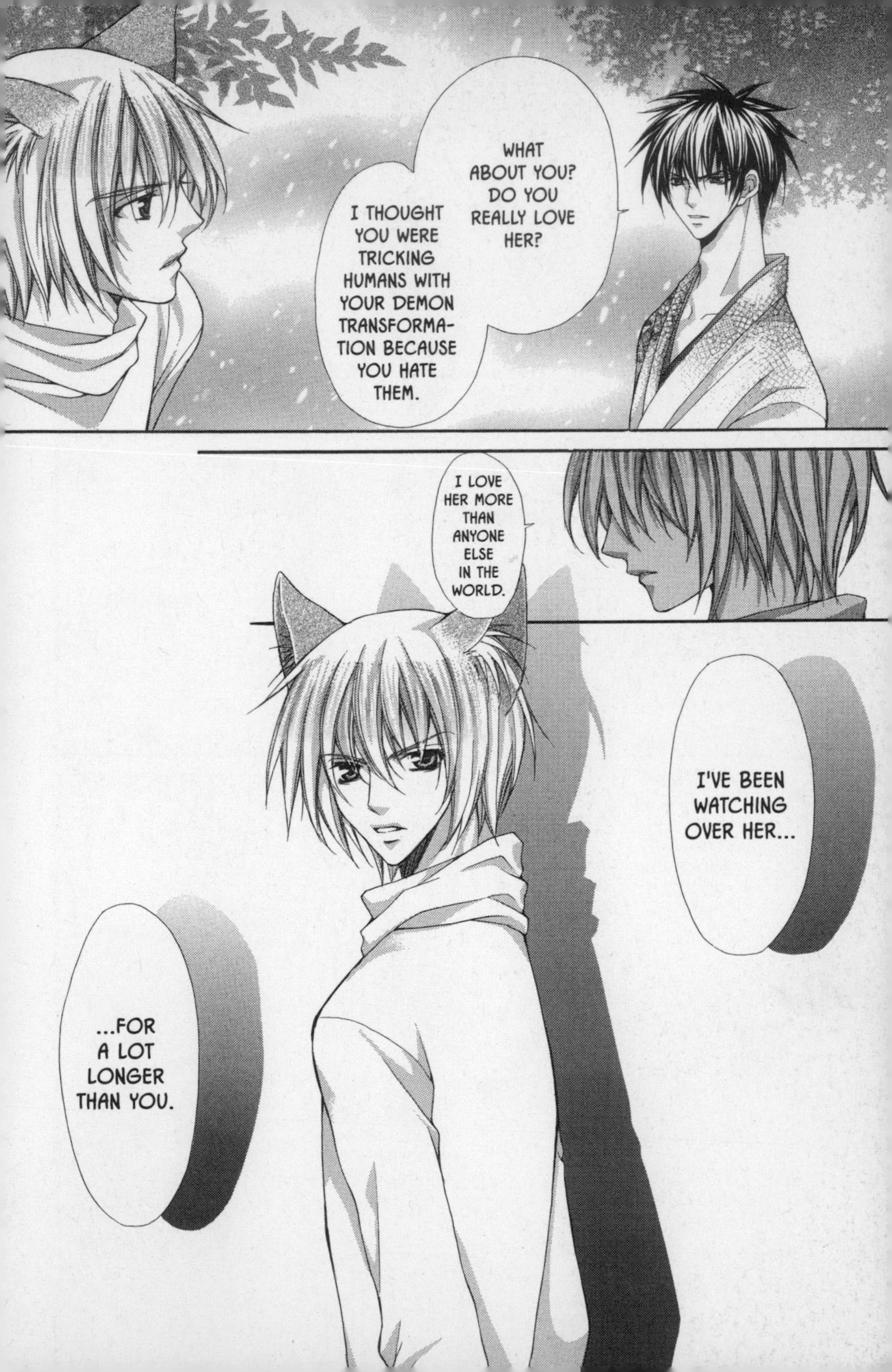
WHAT ABOUT YOU? DO YOU REALLY LOVE HER?
I THOUGHT YOU WERE TRICKING HUMANS WITH YOUR DEMON TRANSFORMATION BECAUSE YOU HATE THEM.
I LOVE HER MORE THAN ANYONE ELSE IN THE WORLD.
I'VE BEEN WATCHING OVER HER...
...FOR A LOT LONGER THAN YOU.

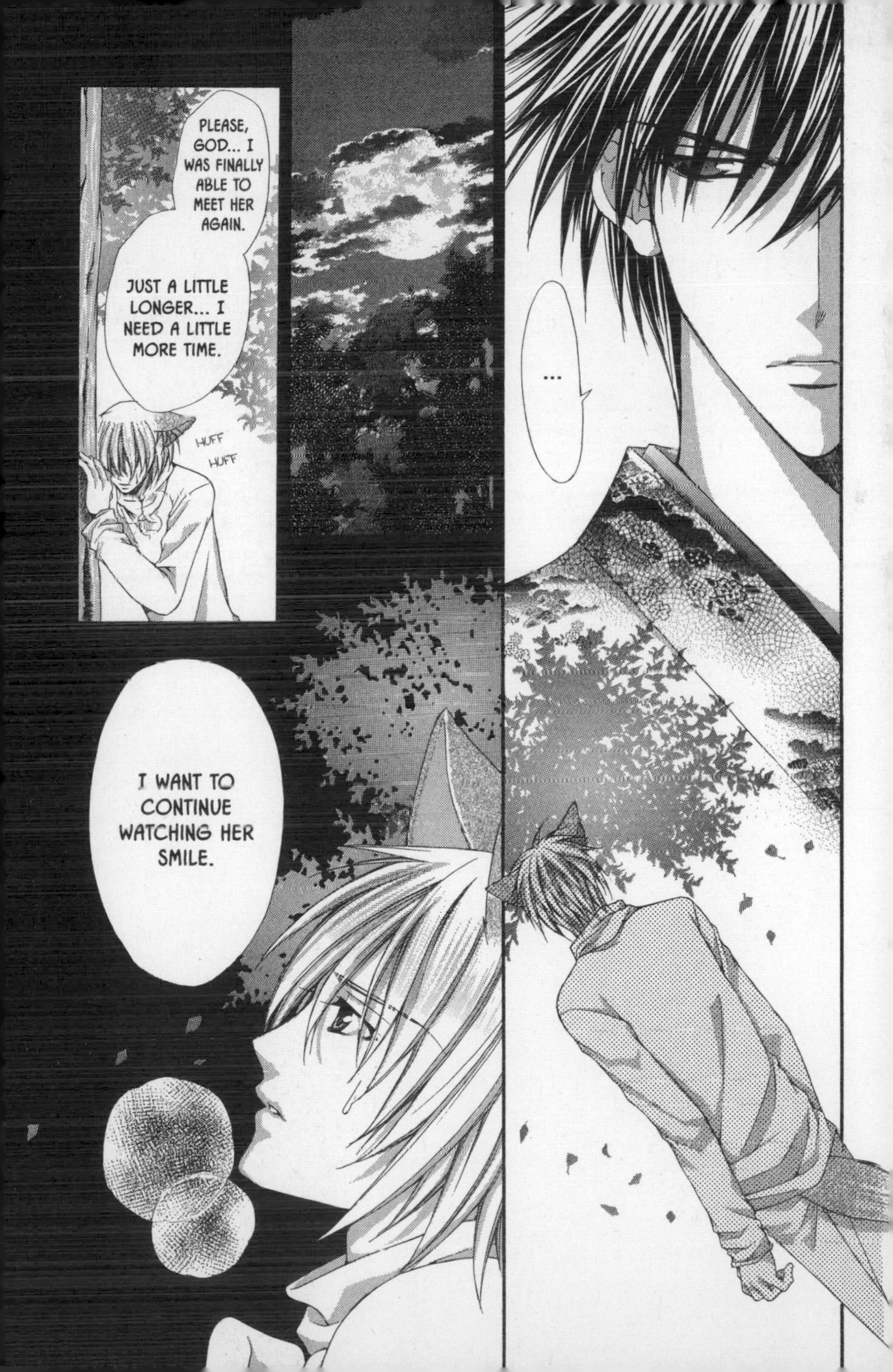
...
PLEASE, GOD... I WAS FINALLY ABLE TO MEET HER AGAIN.
JUST A LITTLE LONGER... I NEED A LITTLE MORE TIME.
HUFF
HUFF
I WANT TO CONTINUE WATCHING HER SMILE.

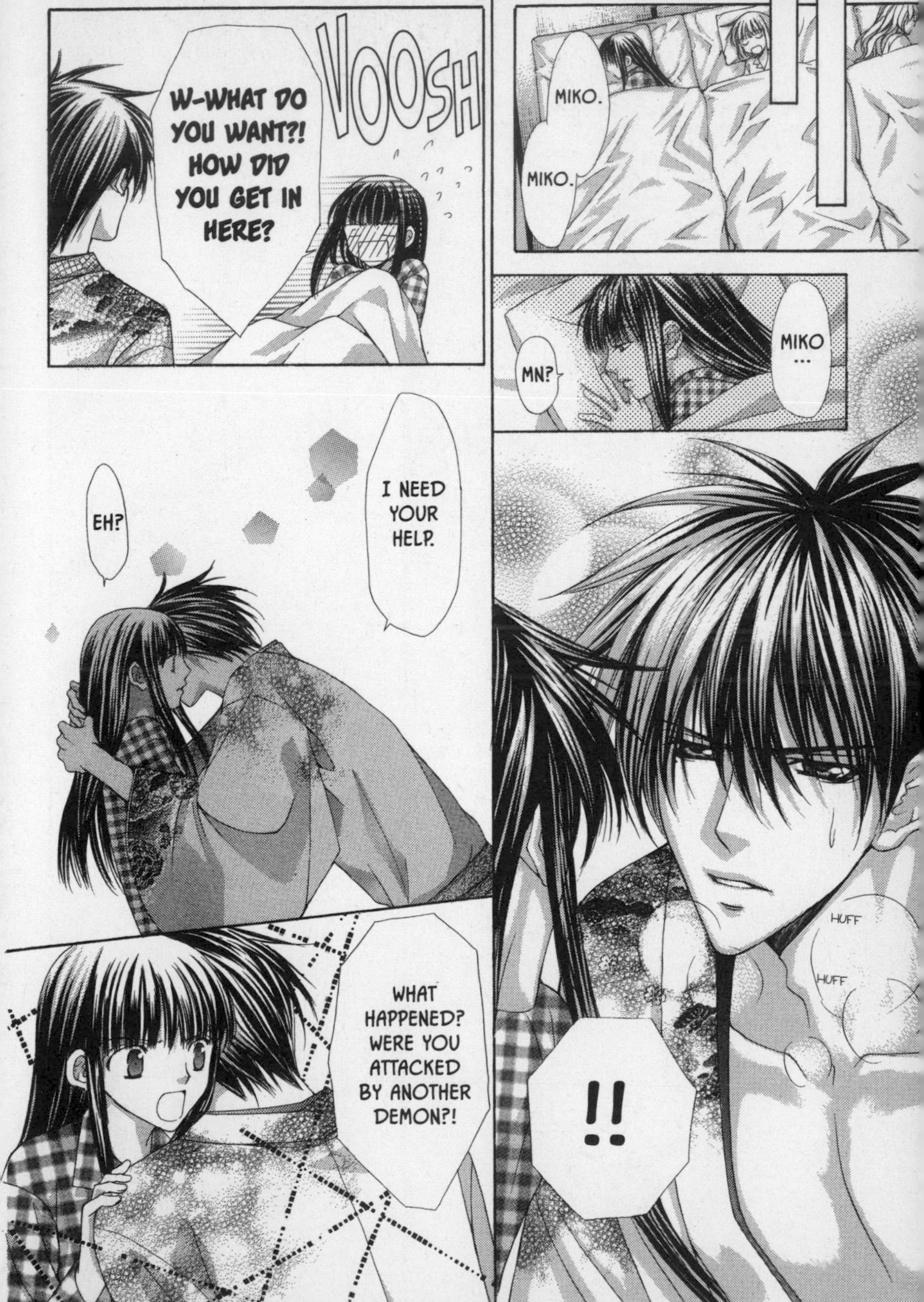
MIKO.
MIKO.
MIKO ...
MN?
HUFF
HUFF
!!
VOOSH
W-WHAT DO YOU WANT?! HOW DID YOU GET IN HERE?
I NEED YOUR HELP.
EH?
WHAT HAPPENED? WERE YOU ATTACKED BY ANOTHER DEMON?!

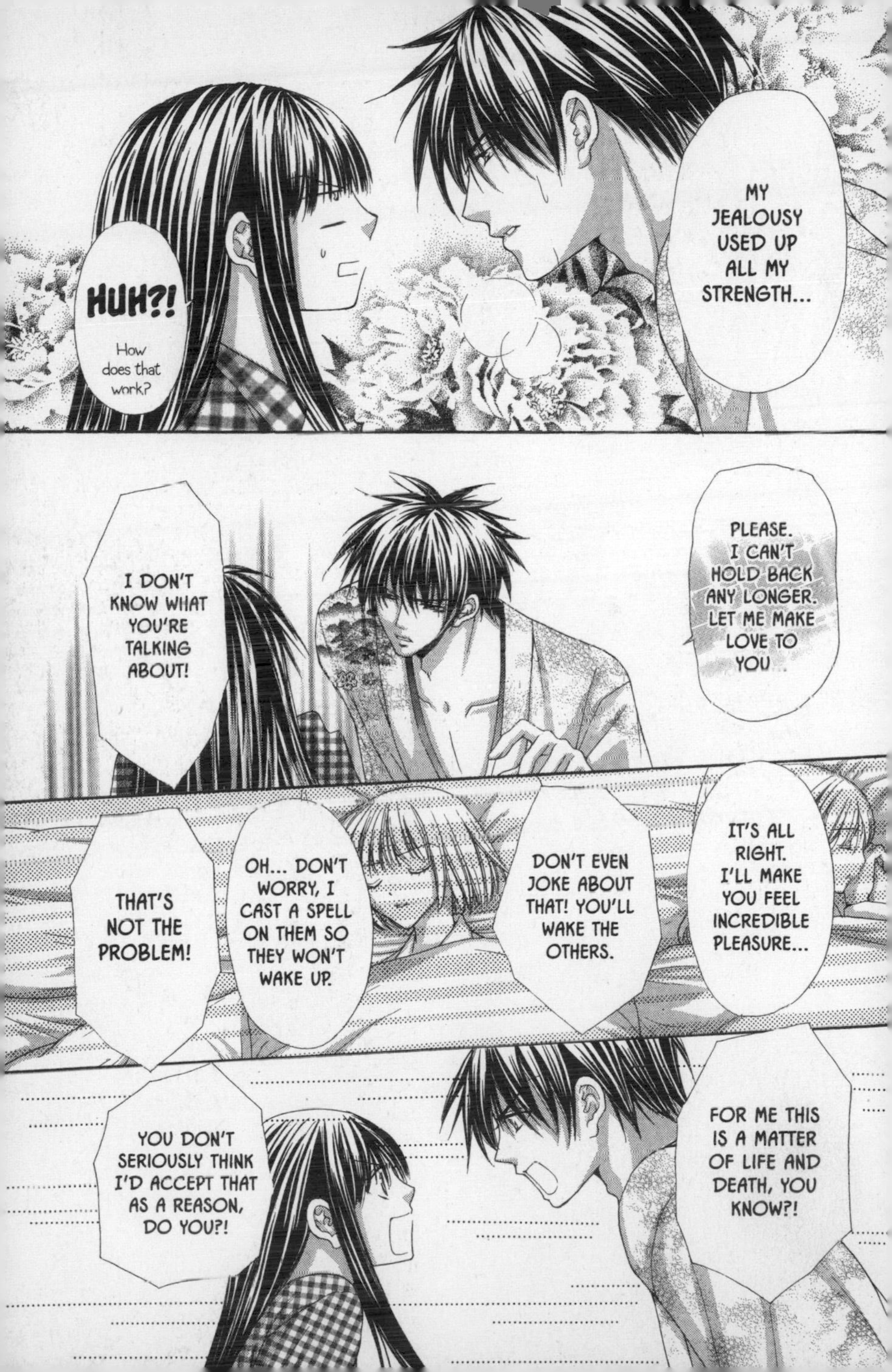
MY JEALOUSY USED UP ALL MY STRENGTH...
HUH?!
How does that work?
PLEASE. I CAN'T HOLD BACK ANY LONGER. LET ME MAKE LOVE TO YOU...
I DON'T KNOW WHAT YOU'RE TALKING ABOUT!
IT'S ALL RIGHT. I'LL MAKE YOU FEEL INCREDIBLE PLEASURE...
DON'T EVEN JOKE ABOUT THAT! YOU'LL WAKE THE OTHERS.
OH... DON'T WORRY, I CAST A SPELL ON THEM SO THEY WON'T WAKE UP.
THAT'S NOT THE PROBLEM!
FOR ME THIS IS A MATTER OF LIFE AND DEATH, YOU KNOW?!
YOU DON'T SERIOUSLY THINK I'D ACCEPT THAT AS A REASON, DO YOU?!

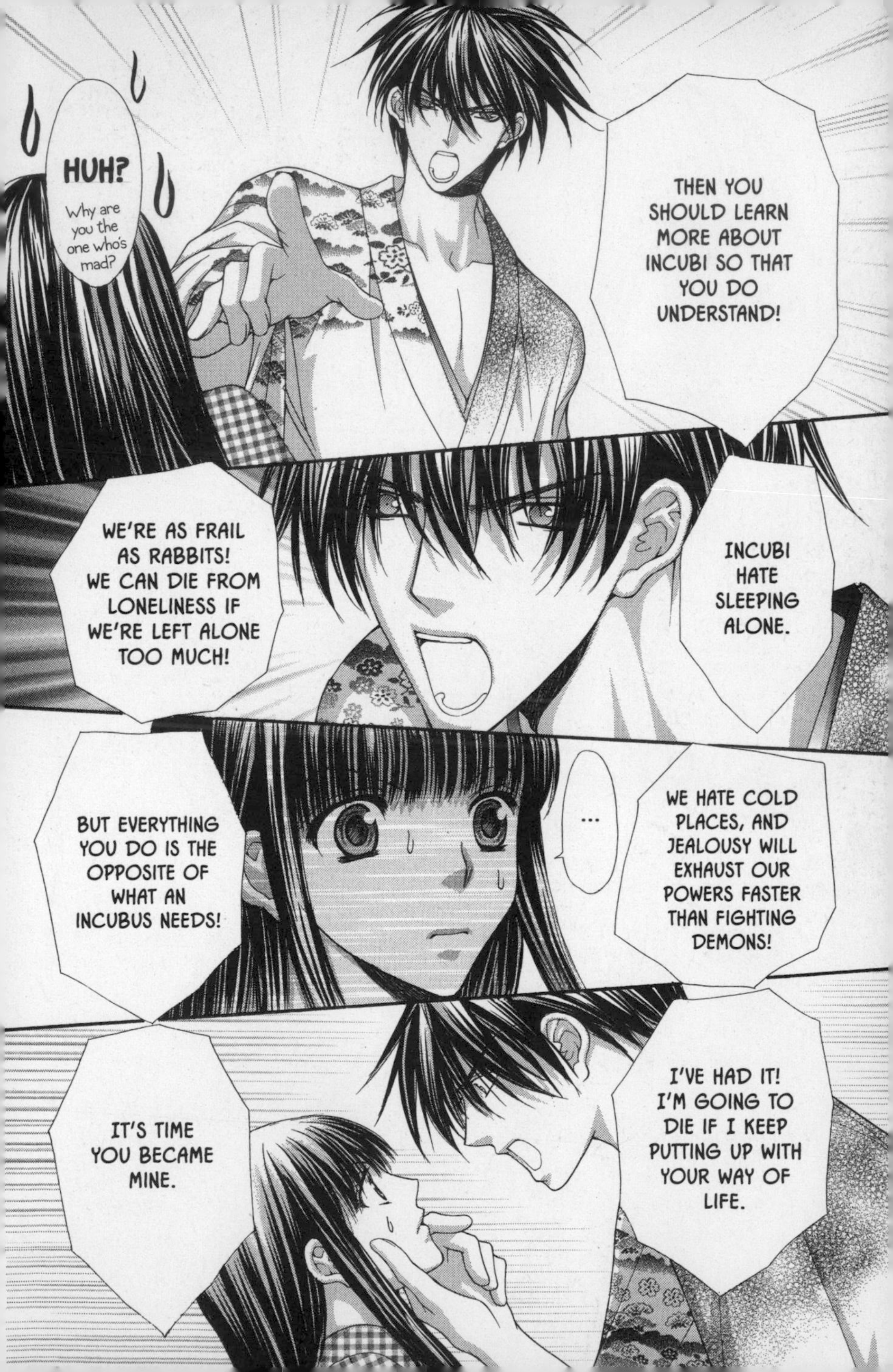
THEN YOU SHOULD LEARN MORE ABOUT INCUBI SO THAT YOU DO UNDERSTAND!
HUH?
Why are you the one who's mad?
INCUBI HATE SLEEPING ALONE.
WE'RE AS FRAIL AS RABBITS! WE CAN DIE FROM LONELINESS IF WE'RE LEFT ALONE TOO MUCH!
WE HATE COLD PLACES, AND JEALOUSY WILL EXHAUST OUR POWERS FASTER THAN FIGHTING DEMONS!
...
BUT EVERYTHING YOU DO IS THE OPPOSITE OF WHAT AN INCUBUS NEEDS!
I'VE HAD IT! I'M GOING TO DIE IF I KEEP PUTTING UP WITH YOUR WAY OF LIFE.
IT'S TIME YOU BECAME MINE.

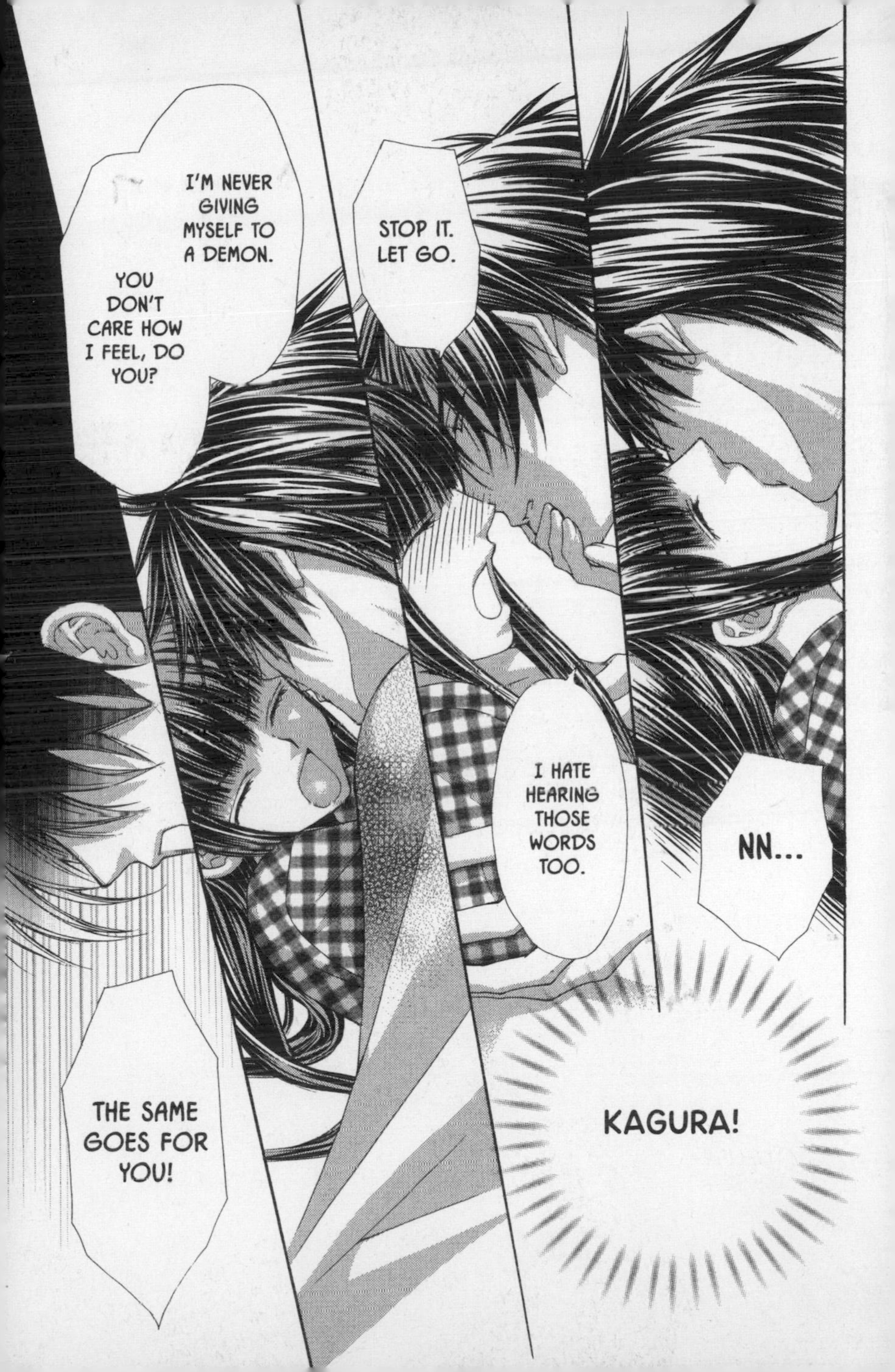
NN...
STOP IT. LET GO.
I HATE HEARING THOSE WORDS TOO.
I'M NEVER GIVING MYSELF TO A DEMON.
YOU DON'T CARE HOW I FEEL, DO YOU?
THE SAME GOES FOR YOU!
KAGURA!

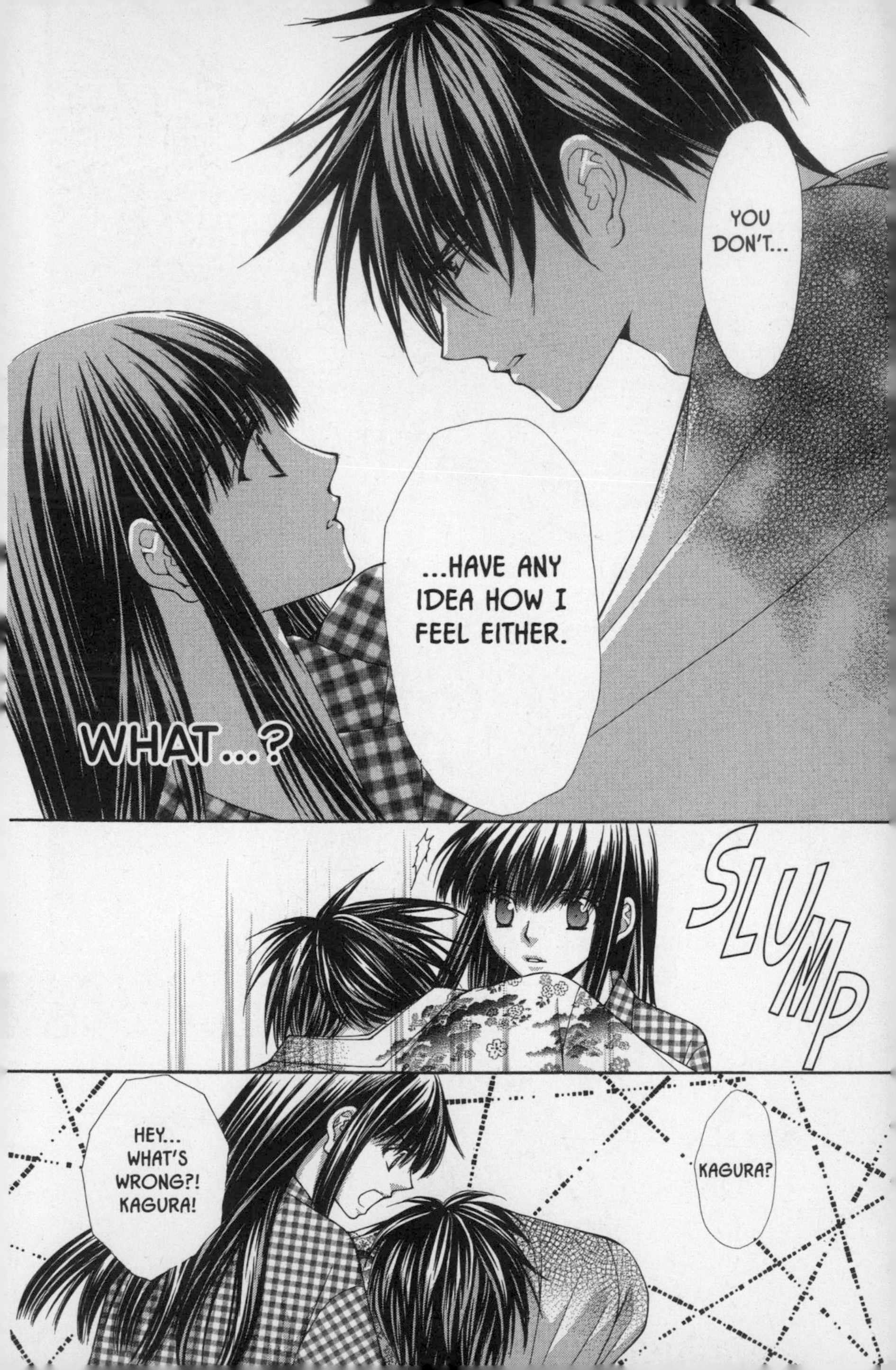
YOU DON'T...
...HAVE ANY IDEA HOW I FEEL EITHER.
WHAT...?
SLUMP
KAGURA?
HEY... WHAT'S WRONG?! KAGURA!

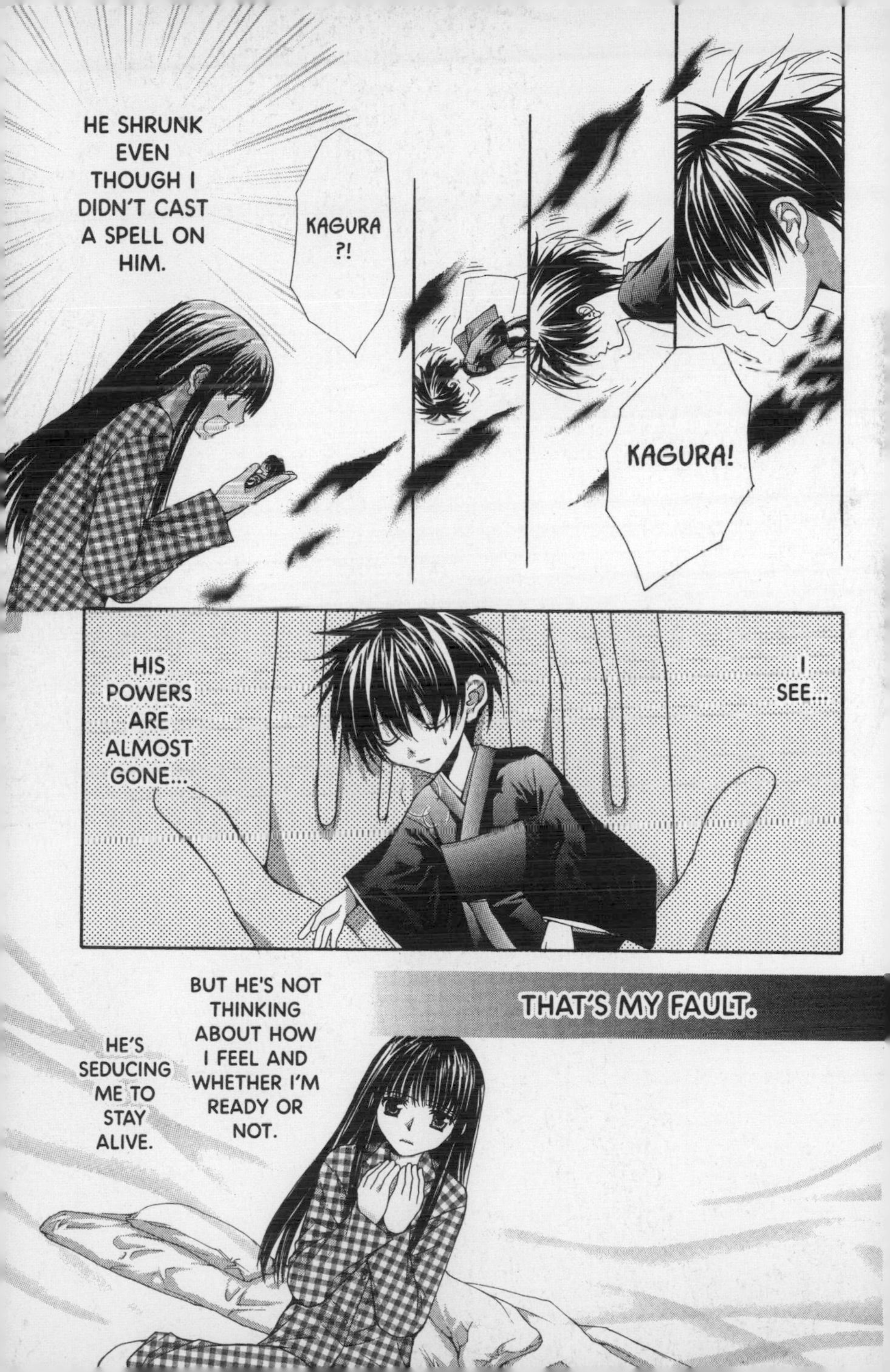
KAGURA!
KAGURA ?!
HE SHRUNK EVEN THOUGH I DIDN'T CAST A SPELL ON HIM.
I SEE...
HIS POWERS ARE ALMOST GONE...
THAT'S MY FAULT.
BUT HE'S NOT THINKING ABOUT HOW I FEEL AND WHETHER I'M READY OR NOT.
HE'S SEDUCING ME TO STAY ALIVE.

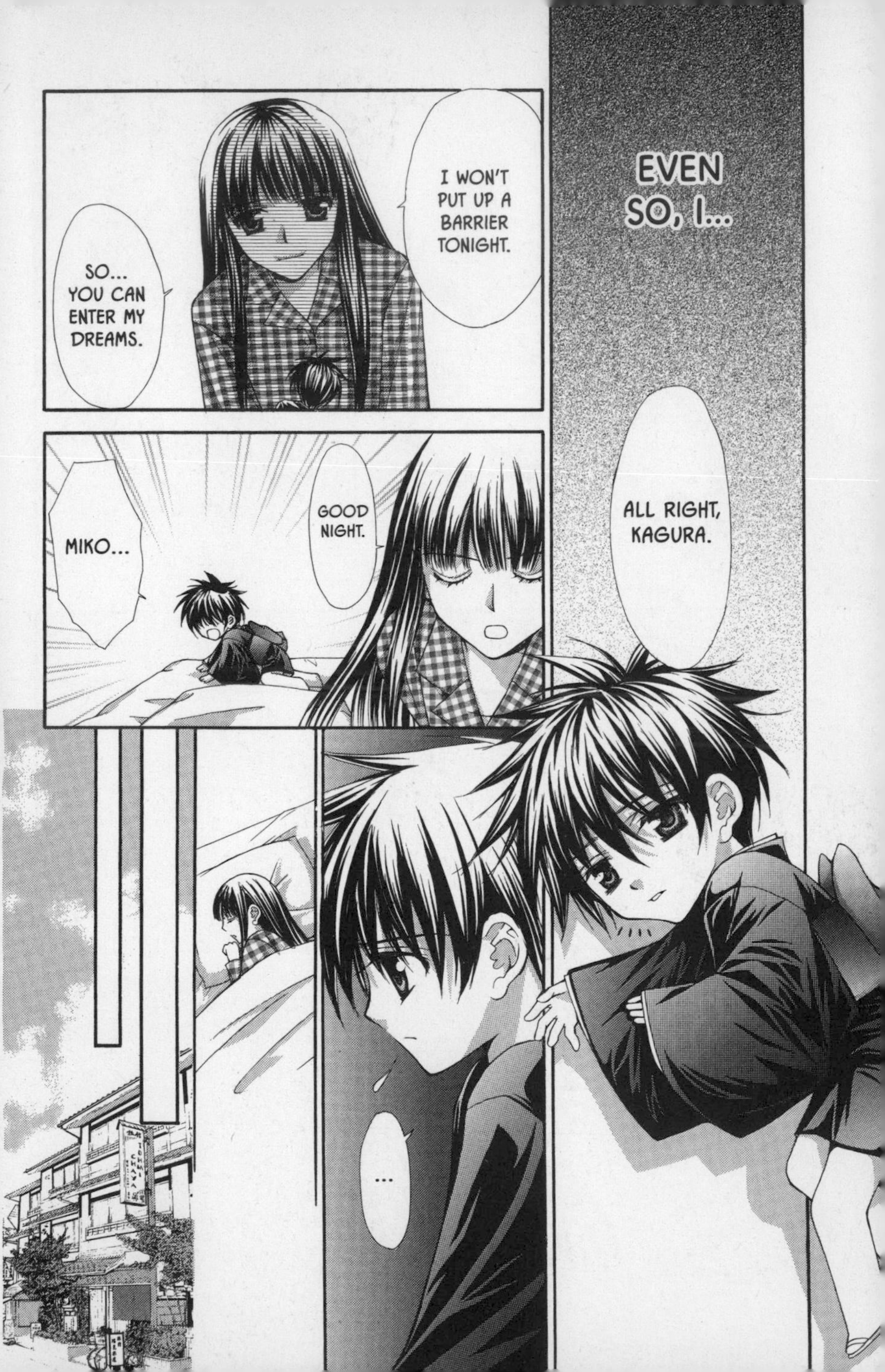
EVEN SO, I...
ALL RIGHT, KAGURA.
I WON'T PUT UP A BARRIER TONIGHT.
SO... YOU CAN ENTER MY DREAMS.
GOOD NIGHT.
MIKO...
...

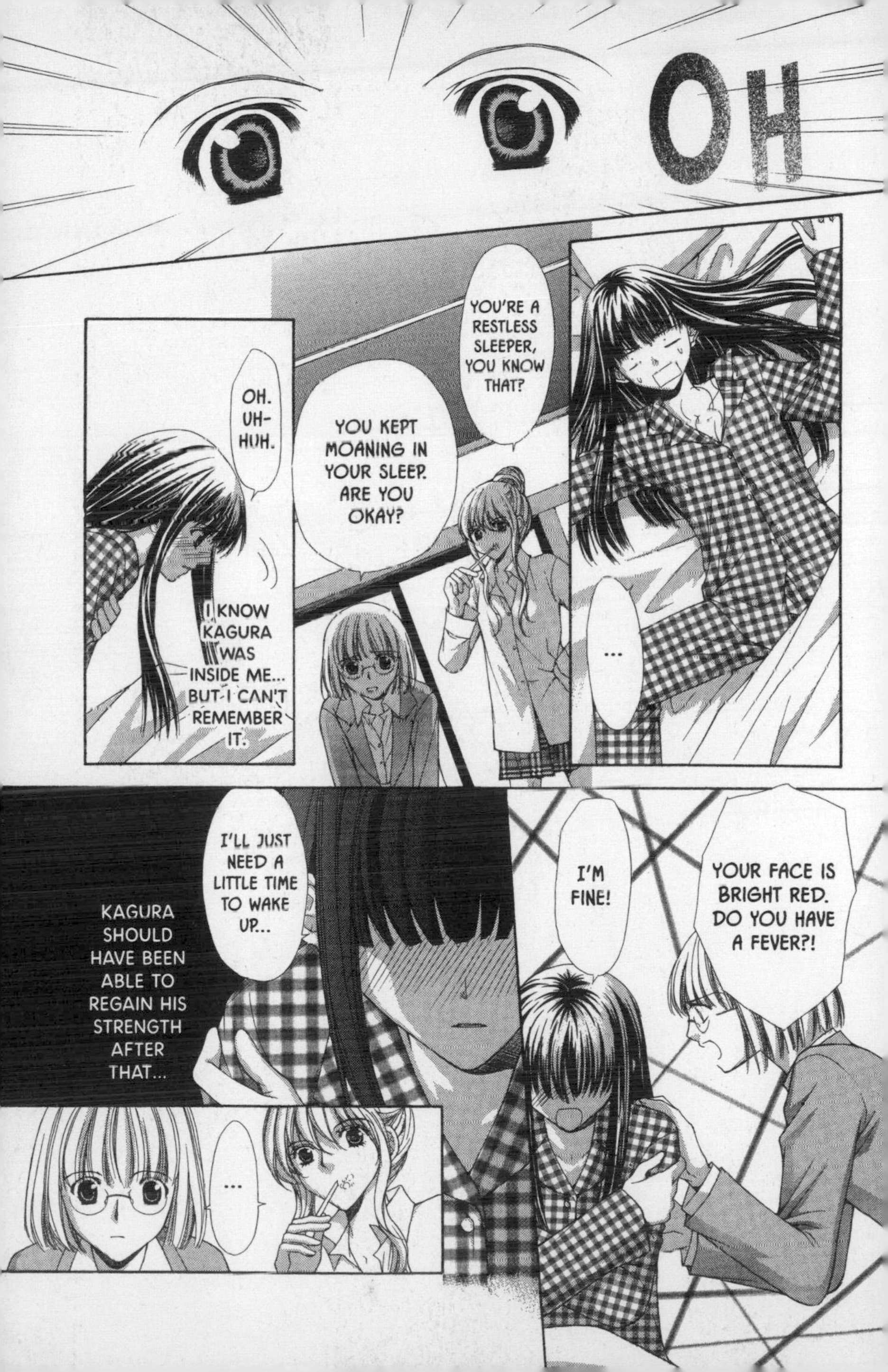
OH
...
YOU'RE A RESTLESS SLEEPER, YOU KNOW THAT?
YOU KEPT MOANING IN YOUR SLEEP. ARE YOU OKAY?
OH. UH-HUH.
I KNOW KAGURA WAS INSIDE ME... BUT I CAN'T REMEMBER IT.
YOUR FACE IS BRIGHT RED. DO YOU HAVE A FEVER?!
I'M FINE!
I'LL JUST NEED A LITTLE TIME TO WAKE UP...
KAGURA SHOULD HAVE BEEN ABLE TO REGAIN HIS STRENGTH AFTER THAT...
...

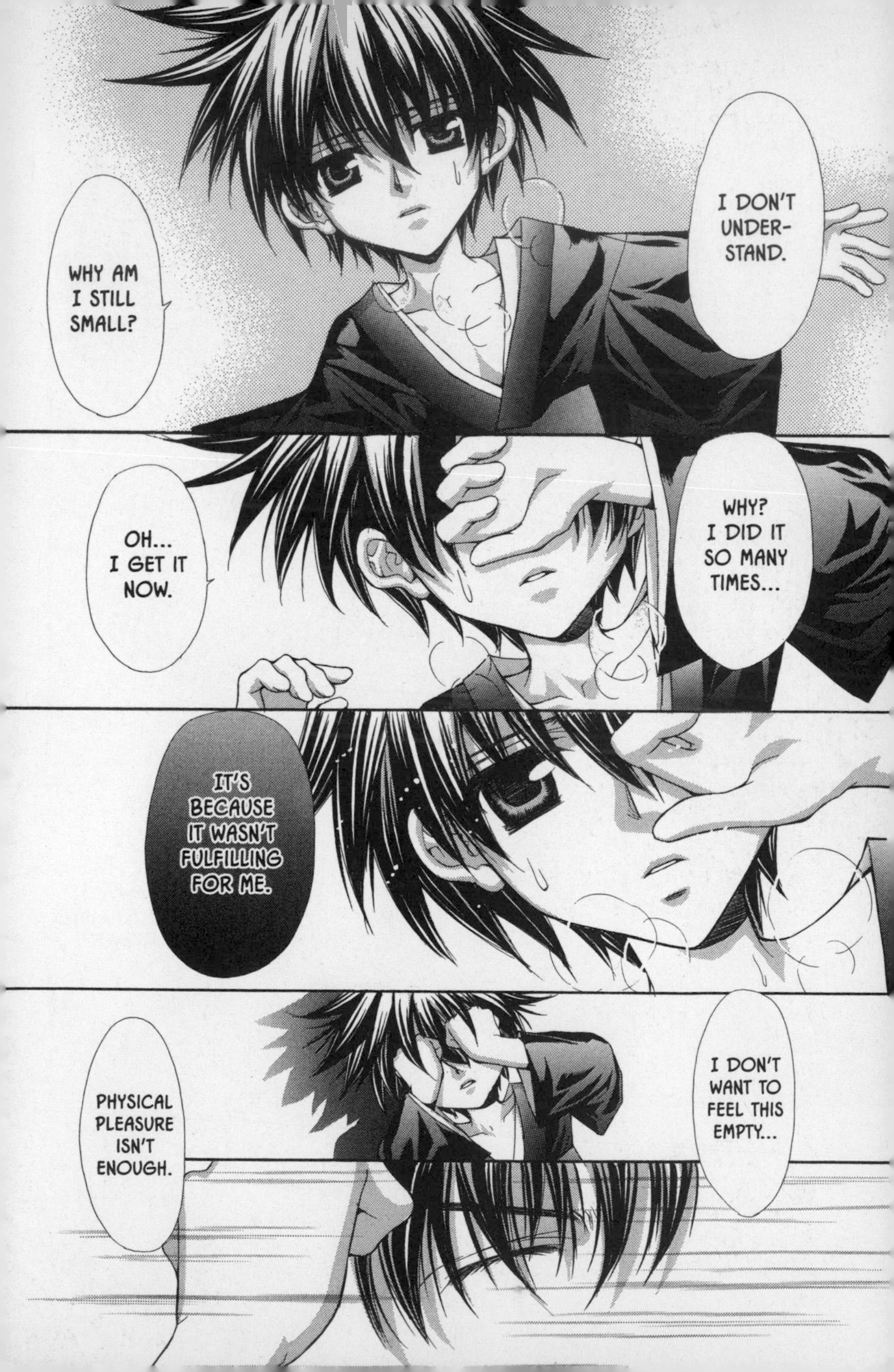
I DON'T UNDER-STAND.
WHY AM I STILL SMALL?
WHY? I DID IT SO MANY TIMES...
OH... I GET IT NOW.
IT'S BECAUSE IT WASN'T FULFILLING FOR ME.
I DON'T WANT TO FEEL THIS EMPTY...
PHYSICAL PLEASURE ISN'T ENOUGH.

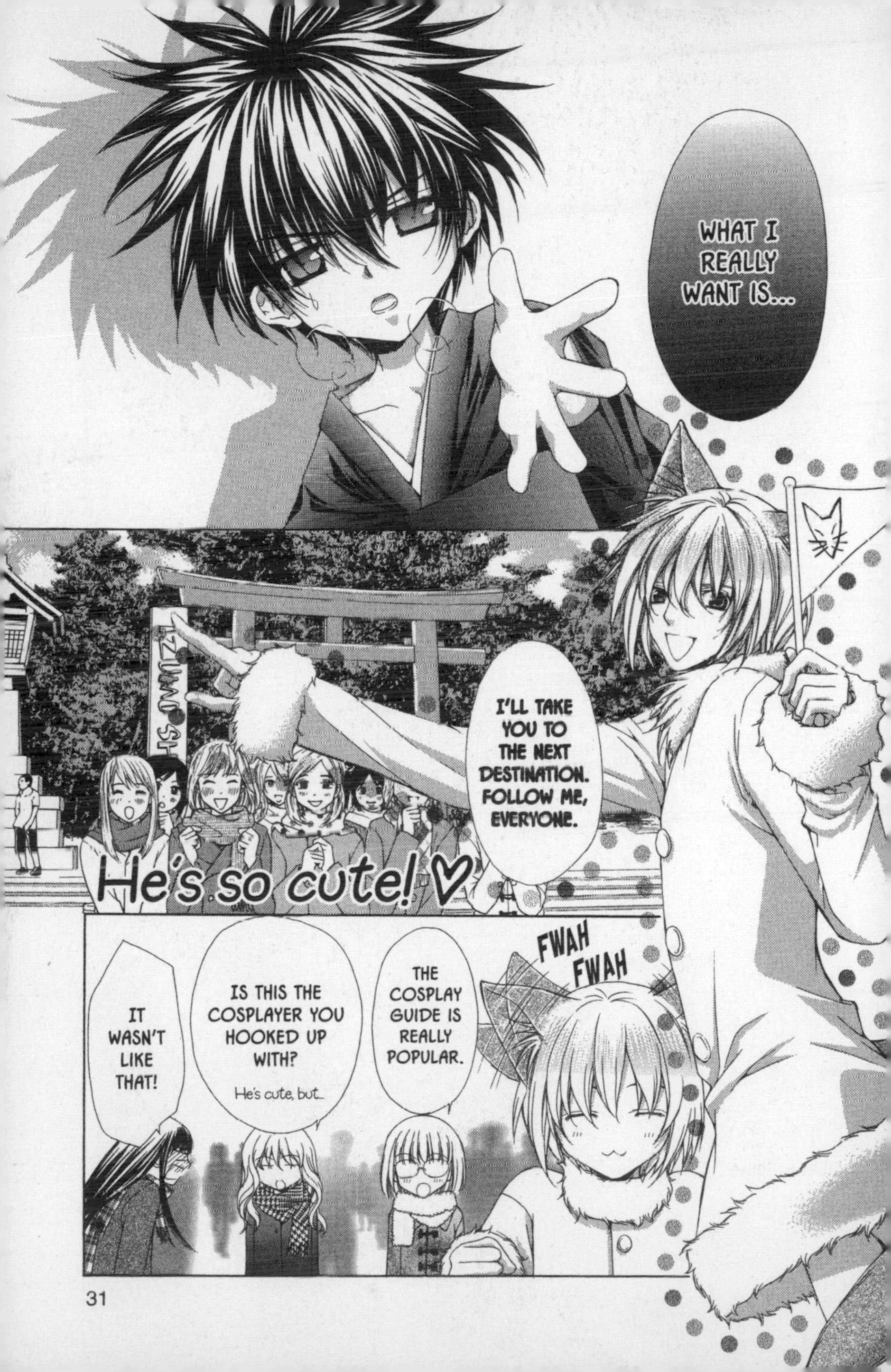
WHAT I REALLY WANT IS...
I'LL TAKE YOU TO THE NEXT DESTINATION. FOLLOW ME, EVERYONE.
He's so cute! ♥
FWAH FWAH
THE COSPLAY GUIDE IS REALLY POPULAR.
IS THIS THE COSPLAYER YOU HOOKED UP WITH?
He's cute, but...
IT WASN'T LIKE THAT!

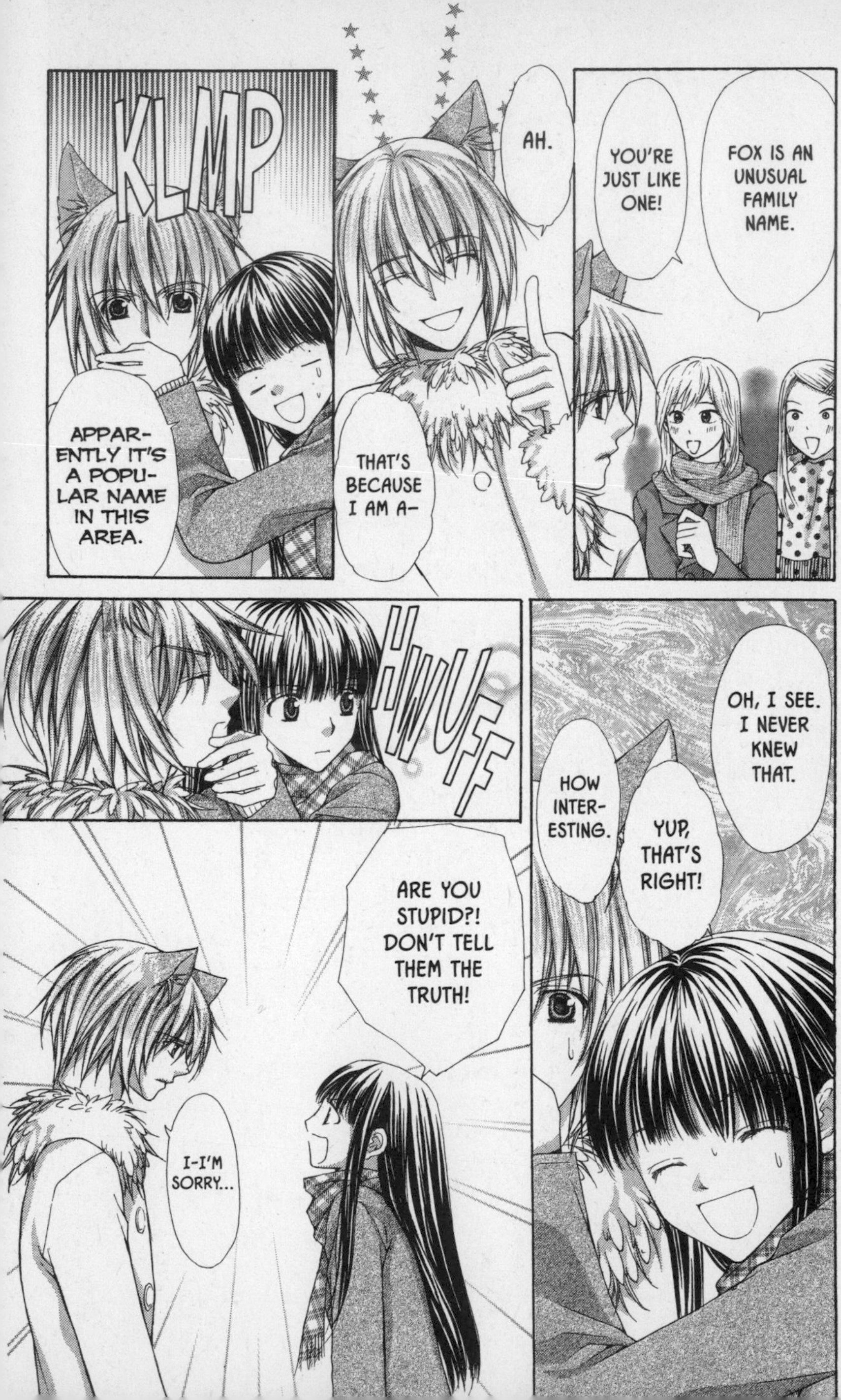
FOX IS AN UNUSUAL FAMILY NAME.
YOU'RE JUST LIKE ONE!
AH.
THAT'S BECAUSE I AM A-
KLMP
APPARENTLY IT'S A POPULAR NAME IN THIS AREA.
OH, I SEE. I NEVER KNEW THAT.
YUP, THAT'S RIGHT!
HOW INTERESTING.
HWUFF
ARE YOU STUPID?! DON'T TELL THEM THE TRUTH!
I-I'M SORRY...

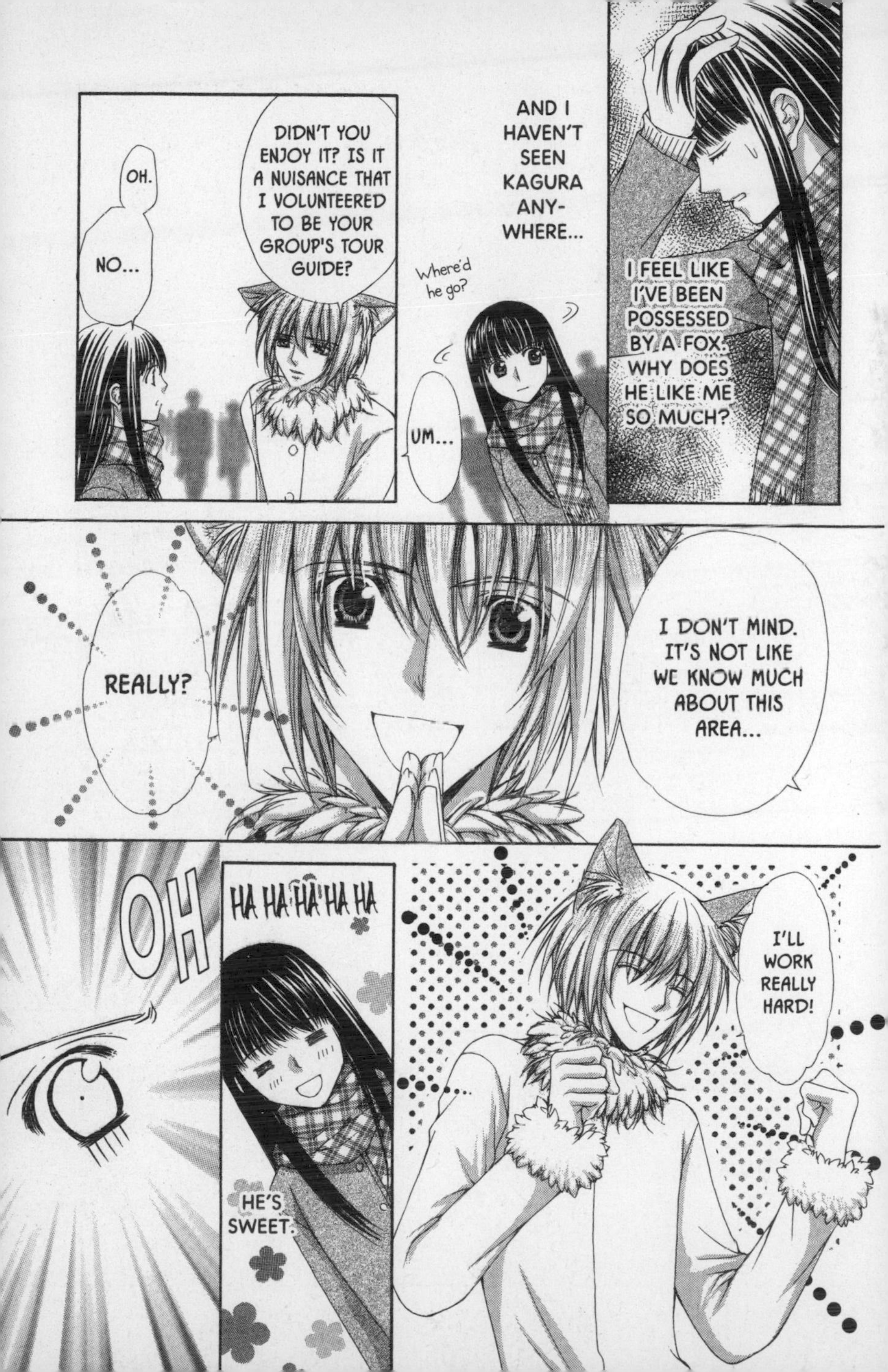

I FEEL LIKE I'VE BEEN POSSESSED BY A FOX. WHY DOES HE LIKE ME SO MUCH?
AND I HAVEN'T SEEN KAGURA ANY-WHERE...
Where'd he go?
UM...
DIDN'T YOU ENJOY IT? IS IT A NUISANCE THAT I VOLUNTEERED TO BE YOUR GROUP'S TOUR GUIDE?
OH.
NO...
I DON'T MIND. IT'S NOT LIKE WE KNOW MUCH ABOUT THIS AREA...
REALLY?
I'LL WORK REALLY HARD!
HA HA HA HA HA
HE'S SWEET.
OH

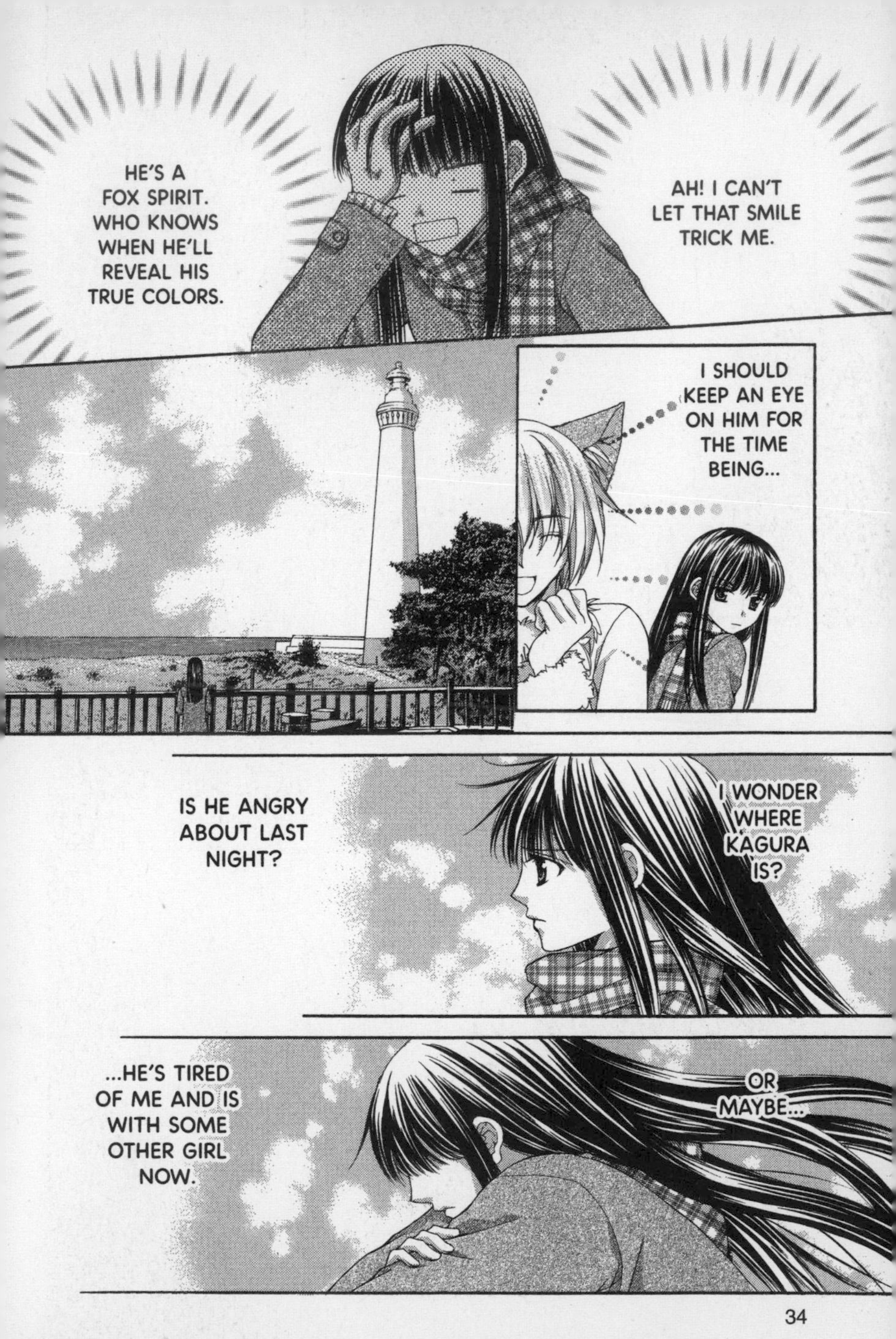
AH! I CAN'T LET THAT SMILE TRICK ME.
HE'S A FOX SPIRIT. WHO KNOWS WHEN HE'LL REVEAL HIS TRUE COLORS.
I SHOULD KEEP AN EYE ON HIM FOR THE TIME BEING...
I WONDER WHERE KAGURA IS?
IS HE ANGRY ABOUT LAST NIGHT?
OR MAYBE...
...HE'S TIRED OF ME AND IS WITH SOME OTHER GIRL NOW.

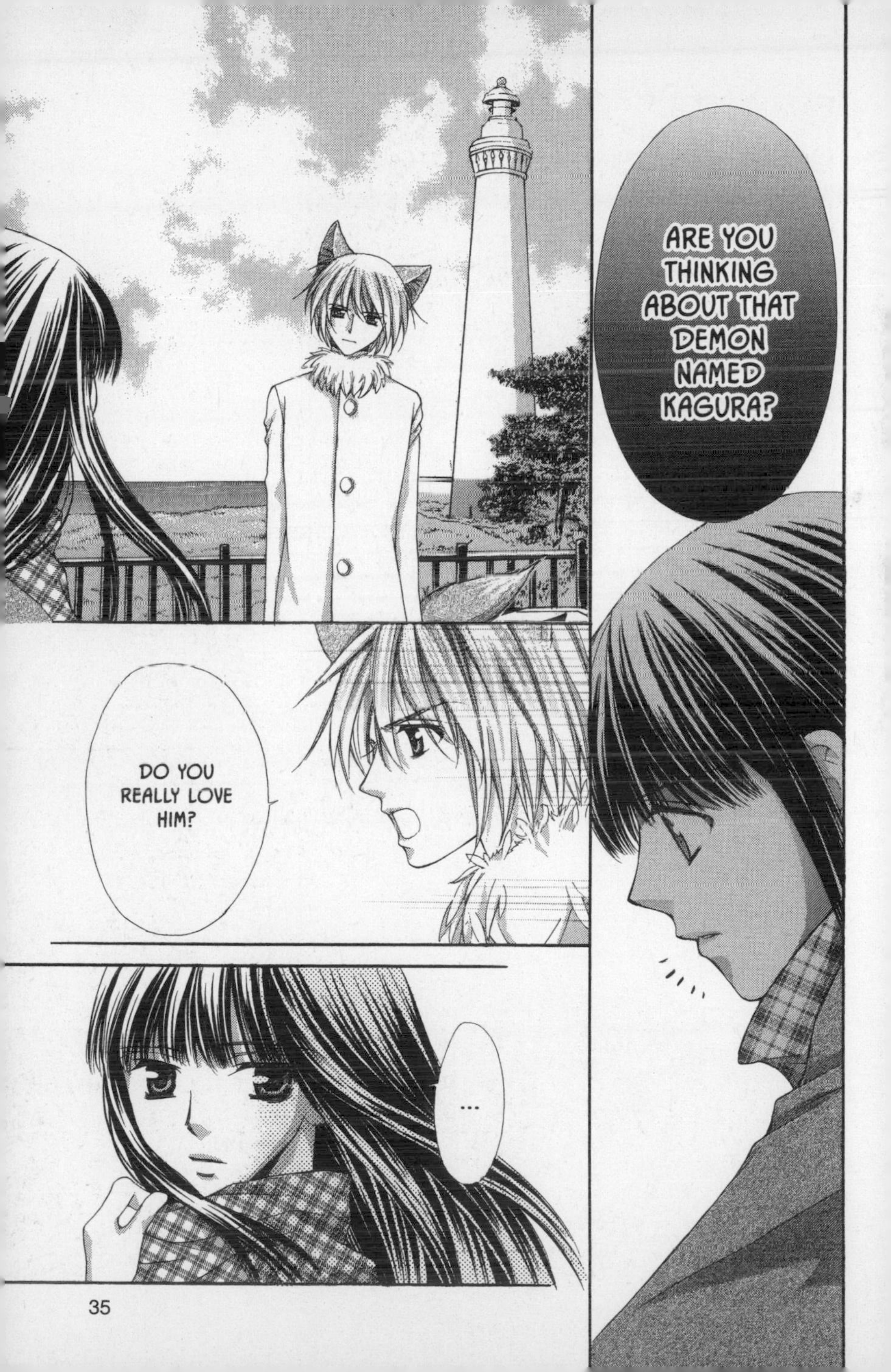
ARE YOU THINKING ABOUT THAT DEMON NAMED KAGURA?
DO YOU REALLY LOVE HIM?
...

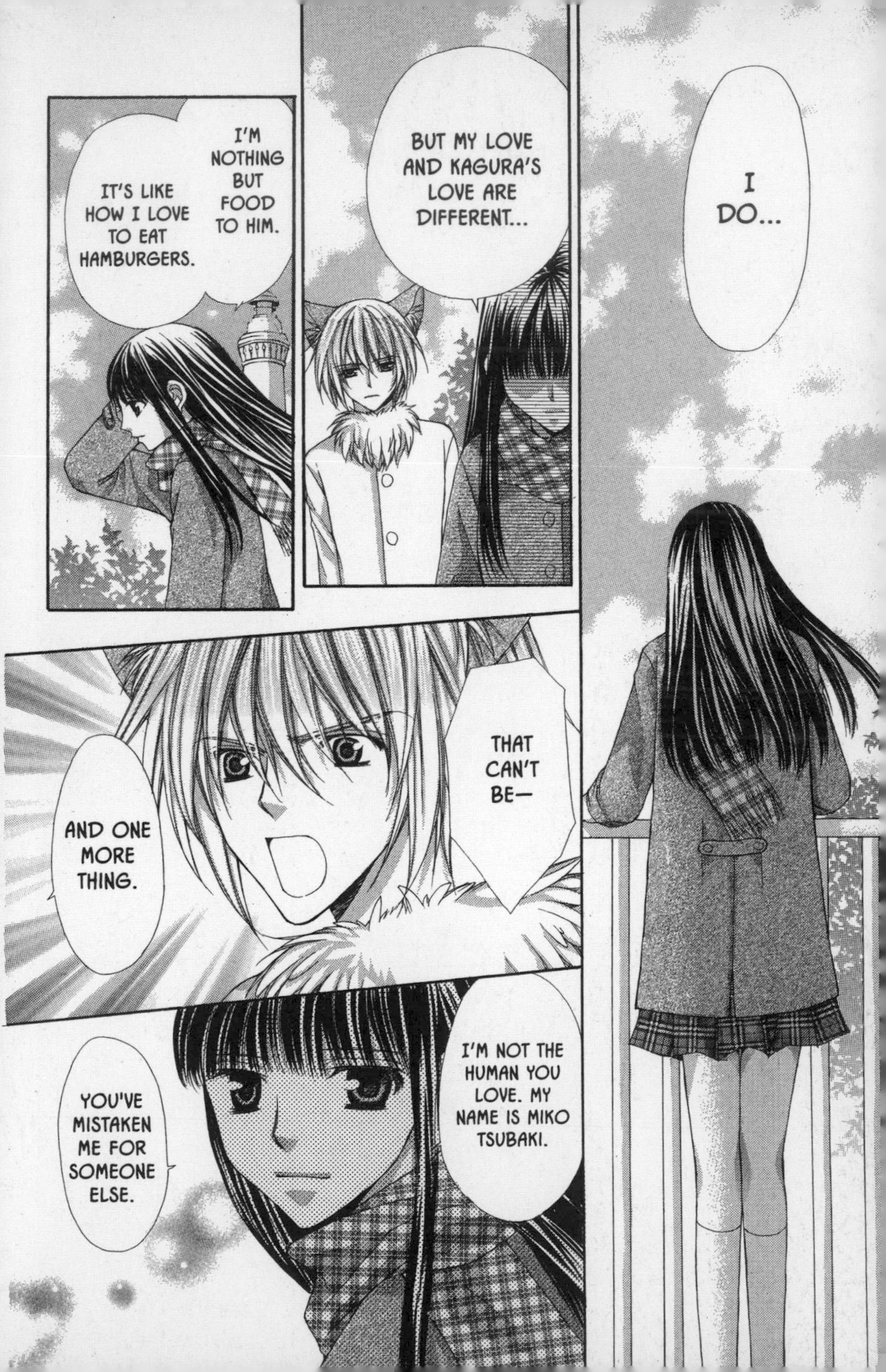
I DO...
BUT MY LOVE AND KAGURA'S LOVE ARE DIFFERENT...
I'M NOTHING BUT FOOD TO HIM.
IT'S LIKE HOW I LOVE TO EAT HAMBURGERS.
THAT CAN'T BE—
AND ONE MORE THING.
I'M NOT THE HUMAN YOU LOVE. MY NAME IS MIKO TSUBAKI.
YOU'VE MISTAKEN ME FOR SOMEONE ELSE.

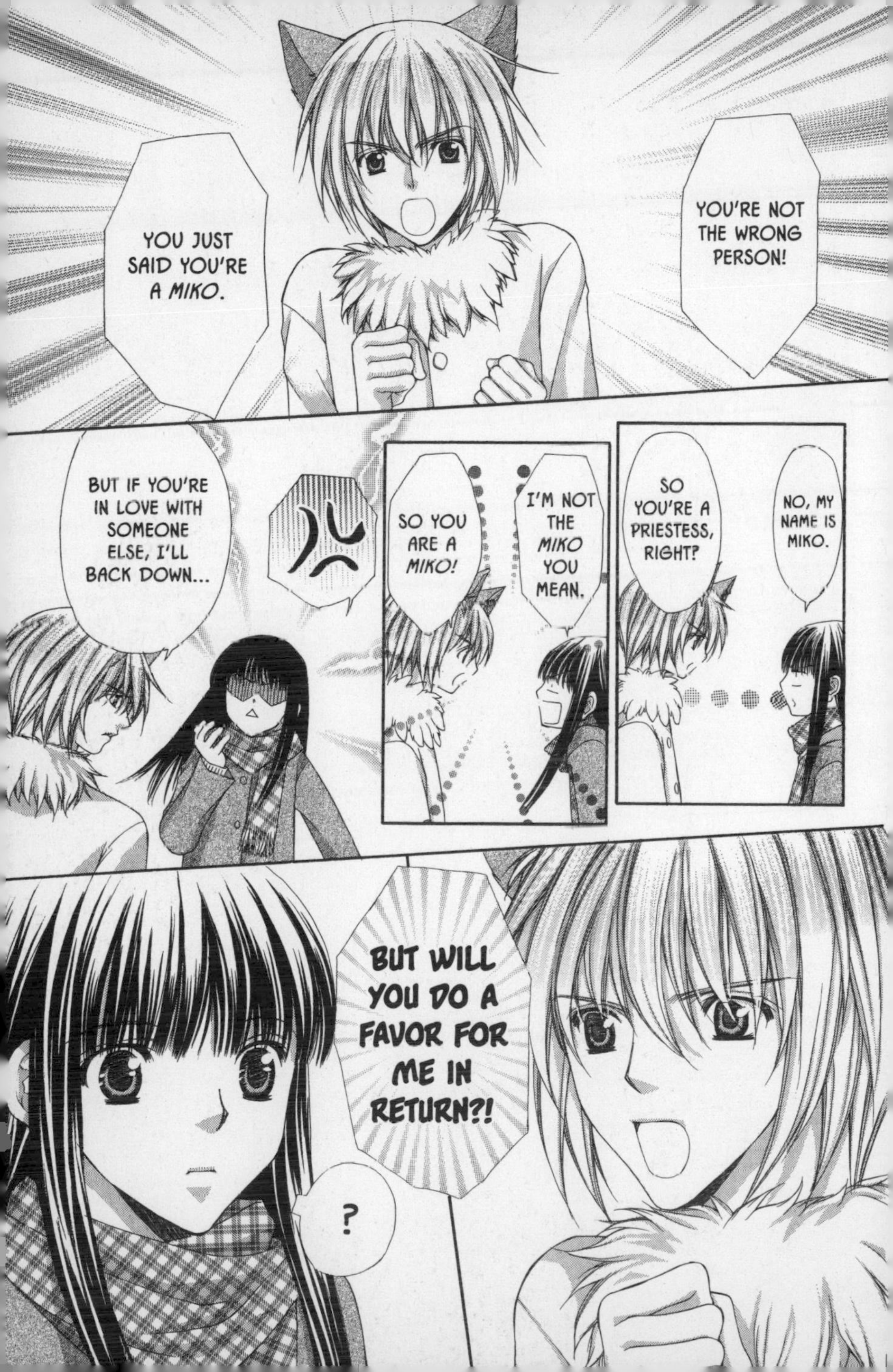
YOU'RE NOT THE WRONG PERSON!
YOU JUST SAID YOU'RE A *MIKO*.
NO, MY NAME IS MIKO.
SO YOU'RE A PRIESTESS, RIGHT?
I'M NOT THE *MIKO* YOU MEAN.
SO YOU ARE A *MIKO!*
BUT IF YOU'RE IN LOVE WITH SOMEONE ELSE, I'LL BACK DOWN...
BUT WILL YOU DO A FAVOR FOR ME IN RETURN?!
?

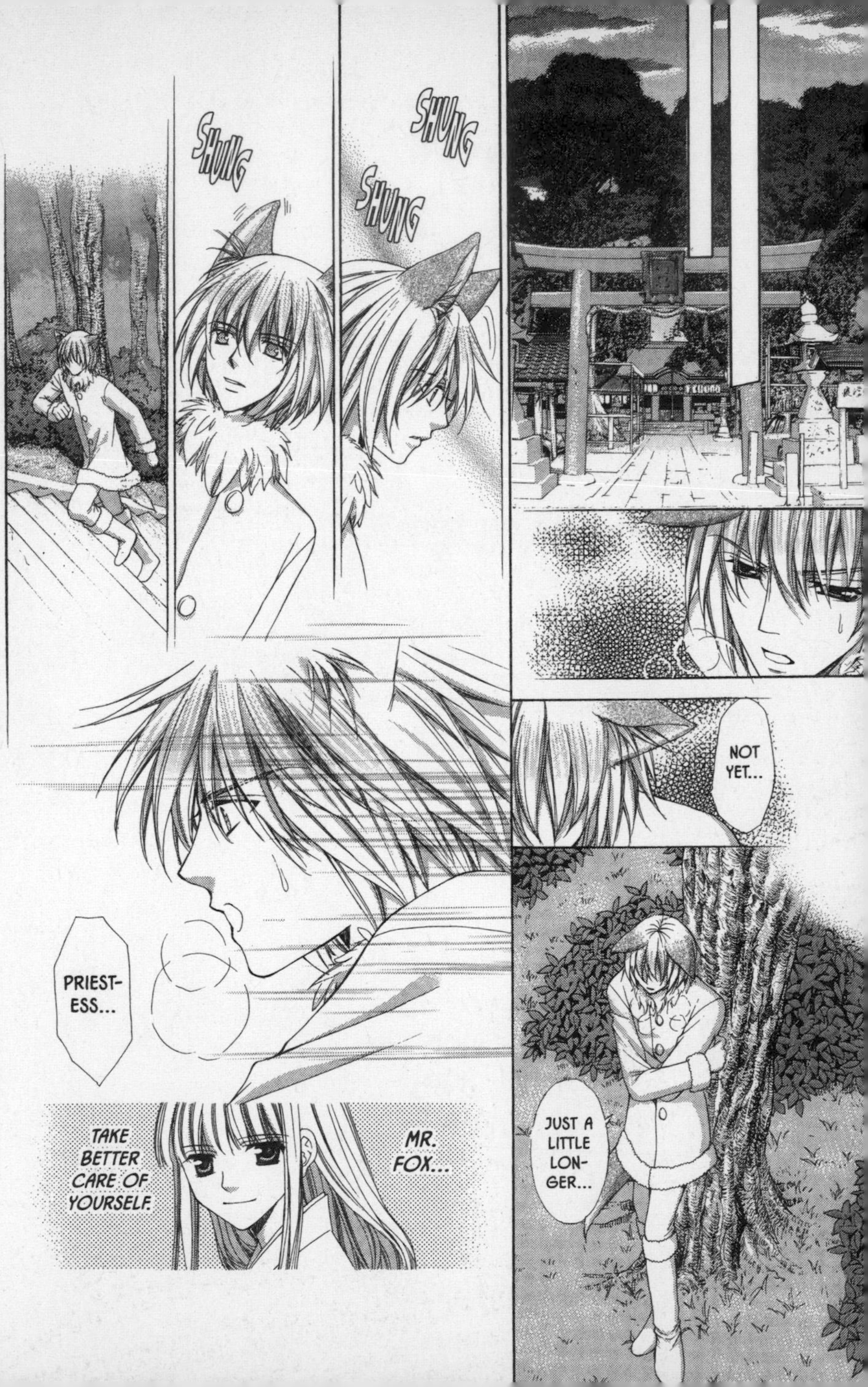
NOT YET...
JUST A LITTLE LONG-GER...
SHUNG
SHUNG
SHUNG
PRIEST-ESS...
MR. FOX...
TAKE BETTER CARE OF YOURSELF.

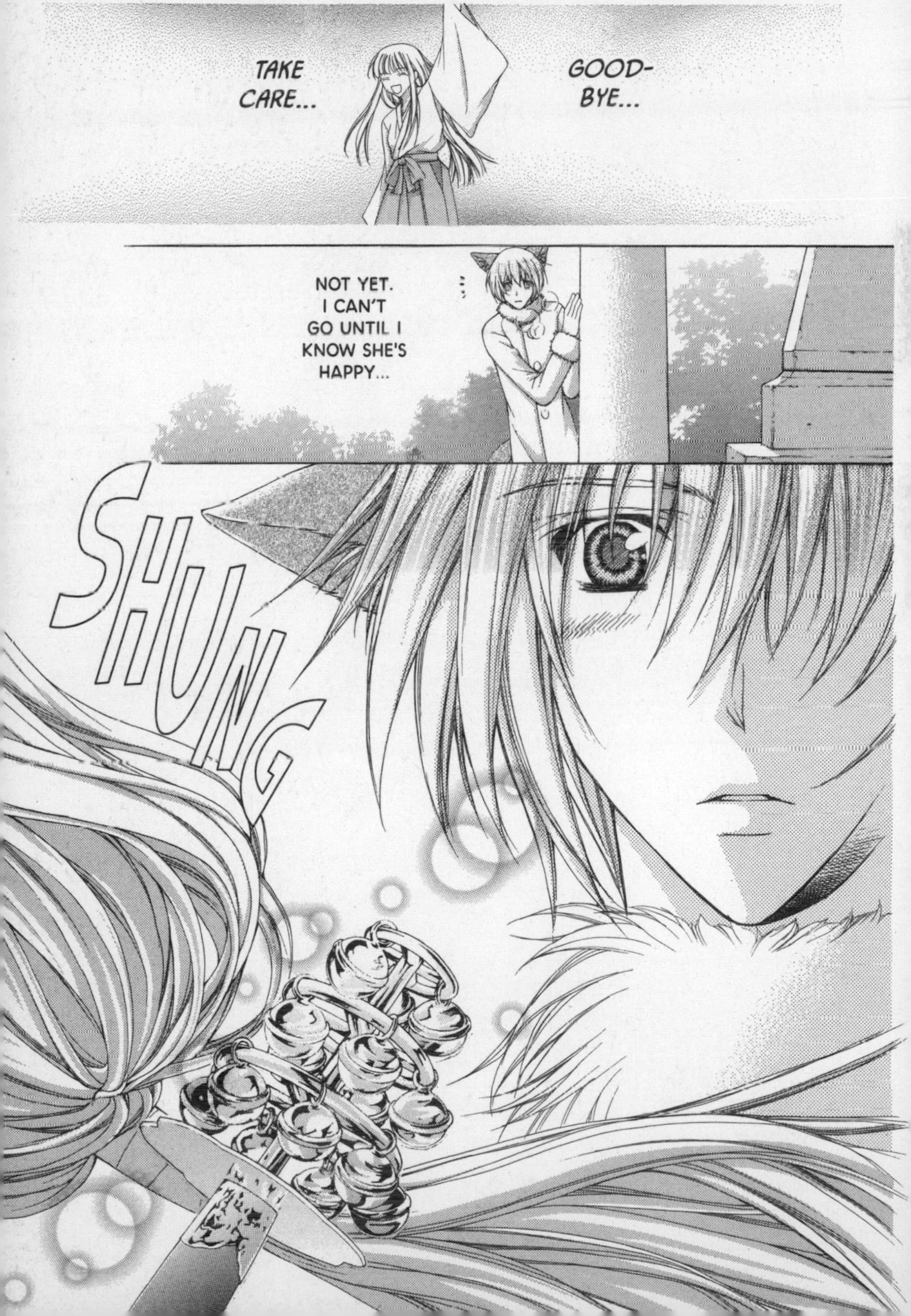
GOOD-BYE...
TAKE CARE...
NOT YET. I CAN'T GO UNTIL I KNOW SHE'S HAPPY...
SHUNG

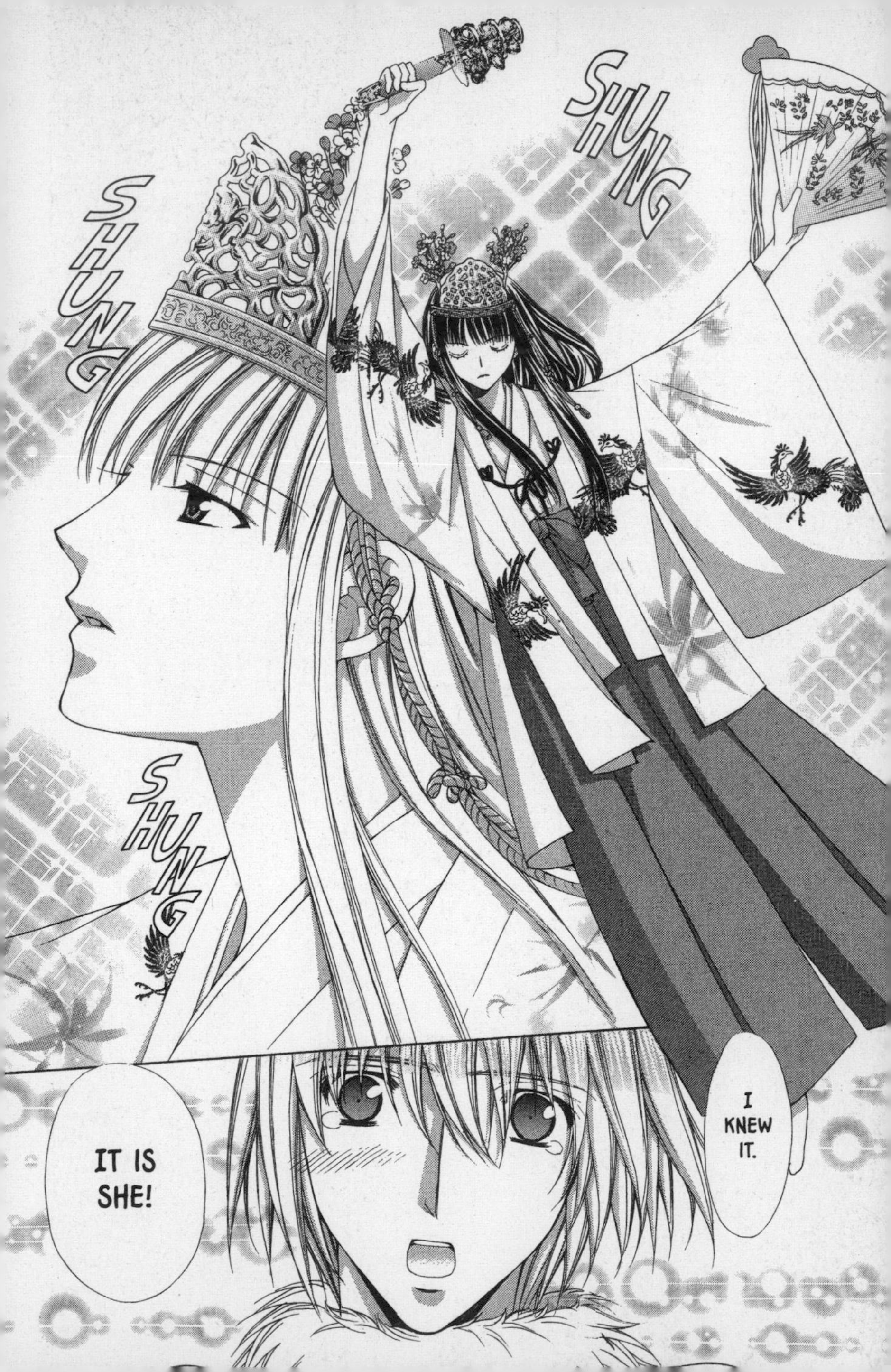
SHUNG
SHUNG
SHUNG
I KNEW IT.
IT IS SHE!

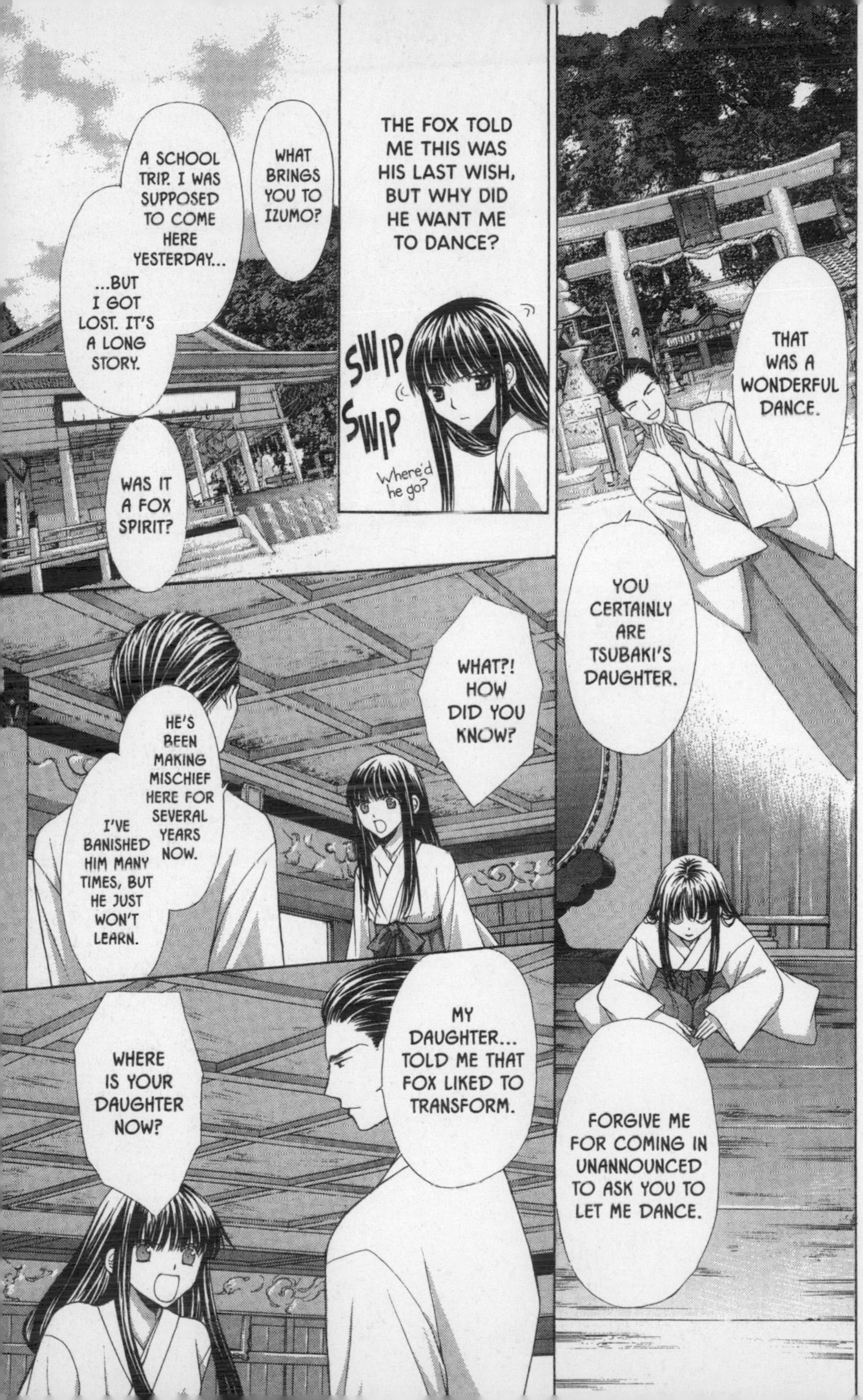
THAT WAS A WONDERFUL DANCE.
YOU CERTAINLY ARE TSUBAKI'S DAUGHTER.
FORGIVE ME FOR COMING IN UNANNOUNCED TO ASK YOU TO LET ME DANCE.
THE FOX TOLD ME THIS WAS HIS LAST WISH, BUT WHY DID HE WANT ME TO DANCE?
SWIP SWIP
Where'd he go?
WHAT BRINGS YOU TO IZUMO?
A SCHOOL TRIP. I WAS SUPPOSED TO COME HERE YESTERDAY...
...BUT I GOT LOST. IT'S A LONG STORY.
WAS IT A FOX SPIRIT?
WHAT?! HOW DID YOU KNOW?
HE'S BEEN MAKING MISCHIEF HERE FOR SEVERAL YEARS NOW.
I'VE BANISHED HIM MANY TIMES, BUT HE JUST WON'T LEARN.
MY DAUGHTER... TOLD ME THAT FOX LIKED TO TRANSFORM.
WHERE IS YOUR DAUGHTER NOW?

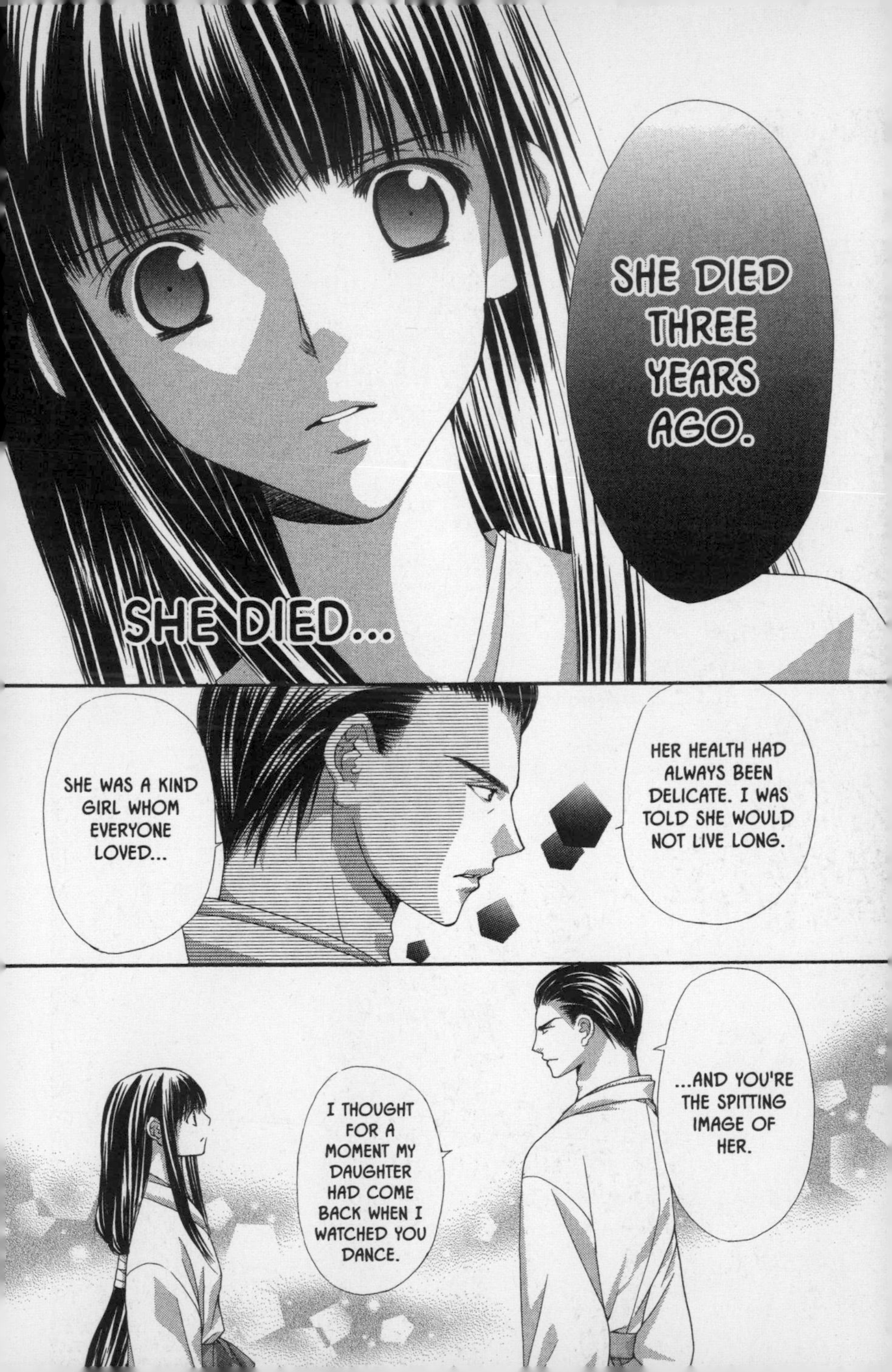
SHE DIED THREE YEARS AGO.
SHE DIED...
HER HEALTH HAD ALWAYS BEEN DELICATE. I WAS TOLD SHE WOULD NOT LIVE LONG.
SHE WAS A KIND GIRL WHOM EVERYONE LOVED...
...AND YOU'RE THE SPITTING IMAGE OF HER.
I THOUGHT FOR A MOMENT MY DAUGHTER HAD COME BACK WHEN I WATCHED YOU DANCE.

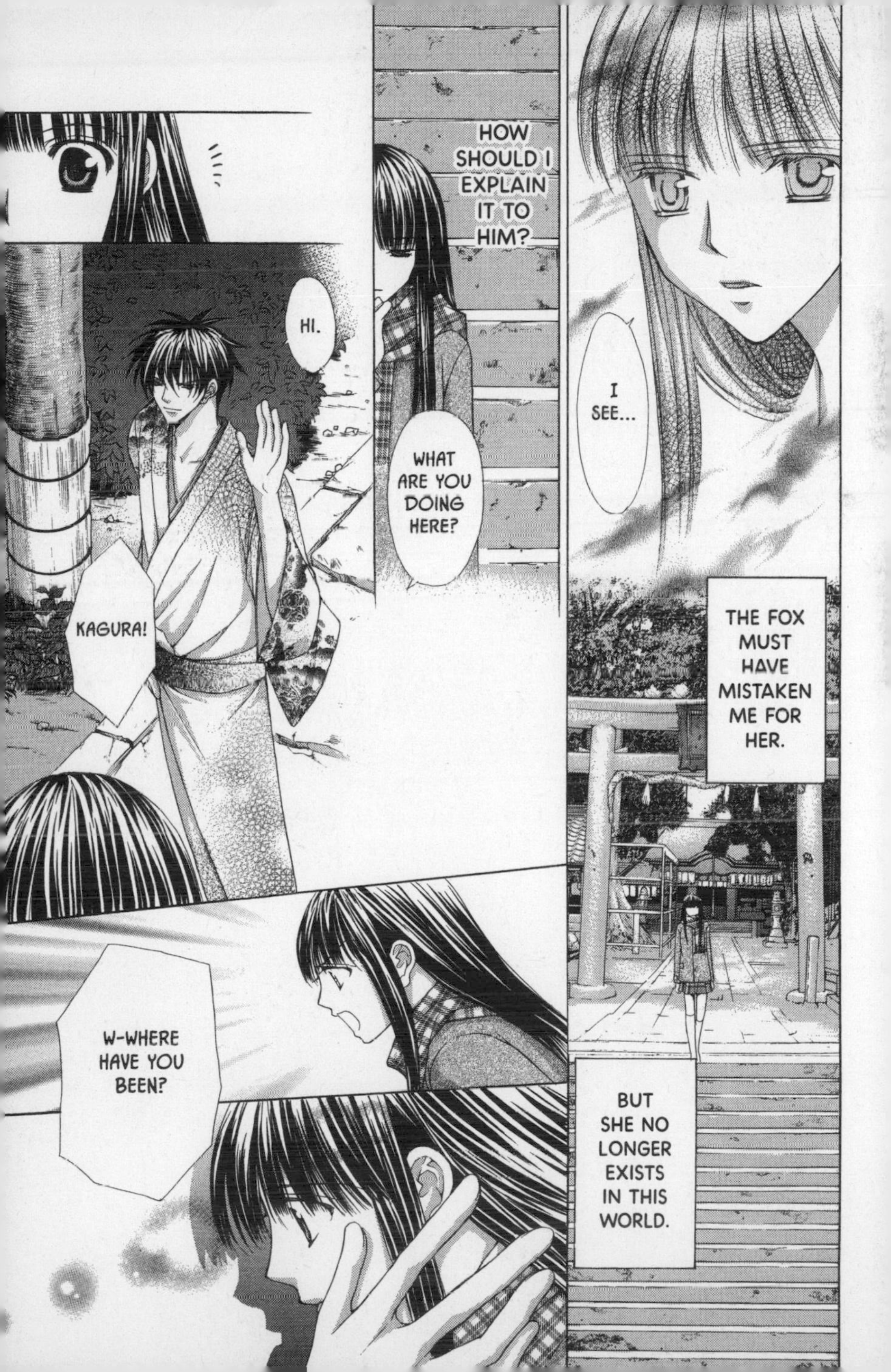
I SEE...
THE FOX MUST HAVE MISTAKEN ME FOR HER.
BUT SHE NO LONGER EXISTS IN THIS WORLD.
HOW SHOULD I EXPLAIN IT TO HIM?
WHAT ARE YOU DOING HERE?
HI.
KAGURA!
W-WHERE HAVE YOU BEEN?

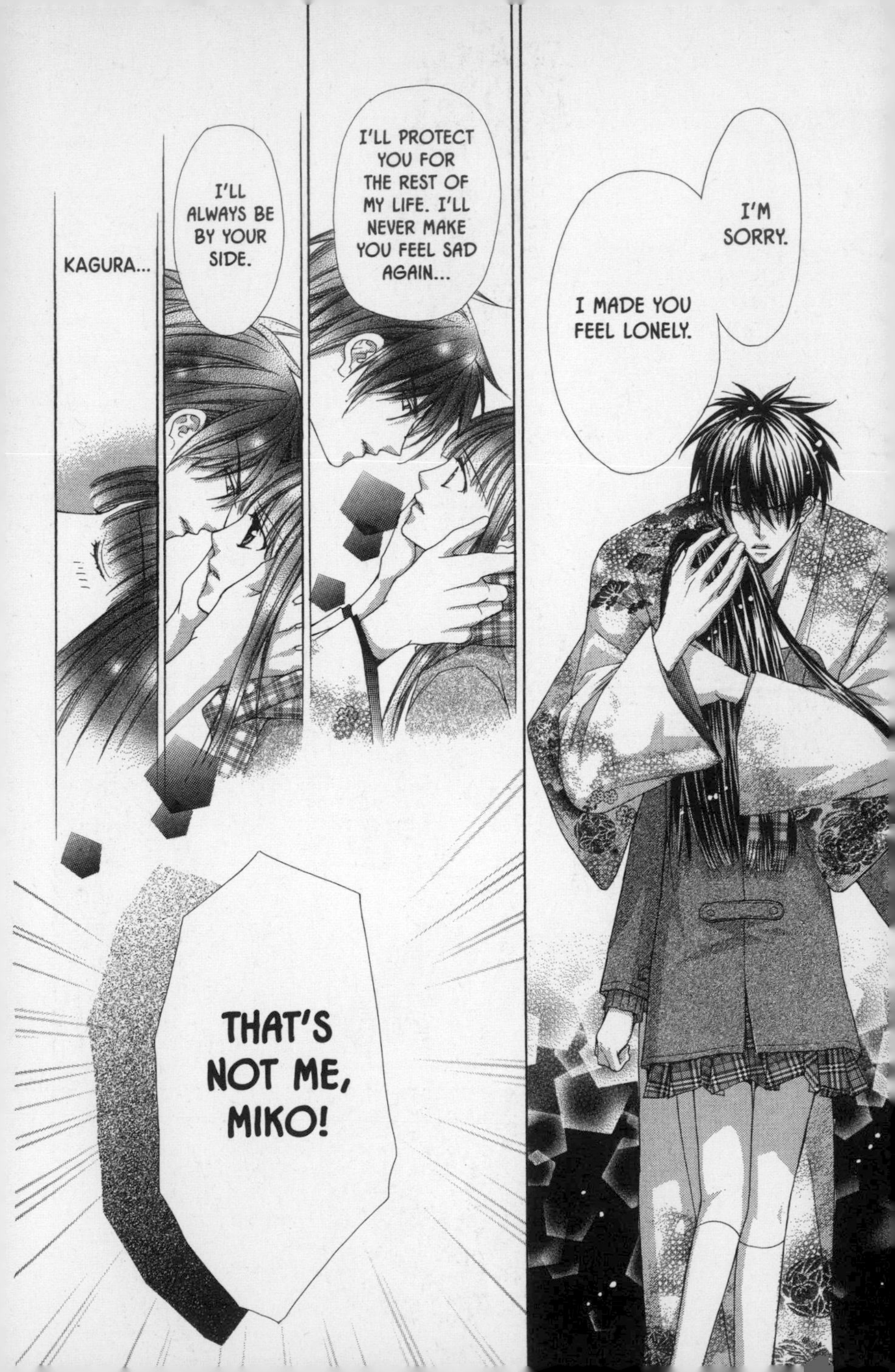
I'M SORRY.
I MADE YOU FEEL LONELY.
I'LL PROTECT YOU FOR THE REST OF MY LIFE. I'LL NEVER MAKE YOU FEEL SAD AGAIN...
I'LL ALWAYS BE BY YOUR SIDE.
KAGURA...
THAT'S NOT ME, MIKO!

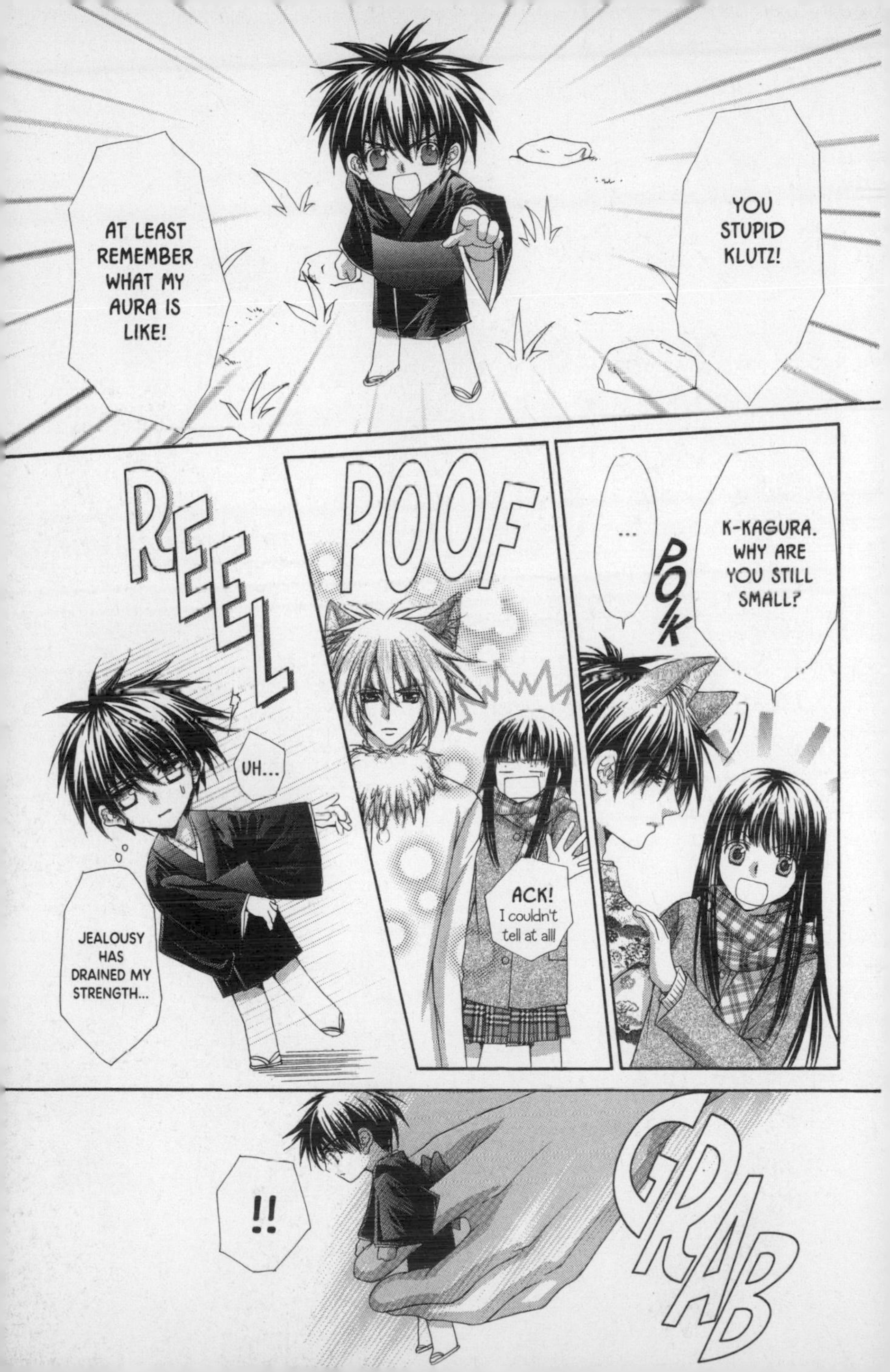
YOU STUPID KLUTZ!
AT LEAST REMEMBER WHAT MY AURA IS LIKE!
K-KAGURA. WHY ARE YOU STILL SMALL?
...
POK
POOF
ACK! I couldn't tell at all!
REEL
UH...
JEALOUSY HAS DRAINED MY STRENGTH...
GRAB
!!

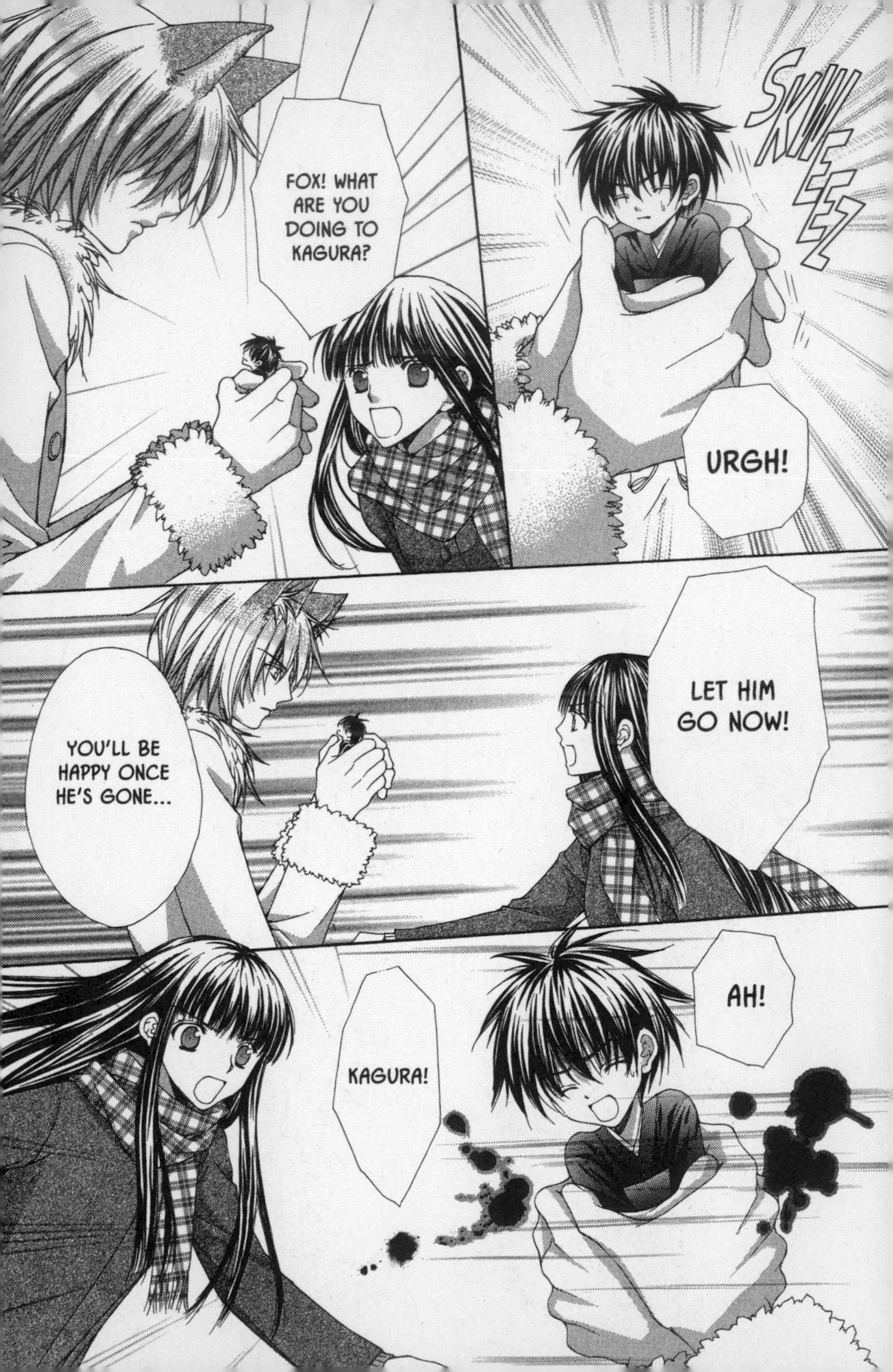
SKWEEZ
URGH!
FOX! WHAT ARE YOU DOING TO KAGURA?
LET HIM GO NOW!
YOU'LL BE HAPPY ONCE HE'S GONE...
AH!
KAGURA!

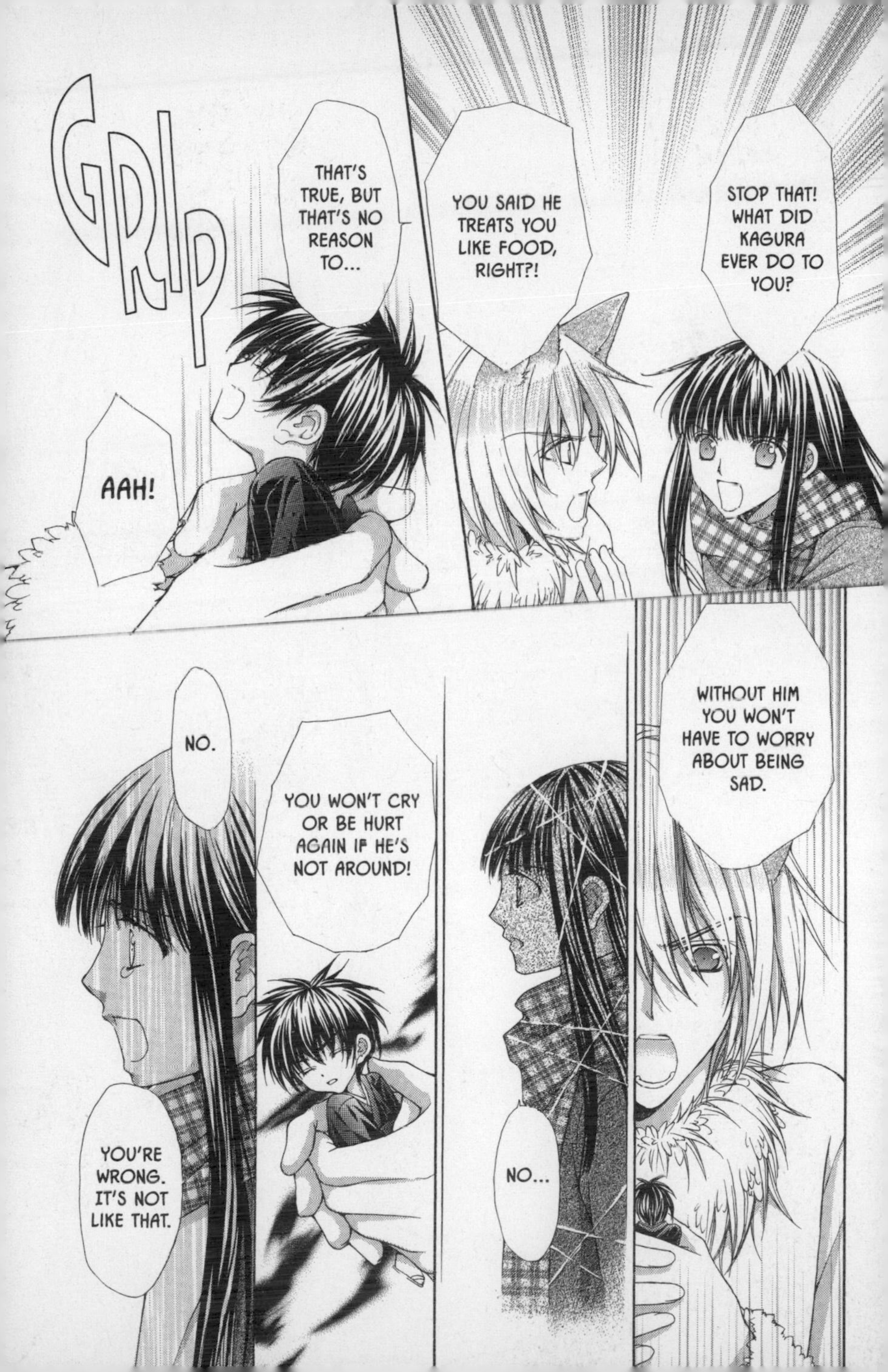
STOP THAT! WHAT DID KAGURA EVER DO TO YOU?
YOU SAID HE TREATS YOU LIKE FOOD, RIGHT?!
THAT'S TRUE, BUT THAT'S NO REASON TO...
GRIP
AAH!
WITHOUT HIM YOU WON'T HAVE TO WORRY ABOUT BEING SAD.
NO...
YOU WON'T CRY OR BE HURT AGAIN IF HE'S NOT AROUND!
NO.
YOU'RE WRONG. IT'S NOT LIKE THAT.

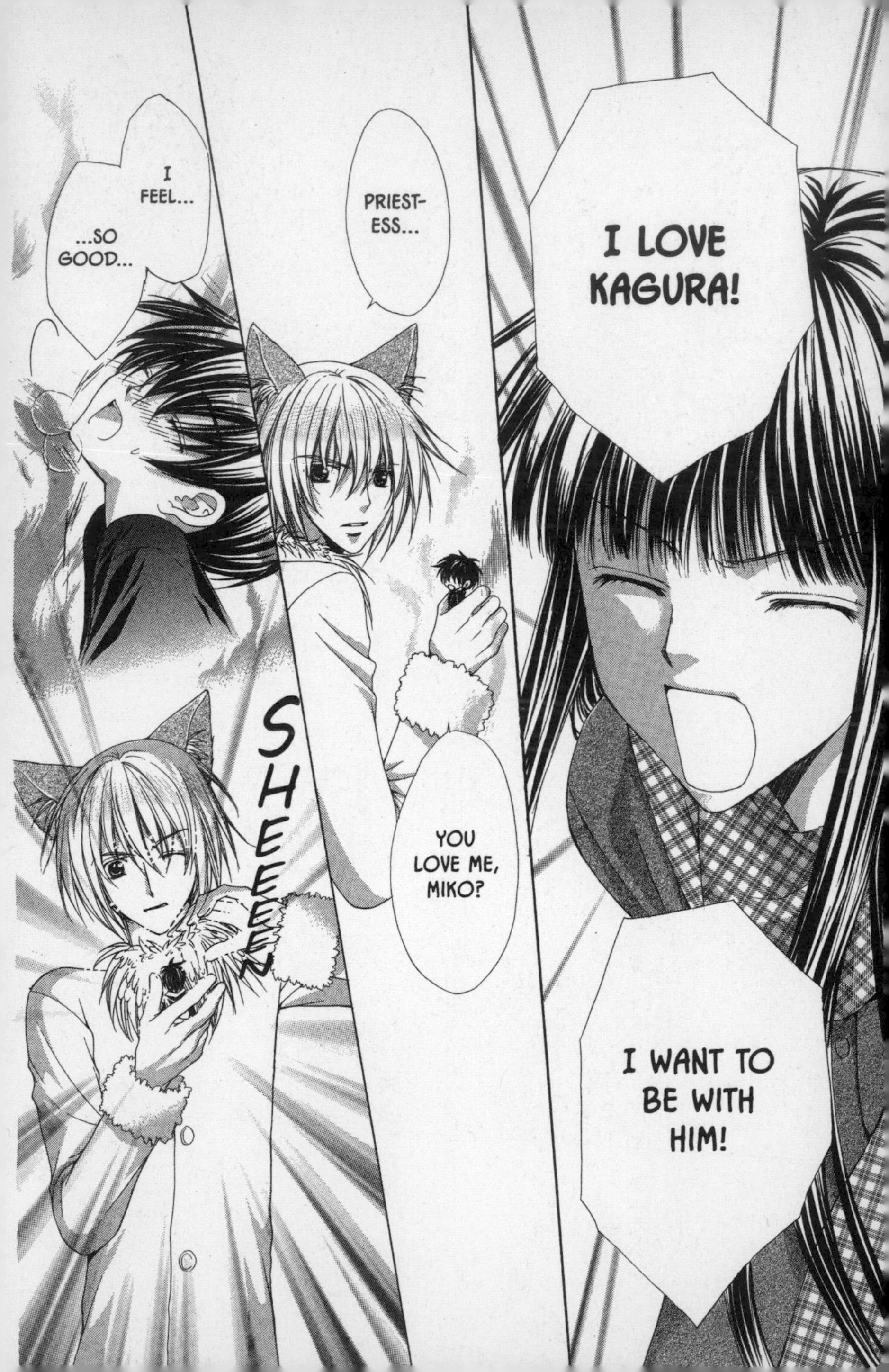
I LOVE KAGURA!
I WANT TO BE WITH HIM!
PRIEST-ESS...
YOU LOVE ME, MIKO?
SHEEEEEN
I FEEL...
...SO GOOD...

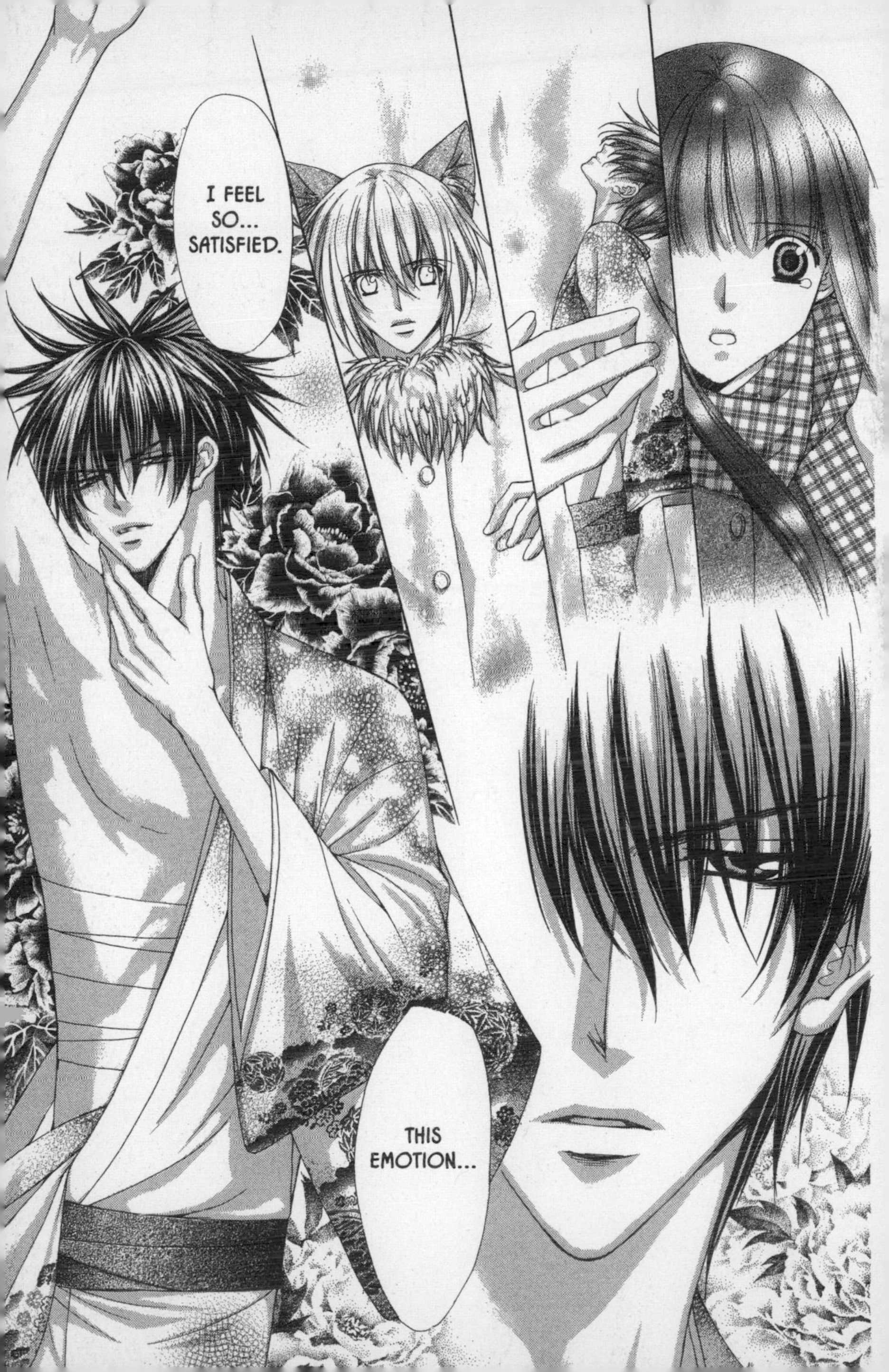
I FEEL SO... SATISFIED.
THIS EMOTION...

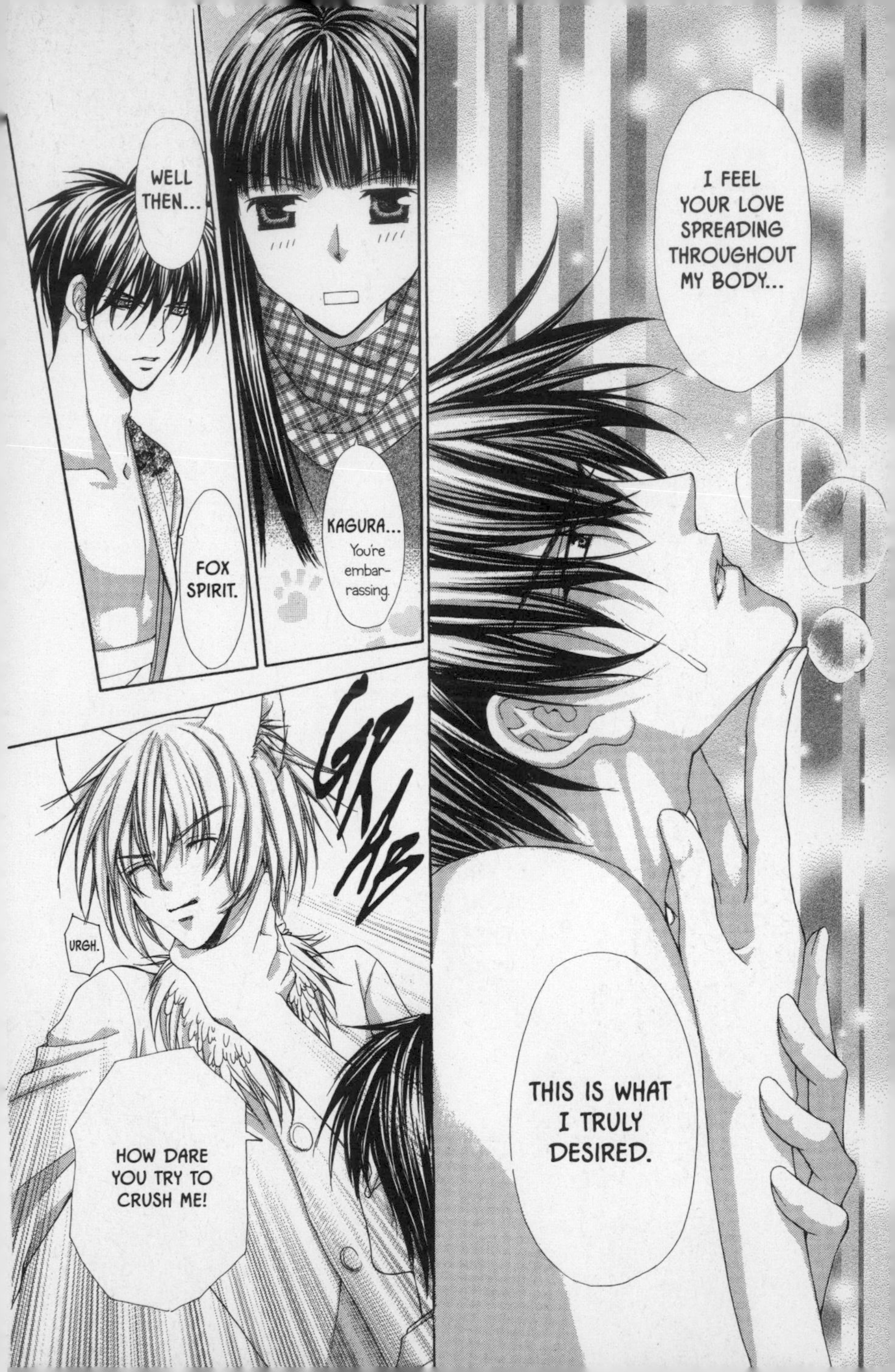
I FEEL YOUR LOVE SPREADING THROUGHOUT MY BODY...
THIS IS WHAT I TRULY DESIRED.
KAGURA...
You're embarrassing.
WELL THEN...
FOX SPIRIT.
GRAB
URGH.
HOW DARE YOU TRY TO CRUSH ME!

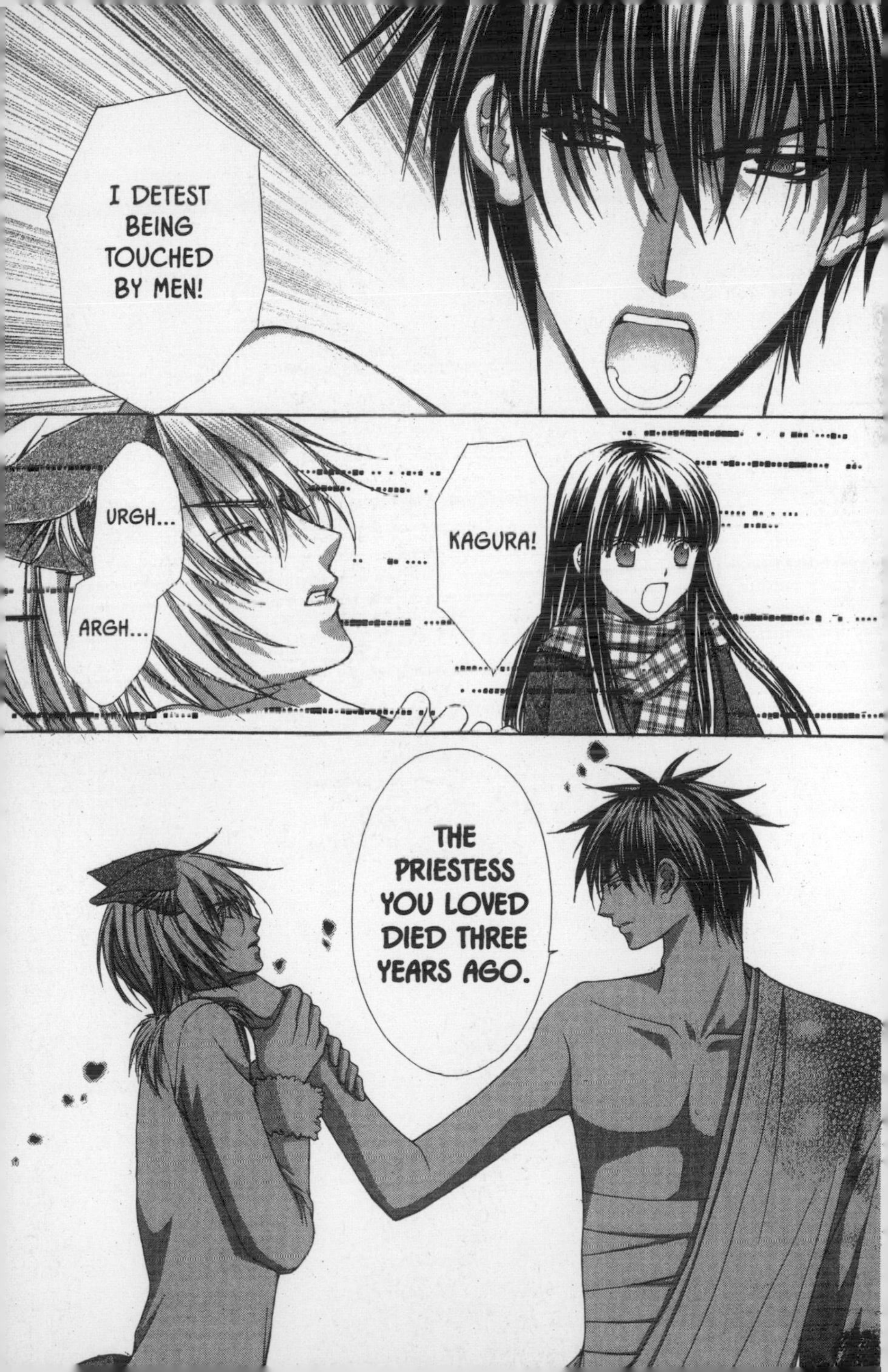
I DETEST BEING TOUCHED BY MEN!
KAGURA!
URGH... ARGH...
THE PRIESTESS YOU LOVED DIED THREE YEARS AGO.

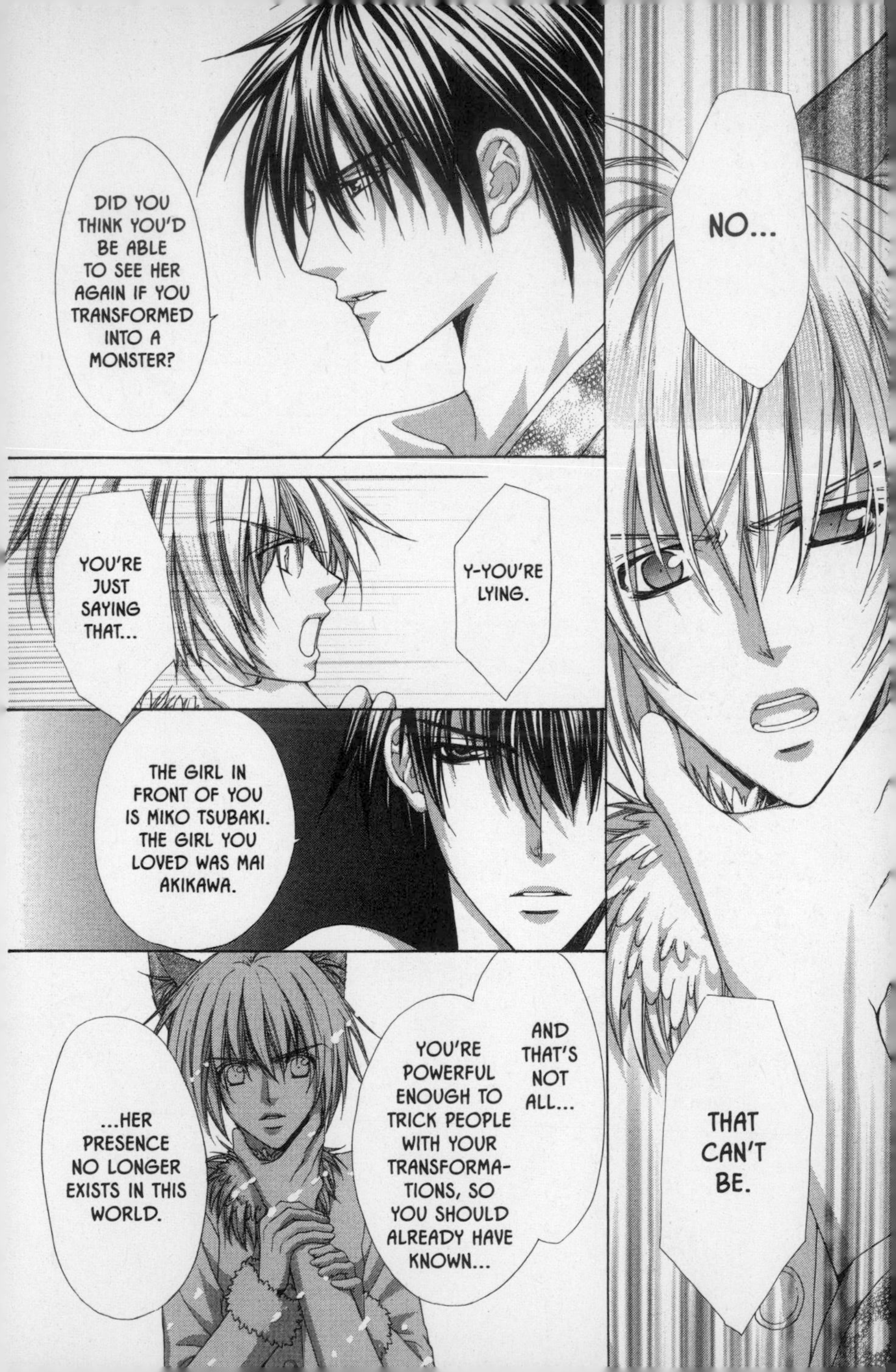
NO...
THAT CAN'T BE.
DID YOU THINK YOU'D BE ABLE TO SEE HER AGAIN IF YOU TRANSFORMED INTO A MONSTER?
Y-YOU'RE LYING.
YOU'RE JUST SAYING THAT...
THE GIRL IN FRONT OF YOU IS MIKO TSUBAKI. THE GIRL YOU LOVED WAS MAI AKIKAWA.
AND THAT'S NOT ALL...
YOU'RE POWERFUL ENOUGH TO TRICK PEOPLE WITH YOUR TRANSFORMA-TIONS, SO YOU SHOULD ALREADY HAVE KNOWN...
...HER PRESENCE NO LONGER EXISTS IN THIS WORLD.

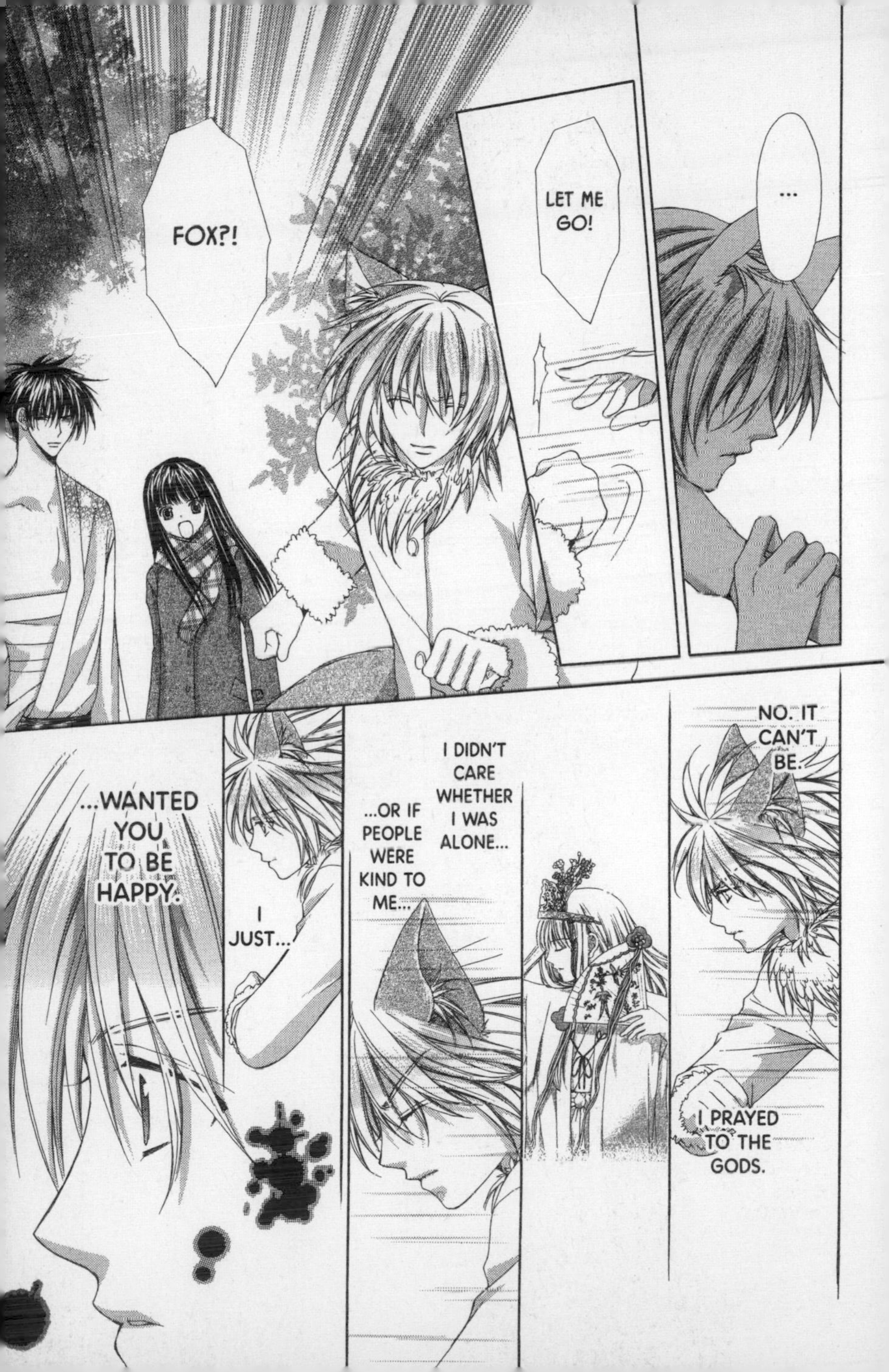
...
LET ME GO!
FOX?!
NO. IT CAN'T BE.
I PRAYED TO THE GODS.
I DIDN'T CARE WHETHER I WAS ALONE...
...OR IF PEOPLE WERE KIND TO ME...
I JUST...
...WANTED YOU TO BE HAPPY.

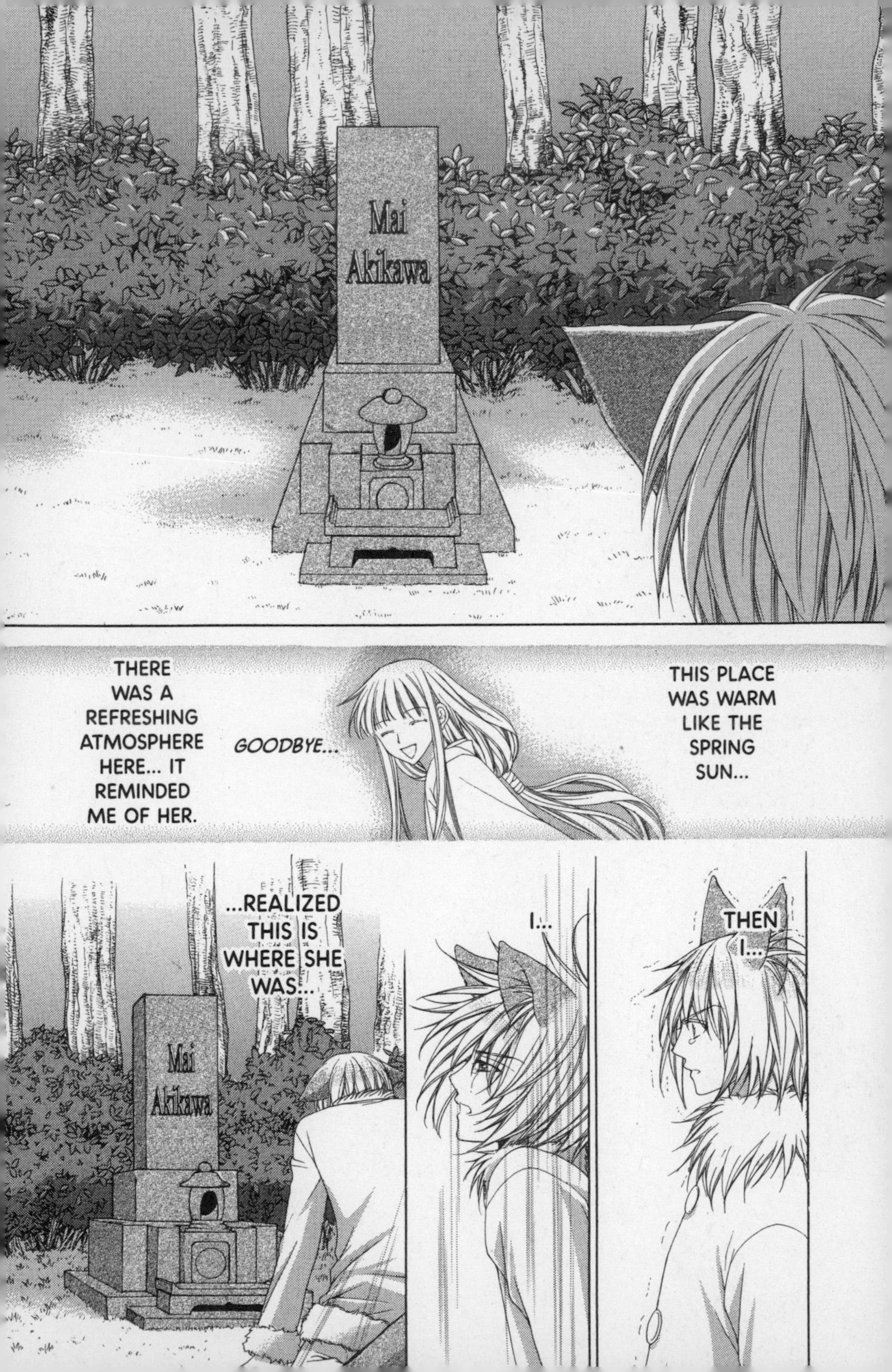
Mai Akikawa
THIS PLACE WAS WARM LIKE THE SPRING SUN...
GOODBYE...
THERE WAS A REFRESHING ATMOSPHERE HERE... IT REMINDED ME OF HER.
THEN I...
I...
...REALIZED THIS IS WHERE SHE WAS...
Mai Akikawa

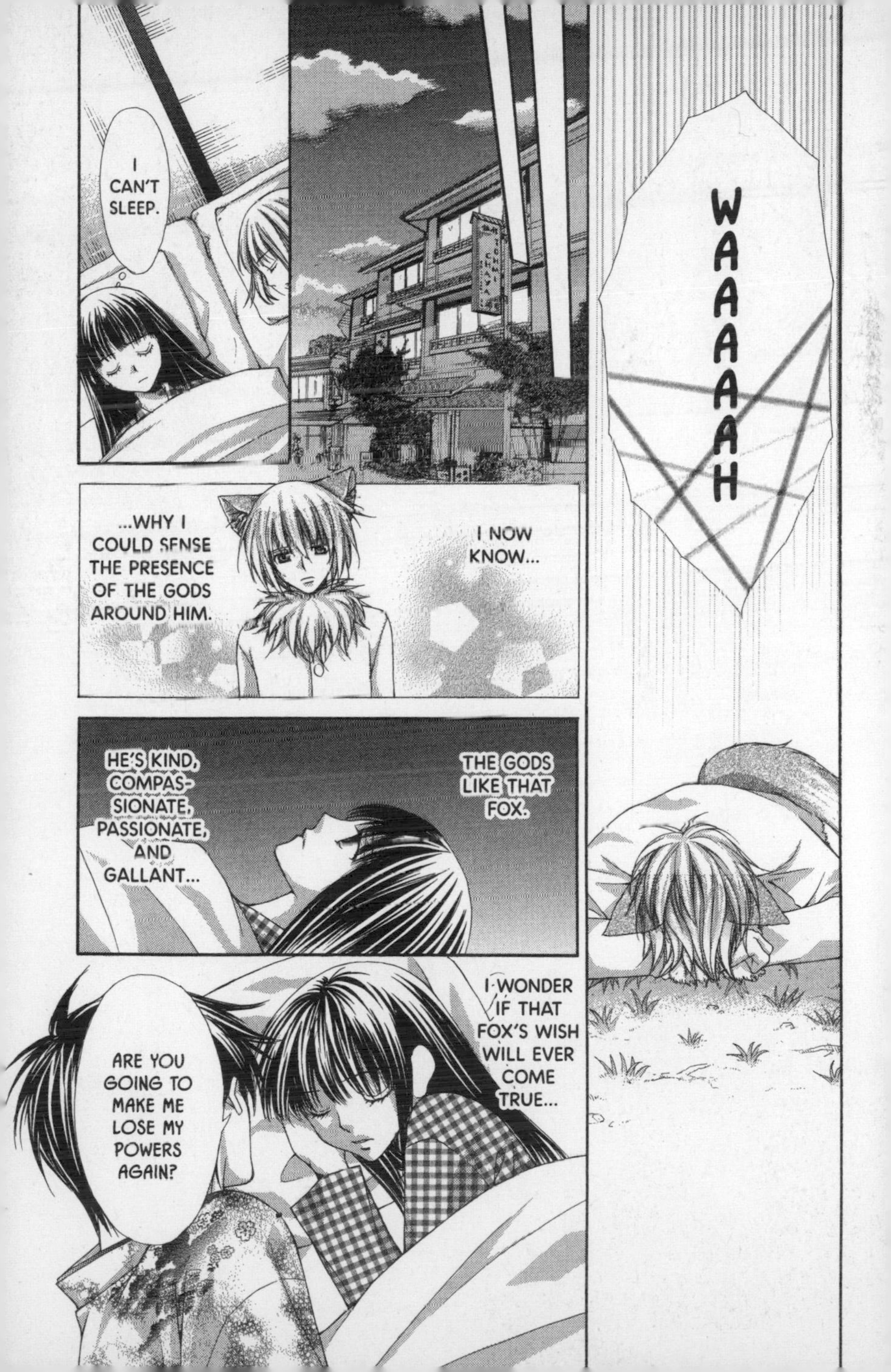
WAAAAAAH
I CAN'T SLEEP.
I NOW KNOW...
...WHY I COULD SENSE THE PRESENCE OF THE GODS AROUND HIM.
THE GODS LIKE THAT FOX.
HE'S KIND, COMPAS-SIONATE, PASSIONATE, AND GALLANT...
I WONDER IF THAT FOX'S WISH WILL EVER COME TRUE...
ARE YOU GOING TO MAKE ME LOSE MY POWERS AGAIN?

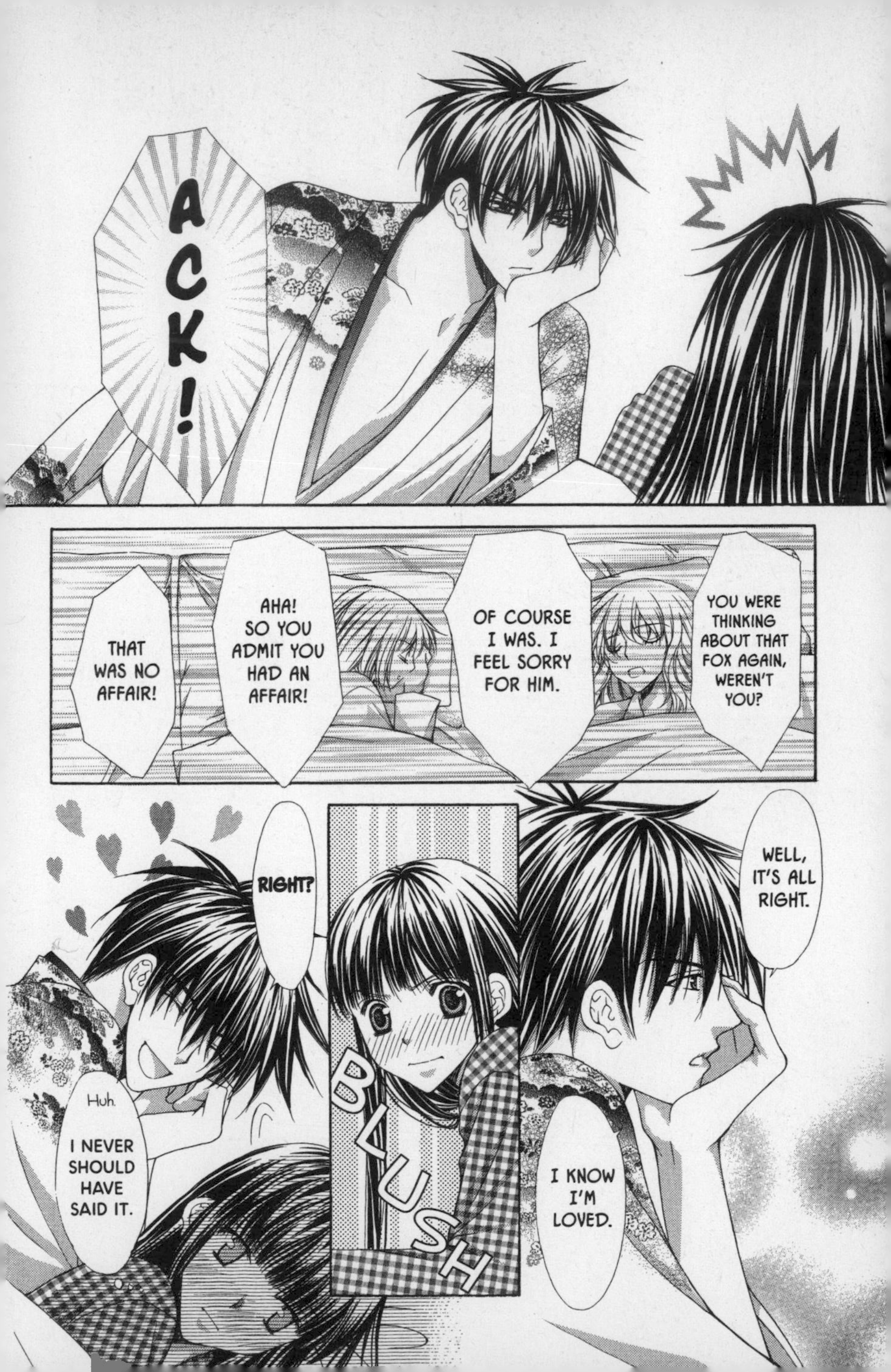

ACK!
YOU WERE THINKING ABOUT THAT FOX AGAIN, WEREN'T YOU?
OF COURSE I WAS. I FEEL SORRY FOR HIM.
AHA! SO YOU ADMIT YOU HAD AN AFFAIR!
THAT WAS NO AFFAIR!
WELL, IT'S ALL RIGHT.
I KNOW I'M LOVED.
RIGHT?
BLUSH
Huh.
I NEVER SHOULD HAVE SAID IT.

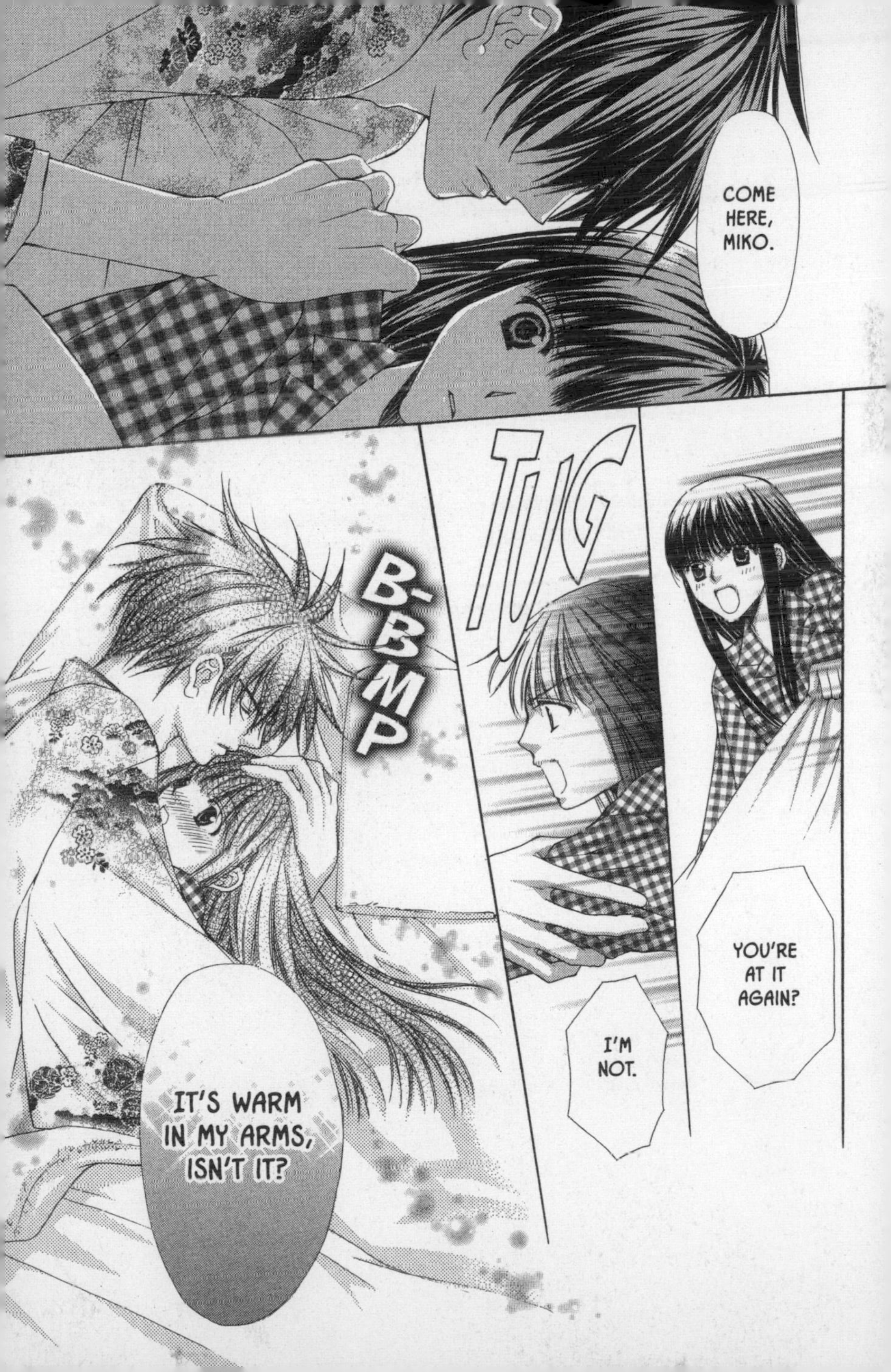
COME HERE, MIKO.
YOU'RE AT IT AGAIN?
TUG
I'M NOT.
B-BMP
IT'S WARM IN MY ARMS, ISN'T IT?

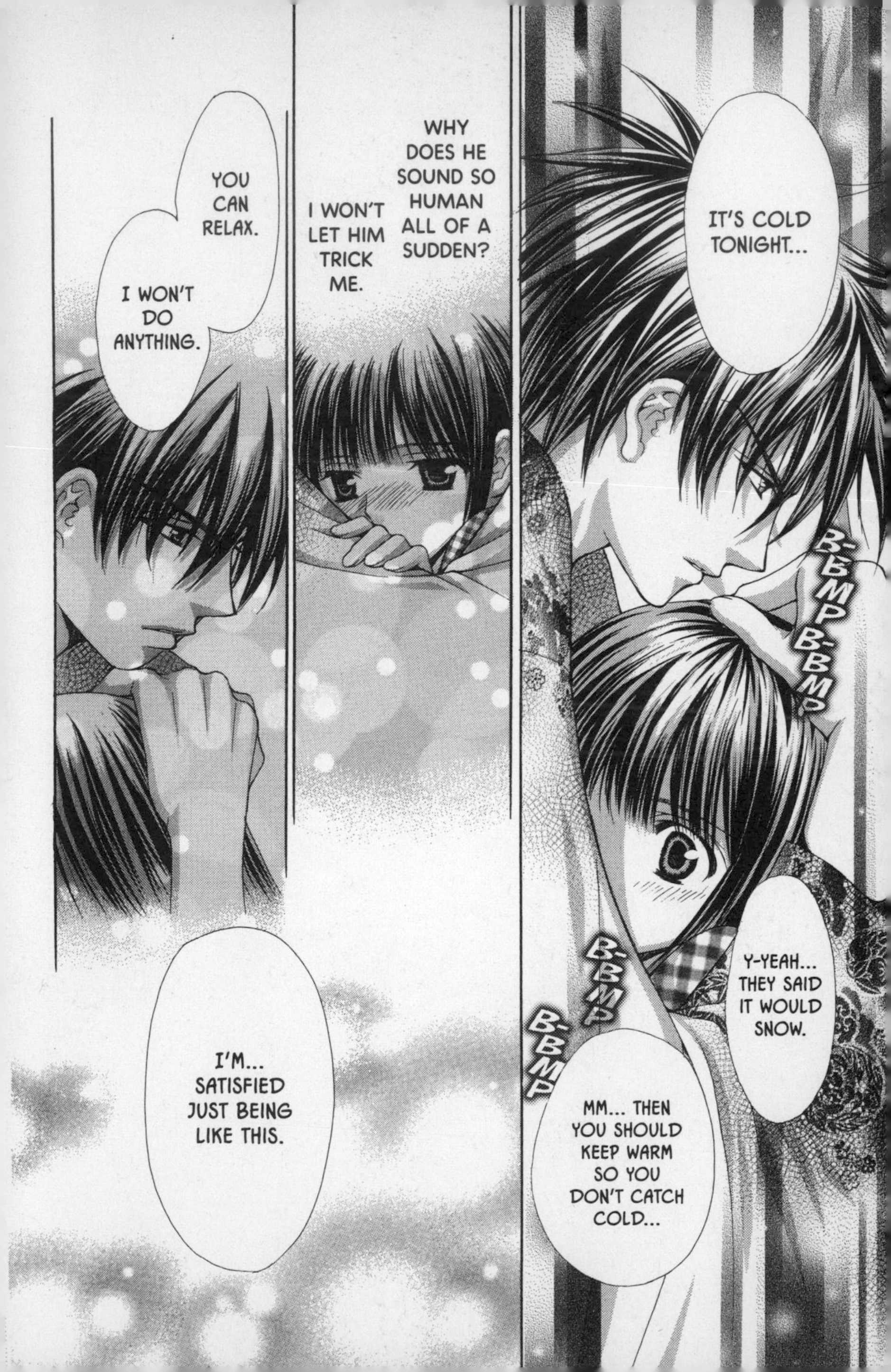
IT'S COLD TONIGHT...
B-BMP B-BMP
Y-YEAH... THEY SAID IT WOULD SNOW.
B-BMP B-BMP
MM... THEN YOU SHOULD KEEP WARM SO YOU DON'T CATCH COLD...
WHY DOES HE SOUND SO HUMAN ALL OF A SUDDEN?
I WON'T LET HIM TRICK ME.
YOU CAN RELAX.
I WON'T DO ANYTHING.
I'M... SATISFIED JUST BEING LIKE THIS.

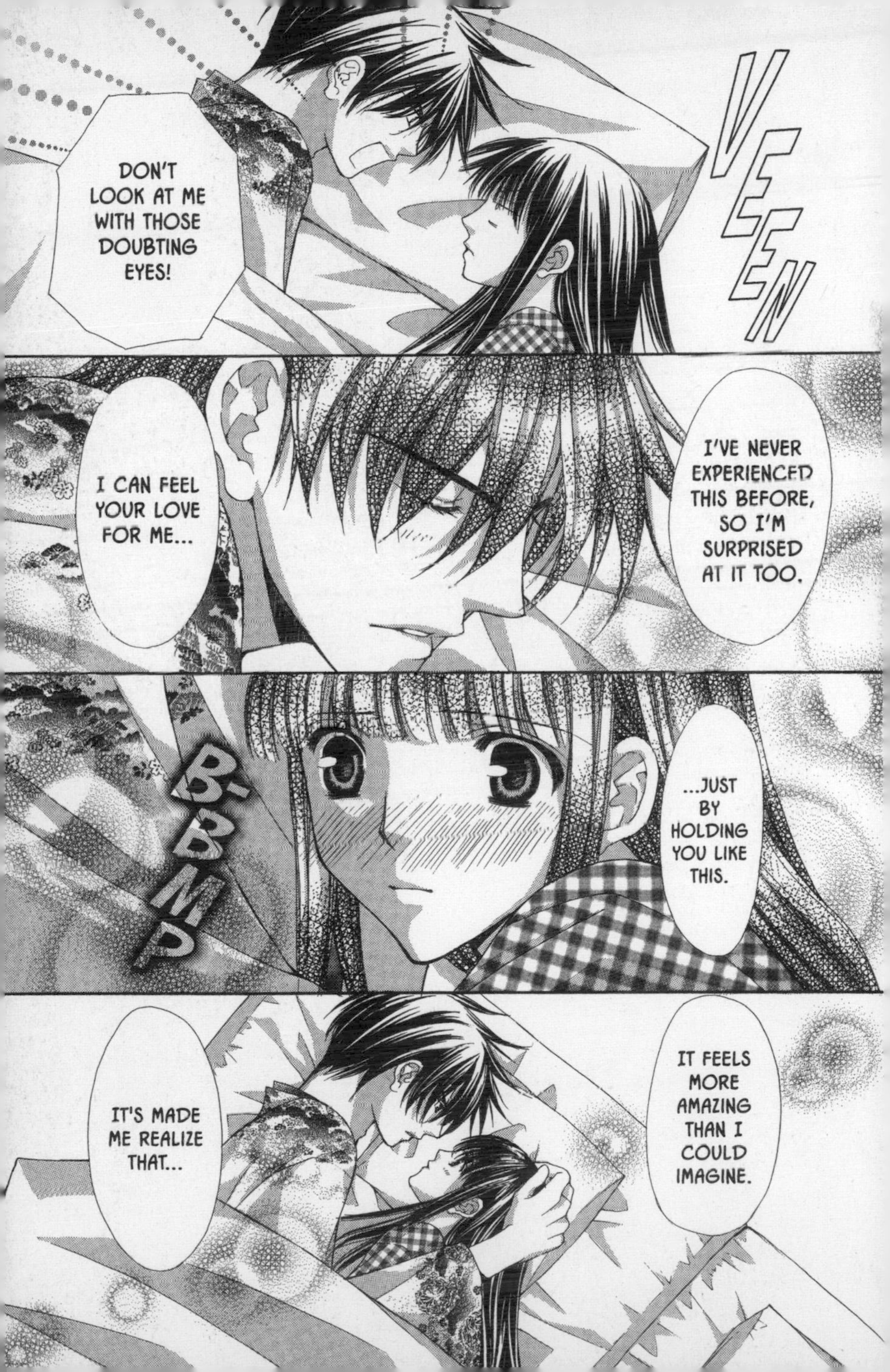
VEEN
DON'T LOOK AT ME WITH THOSE DOUBTING EYES!
I'VE NEVER EXPERIENCED THIS BEFORE, SO I'M SURPRISED AT IT TOO.
I CAN FEEL YOUR LOVE FOR ME...
...JUST BY HOLDING YOU LIKE THIS.
B-BMP
IT FEELS MORE AMAZING THAN I COULD IMAGINE.
IT'S MADE ME REALIZE THAT...

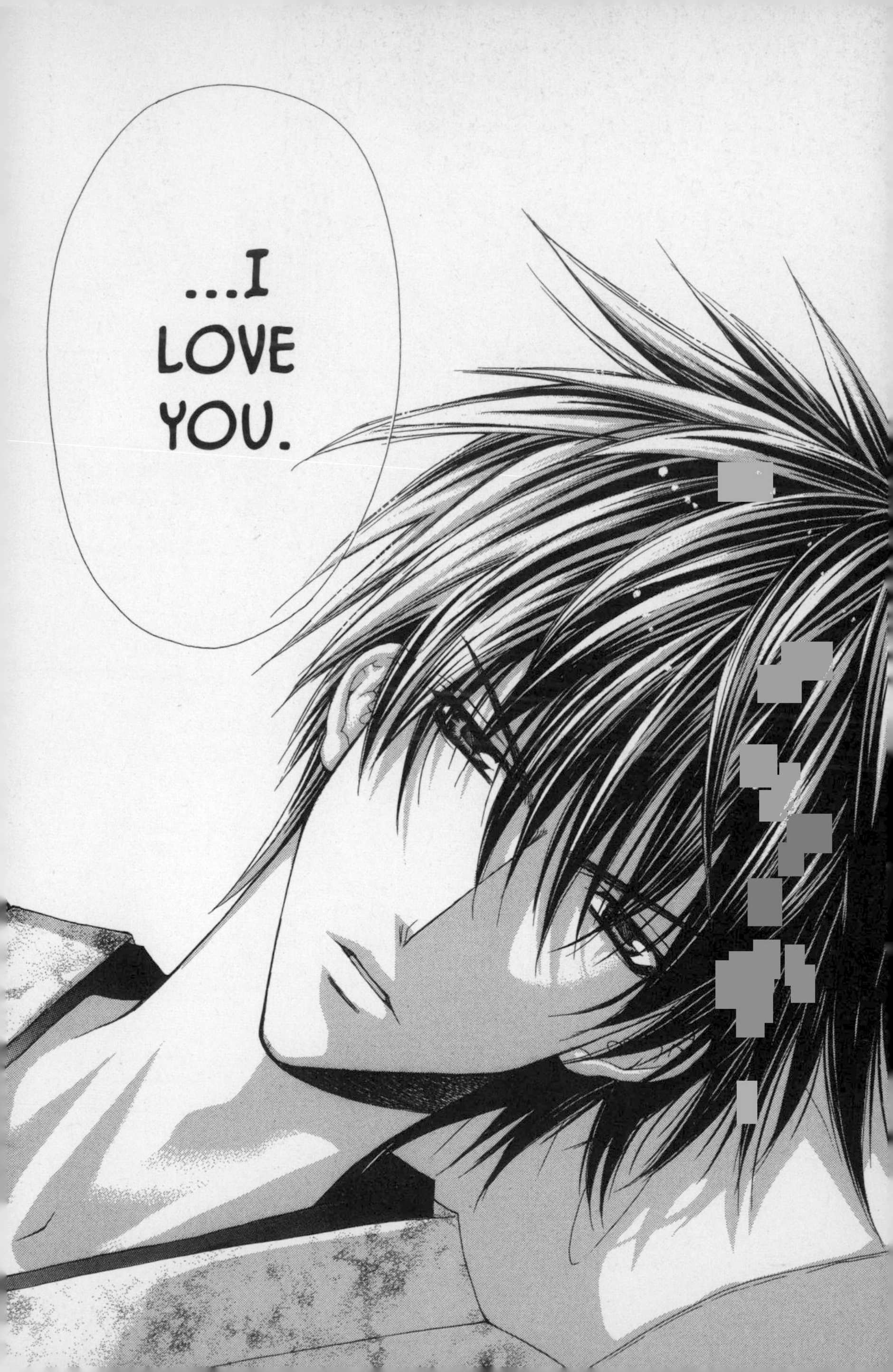
...I LOVE YOU.

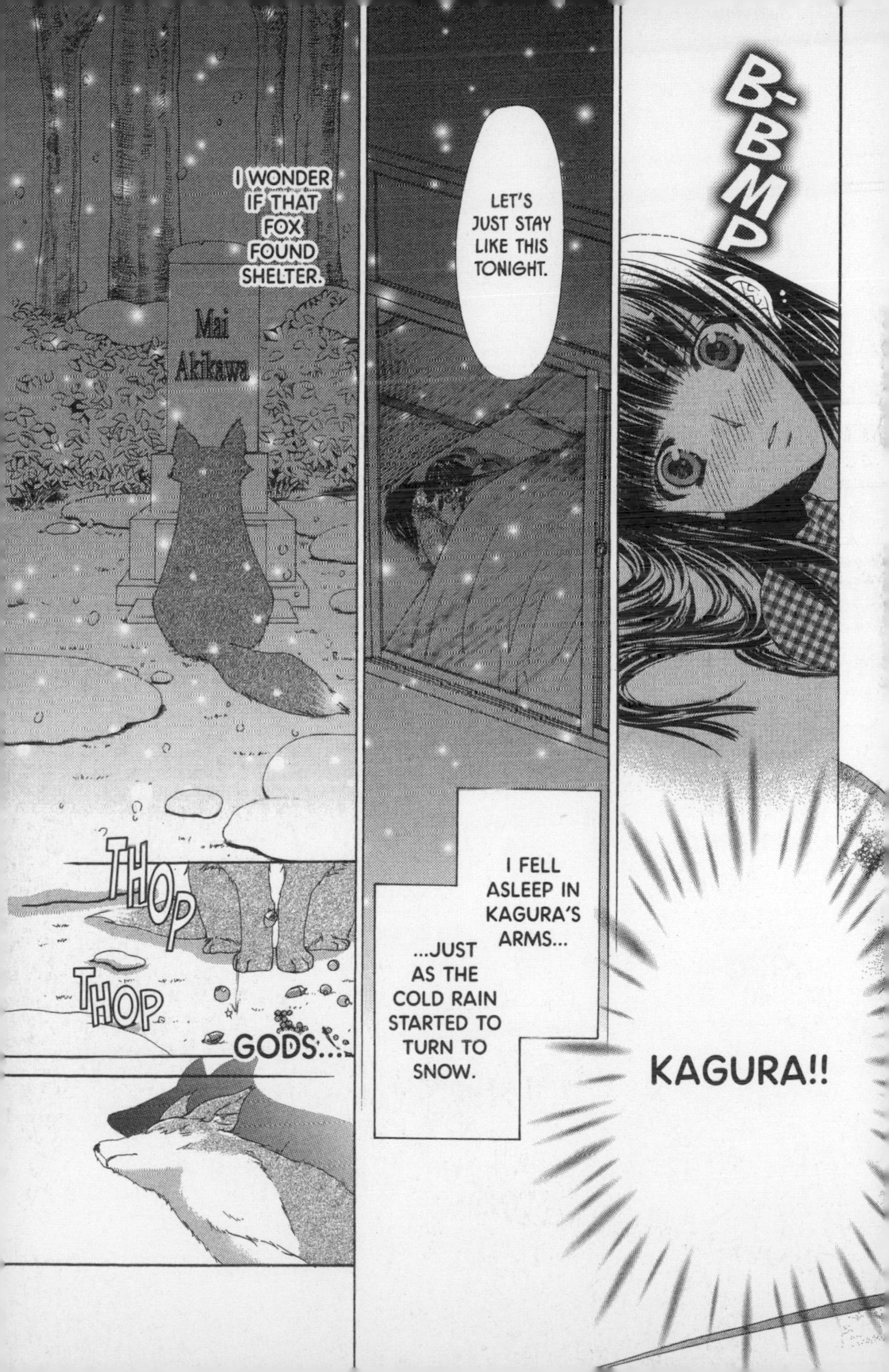
B-BMP
KAGURA!!
LET'S JUST STAY LIKE THIS TONIGHT.
I FELL ASLEEP IN KAGURA'S ARMS...
...JUST AS THE COLD RAIN STARTED TO TURN TO SNOW.
I WONDER IF THAT FOX FOUND SHELTER.
Mai Akikawa
THOP
THOP
GODS...

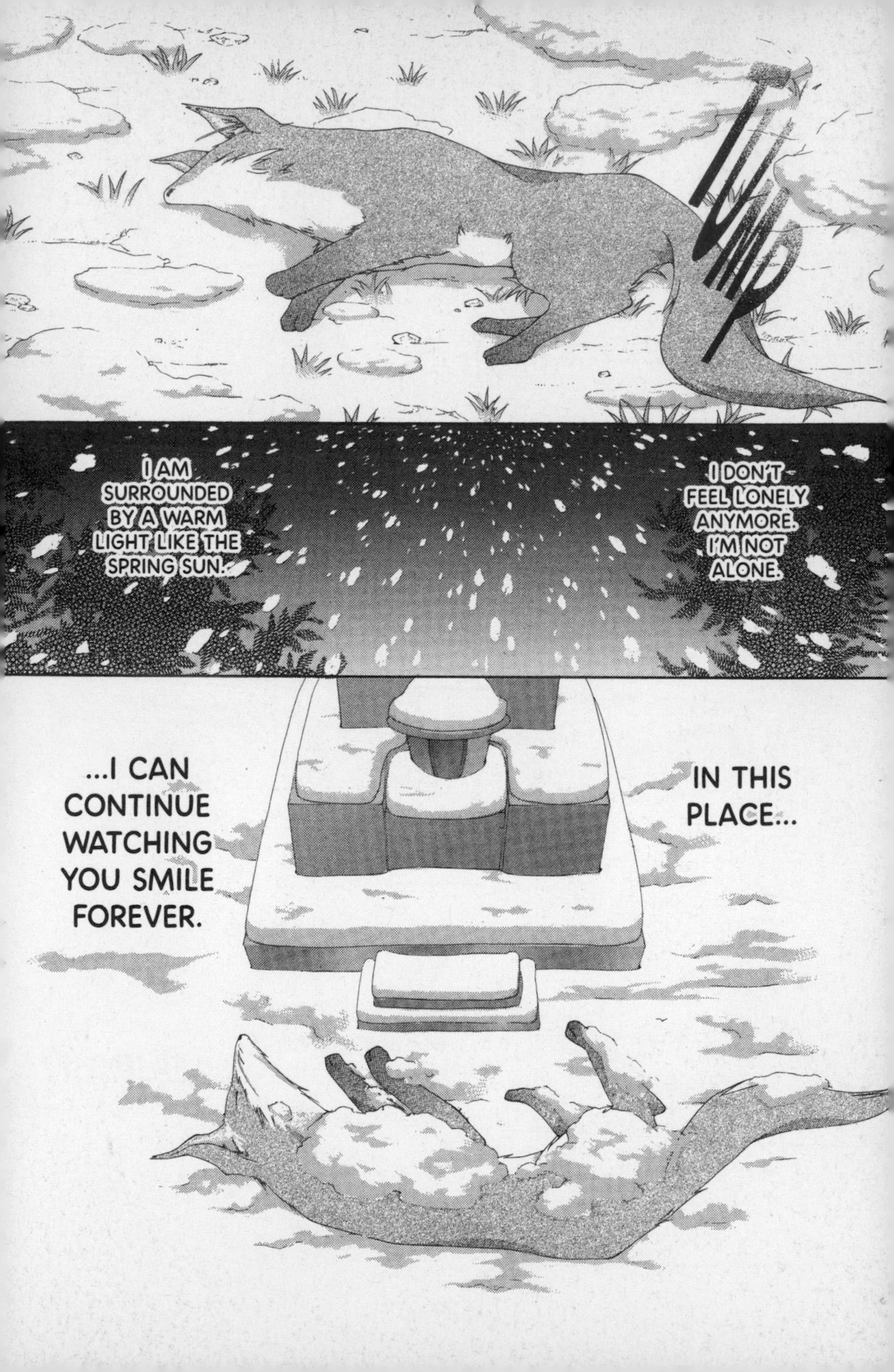
THUMP
I DON'T FEEL LONELY ANYMORE. I'M NOT ALONE.
I AM SURROUNDED BY A WARM LIGHT LIKE THE SPRING SUN.
IN THIS PLACE...
...I CAN CONTINUE WATCHING YOU SMILE FOREVER.

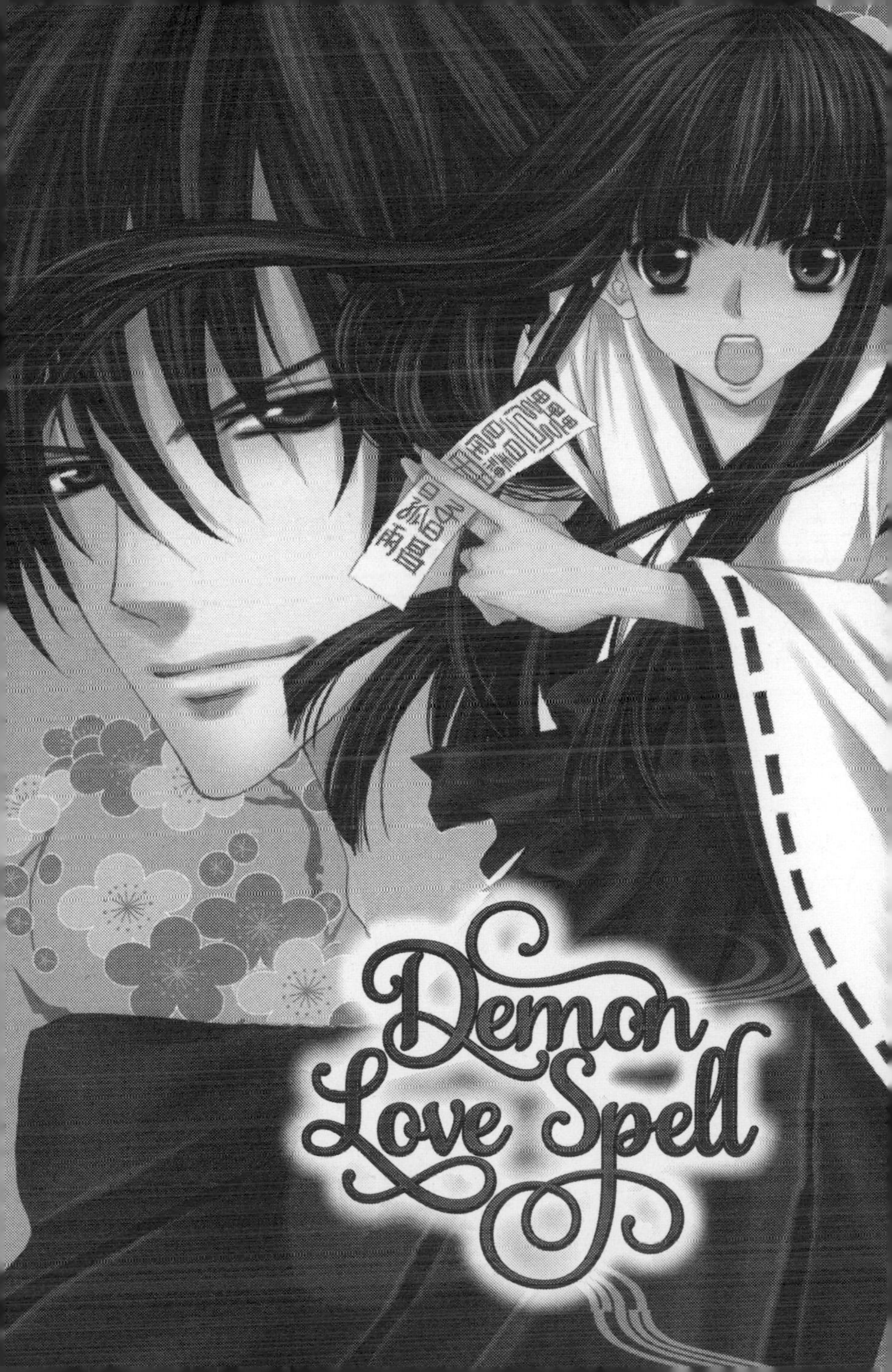
Demon Love Spell

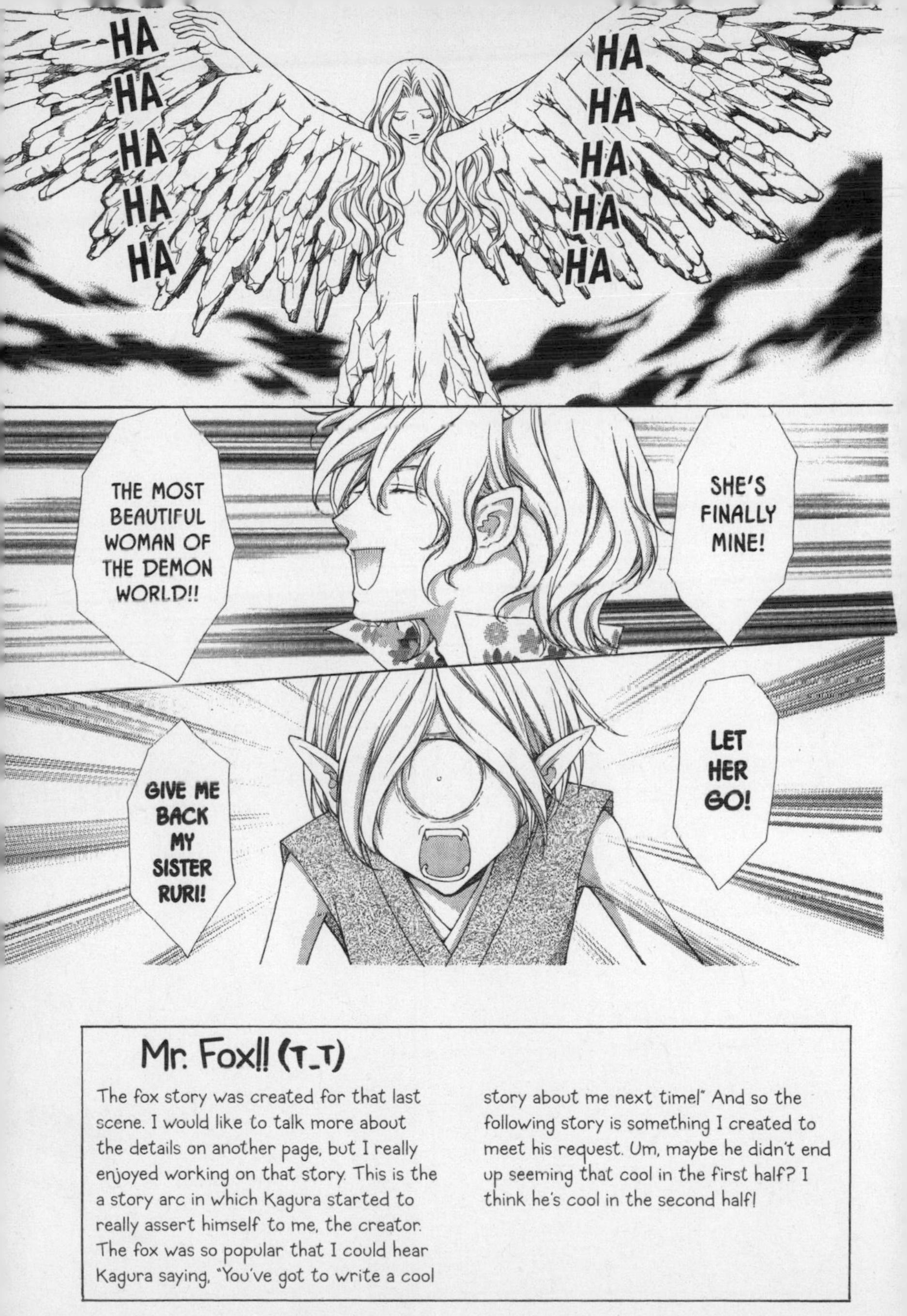
HA HA HA HA HA
HA HA HA HA HA
SHE'S FINALLY MINE!
THE MOST BEAUTIFUL WOMAN OF THE DEMON WORLD!!
LET HER GO!
GIVE ME BACK MY SISTER RURI!

Mr. Fox!! (T_T)

The fox story was created for that last scene. I would like to talk more about the details on another page, but I really enjoyed working on that story. This is the a story arc in which Kagura started to really assert himself to me, the creator. The fox was so popular that I could hear Kagura saying, "You've got to write a cool story about me next time!" And so the following story is something I created to meet his request. Um, maybe he didn't end up seeming that cool in the first half? I think he's cool in the second half!

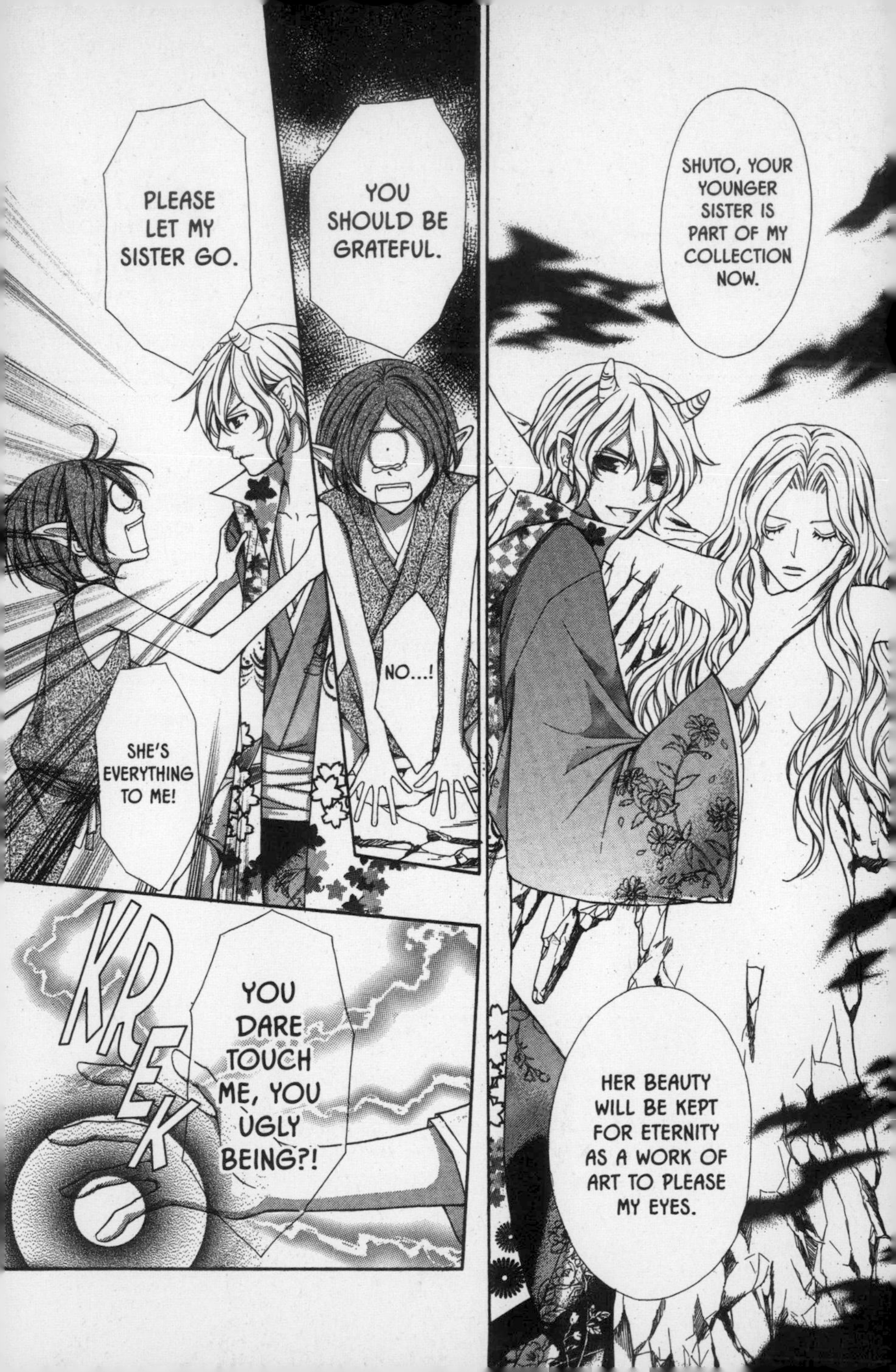
SHUTO, YOUR YOUNGER SISTER IS PART OF MY COLLECTION NOW.
HER BEAUTY WILL BE KEPT FOR ETERNITY AS A WORK OF ART TO PLEASE MY EYES.
YOU SHOULD BE GRATEFUL.
NO...!
PLEASE LET MY SISTER GO.
SHE'S EVERYTHING TO ME!
KREK
YOU DARE TOUCH ME, YOU UGLY BEING?!

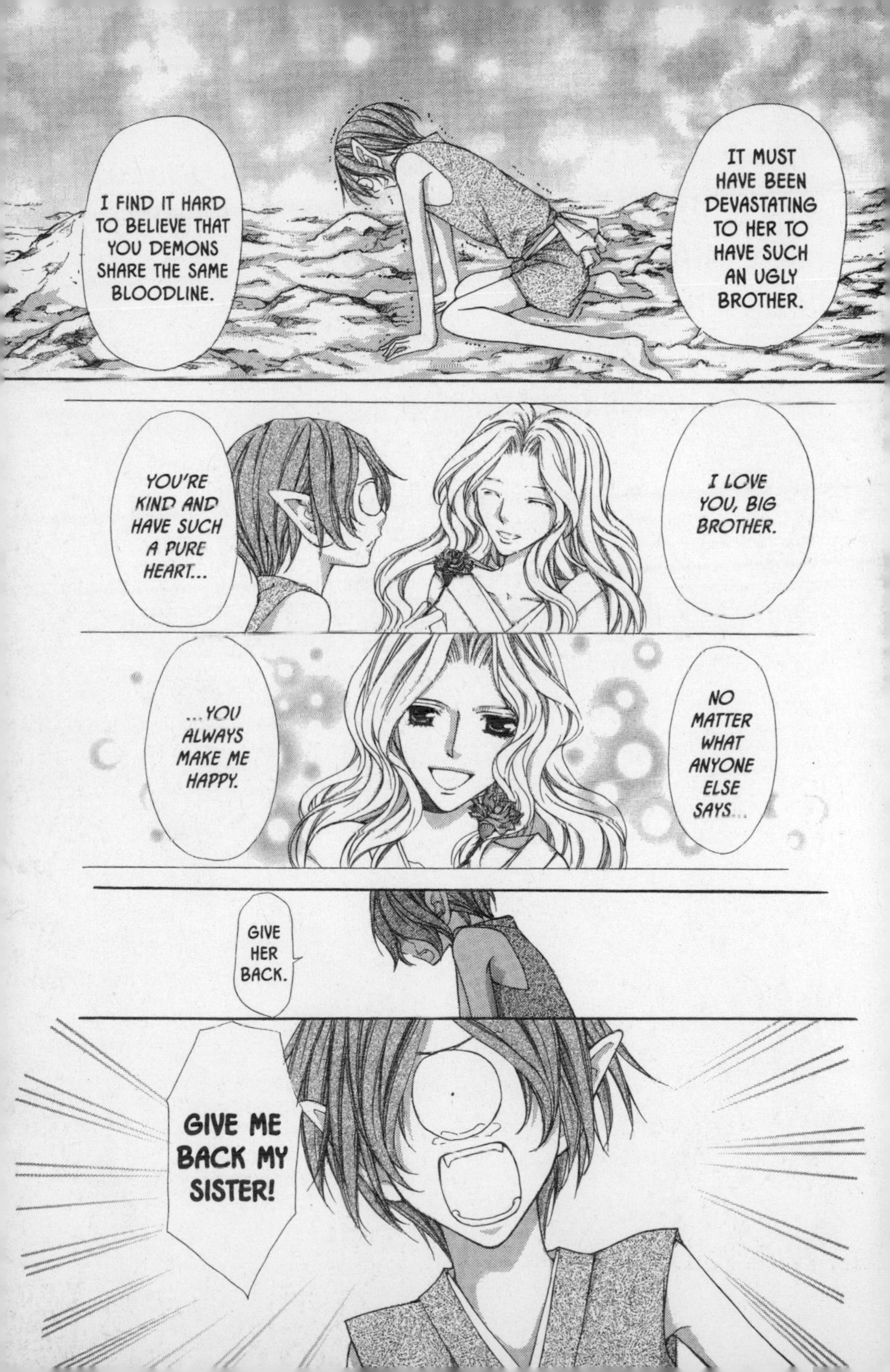
IT MUST HAVE BEEN DEVASTATING TO HER TO HAVE SUCH AN UGLY BROTHER.
I FIND IT HARD TO BELIEVE THAT YOU DEMONS SHARE THE SAME BLOODLINE.
I LOVE YOU, BIG BROTHER.
YOU'RE KIND AND HAVE SUCH A PURE HEART...
NO MATTER WHAT ANYONE ELSE SAYS...
...YOU ALWAYS MAKE ME HAPPY.
GIVE HER BACK.
GIVE ME BACK MY SISTER!

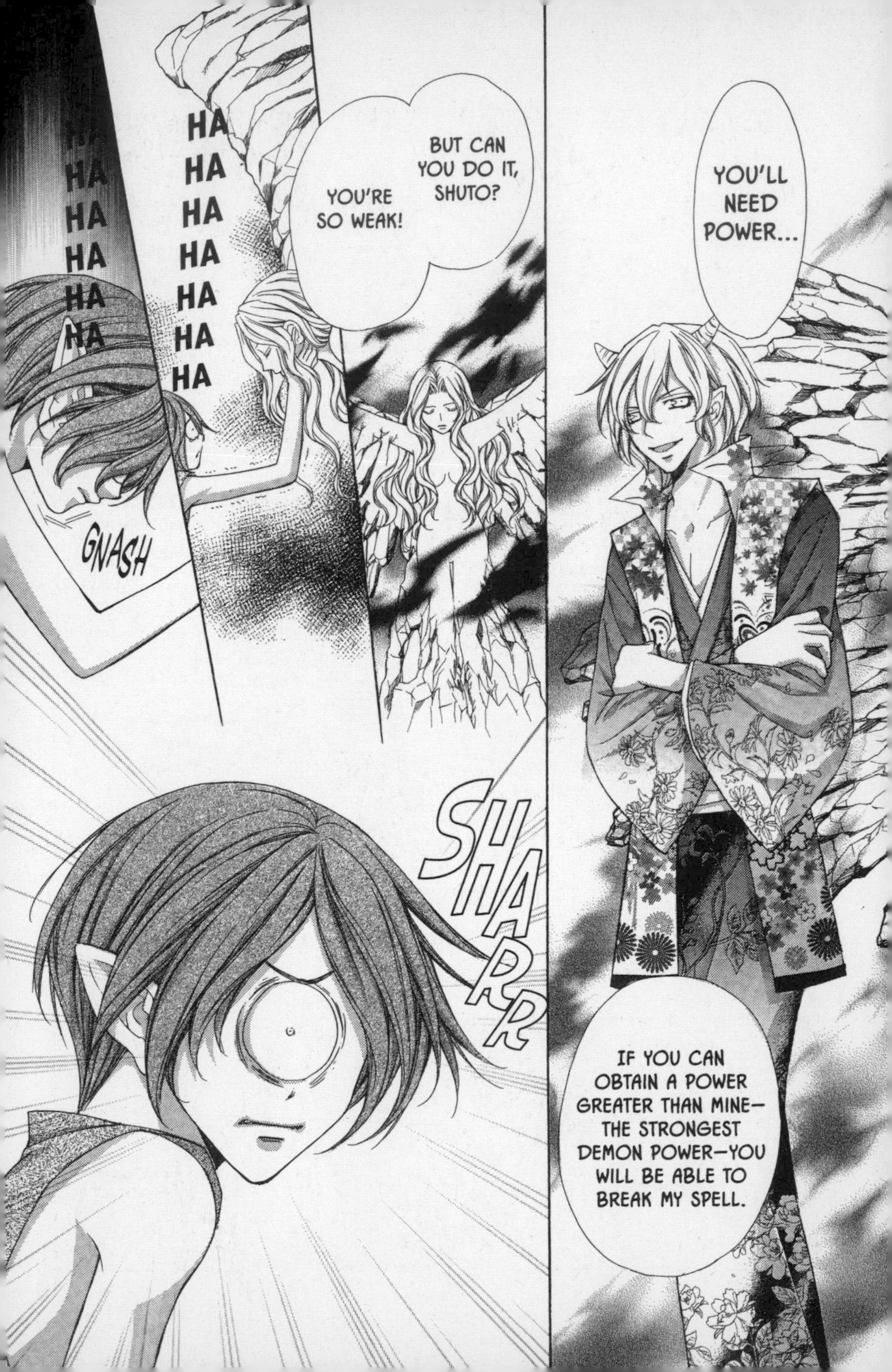
YOU'LL NEED POWER...
IF YOU CAN OBTAIN A POWER GREATER THAN MINE—THE STRONGEST DEMON POWER—YOU WILL BE ABLE TO BREAK MY SPELL.
BUT CAN YOU DO IT, SHUTO?
YOU'RE SO WEAK!
HA HA HA HA HA HA HA
HA HA HA HA HA
GNASH
SHARR

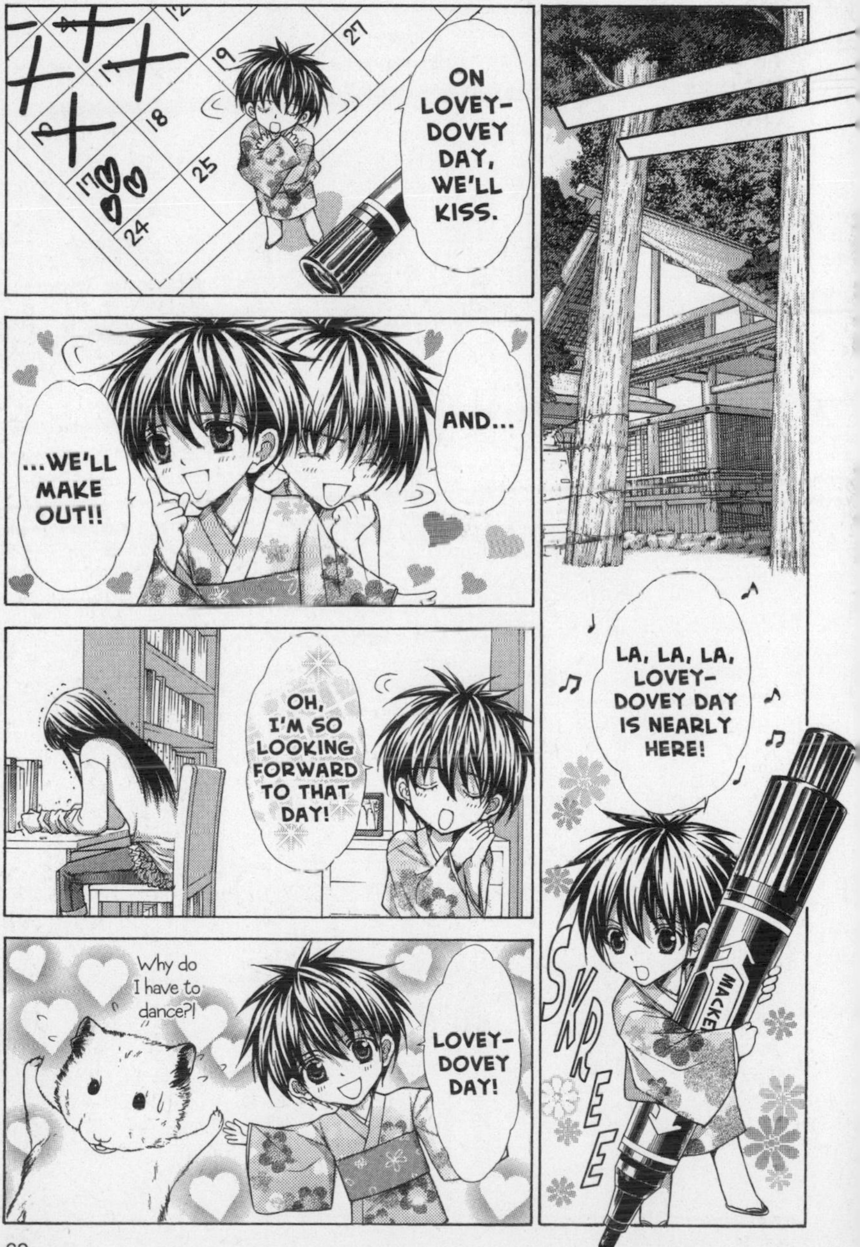
LA, LA, LA, LOVEY-DOVEY DAY IS NEARLY HERE!
SKREE
ON LOVEY-DOVEY DAY, WE'LL KISS.
AND...
...WE'LL MAKE OUT!!
OH, I'M SO LOOKING FORWARD TO THAT DAY!
LOVEY-DOVEY DAY!
Why do I have to dance?!

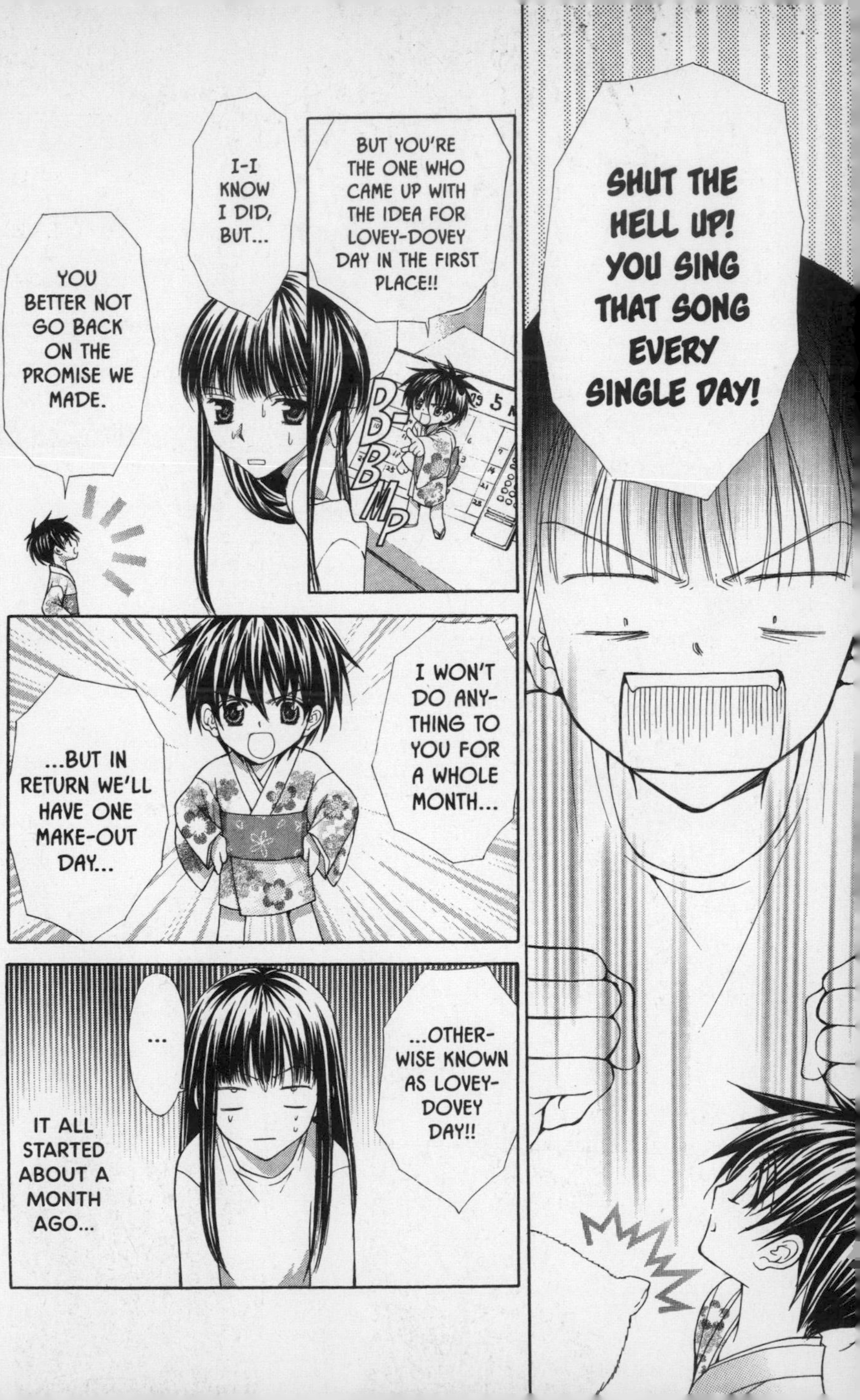
SHUT THE HELL UP! YOU SING THAT SONG EVERY SINGLE DAY!
BUT YOU'RE THE ONE WHO CAME UP WITH THE IDEA FOR LOVEY-DOVEY DAY IN THE FIRST PLACE!!
B-BUMP
I-I KNOW I DID, BUT...
YOU BETTER NOT GO BACK ON THE PROMISE WE MADE.
I WON'T DO ANY-THING TO YOU FOR A WHOLE MONTH...
...BUT IN RETURN WE'LL HAVE ONE MAKE-OUT DAY...
...OTHER-WISE KNOWN AS LOVEY-DOVEY DAY!!
...
IT ALL STARTED ABOUT A MONTH AGO...

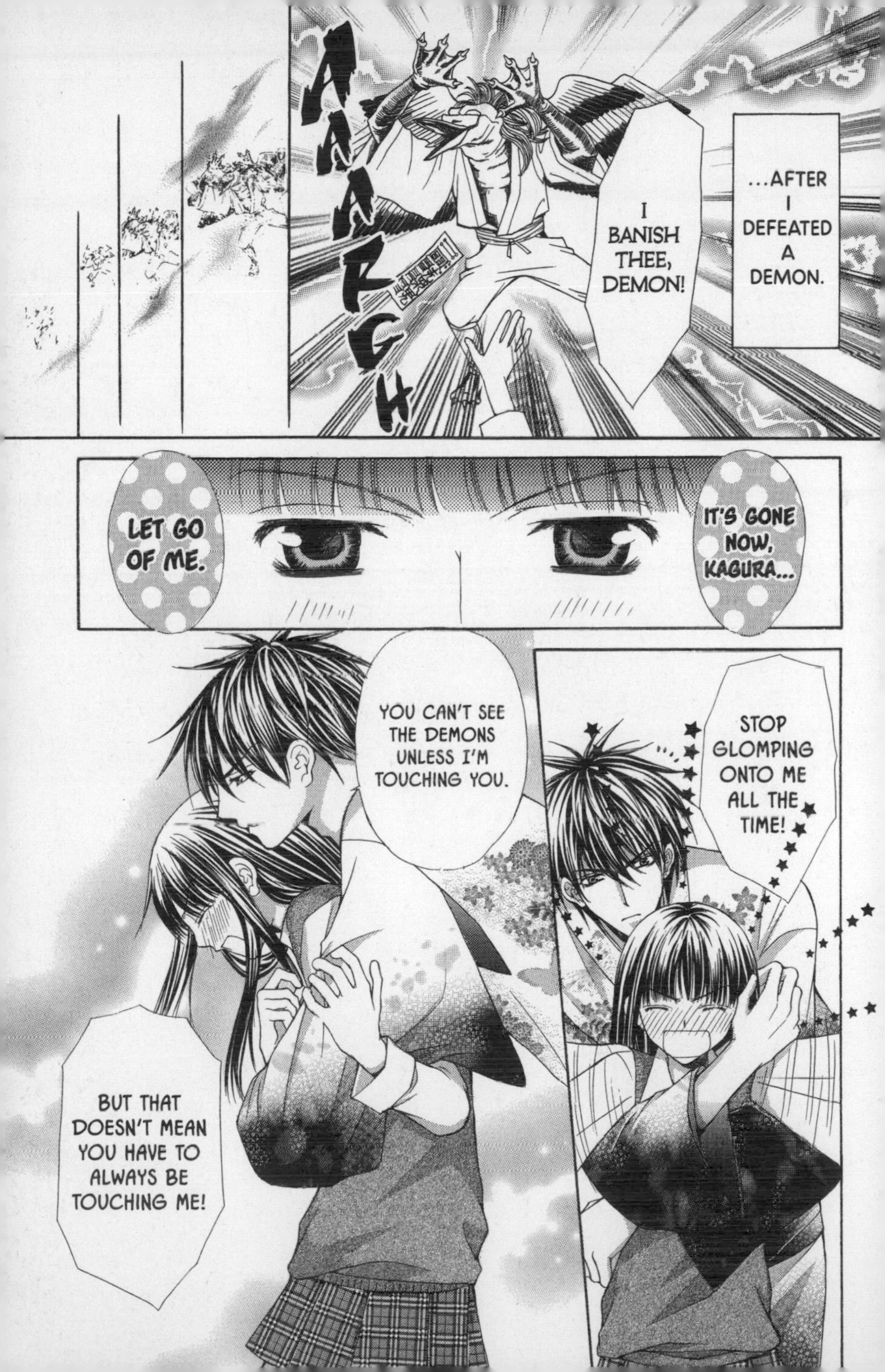
...AFTER I DEFEATED A DEMON.
I BANISH THEE, DEMON!
AAARGH
IT'S GONE NOW, KAGURA...
LET GO OF ME.
STOP GLOMPING ONTO ME ALL THE TIME!
YOU CAN'T SEE THE DEMONS UNLESS I'M TOUCHING YOU.
BUT THAT DOESN'T MEAN YOU HAVE TO ALWAYS BE TOUCHING ME!

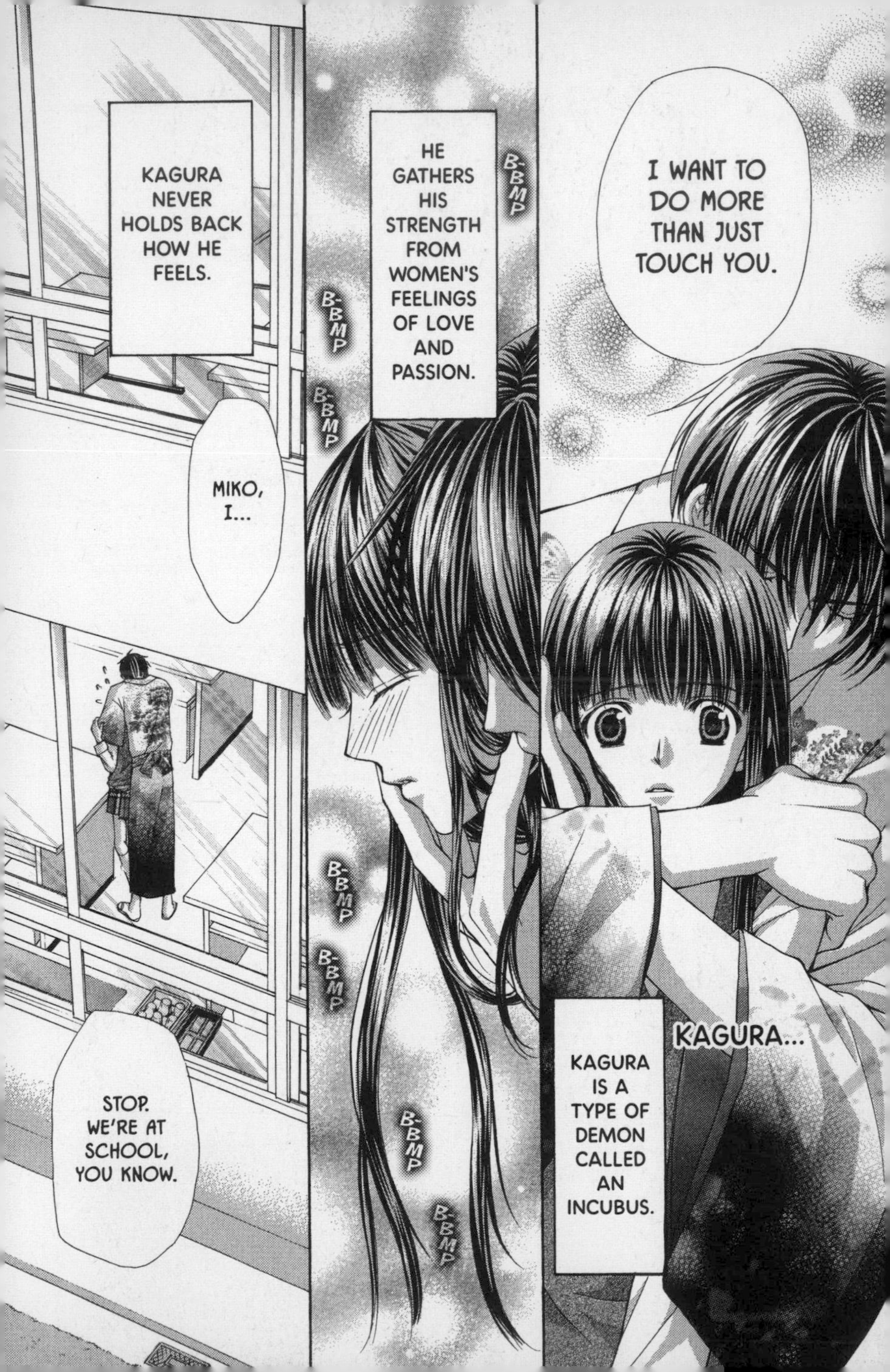
I WANT TO DO MORE THAN JUST TOUCH YOU.
KAGURA...
KAGURA IS A TYPE OF DEMON CALLED AN INCUBUS.
HE GATHERS HIS STRENGTH FROM WOMEN'S FEELINGS OF LOVE AND PASSION.
B-BMP
B-BMP
B-BMP
B-BMP
B-BMP
B-BMP
B-BMP
KAGURA NEVER HOLDS BACK HOW HE FEELS.
MIKO, I...
STOP. WE'RE AT SCHOOL, YOU KNOW.

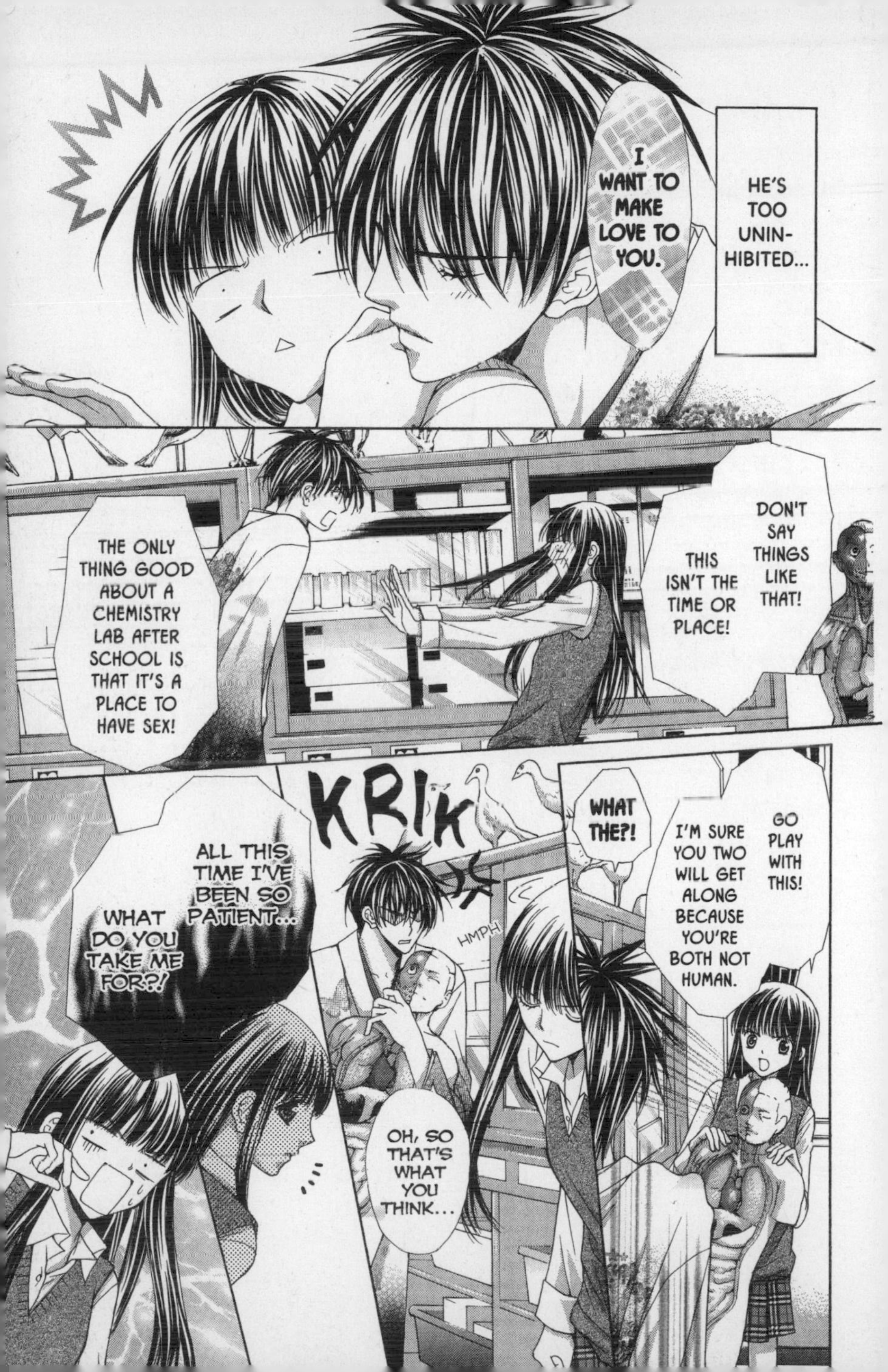
HE'S TOO UNIN-HIBITED...
I WANT TO MAKE LOVE TO YOU.
DON'T SAY THINGS LIKE THAT!
THIS ISN'T THE TIME OR PLACE!
THE ONLY THING GOOD ABOUT A CHEMISTRY LAB AFTER SCHOOL IS THAT IT'S A PLACE TO HAVE SEX!
GO PLAY WITH THIS!
I'M SURE YOU TWO WILL GET ALONG BECAUSE YOU'RE BOTH NOT HUMAN.
WHAT THE?!
KRIK
HMPH
OH, SO THAT'S WHAT YOU THINK...
ALL THIS TIME I'VE BEEN SO PATIENT...
WHAT DO YOU TAKE ME FOR?!

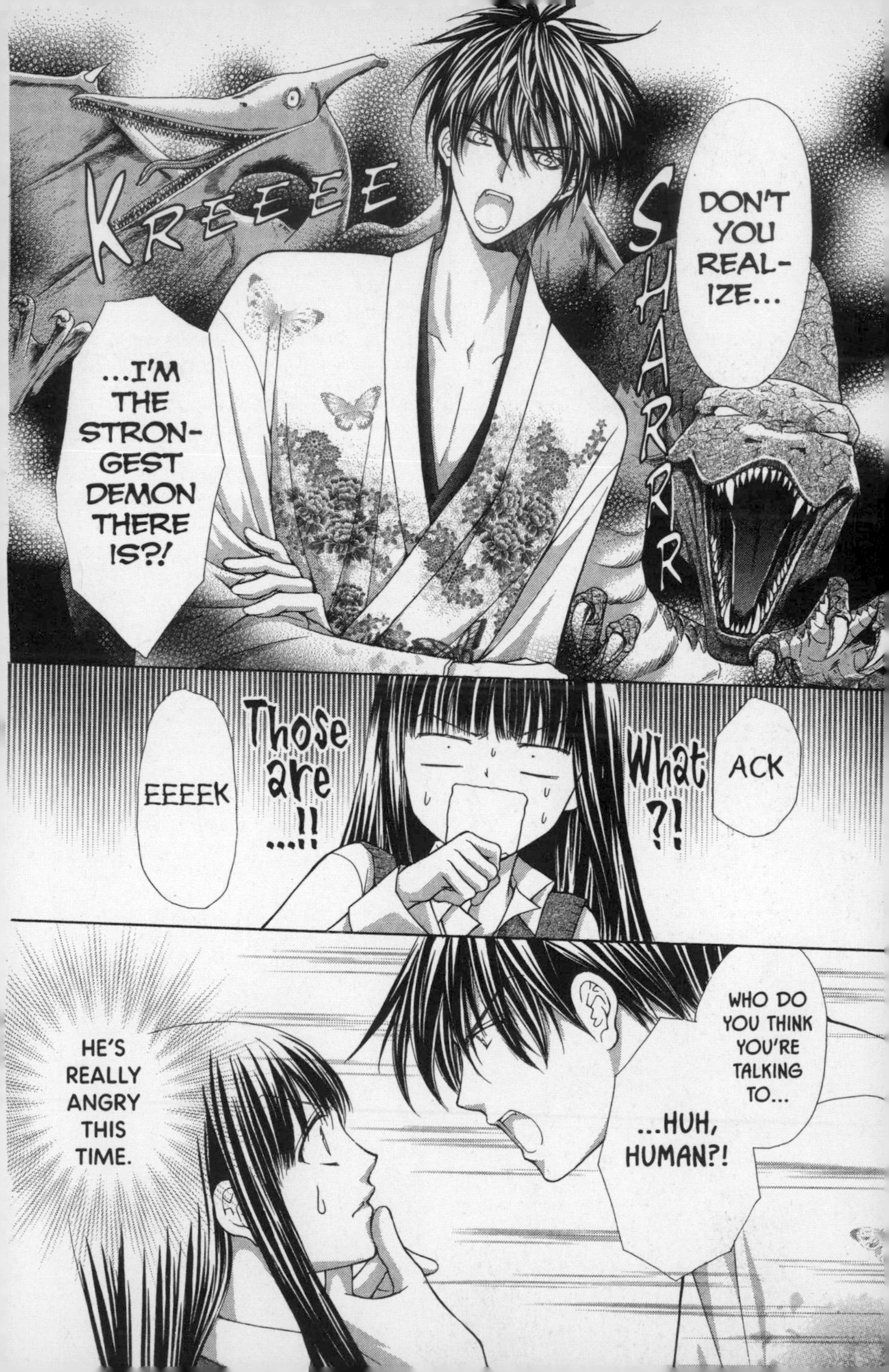
DON'T YOU REAL-IZE...
SHARRR
KREEEE
...I'M THE STRON-GEST DEMON THERE IS?!
ACK
What?!
Those are...!!
EEEEK
WHO DO YOU THINK YOU'RE TALKING TO...
...HUH, HUMAN?!
HE'S REALLY ANGRY THIS TIME.

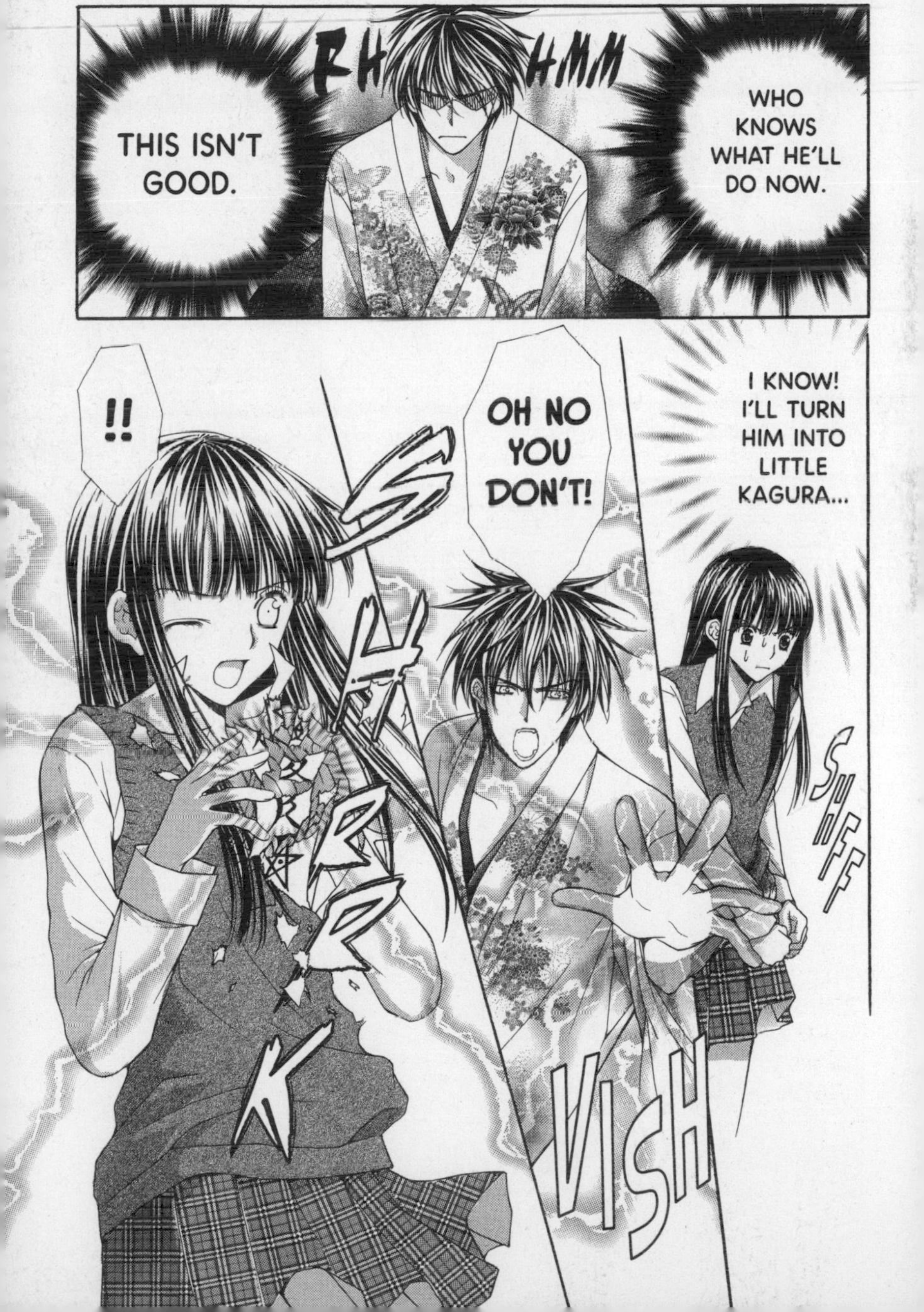
WHO KNOWS WHAT HE'LL DO NOW.
RH HMM
THIS ISN'T GOOD.
I KNOW! I'LL TURN HIM INTO LITTLE KAGURA...
SHFF
OH NO YOU DON'T!
VISH
!!

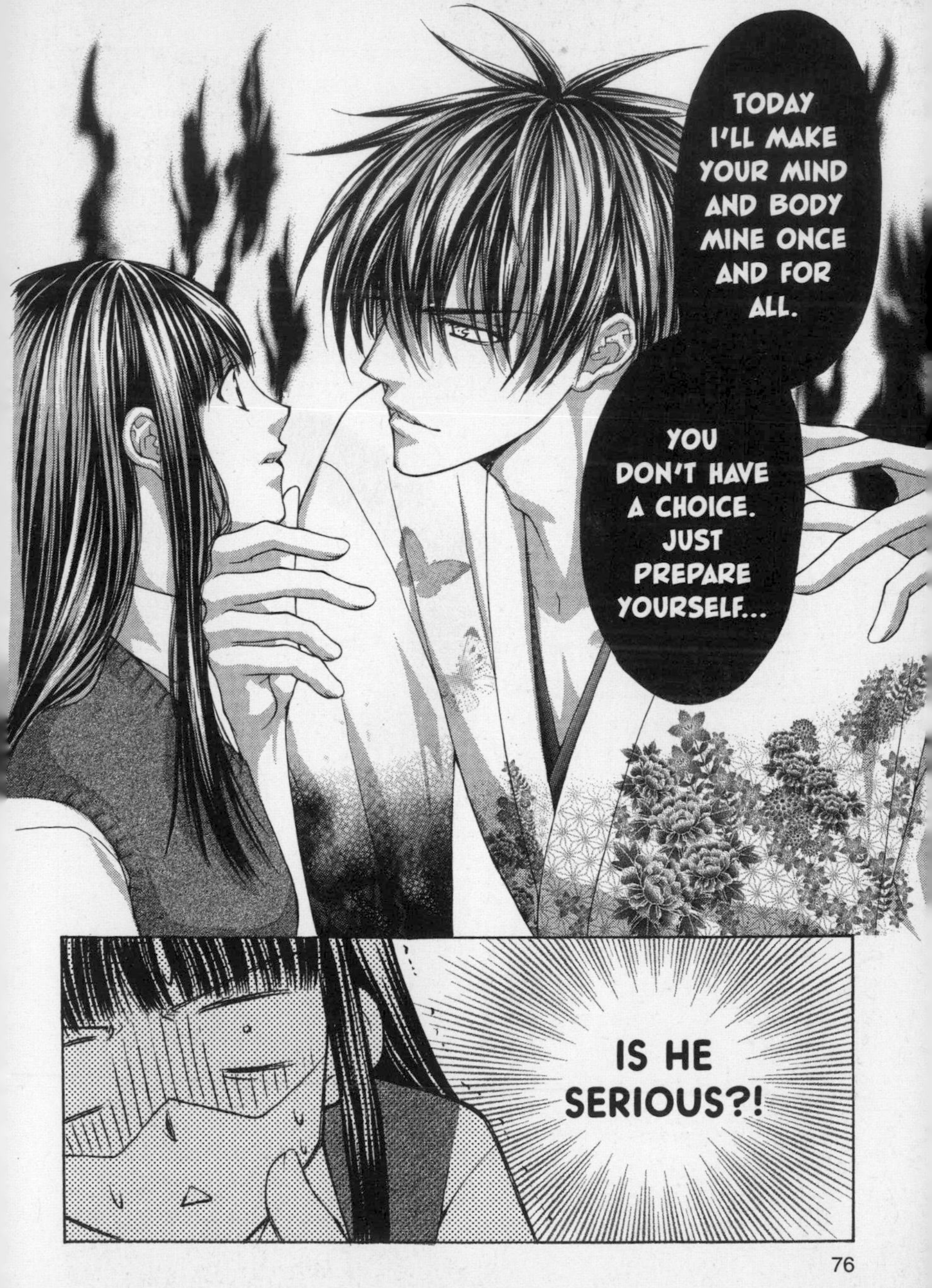
TODAY I'LL MAKE YOUR MIND AND BODY MINE ONCE AND FOR ALL.
YOU DON'T HAVE A CHOICE. JUST PREPARE YOURSELF...
...
IS HE SERIOUS?!

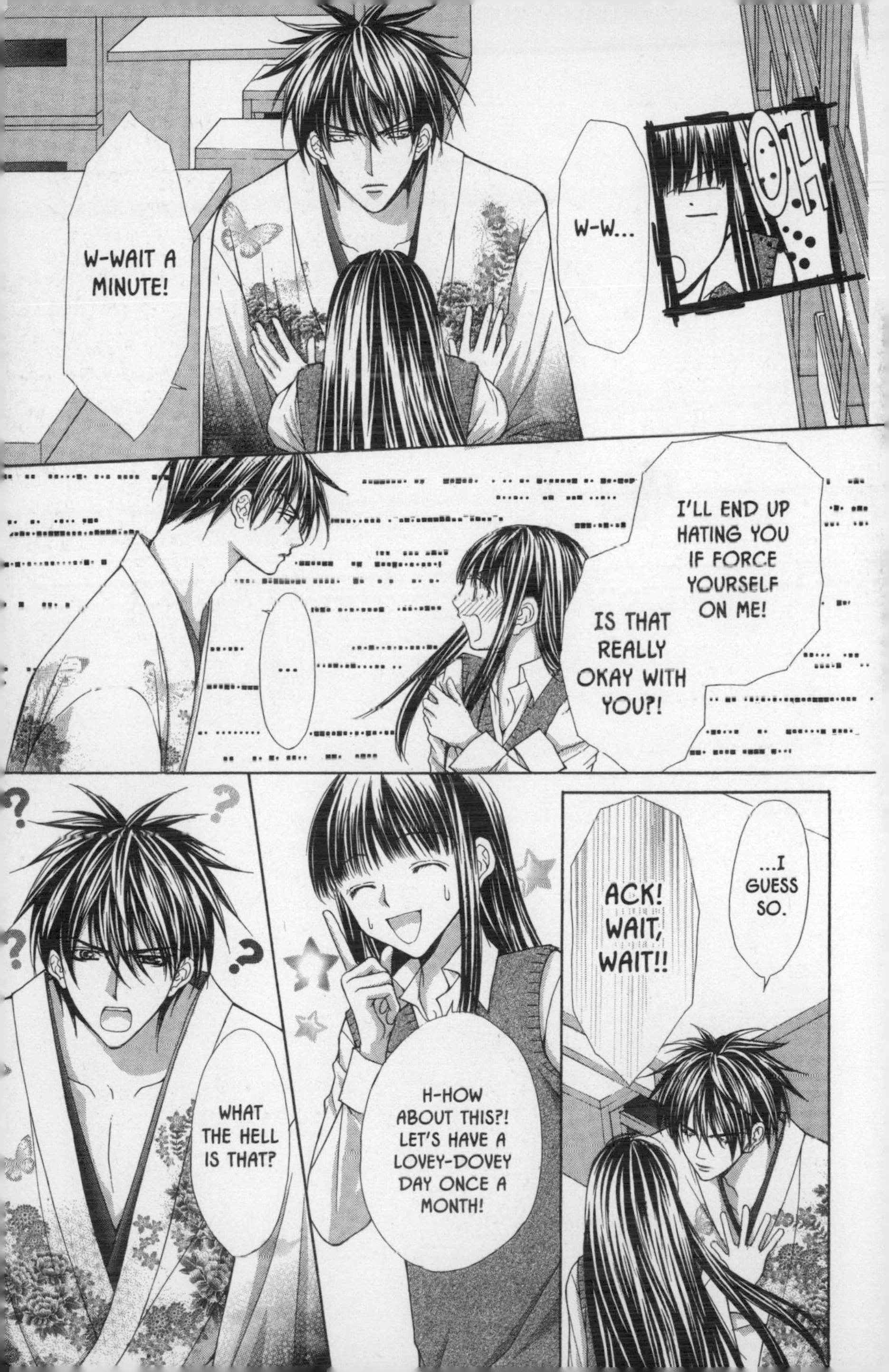
OH!
W-W...
W-WAIT A MINUTE!
I'LL END UP HATING YOU IF FORCE YOURSELF ON ME!
IS THAT REALLY OKAY WITH YOU?!
...
...I GUESS SO.
ACK! WAIT, WAIT!!
H-HOW ABOUT THIS?! LET'S HAVE A LOVEY-DOVEY DAY ONCE A MONTH!
WHAT THE HELL IS THAT?

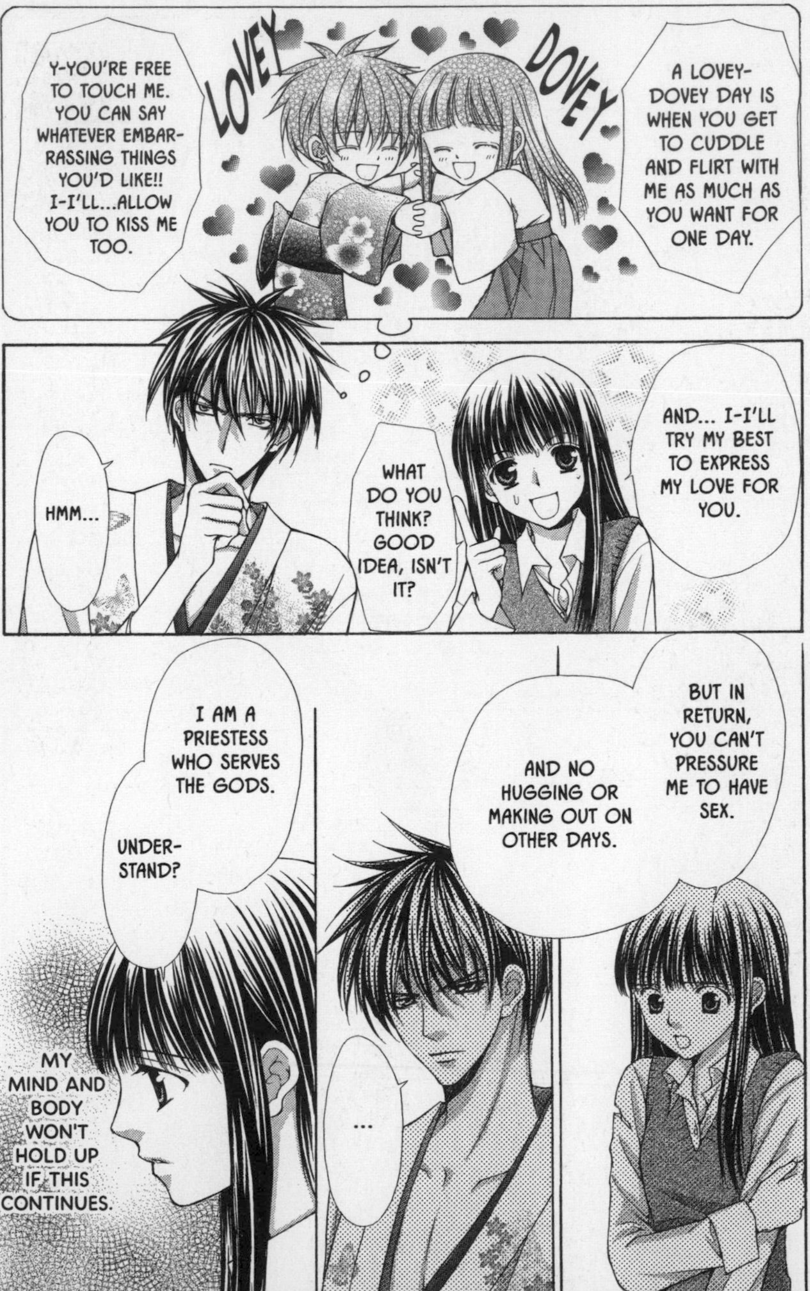
A LOVEY-DOVEY DAY IS WHEN YOU GET TO CUDDLE AND FLIRT WITH ME AS MUCH AS YOU WANT FOR ONE DAY.
LOVEY DOVEY
Y-YOU'RE FREE TO TOUCH ME. YOU CAN SAY WHATEVER EMBARRASSING THINGS YOU'D LIKE!! I-I'LL...ALLOW YOU TO KISS ME TOO.
AND... I-I'LL TRY MY BEST TO EXPRESS MY LOVE FOR YOU.
WHAT DO YOU THINK? GOOD IDEA, ISN'T IT?
HMM...
BUT IN RETURN, YOU CAN'T PRESSURE ME TO HAVE SEX.
AND NO HUGGING OR MAKING OUT ON OTHER DAYS.
...
I AM A PRIESTESS WHO SERVES THE GODS.
UNDERSTAND?
MY MIND AND BODY WON'T HOLD UP IF THIS CONTINUES.

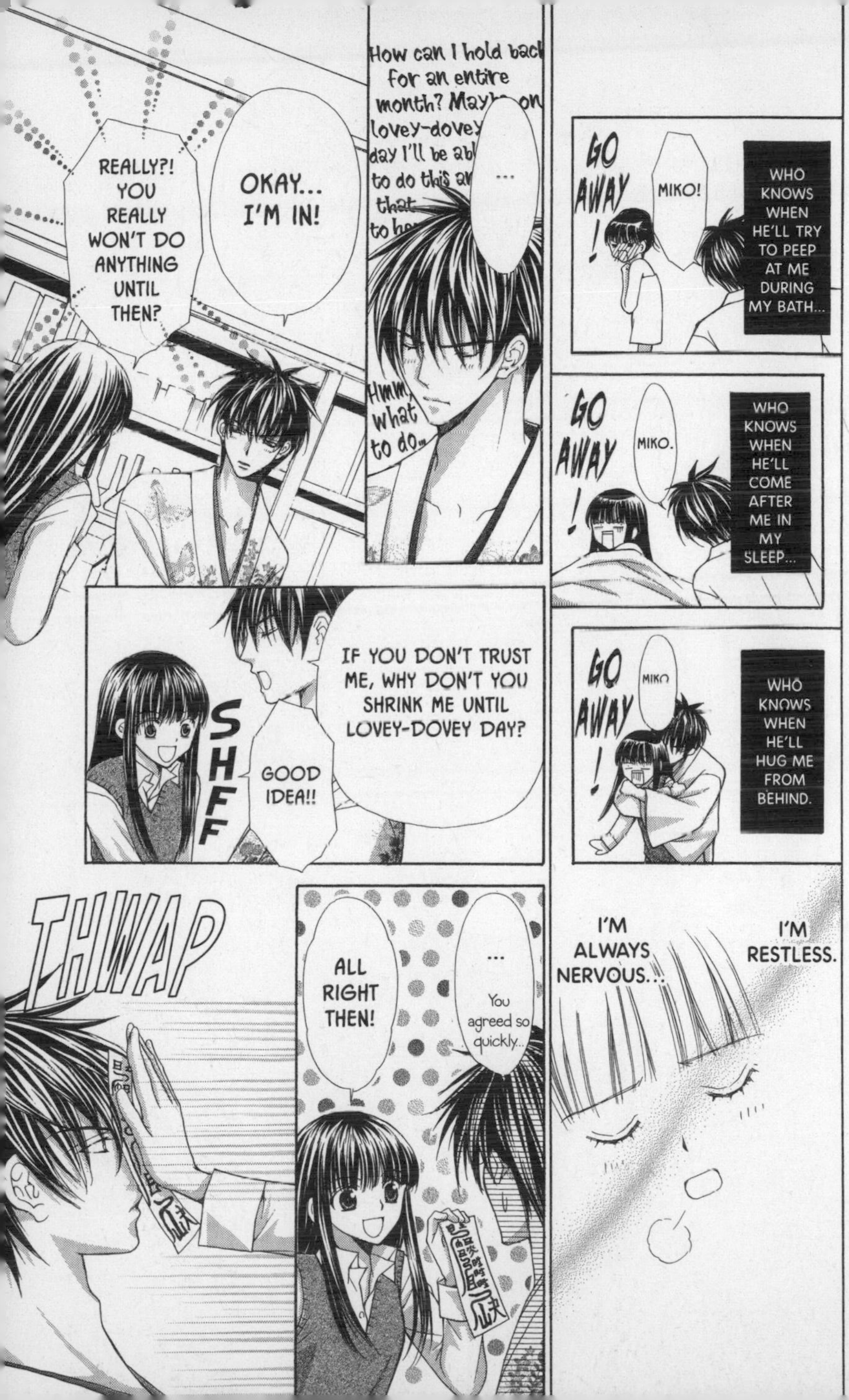
WHO KNOWS WHEN HE'LL TRY TO PEEP AT ME DURING MY BATH...
MIKO!
GO AWAY!
WHO KNOWS WHEN HE'LL COME AFTER ME IN MY SLEEP...
MIKO.
GO AWAY!
WHO KNOWS WHEN HE'LL HUG ME FROM BEHIND.
MIKO
GO AWAY!
I'M RESTLESS.
I'M ALWAYS NERVOUS...
How can I hold back for an entire month? Mayb on lovey-dovey day I'll be abl to do this an that to he
...
Hmm, what to do...
REALLY?! YOU REALLY WON'T DO ANYTHING UNTIL THEN?
OKAY... I'M IN!
IF YOU DON'T TRUST ME, WHY DON'T YOU SHRINK ME UNTIL LOVEY-DOVEY DAY?
GOOD IDEA!!
SHFF
...
You agreed so quickly...
ALL RIGHT THEN!
THWAP

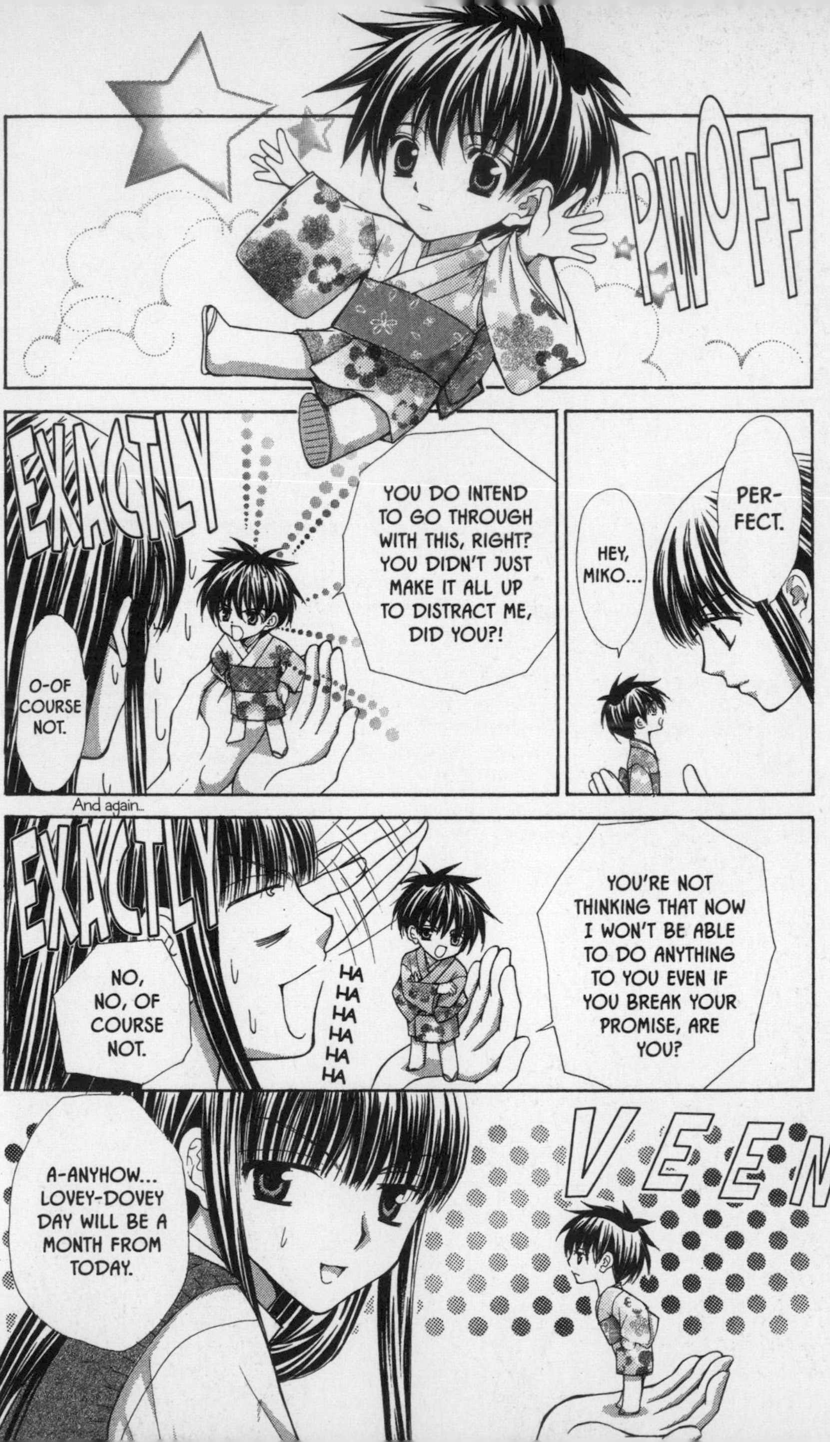
PWOFF
PER-FECT.
HEY, MIKO...
YOU DO INTEND TO GO THROUGH WITH THIS, RIGHT? YOU DIDN'T JUST MAKE IT ALL UP TO DISTRACT ME, DID YOU?!
EXACTLY
O-OF COURSE NOT.
And again...
YOU'RE NOT THINKING THAT NOW I WON'T BE ABLE TO DO ANYTHING TO YOU EVEN IF YOU BREAK YOUR PROMISE, ARE YOU?
HA HA HA HA HA HA
EXACTLY
NO, NO, OF COURSE NOT.
VEEN
A-ANYHOW... LOVEY-DOVEY DAY WILL BE A MONTH FROM TODAY.

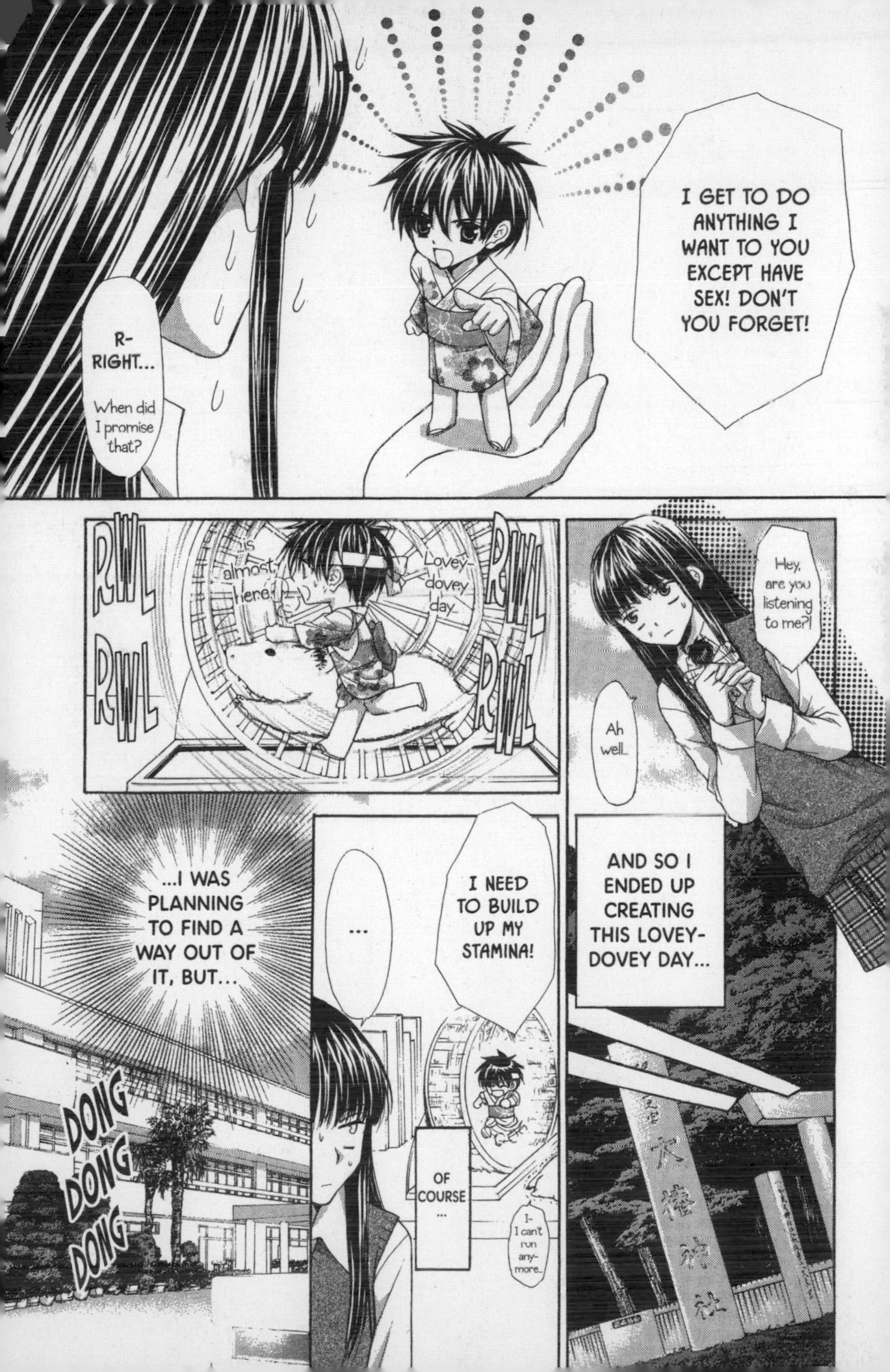
I GET TO DO ANYTHING I WANT TO YOU EXCEPT HAVE SEX! DON'T YOU FORGET!
R-RIGHT...
When did I promise that?
Hey, are you listening to me?!
Ah well...
RWL RWL
Lovey-dovey day...
is almost here.
RWL RWL
AND SO I ENDED UP CREATING THIS LOVEY-DOVEY DAY...
I NEED TO BUILD UP MY STAMINA!
...
OF COURSE...
I-I can't run any-more...
...I WAS PLANNING TO FIND A WAY OUT OF IT, BUT...
DONG DONG DONG

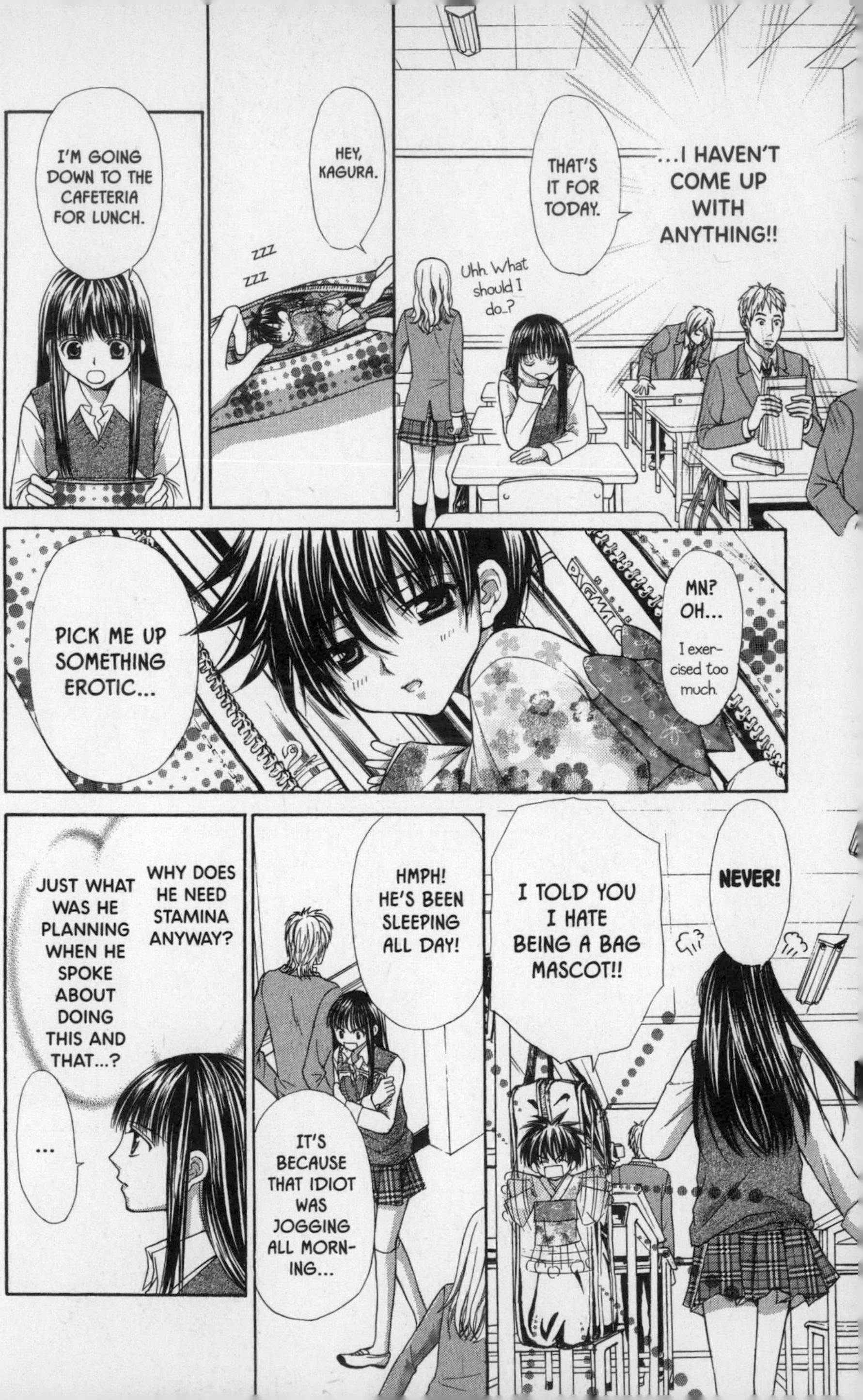
...I HAVEN'T COME UP WITH ANYTHING!!
THAT'S IT FOR TODAY.
Uhh. What should I do..?
HEY, KAGURA.
ZZZ
ZZZ
I'M GOING DOWN TO THE CAFETERIA FOR LUNCH.
MN? OH...
I exercised too much.
PICK ME UP SOMETHING EROTIC...
NEVER!
I TOLD YOU I HATE BEING A BAG MASCOT!!
HMPH! HE'S BEEN SLEEPING ALL DAY!
IT'S BECAUSE THAT IDIOT WAS JOGGING ALL MORNING...
WHY DOES HE NEED STAMINA ANYWAY?
JUST WHAT WAS HE PLANNING WHEN HE SPOKE ABOUT DOING THIS AND THAT...?
...

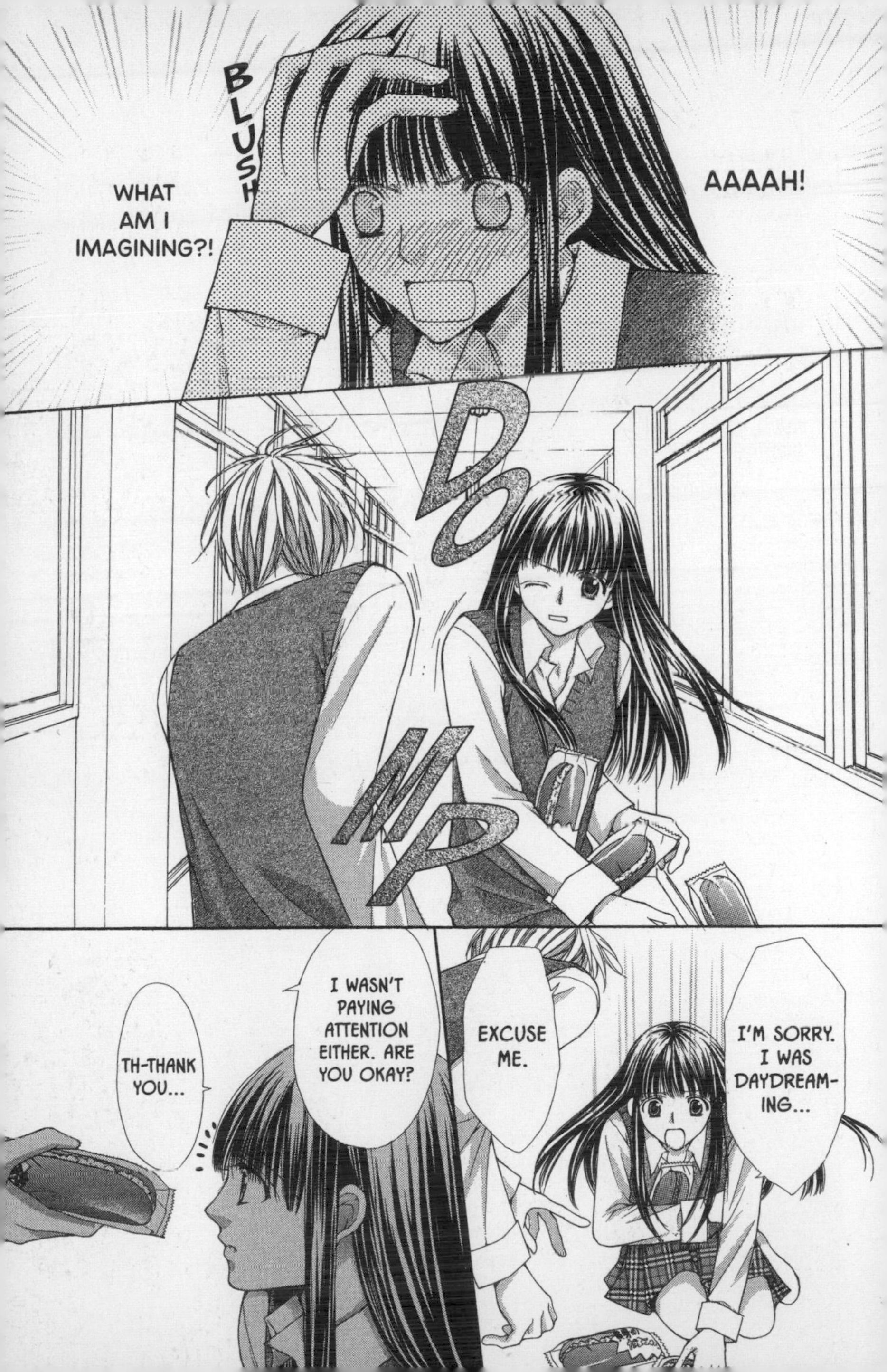
AAAAH!
BLUSH
WHAT AM I IMAGINING?!
DOMP
I'M SORRY. I WAS DAYDREAMING...
EXCUSE ME.
I WASN'T PAYING ATTENTION EITHER. ARE YOU OKAY?
TH-THANK YOU...

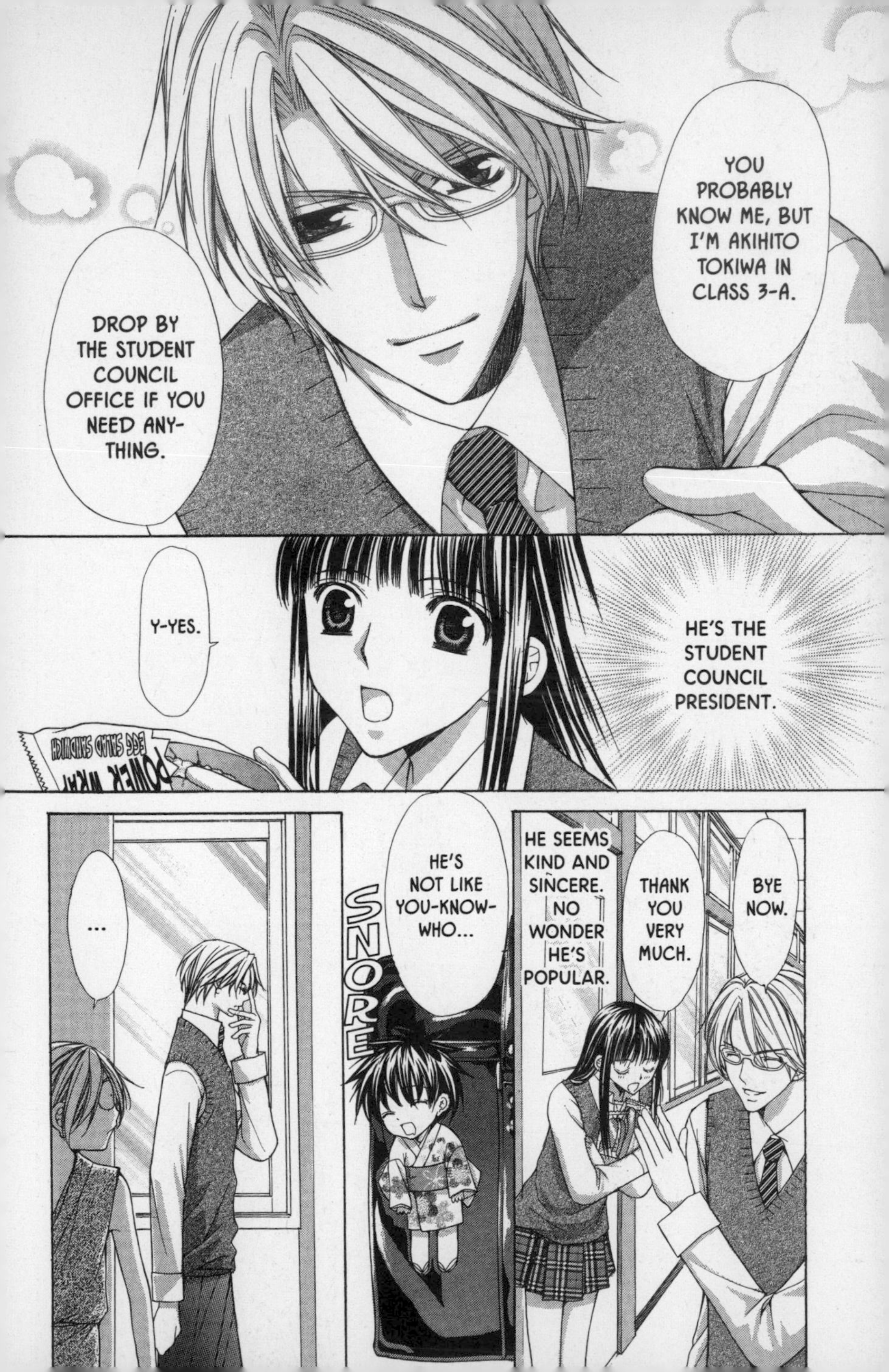
YOU PROBABLY KNOW ME, BUT I'M AKIHITO TOKIWA IN CLASS 3-A.
DROP BY THE STUDENT COUNCIL OFFICE IF YOU NEED ANYTHING.
HE'S THE STUDENT COUNCIL PRESIDENT.
Y-YES.
EGG SALAD SANDWICH
BYE NOW.
THANK YOU VERY MUCH.
HE SEEMS KIND AND SINCERE. NO WONDER HE'S POPULAR.
HE'S NOT LIKE YOU-KNOW-WHO...
SNORE
...

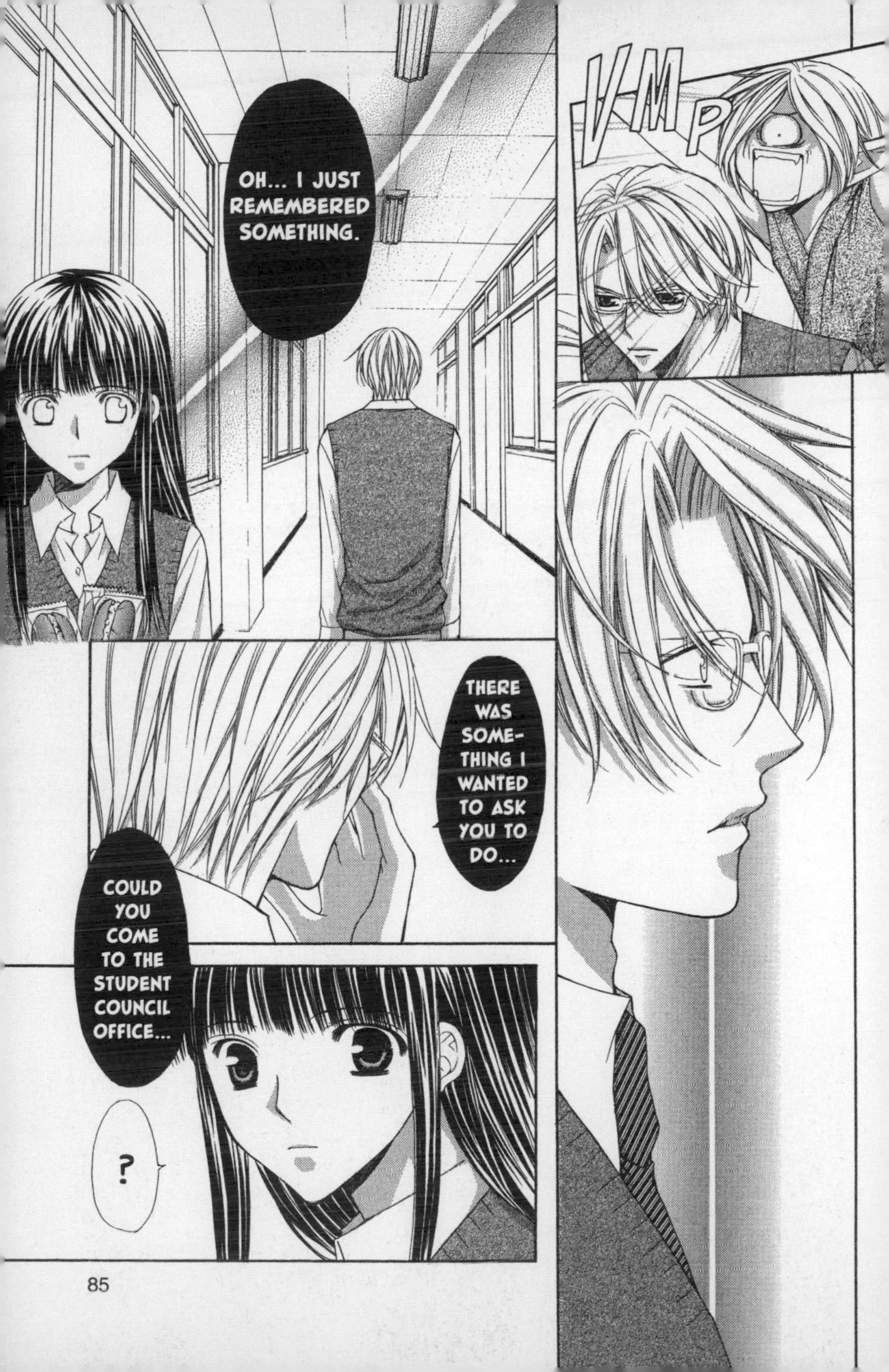
VMP
OH... I JUST REMEMBERED SOMETHING.
THERE WAS SOME-THING I WANTED TO ASK YOU TO DO...
COULD YOU COME TO THE STUDENT COUNCIL OFFICE...
?

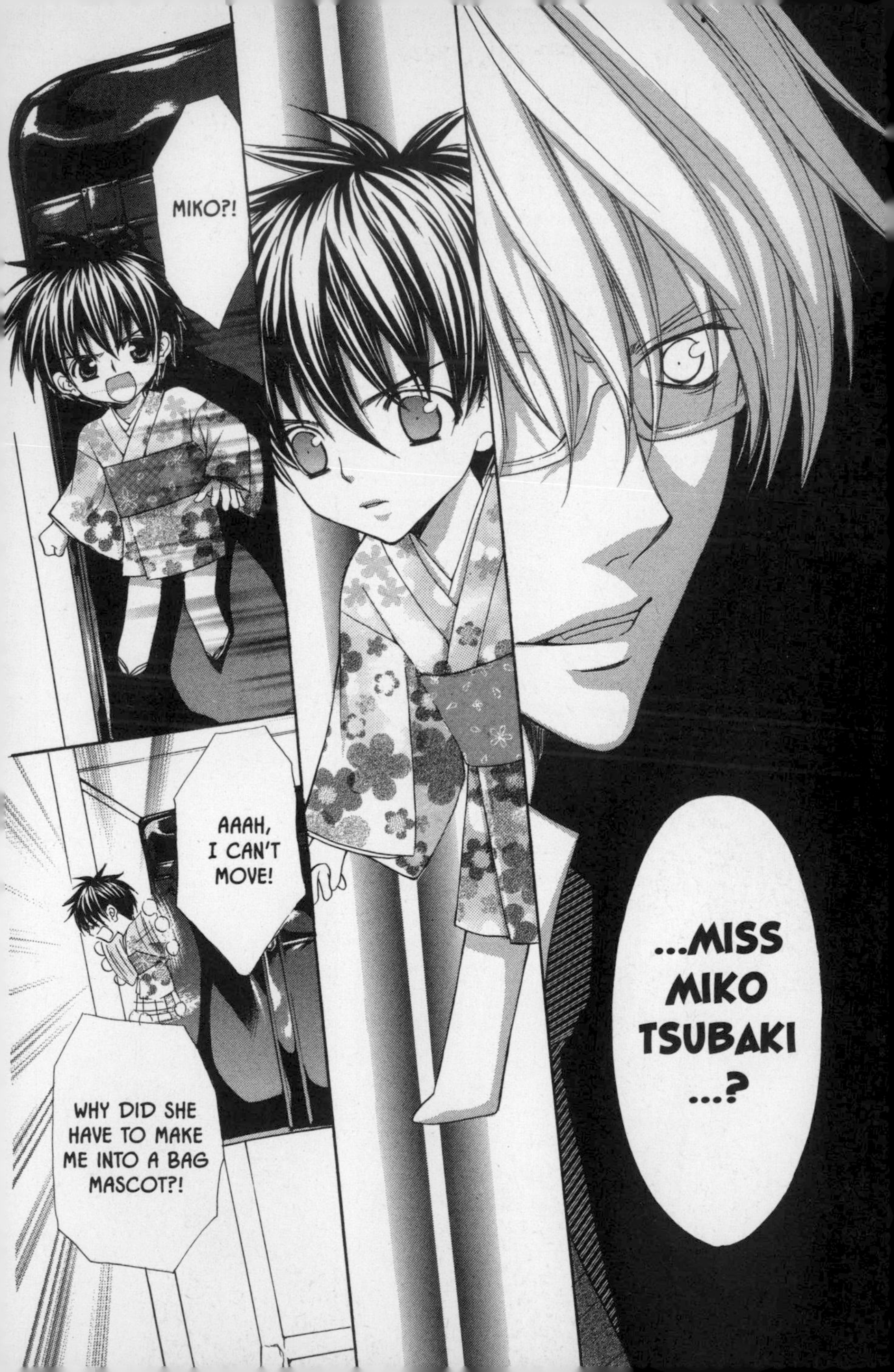
...MISS MIKO TSUBAKI ...?
MIKO?!
AAAH, I CAN'T MOVE!
WHY DID SHE HAVE TO MAKE ME INTO A BAG MASCOT?!

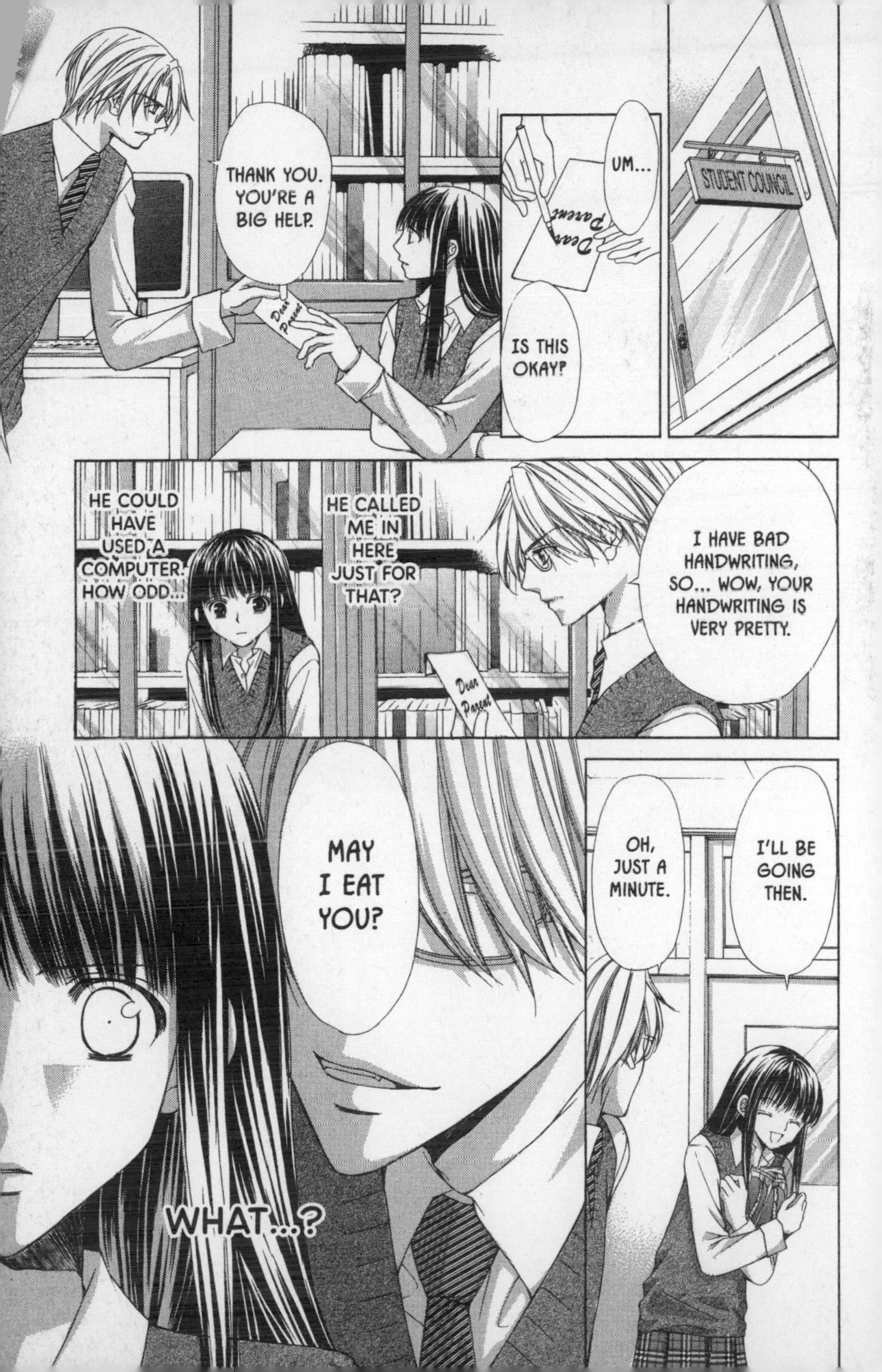
STUDENT COUNCIL
UM...
Dear Parent
IS THIS OKAY?
THANK YOU. YOU'RE A BIG HELP.
I HAVE BAD HANDWRITING, SO... WOW, YOUR HANDWRITING IS VERY PRETTY.
HE CALLED ME IN HERE JUST FOR THAT?
HE COULD HAVE USED A COMPUTER. HOW ODD...
I'LL BE GOING THEN.
OH, JUST A MINUTE.
MAY I EAT YOU?
WHAT...?

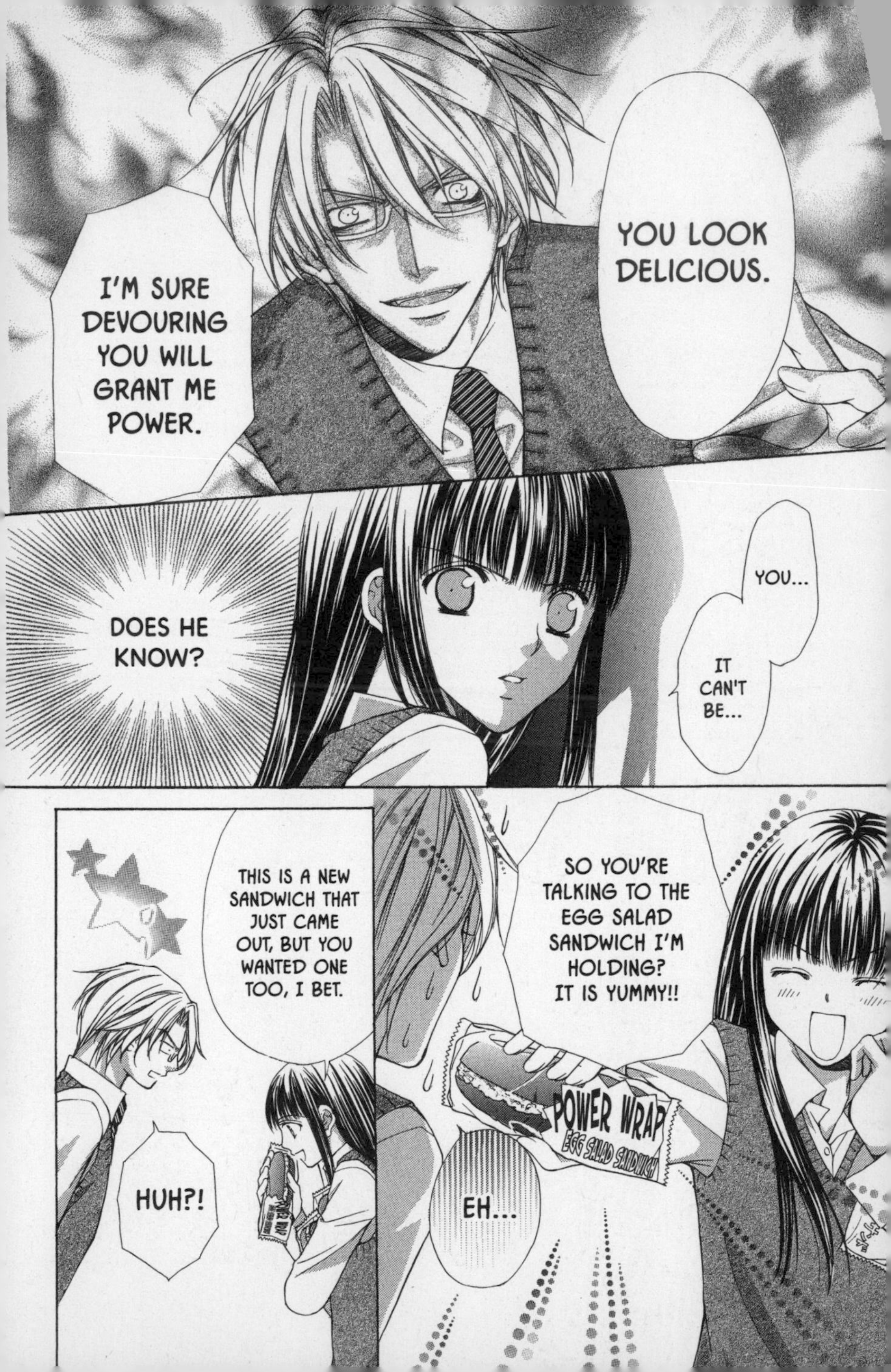
YOU LOOK DELICIOUS.
I'M SURE DEVOURING YOU WILL GRANT ME POWER.
YOU...
IT CAN'T BE...
DOES HE KNOW?
SO YOU'RE TALKING TO THE EGG SALAD SANDWICH I'M HOLDING? IT IS YUMMY!!
POWER WRAP
EGG SALAD SANDWICH
EH...
THIS IS A NEW SANDWICH THAT JUST CAME OUT, BUT YOU WANTED ONE TOO, I BET.
HUH?!

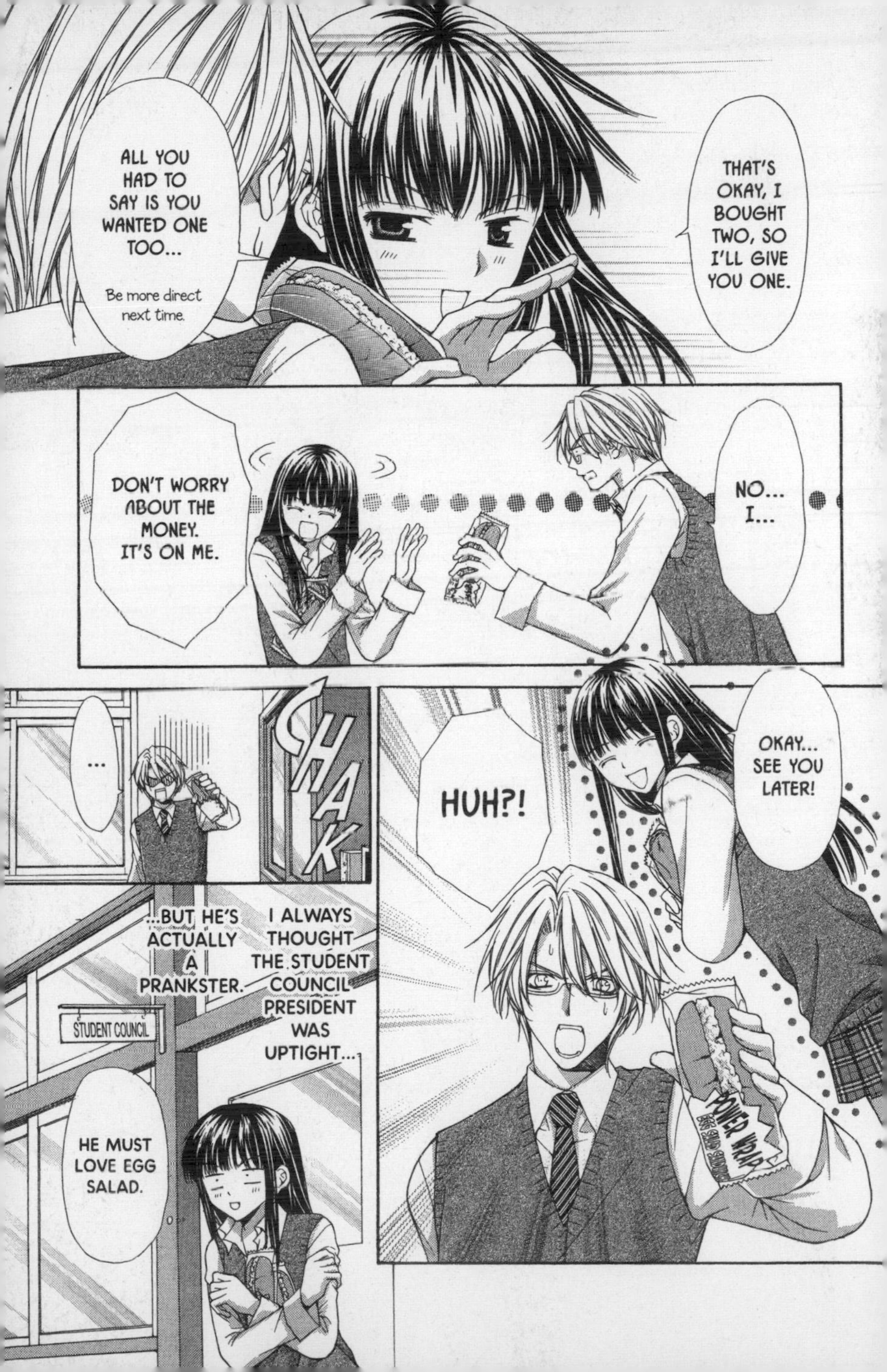
THAT'S OKAY, I BOUGHT TWO, SO I'LL GIVE YOU ONE.
ALL YOU HAD TO SAY IS YOU WANTED ONE TOO...
Be more direct next time.
NO... I...
DON'T WORRY ABOUT THE MONEY. IT'S ON ME.
OKAY... SEE YOU LATER!
HUH?!
POWER WRAP
CHAK
...
I ALWAYS THOUGHT THE STUDENT COUNCIL PRESIDENT WAS UPTIGHT...
...BUT HE'S ACTUALLY A PRANKSTER.
STUDENT COUNCIL
HE MUST LOVE EGG SALAD.

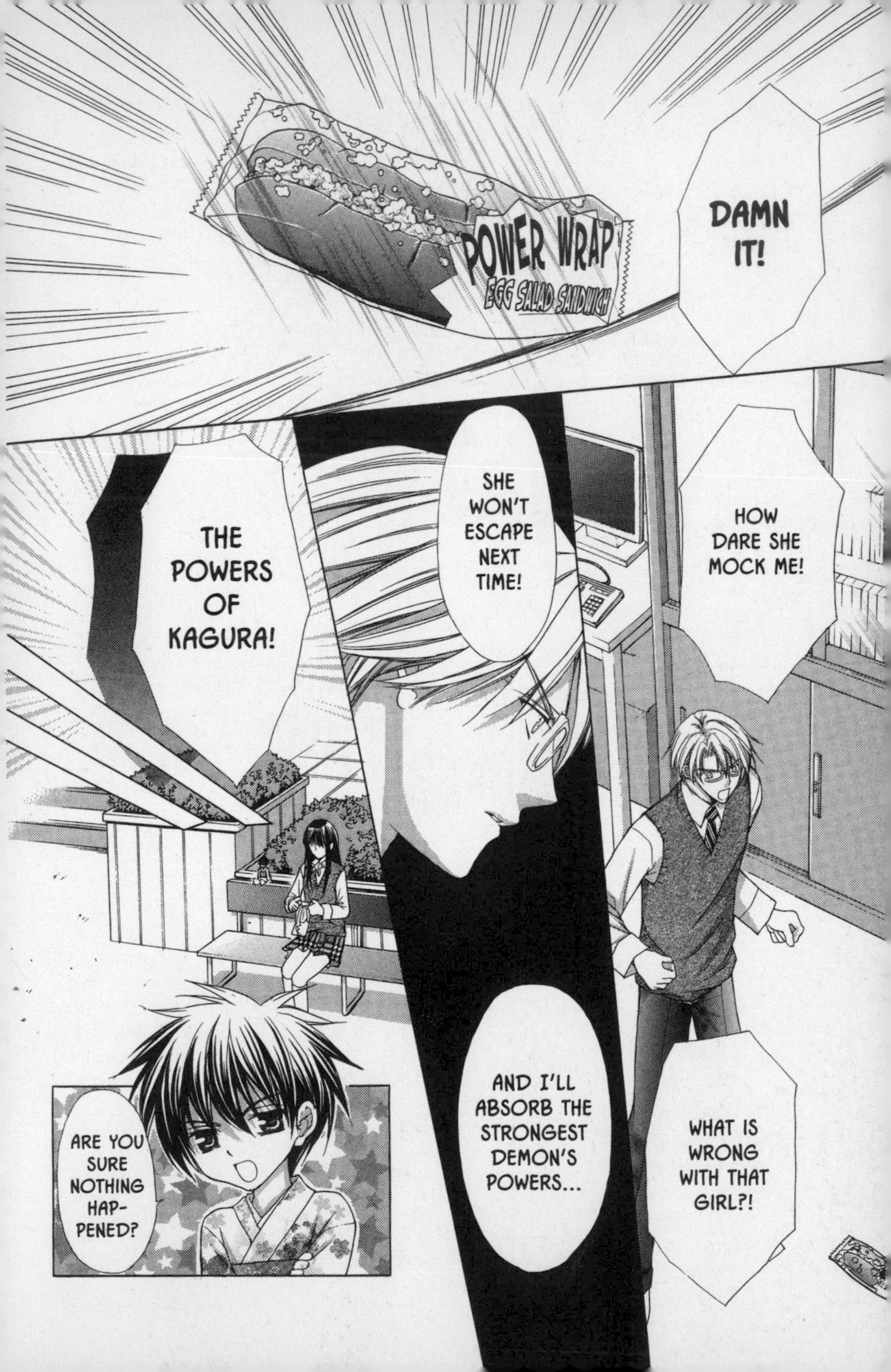
DAMN IT!
POWER WRAP
EGG SALAD SANDWICH
HOW DARE SHE MOCK ME!
WHAT IS WRONG WITH THAT GIRL?!
SHE WON'T ESCAPE NEXT TIME!
AND I'LL ABSORB THE STRONGEST DEMON'S POWERS...
THE POWERS OF KAGURA!
ARE YOU SURE NOTHING HAP-PENED?

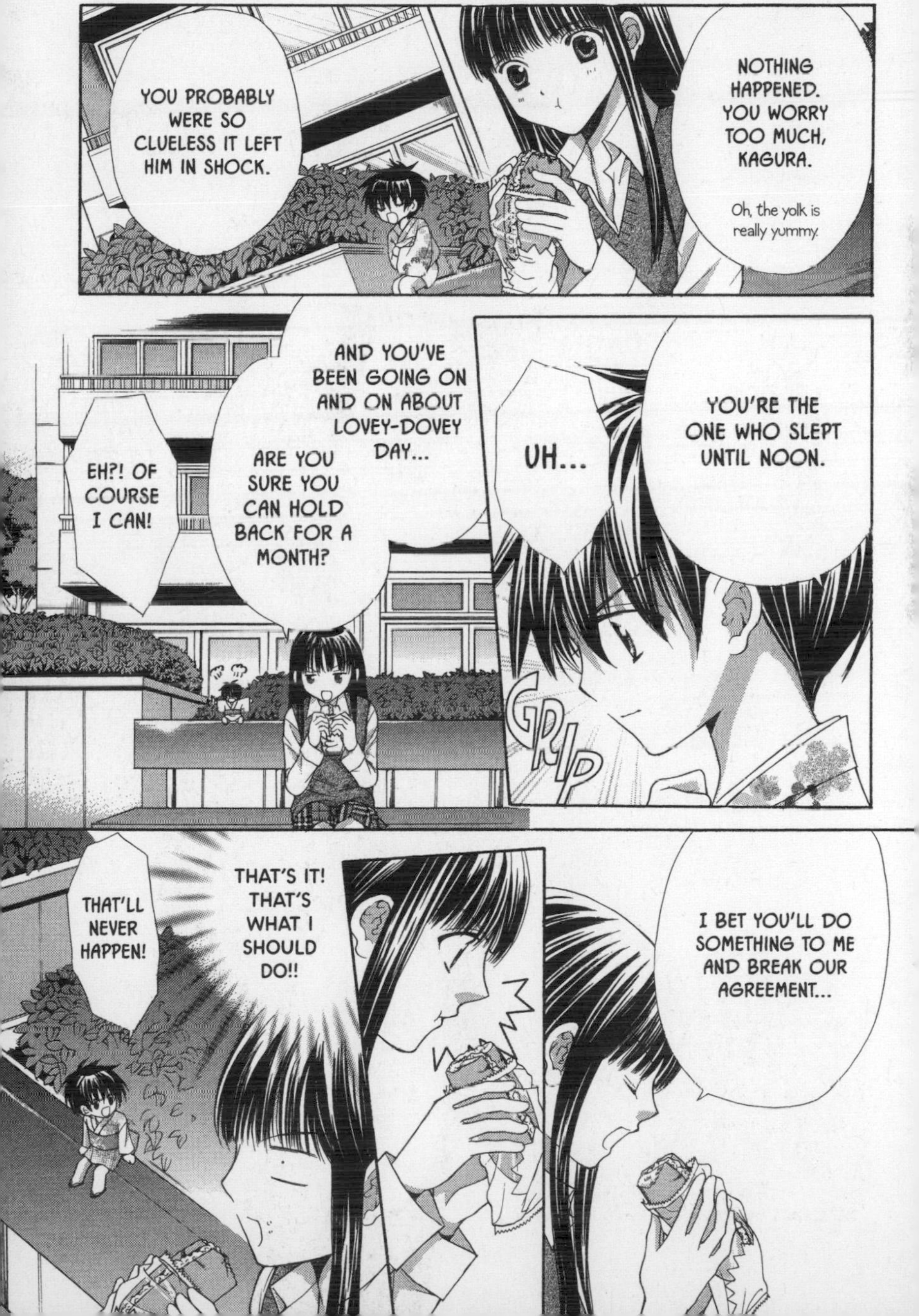
NOTHING HAPPENED. YOU WORRY TOO MUCH, KAGURA.
Oh, the yolk is really yummy.
YOU PROBABLY WERE SO CLUELESS IT LEFT HIM IN SHOCK.
YOU'RE THE ONE WHO SLEPT UNTIL NOON.
UH...
GRIP
AND YOU'VE BEEN GOING ON AND ON ABOUT LOVEY-DOVEY DAY...
ARE YOU SURE YOU CAN HOLD BACK FOR A MONTH?
EH?! OF COURSE I CAN!
I BET YOU'LL DO SOMETHING TO ME AND BREAK OUR AGREEMENT...
THAT'S IT! THAT'S WHAT I SHOULD DO!!
THAT'LL NEVER HAPPEN!

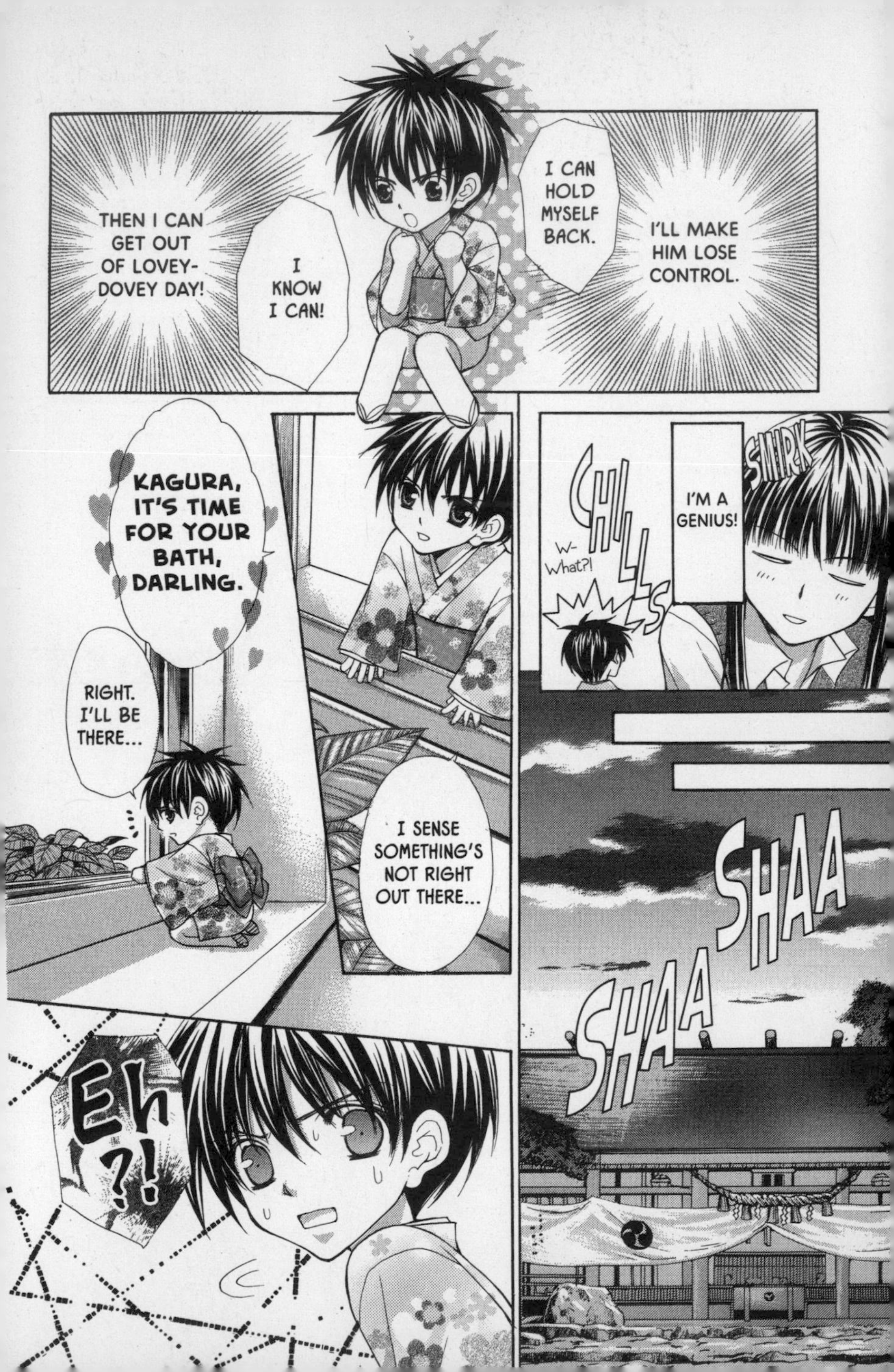
I'LL MAKE HIM LOSE CONTROL.
I CAN HOLD MYSELF BACK.
I KNOW I CAN!
THEN I CAN GET OUT OF LOVEY-DOVEY DAY!
SMIRK
I'M A GENIUS!
CHILLS
W-What?!
I SENSE SOMETHING'S NOT RIGHT OUT THERE...
KAGURA, IT'S TIME FOR YOUR BATH, DARLING.
RIGHT. I'LL BE THERE...
SHAA SHAA SHAA
Eh?!

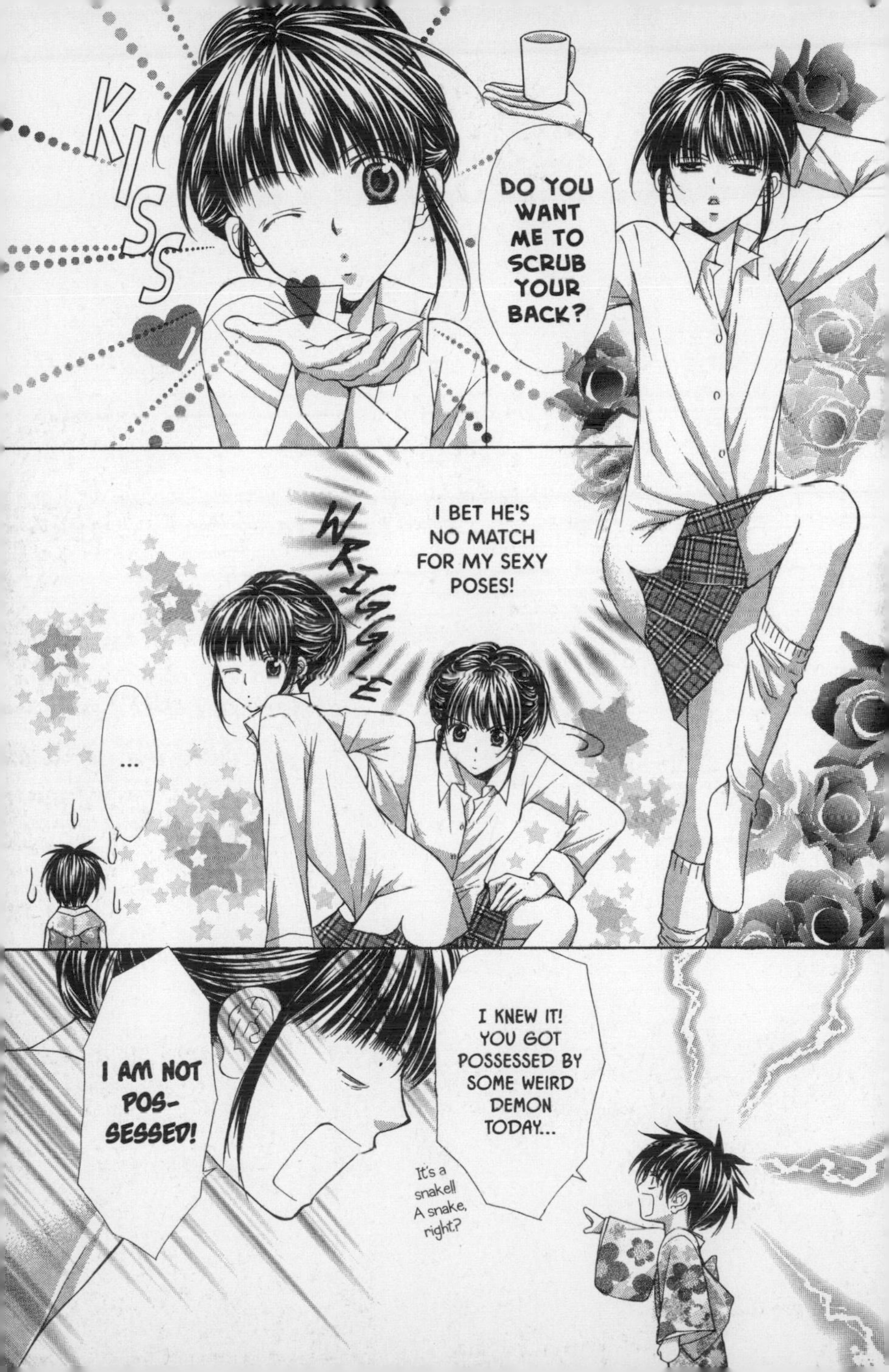

DO YOU WANT ME TO SCRUB YOUR BACK?
KISS
I BET HE'S NO MATCH FOR MY SEXY POSES!
WRIGGLE
...
I KNEW IT! YOU GOT POSSESSED BY SOME WEIRD DEMON TODAY...
It's a snake!! A snake, right?
I AM NOT POS-SESSED!

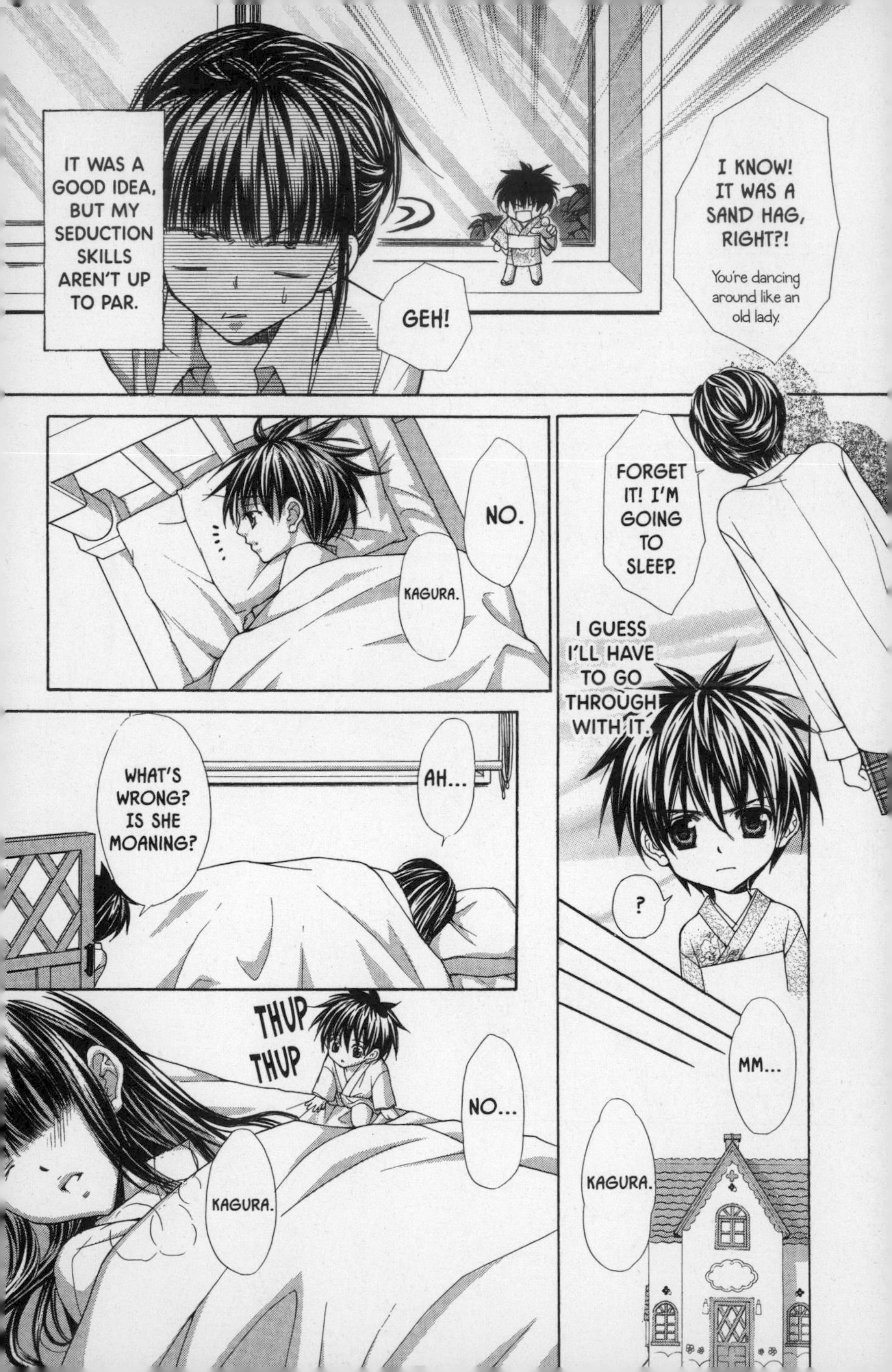
I KNOW! IT WAS A SAND HAG, RIGHT?!
You're dancing around like an old lady.
GEH!
IT WAS A GOOD IDEA, BUT MY SEDUCTION SKILLS AREN'T UP TO PAR.
FORGET IT! I'M GOING TO SLEEP.
I GUESS I'LL HAVE TO GO THROUGH WITH IT.
?
NO.
KAGURA.
AH...
WHAT'S WRONG? IS SHE MOANING?
MM...
KAGURA.
NO...
THUP THUP
KAGURA.

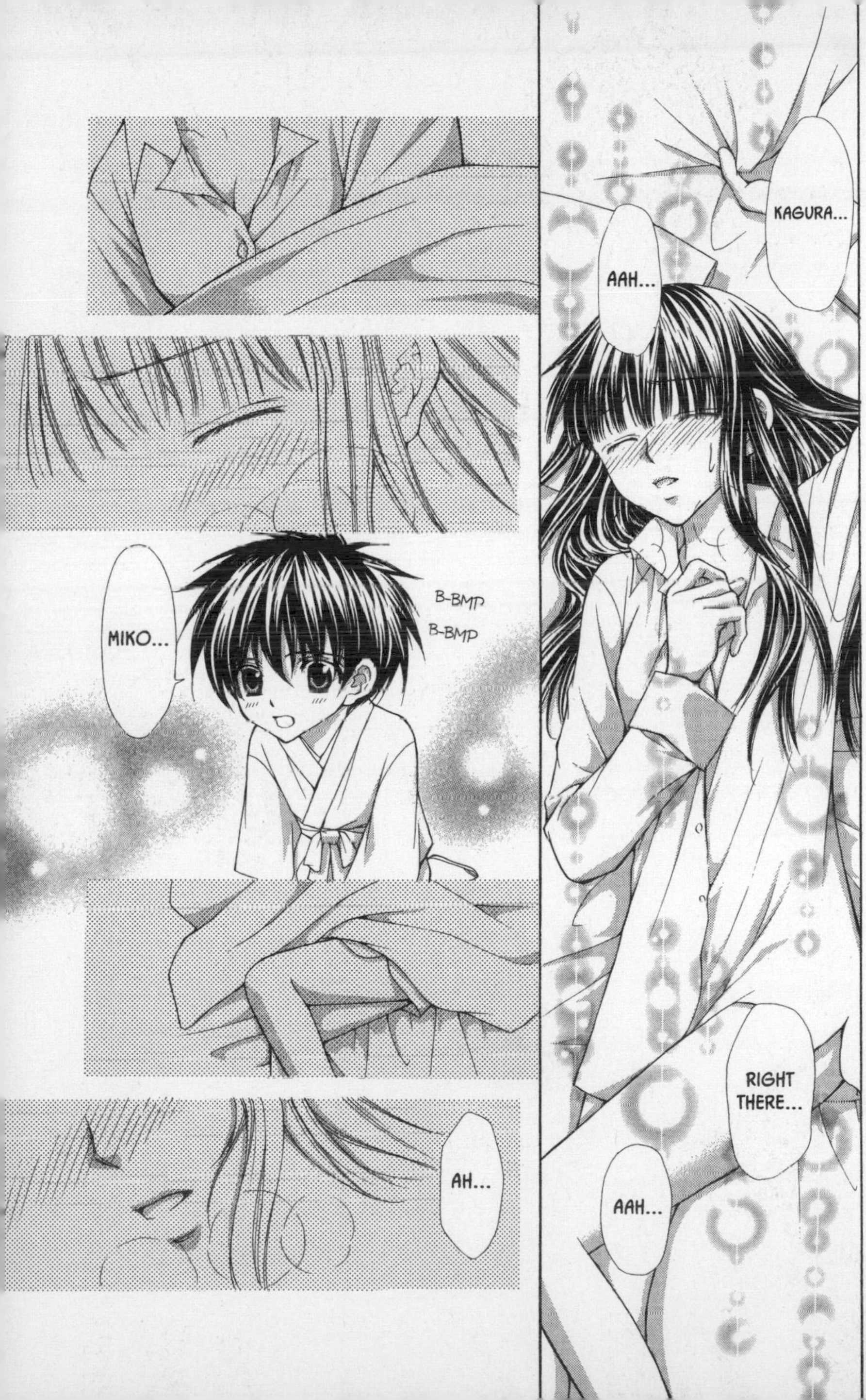
KAGURA...
AAH...
RIGHT THERE...
AAH...
MIKO...
B-BMP
B-BMP
AH...

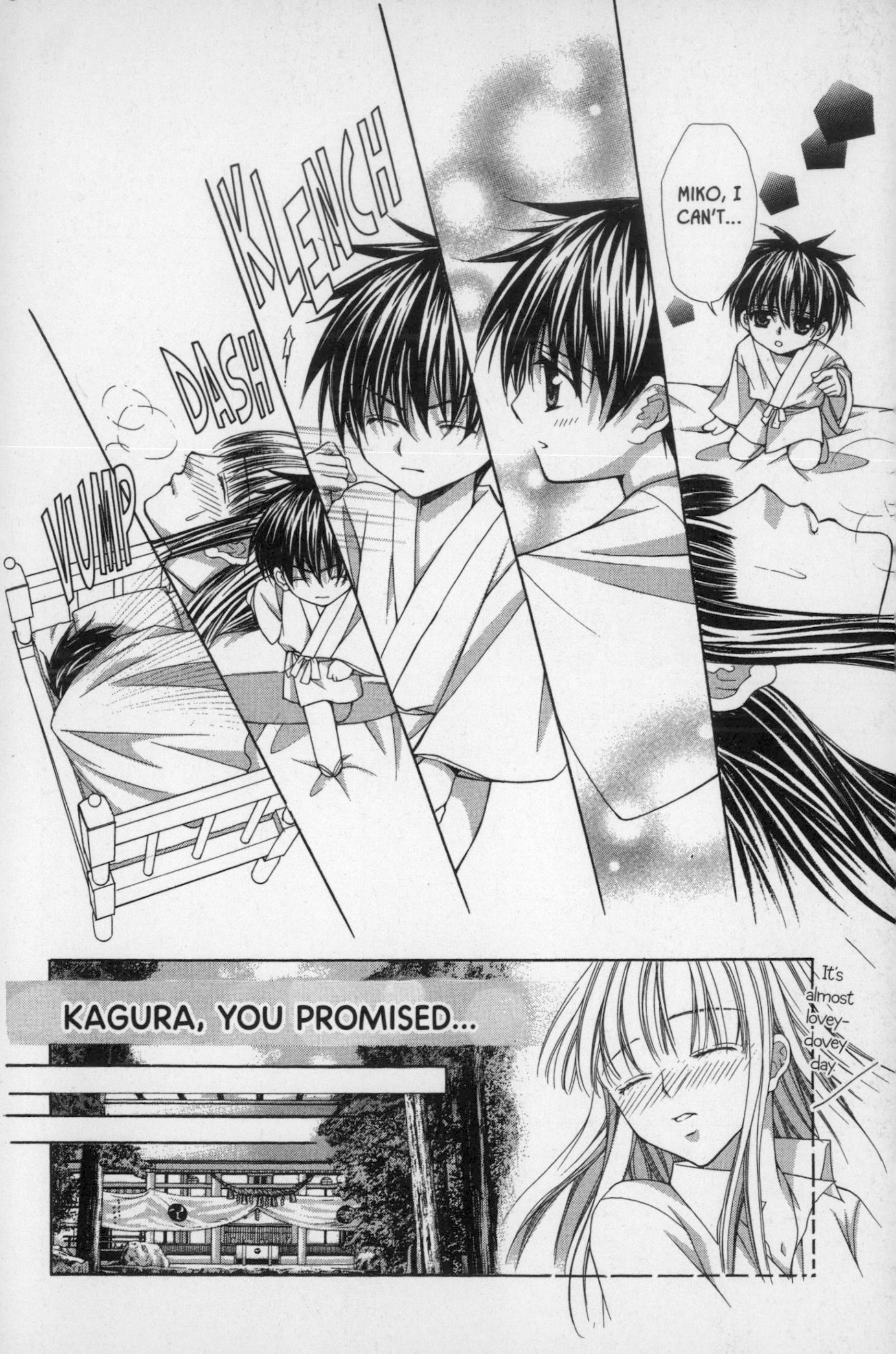
MIKO, I CAN'T...
KLENCH
DASH
VUMP
It's almost lovey-dovey day.
KAGURA, YOU PROMISED...

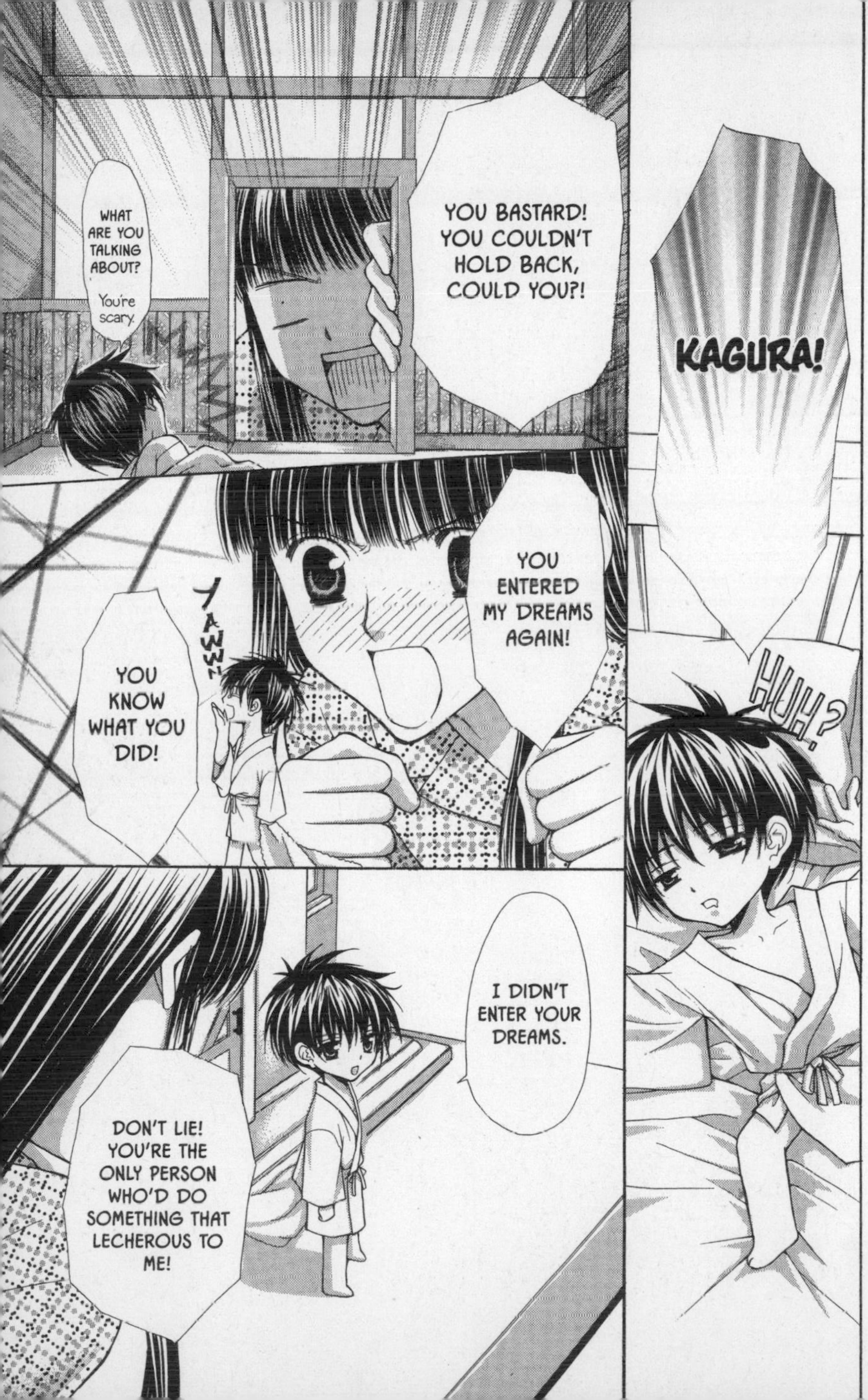
KAGURA!
HUH?
YOU BASTARD! YOU COULDN'T HOLD BACK, COULD YOU?!
WHAT ARE YOU TALKING ABOUT?
You're scary.
YOU ENTERED MY DREAMS AGAIN!
YOU KNOW WHAT YOU DID!
I DIDN'T ENTER YOUR DREAMS.
DON'T LIE! YOU'RE THE ONLY PERSON WHO'D DO SOMETHING THAT LECHEROUS TO ME!

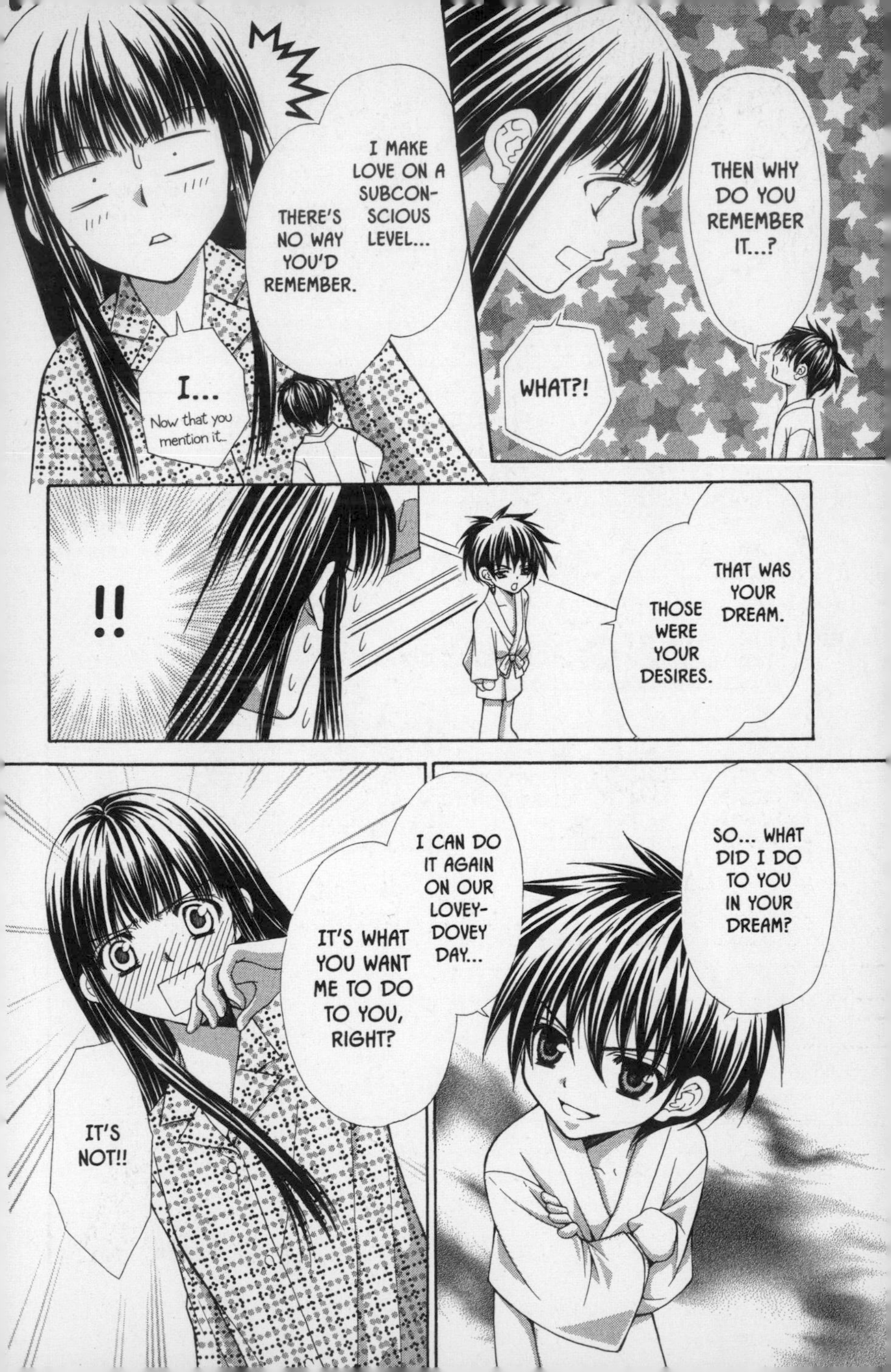
THEN WHY DO YOU REMEMBER IT...?
WHAT?!
I MAKE LOVE ON A SUBCON-SCIOUS LEVEL...
THERE'S NO WAY YOU'D REMEMBER.
I... Now that you mention it...
THAT WAS YOUR DREAM.
THOSE WERE YOUR DESIRES.
!!
SO... WHAT DID I DO TO YOU IN YOUR DREAM?
I CAN DO IT AGAIN ON OUR LOVEY-DOVEY DAY...
IT'S WHAT YOU WANT ME TO DO TO YOU, RIGHT?
IT'S NOT!!

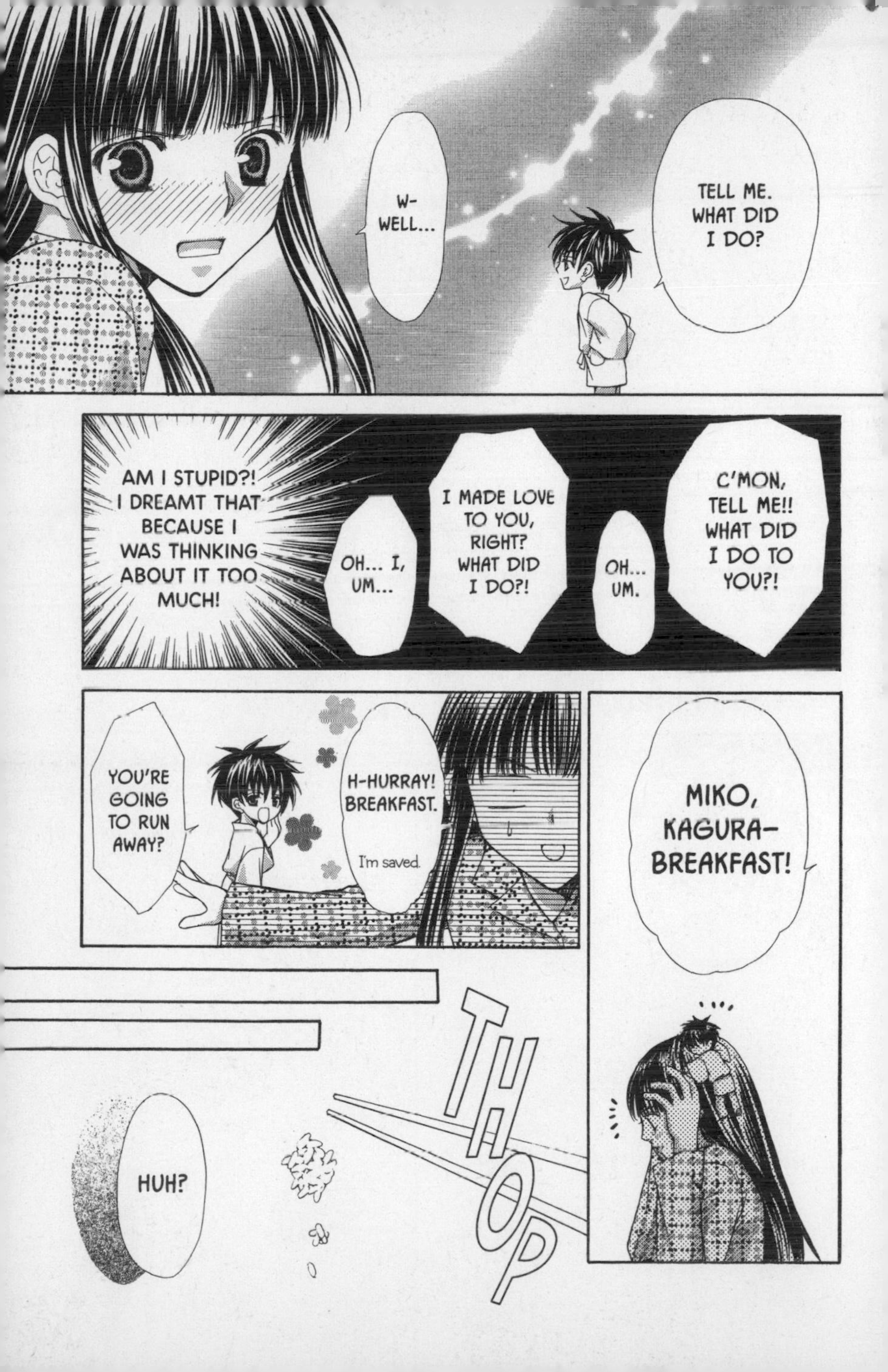
TELL ME. WHAT DID I DO?
W- WELL...
C'MON, TELL ME!! WHAT DID I DO TO YOU?!
OH... UM.
I MADE LOVE TO YOU, RIGHT? WHAT DID I DO?!
OH... I, UM...
AM I STUPID?! I DREAMT THAT BECAUSE I WAS THINKING ABOUT IT TOO MUCH!
MIKO, KAGURA-BREAKFAST!
H-HURRAY! BREAKFAST.
I'm saved.
YOU'RE GOING TO RUN AWAY?
THOOP
HUH?

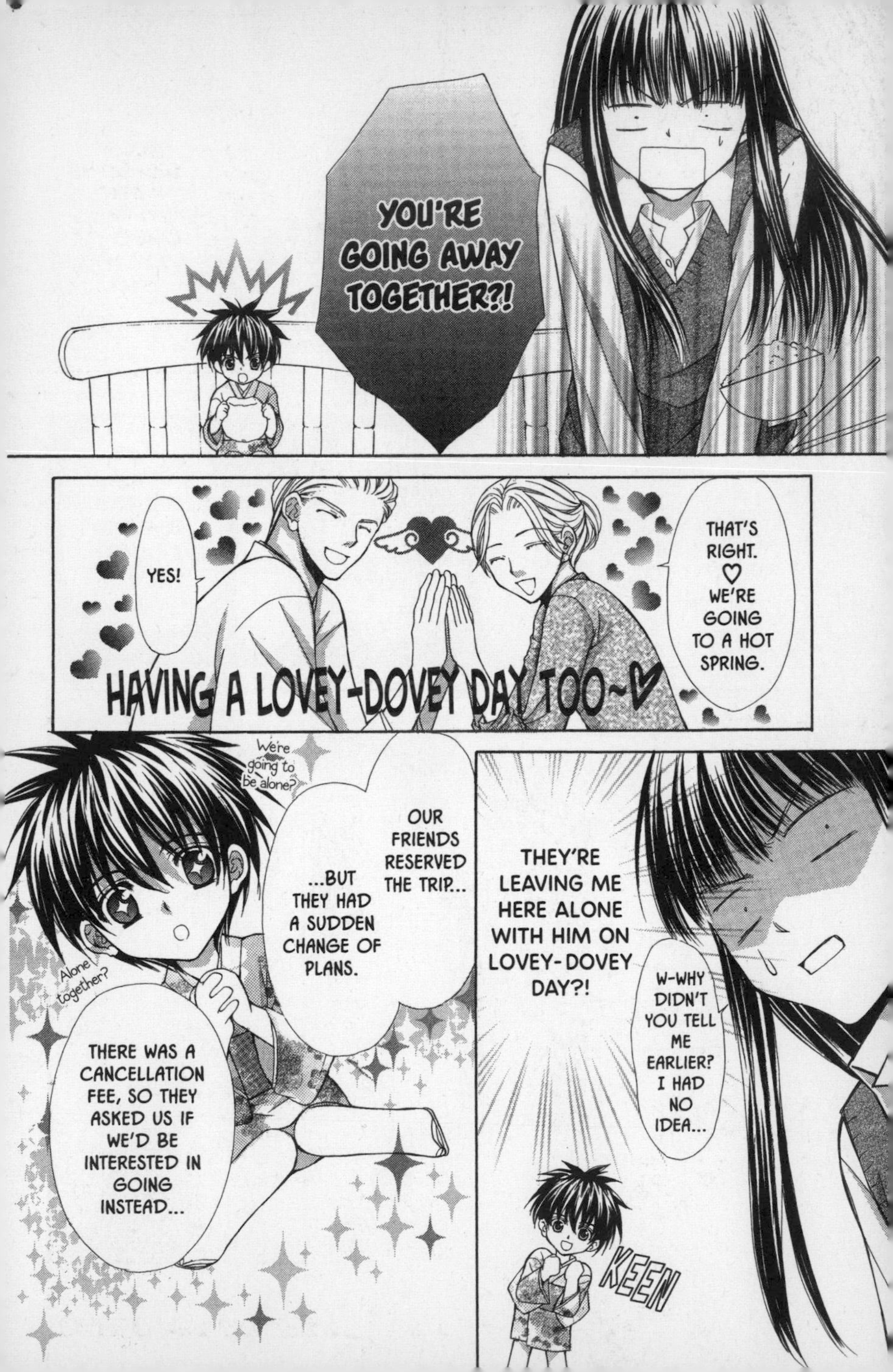

YOU'RE GOING AWAY TOGETHER?!
THAT'S RIGHT. ♡ WE'RE GOING TO A HOT SPRING.
YES!
HAVING A LOVEY-DOVEY DAY TOO~♡
THEY'RE LEAVING ME HERE ALONE WITH HIM ON LOVEY-DOVEY DAY?!
W-WHY DIDN'T YOU TELL ME EARLIER? I HAD NO IDEA...
KEEN
OUR FRIENDS RESERVED THE TRIP...
...BUT THEY HAD A SUDDEN CHANGE OF PLANS.
We're going to be alone?
Alone together?
THERE WAS A CANCELLATION FEE, SO THEY ASKED US IF WE'D BE INTERESTED IN GOING INSTEAD...

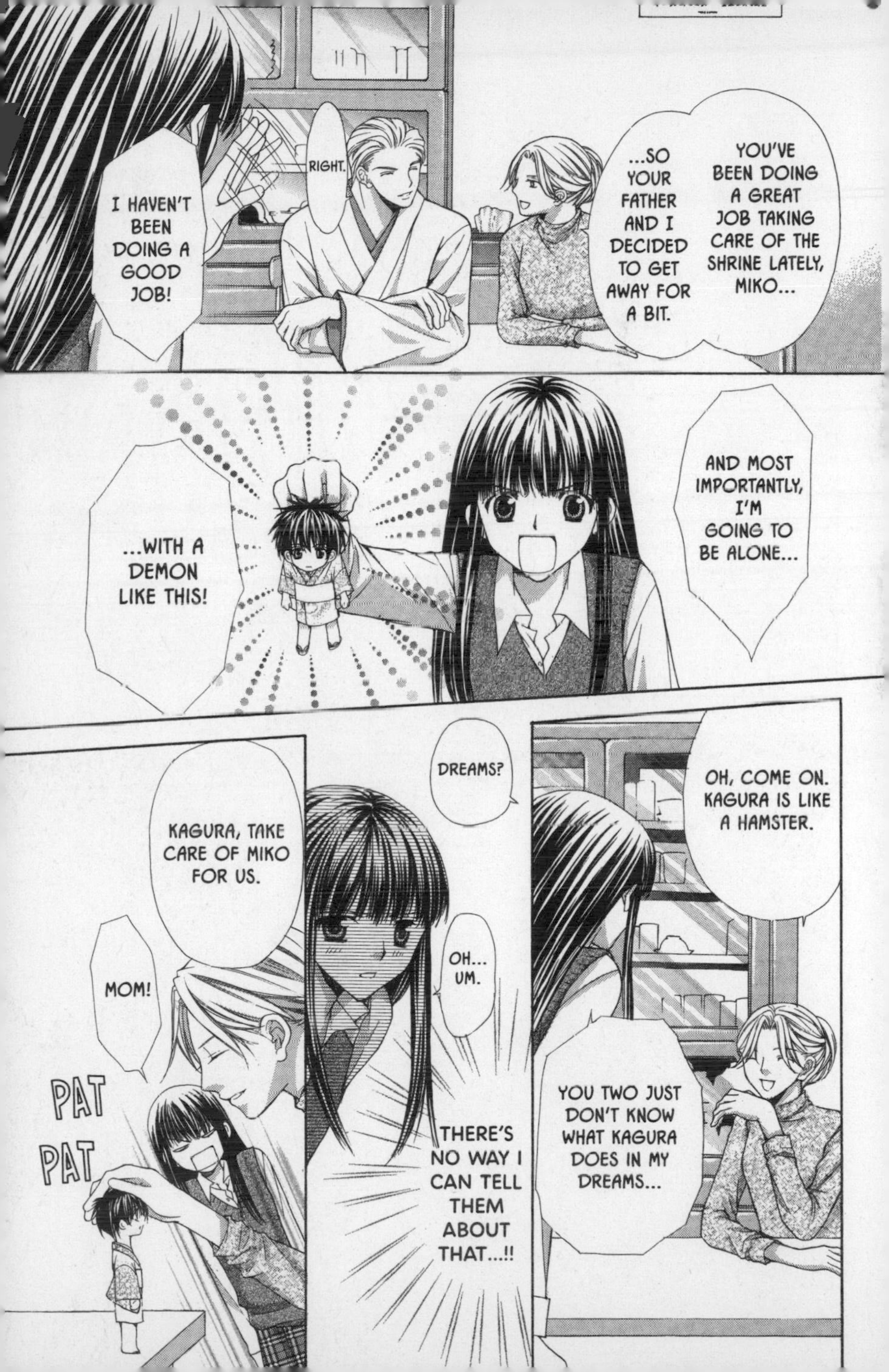
YOU'VE BEEN DOING A GREAT JOB TAKING CARE OF THE SHRINE LATELY, MIKO...
...SO YOUR FATHER AND I DECIDED TO GET AWAY FOR A BIT.
RIGHT.
I HAVEN'T BEEN DOING A GOOD JOB!
AND MOST IMPORTANTLY, I'M GOING TO BE ALONE...
...WITH A DEMON LIKE THIS!
OH, COME ON. KAGURA IS LIKE A HAMSTER.
YOU TWO JUST DON'T KNOW WHAT KAGURA DOES IN MY DREAMS...
DREAMS?
OH... UM.
THERE'S NO WAY I CAN TELL THEM ABOUT THAT...!!
KAGURA, TAKE CARE OF MIKO FOR US.
MOM!
PAT
PAT

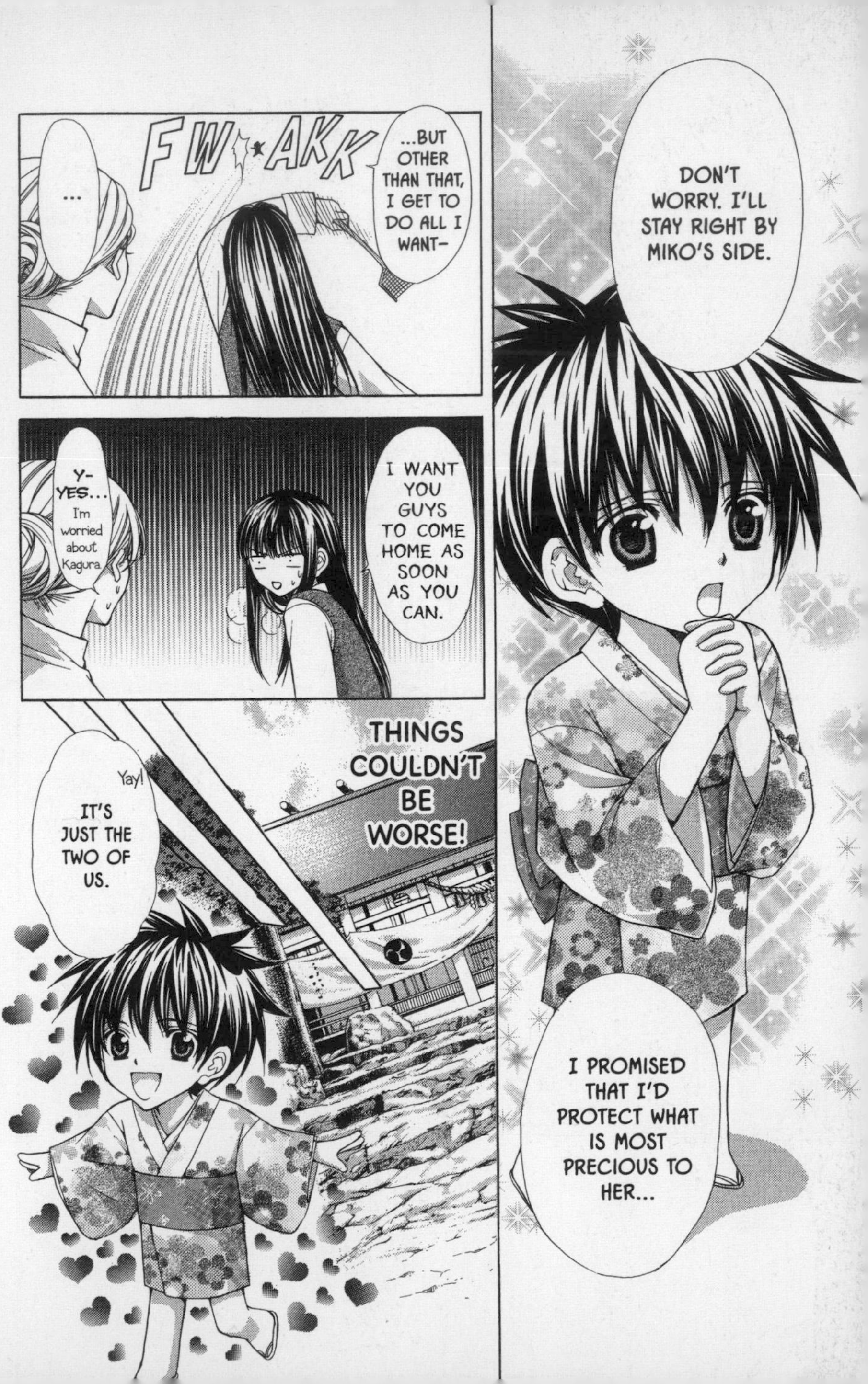
DON'T WORRY. I'LL STAY RIGHT BY MIKO'S SIDE.
I PROMISED THAT I'D PROTECT WHAT IS MOST PRECIOUS TO HER...
...BUT OTHER THAN THAT, I GET TO DO ALL I WANT–
FW★AKK
...
I WANT YOU GUYS TO COME HOME AS SOON AS YOU CAN.
Y-YES...
I'm worried about Kagura.
THINGS COULDN'T BE WORSE!
Yay!
IT'S JUST THE TWO OF US.

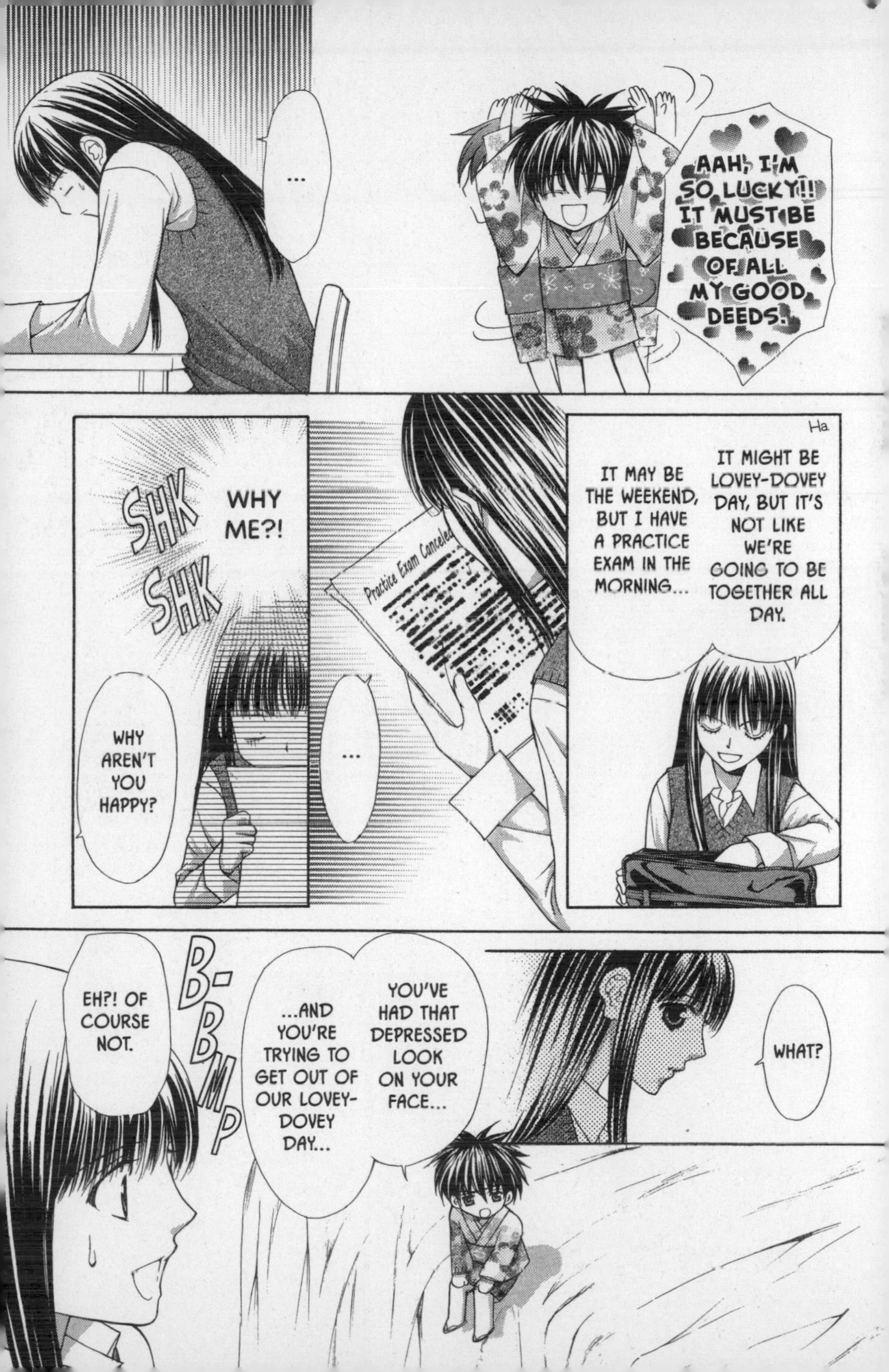
AAH, I'M SO LUCKY!!! IT MUST BE BECAUSE OF ALL MY GOOD DEEDS.
...
Ha.
IT MIGHT BE LOVEY-DOVEY DAY, BUT IT'S NOT LIKE WE'RE GOING TO BE TOGETHER ALL DAY.
IT MAY BE THE WEEKEND, BUT I HAVE A PRACTICE EXAM IN THE MORNING...
Practice Exam Canceled
...
WHY ME?!
SHK SHK
WHY AREN'T YOU HAPPY?
WHAT?
YOU'VE HAD THAT DEPRESSED LOOK ON YOUR FACE...
...AND YOU'RE TRYING TO GET OUT OF OUR LOVEY-DOVEY DAY...
B-BMP
EH?! OF COURSE NOT.

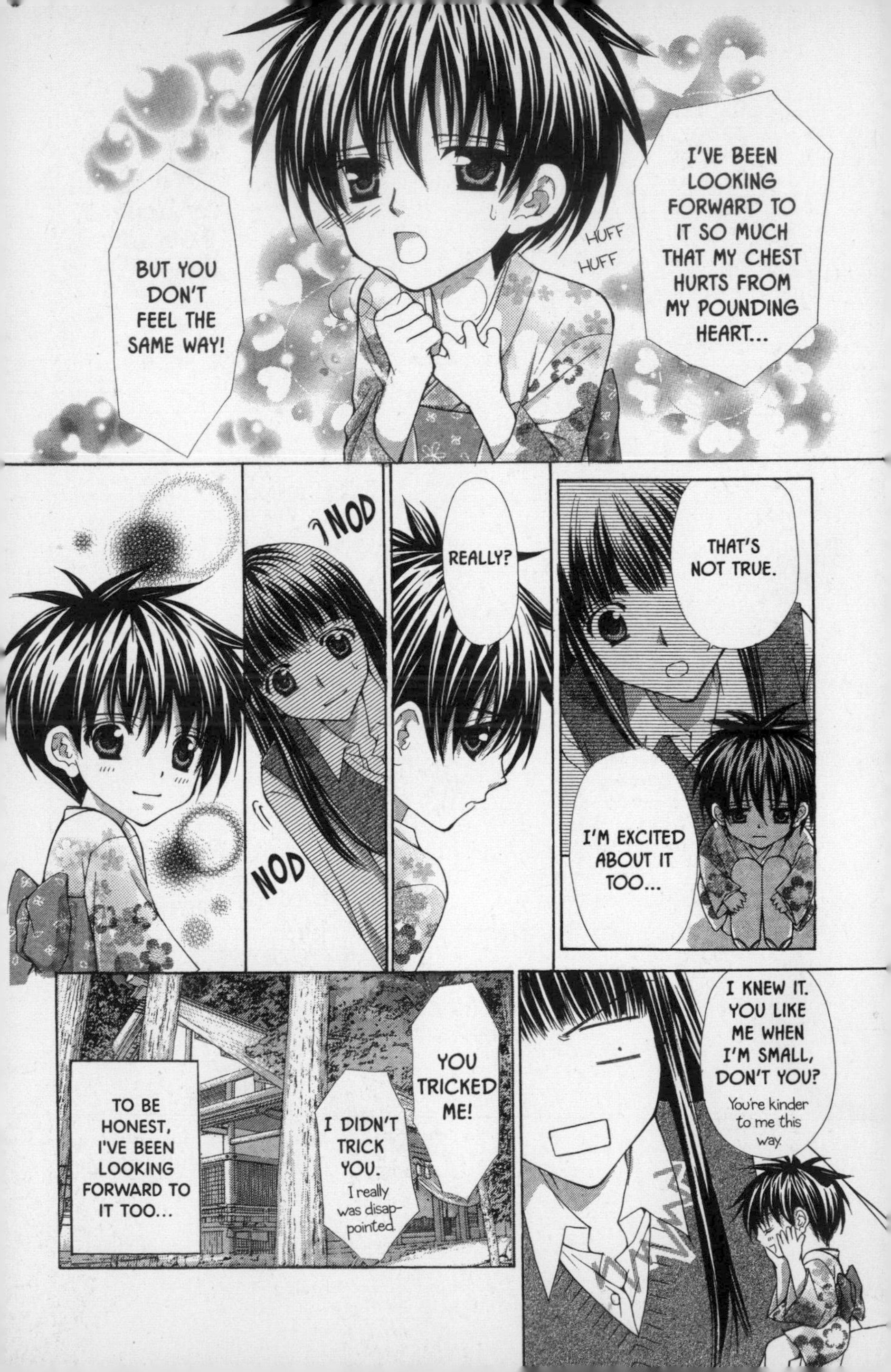
I'VE BEEN LOOKING FORWARD TO IT SO MUCH THAT MY CHEST HURTS FROM MY POUNDING HEART...
HUFF HUFF
BUT YOU DON'T FEEL THE SAME WAY!
THAT'S NOT TRUE.
I'M EXCITED ABOUT IT TOO...
REALLY?
NOD
NOD
I KNEW IT. YOU LIKE ME WHEN I'M SMALL, DON'T YOU?
You're kinder to me this way.
YOU TRICKED ME!
I DIDN'T TRICK YOU.
I really was disap-pointed.
TO BE HONEST, I'VE BEEN LOOKING FORWARD TO IT TOO...

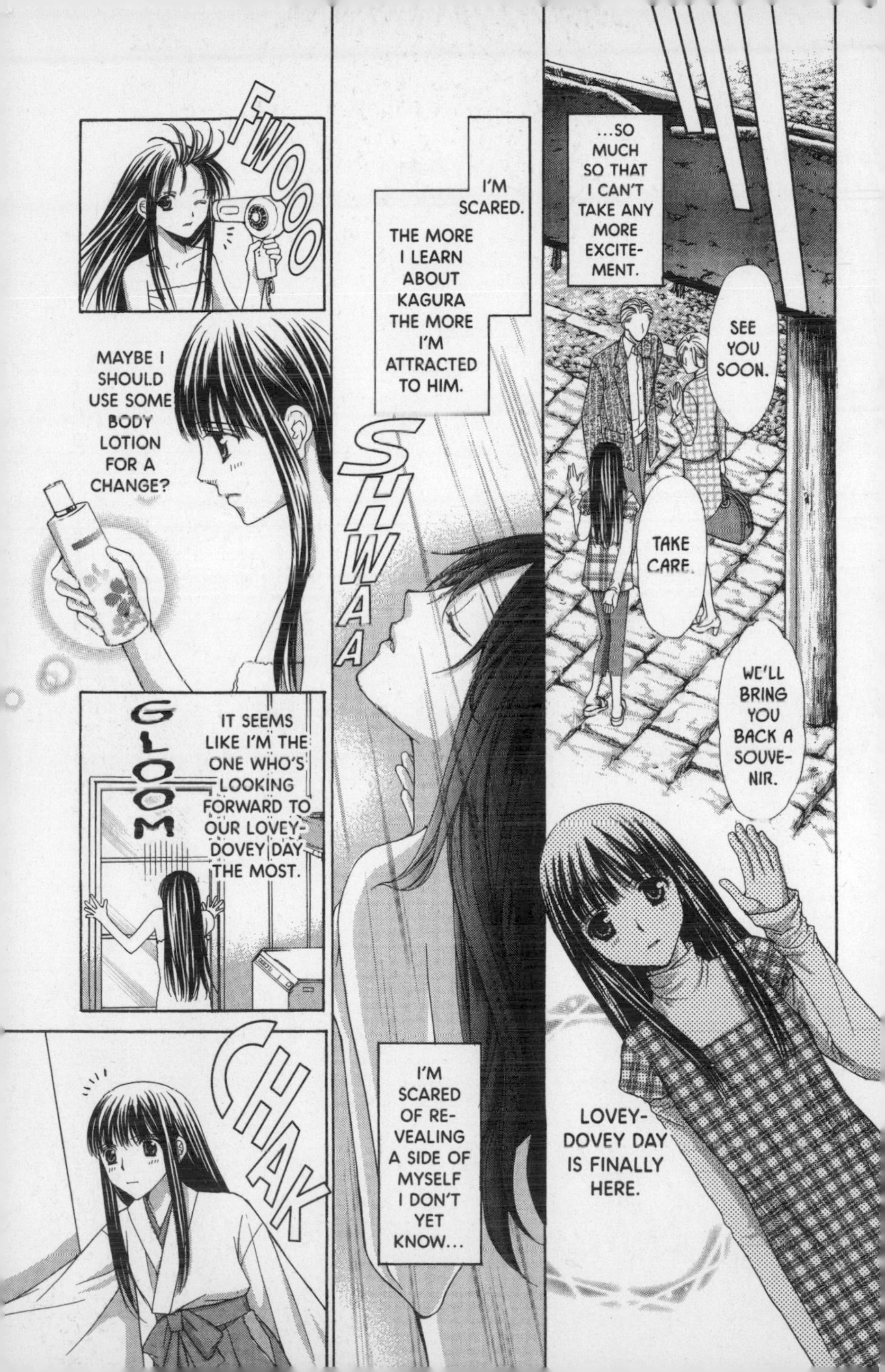
I'M SCARED.
THE MORE I LEARN ABOUT KAGURA THE MORE I'M ATTRACTED TO HIM.
...SO MUCH SO THAT I CAN'T TAKE ANY MORE EXCITE-MENT.
SEE YOU SOON.
TAKE CARE.
WE'LL BRING YOU BACK A SOUVE-NIR.
LOVEY-DOVEY DAY IS FINALLY HERE.
SHWAA
I'M SCARED OF RE-VEALING A SIDE OF MYSELF I DON'T YET KNOW...
FWOOO
MAYBE I SHOULD USE SOME BODY LOTION FOR A CHANGE?
GLOOM
IT SEEMS LIKE I'M THE ONE WHO'S LOOKING FORWARD TO OUR LOVEY-DOVEY DAY THE MOST.
CHAK

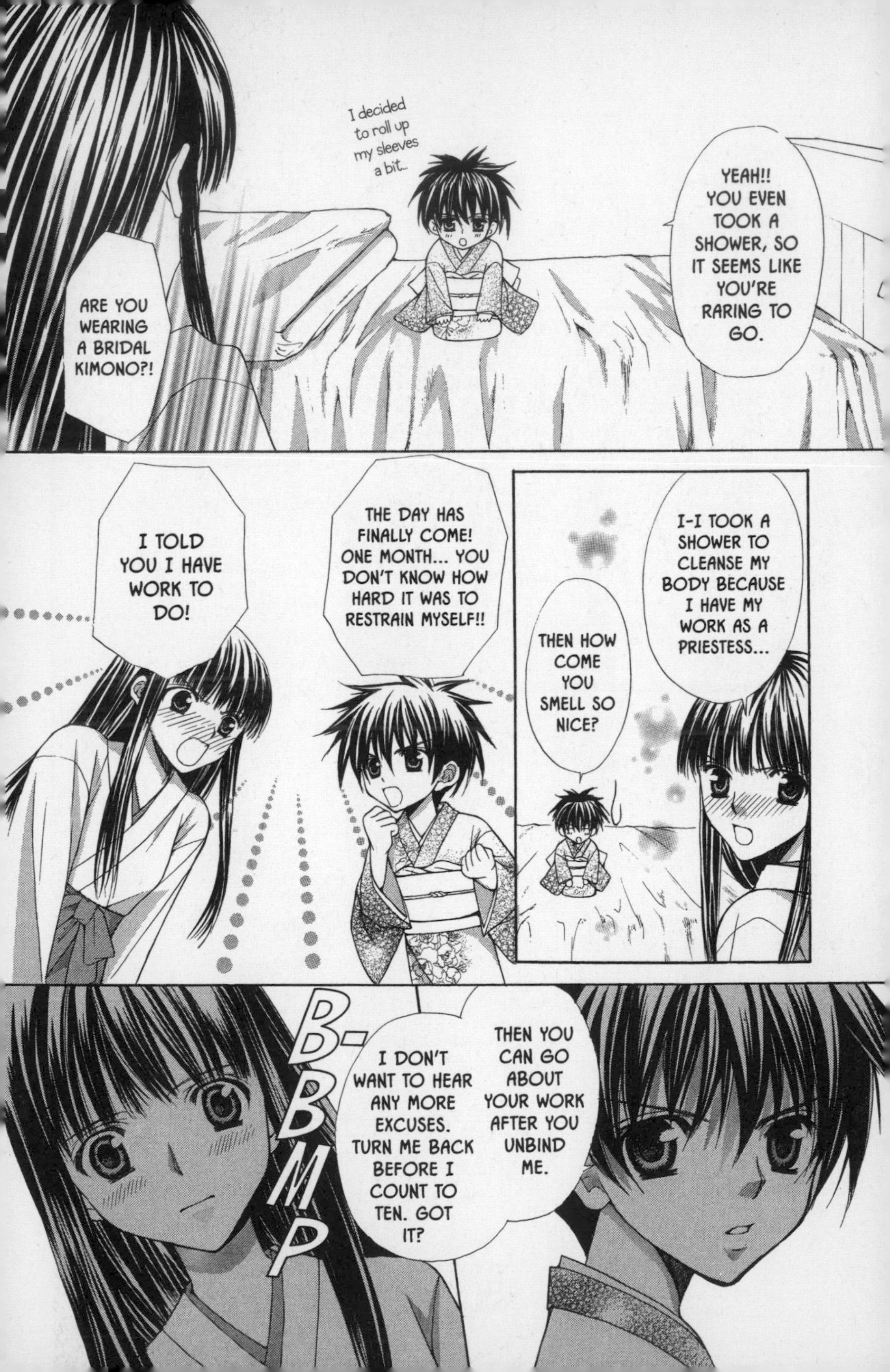
YEAH!! YOU EVEN TOOK A SHOWER, SO IT SEEMS LIKE YOU'RE RARING TO GO.
I decided to roll up my sleeves a bit..
ARE YOU WEARING A BRIDAL KIMONO?!
I-I TOOK A SHOWER TO CLEANSE MY BODY BECAUSE I HAVE MY WORK AS A PRIESTESS...
THEN HOW COME YOU SMELL SO NICE?
THE DAY HAS FINALLY COME! ONE MONTH... YOU DON'T KNOW HOW HARD IT WAS TO RESTRAIN MYSELF!!
I TOLD YOU I HAVE WORK TO DO!
THEN YOU CAN GO ABOUT YOUR WORK AFTER YOU UNBIND ME.
I DON'T WANT TO HEAR ANY MORE EXCUSES. TURN ME BACK BEFORE I COUNT TO TEN. GOT IT?
B-BMP

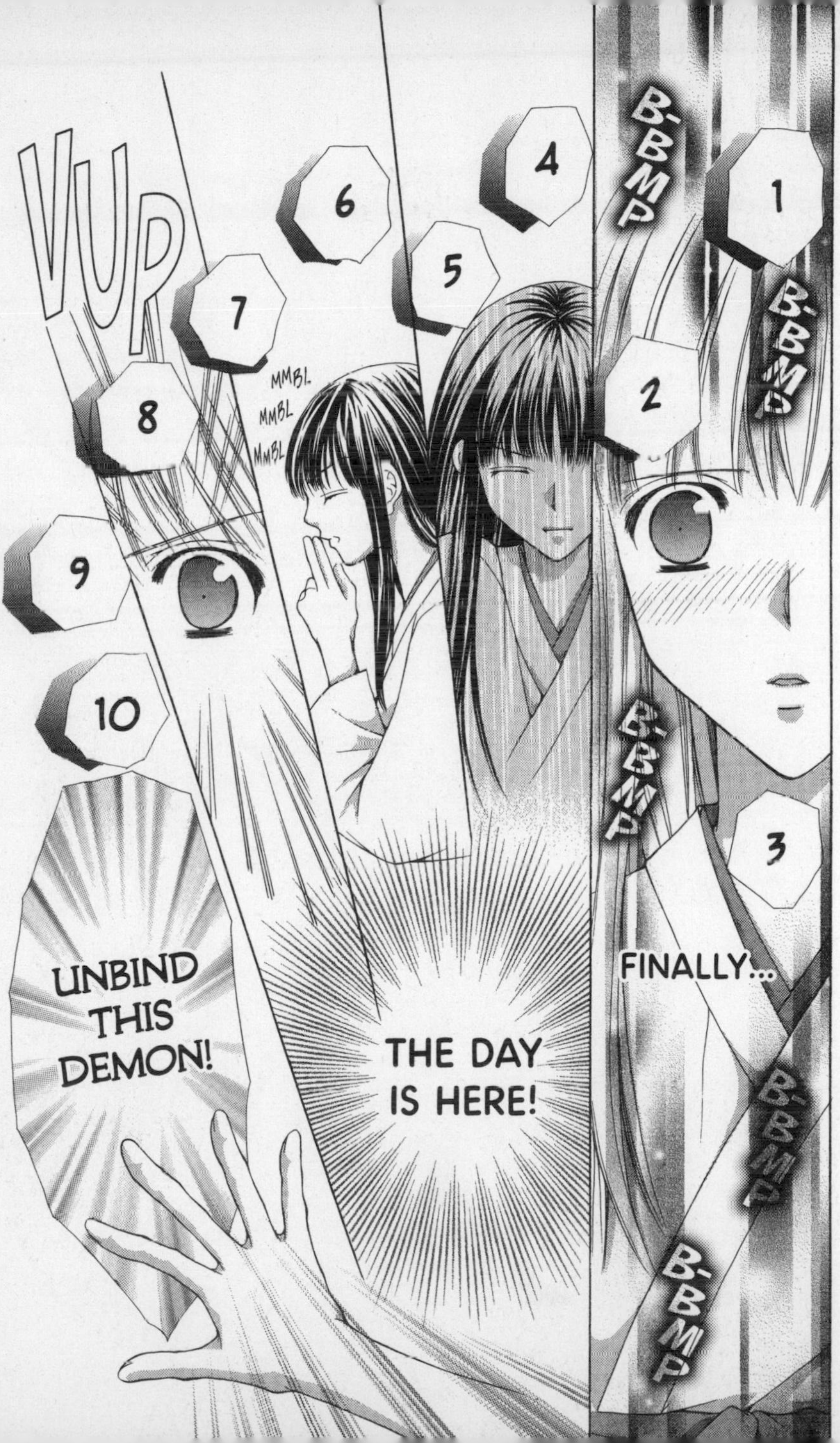
B-BMP
1
B-BMP
2
B-BMP
3
FINALLY...
B-BMP
B-BMP
4
5
THE DAY IS HERE!
6
MMBL
MMBL
MMBL
VUP
7
8
9
10
UNBIND THIS DEMON!

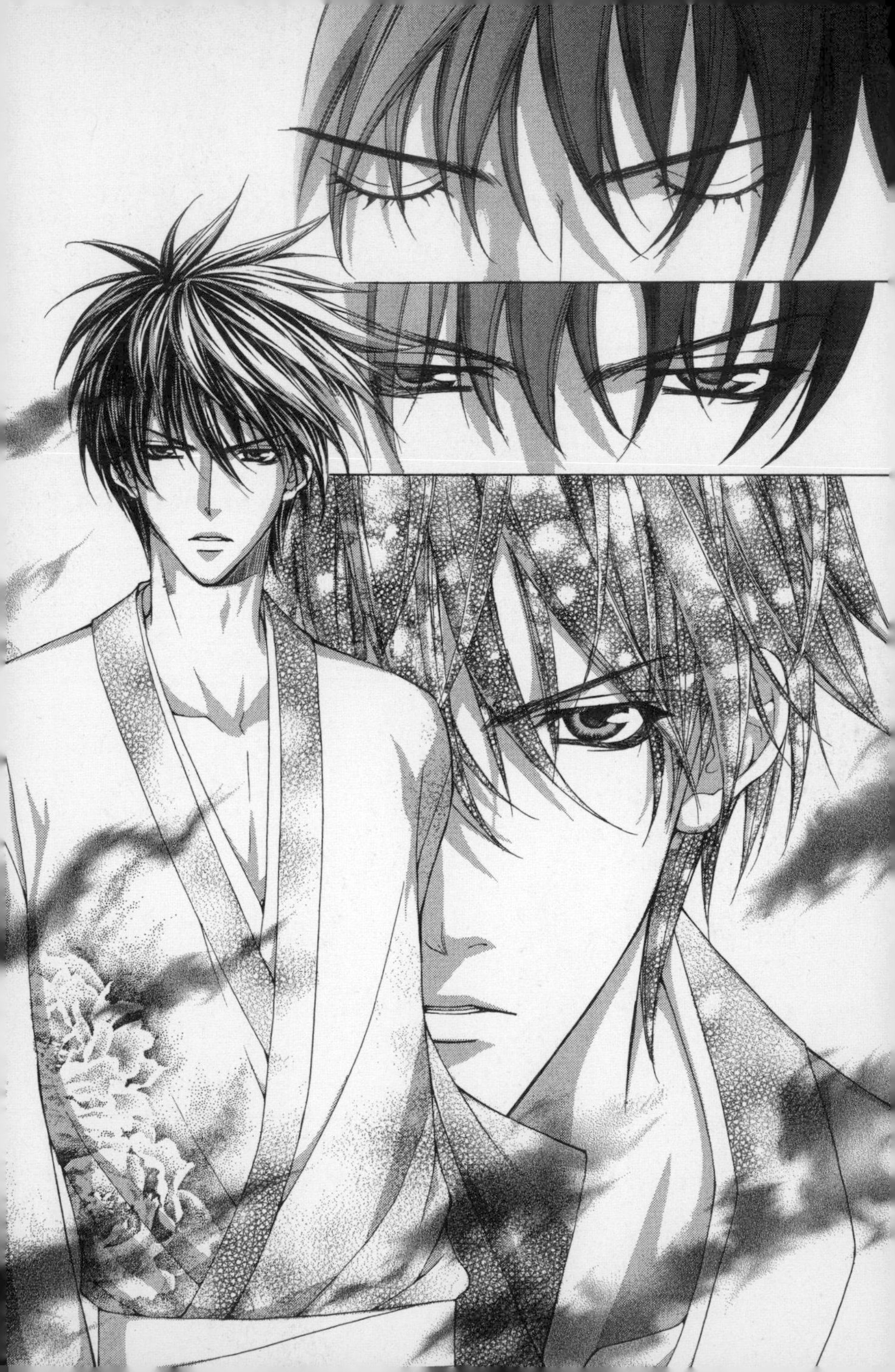

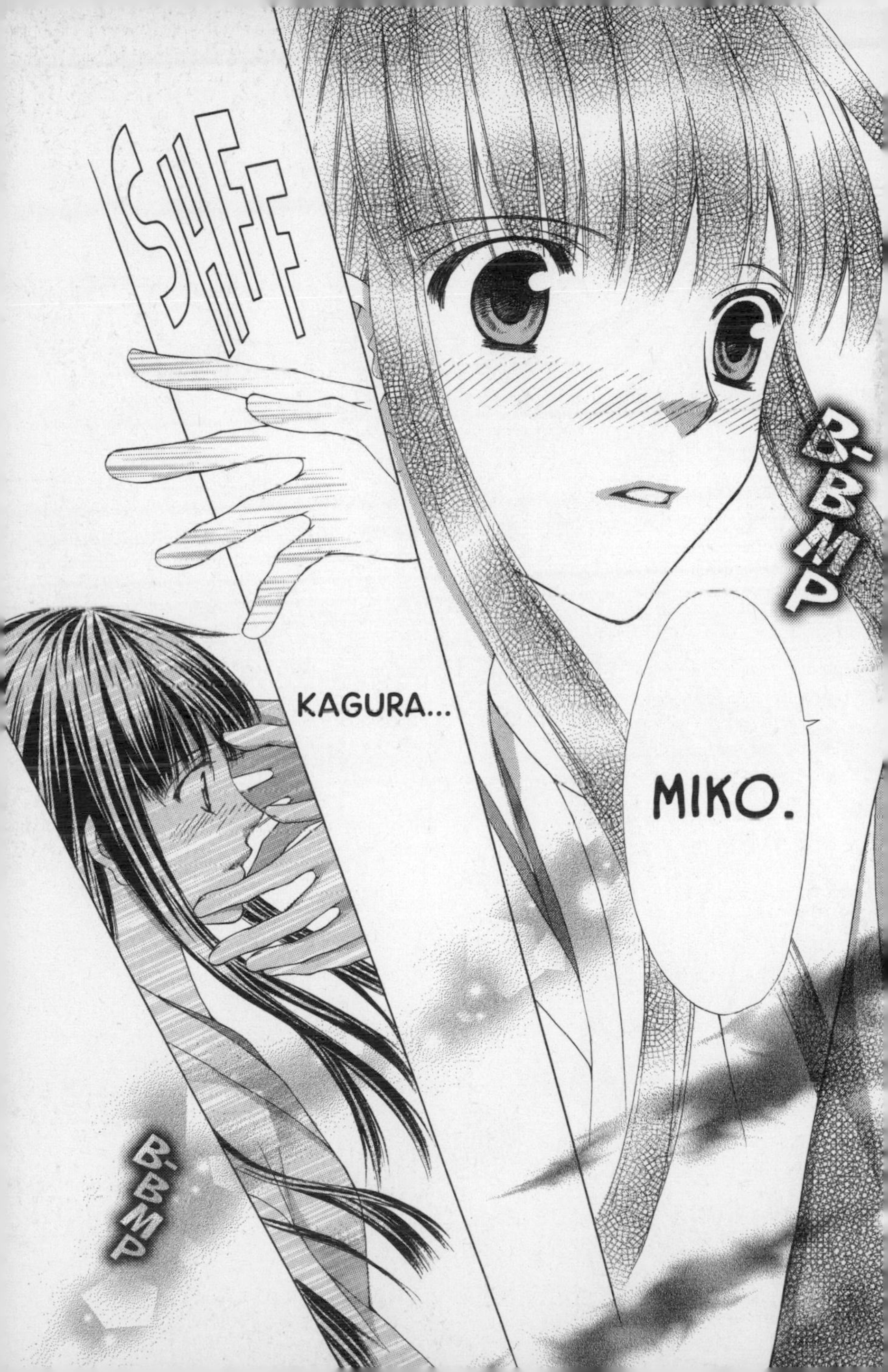
SHFF
B'BMP
MIKO.
KAGURA...
B'BMP

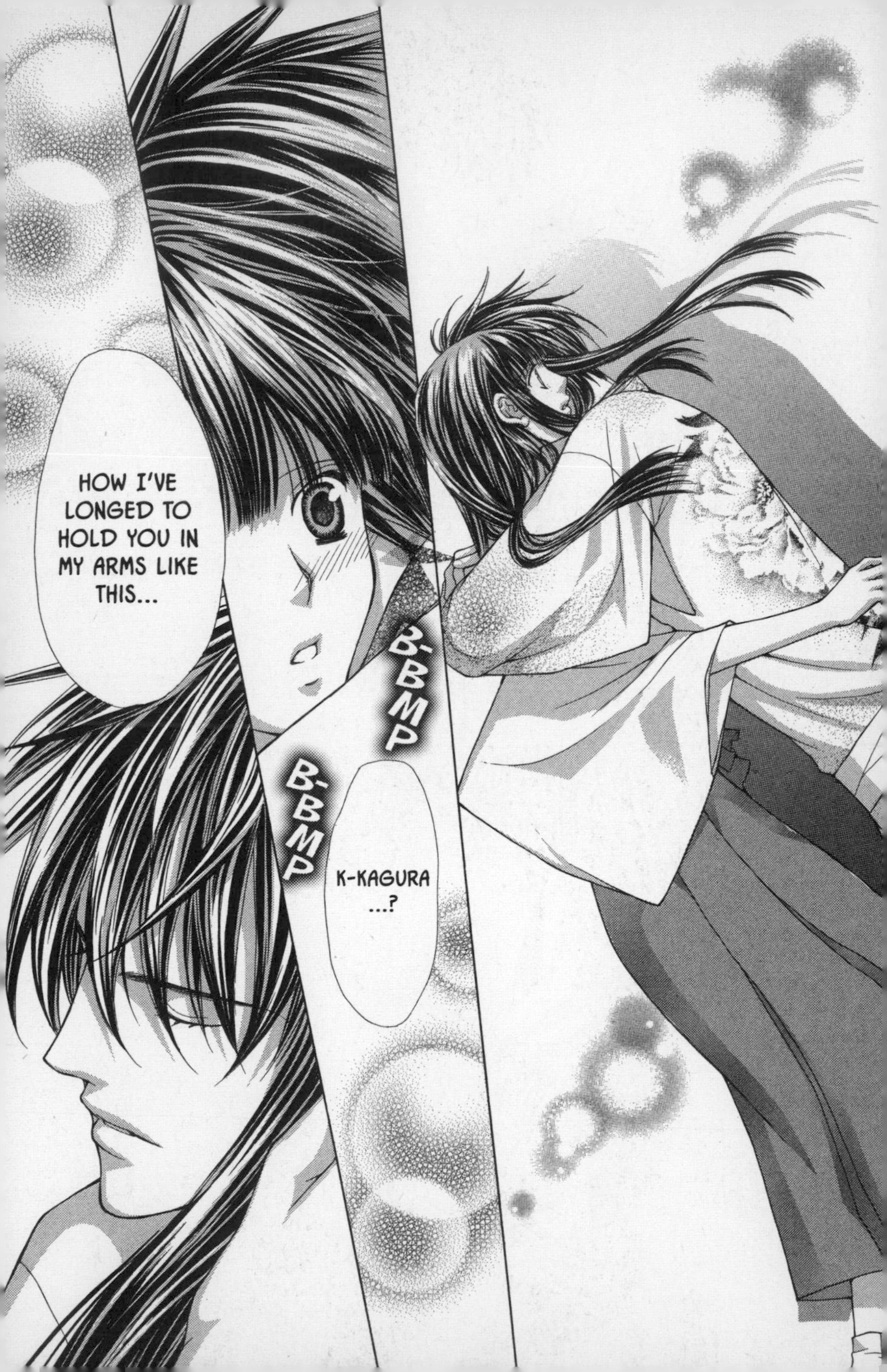
B-BMP
B-BMP
K-KAGURA ...?
HOW I'VE LONGED TO HOLD YOU IN MY ARMS LIKE THIS...

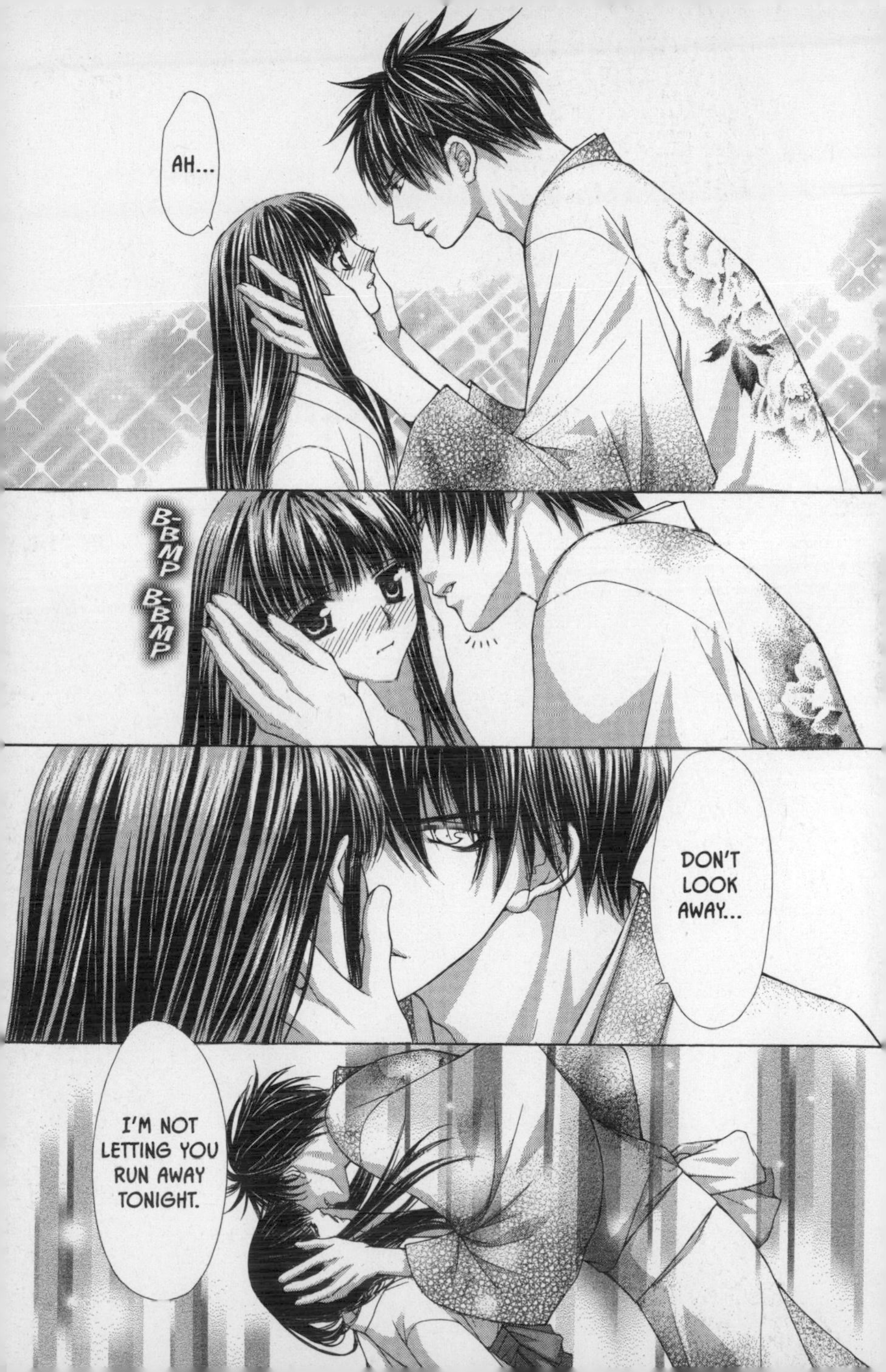
AH...
B-BMP B-BMP
DON'T LOOK AWAY...
I'M NOT LETTING YOU RUN AWAY TONIGHT.

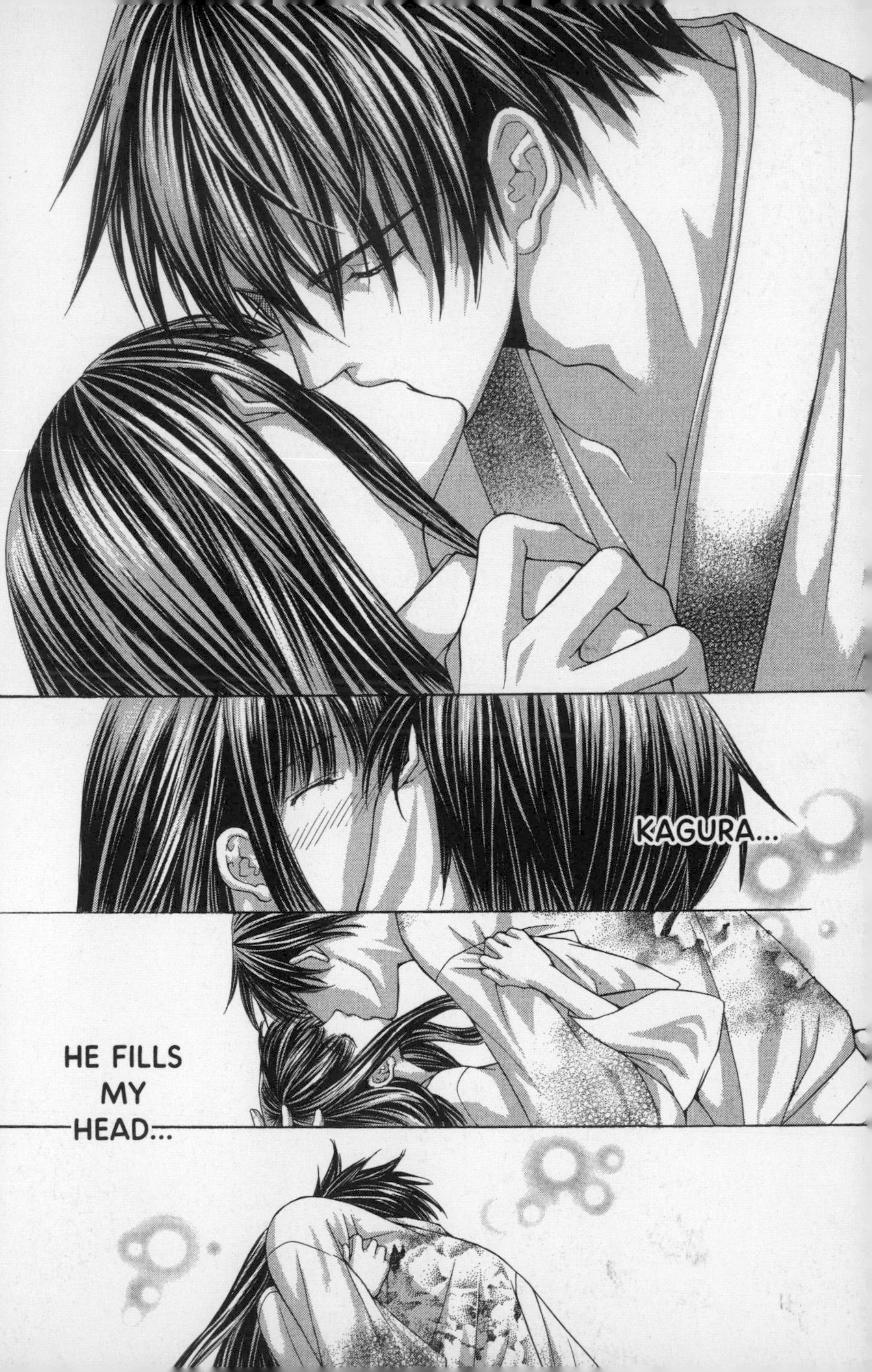
KAGURA...
HE FILLS MY HEAD...

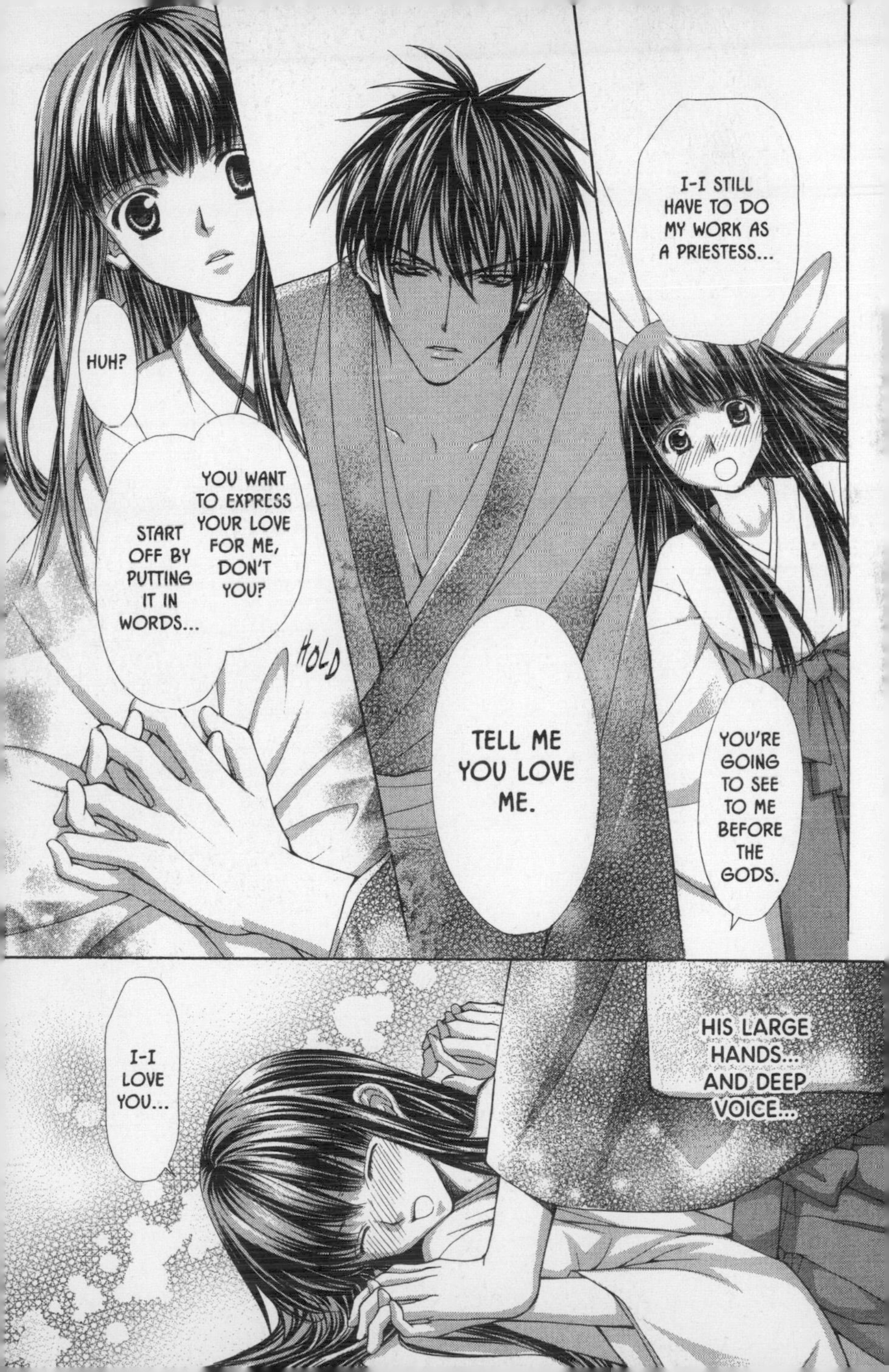
I-I STILL HAVE TO DO MY WORK AS A PRIESTESS...
YOU'RE GOING TO SEE TO ME BEFORE THE GODS.
TELL ME YOU LOVE ME.
HUH?
YOU WANT TO EXPRESS YOUR LOVE FOR ME, DON'T YOU?
START OFF BY PUTTING IT IN WORDS...
HOLD
HIS LARGE HANDS... AND DEEP VOICE...
I-I LOVE YOU...

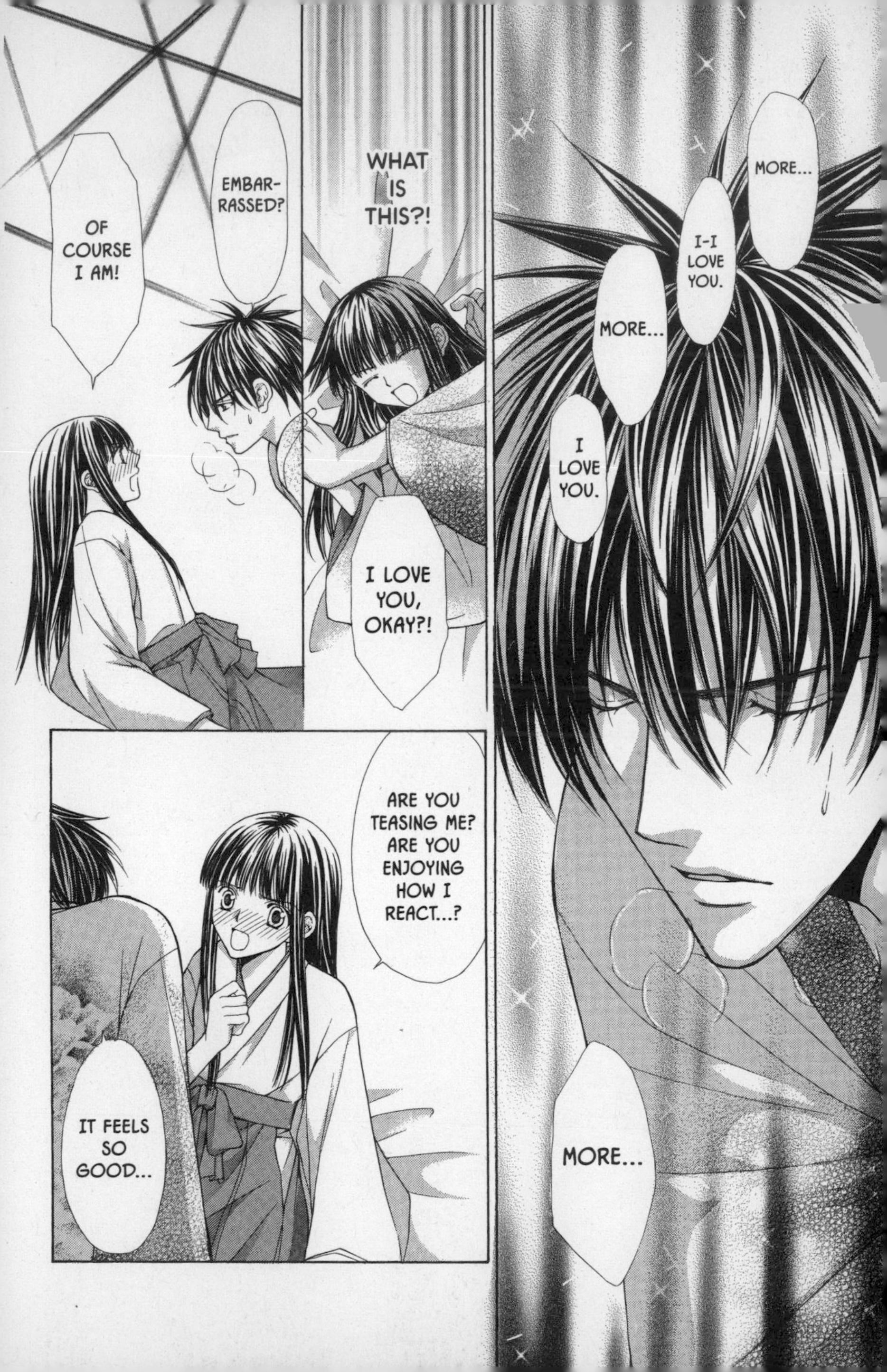
MORE...
I-I LOVE YOU.
MORE...
I LOVE YOU.
MORE...
WHAT IS THIS?!
I LOVE YOU, OKAY?!
EMBAR-RASSED?
OF COURSE I AM!
ARE YOU TEASING ME? ARE YOU ENJOYING HOW I REACT...?
IT FEELS SO GOOD...

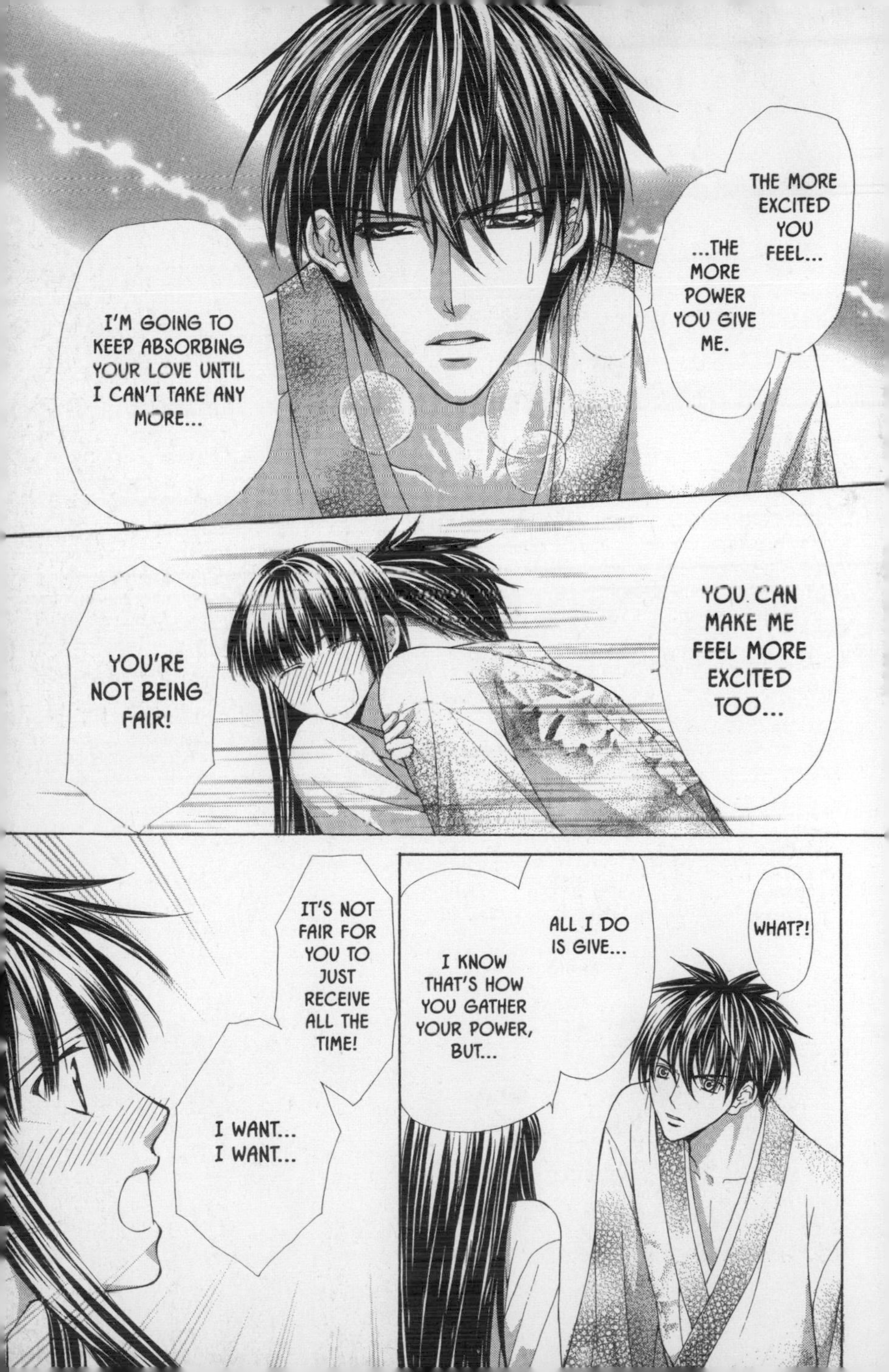
THE MORE EXCITED YOU FEEL...
...THE MORE POWER YOU GIVE ME.
I'M GOING TO KEEP ABSORBING YOUR LOVE UNTIL I CAN'T TAKE ANY MORE...
YOU CAN MAKE ME FEEL MORE EXCITED TOO...
YOU'RE NOT BEING FAIR!
WHAT?!
ALL I DO IS GIVE...
I KNOW THAT'S HOW YOU GATHER YOUR POWER, BUT...
IT'S NOT FAIR FOR YOU TO JUST RECEIVE ALL THE TIME!
I WANT... I WANT...

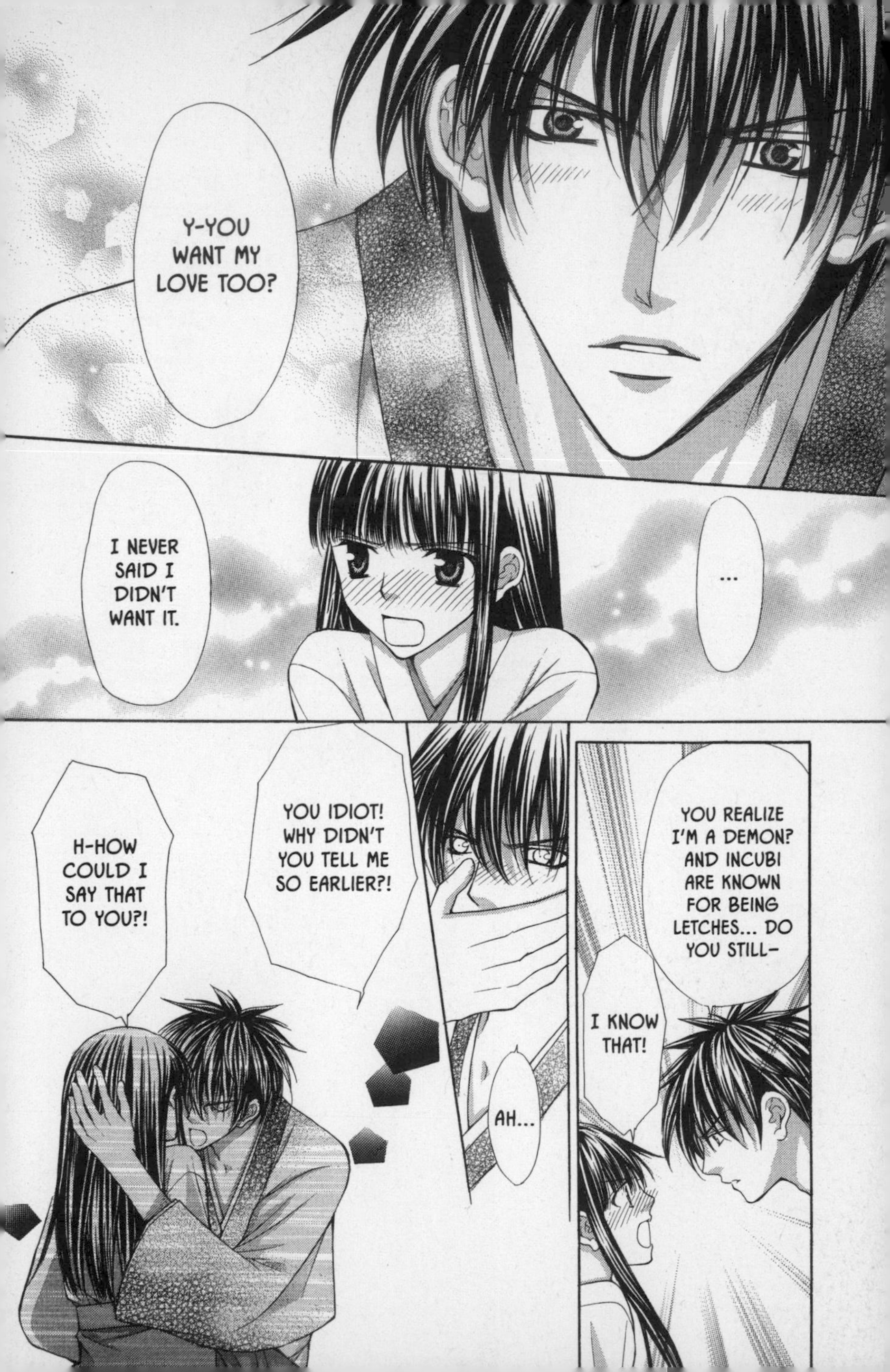
Y-YOU WANT MY LOVE TOO?
...
I NEVER SAID I DIDN'T WANT IT.
YOU REALIZE I'M A DEMON? AND INCUBI ARE KNOWN FOR BEING LETCHES... DO YOU STILL–
I KNOW THAT!
AH...
YOU IDIOT! WHY DIDN'T YOU TELL ME SO EARLIER?!
H-HOW COULD I SAY THAT TO YOU?!

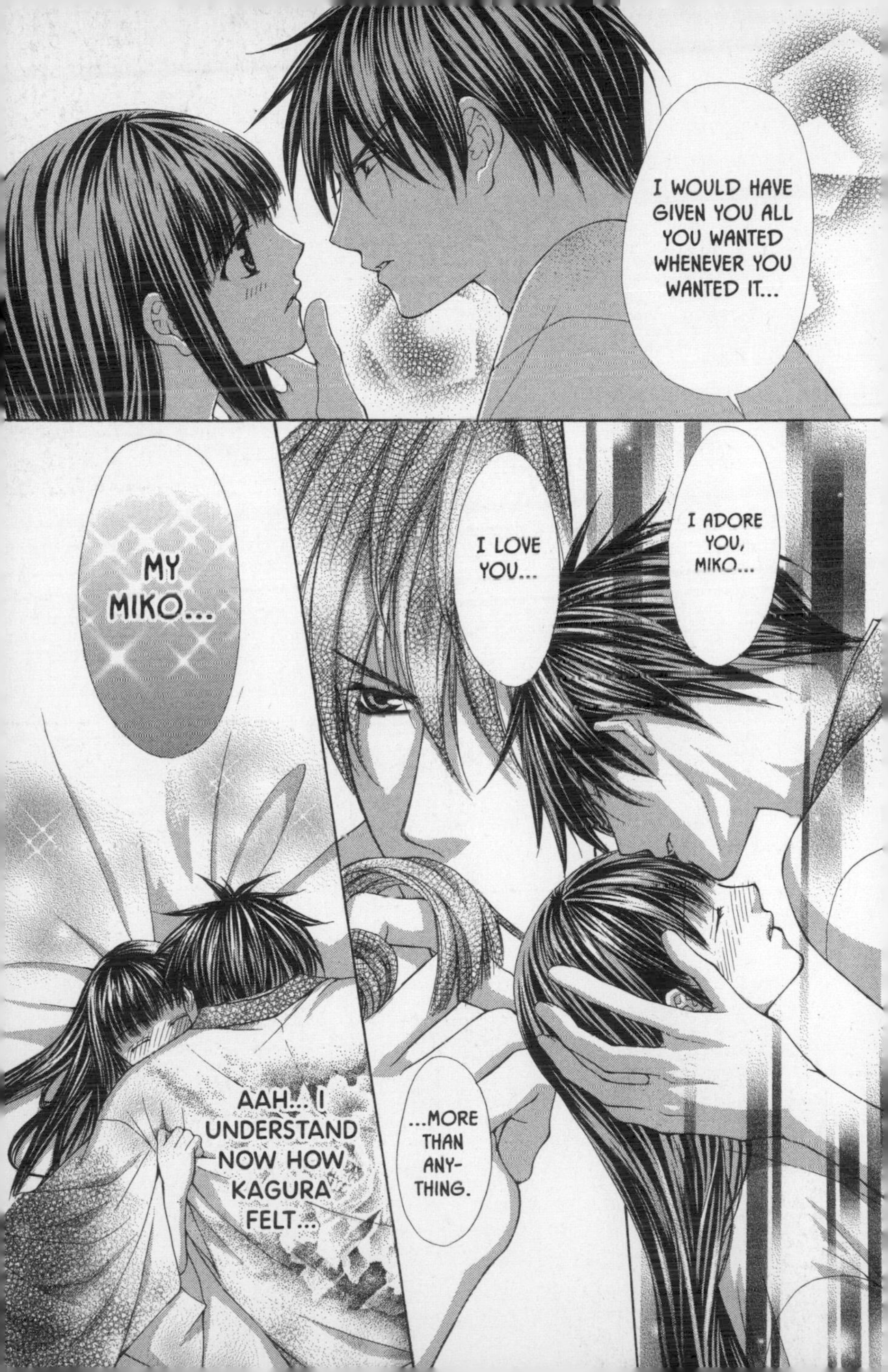
I WOULD HAVE GIVEN YOU ALL YOU WANTED WHENEVER YOU WANTED IT...
I ADORE YOU, MIKO...
I LOVE YOU...
...MORE THAN ANY-THING.
MY MIKO...
AAH... I UNDERSTAND NOW HOW KAGURA FELT...

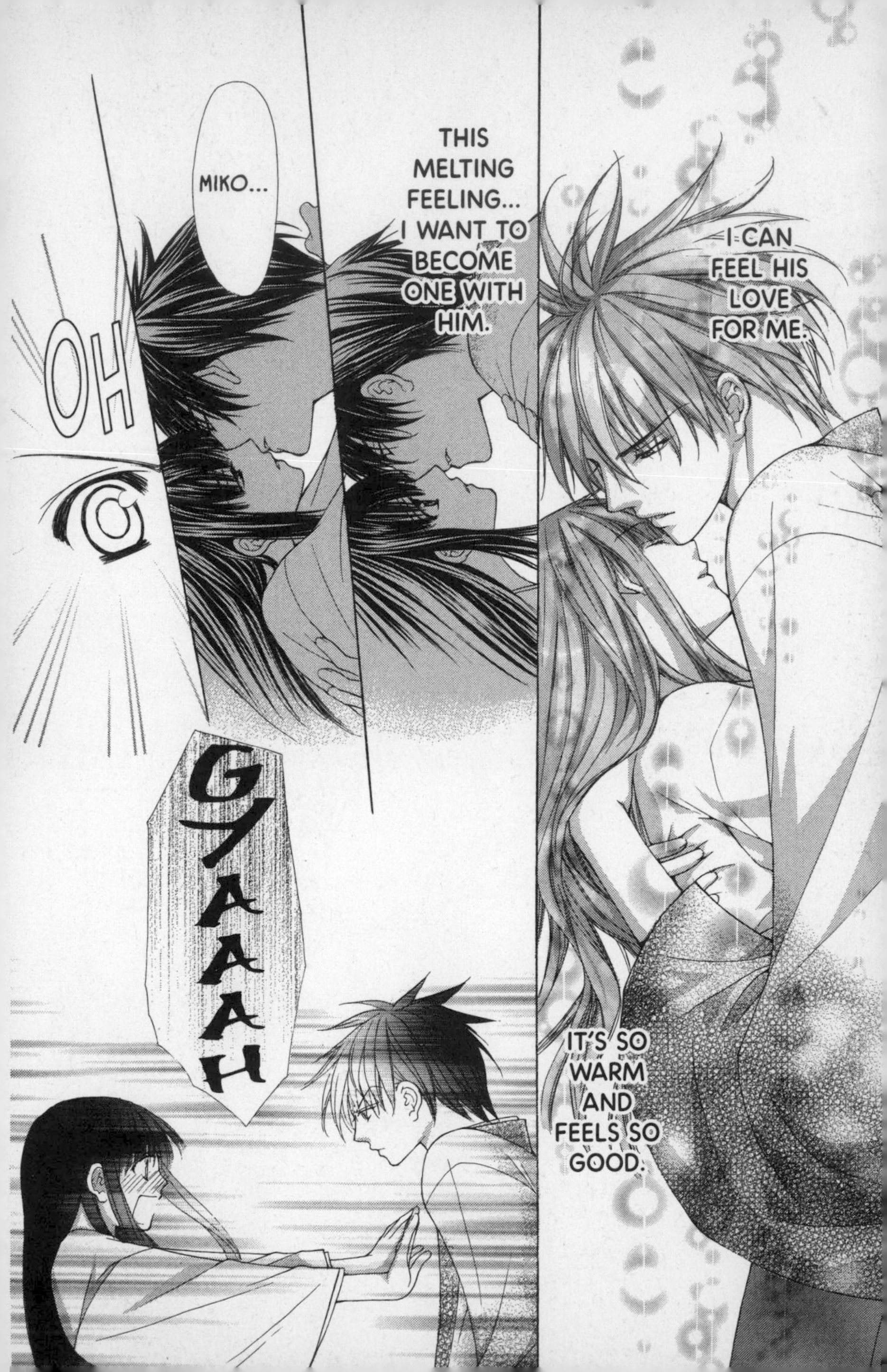
I CAN FEEL HIS LOVE FOR ME.
IT'S SO WARM AND FEELS SO GOOD.
THIS MELTING FEELING... I WANT TO BECOME ONE WITH HIM.
MIKO...
OH
GYAAAH

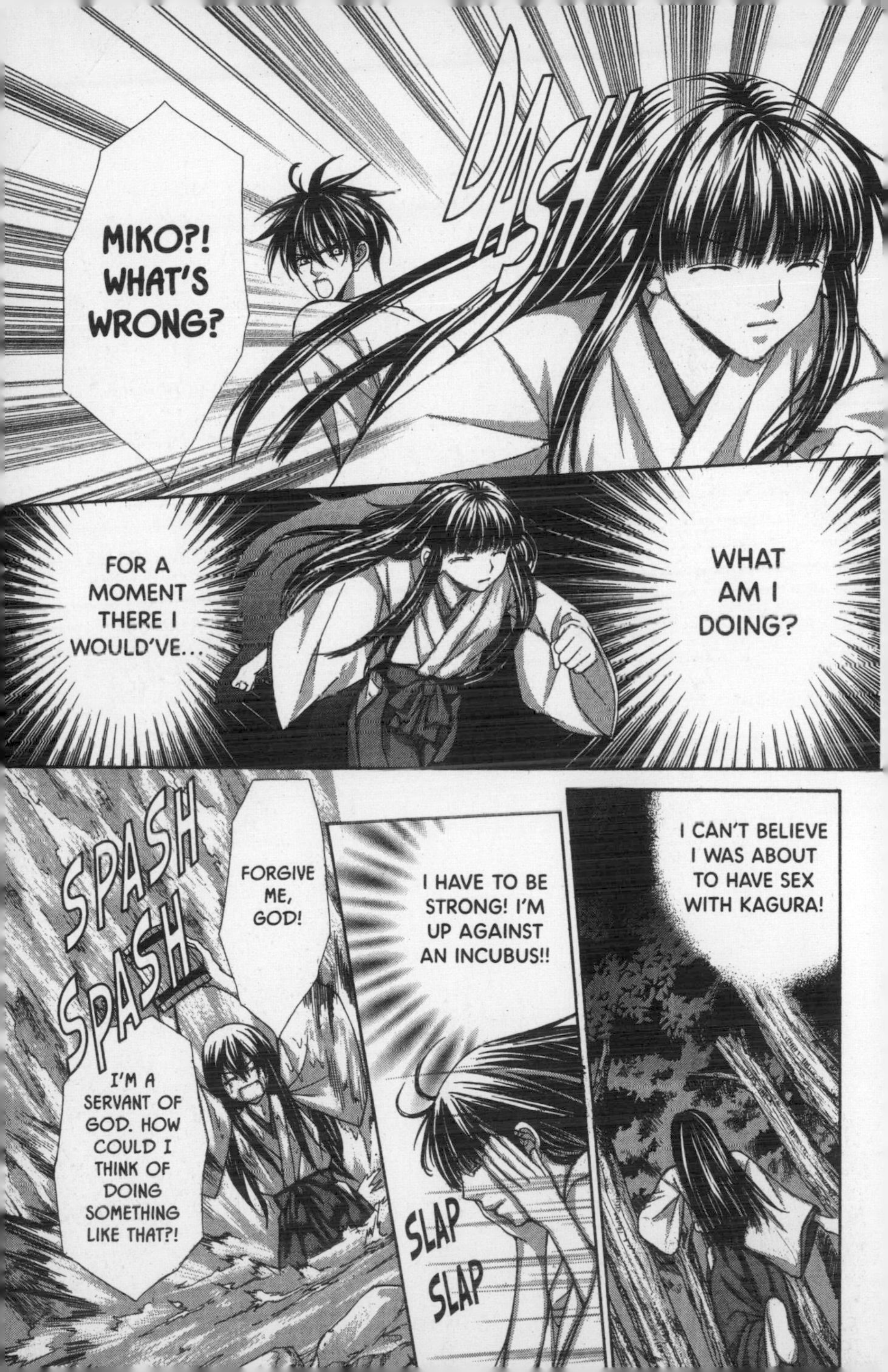
DASH
MIKO?! WHAT'S WRONG?
WHAT AM I DOING?
FOR A MOMENT THERE I WOULD'VE...
I CAN'T BELIEVE I WAS ABOUT TO HAVE SEX WITH KAGURA!
I HAVE TO BE STRONG! I'M UP AGAINST AN INCUBUS!!
SLAP
SLAP
SPASH
SPASH
FORGIVE ME, GOD!
I'M A SERVANT OF GOD. HOW COULD I THINK OF DOING SOMETHING LIKE THAT?!

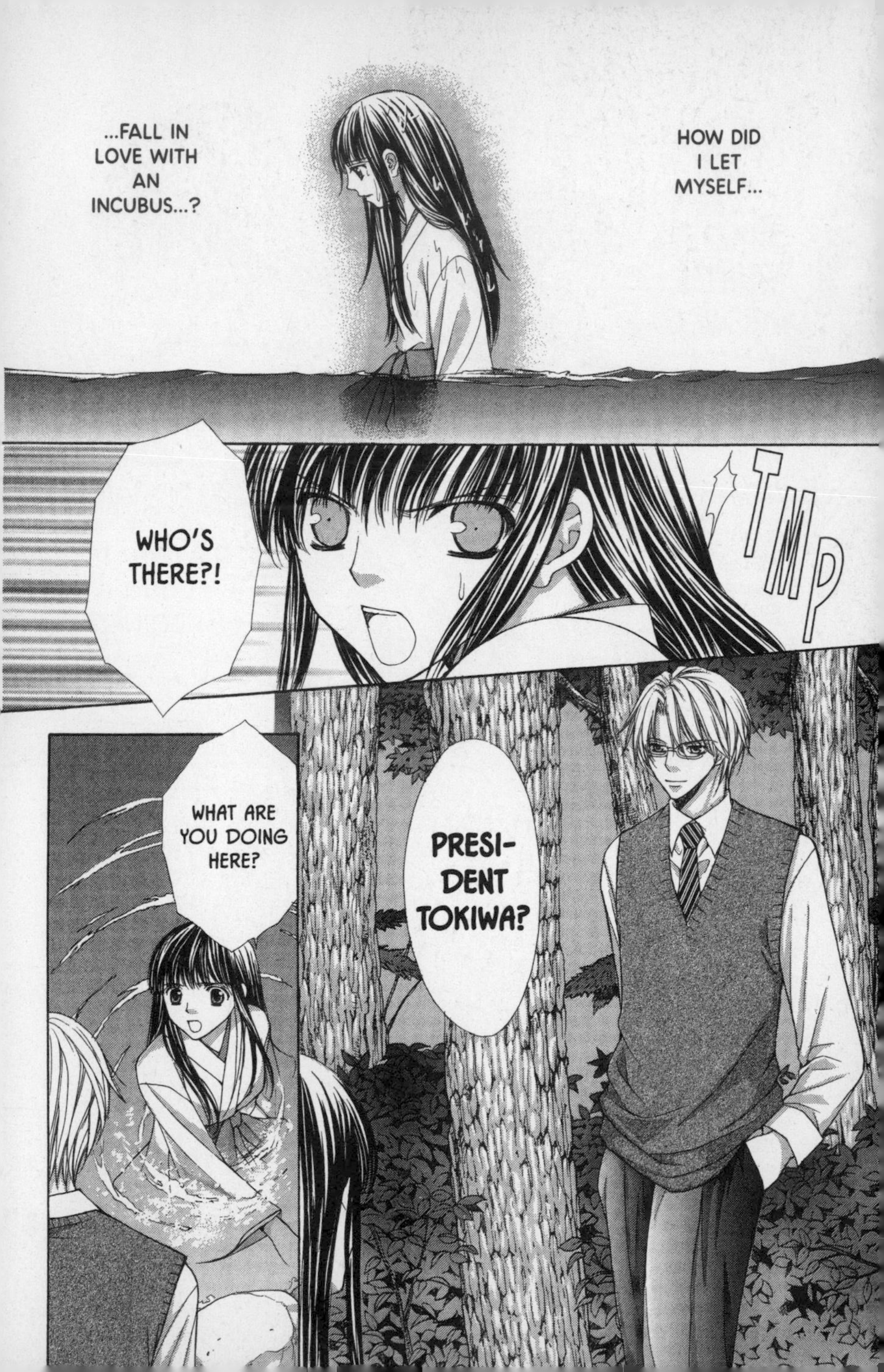
HOW DID I LET MYSELF...
...FALL IN LOVE WITH AN INCUBUS...?
TMP
WHO'S THERE?!
PRESI-DENT TOKIWA?
WHAT ARE YOU DOING HERE?

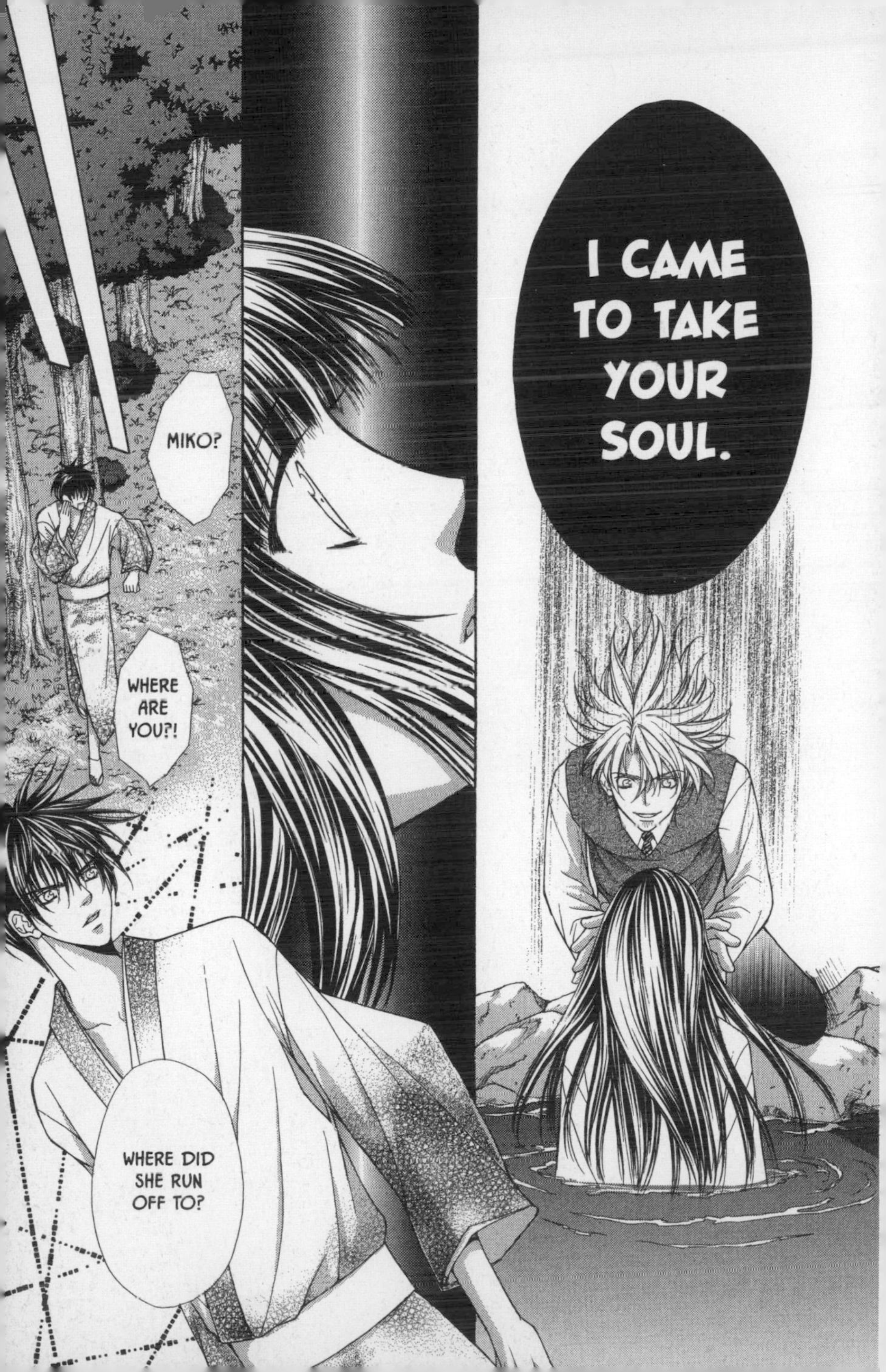
I CAME TO TAKE YOUR SOUL.
MIKO?
WHERE ARE YOU?!
WHERE DID SHE RUN OFF TO?

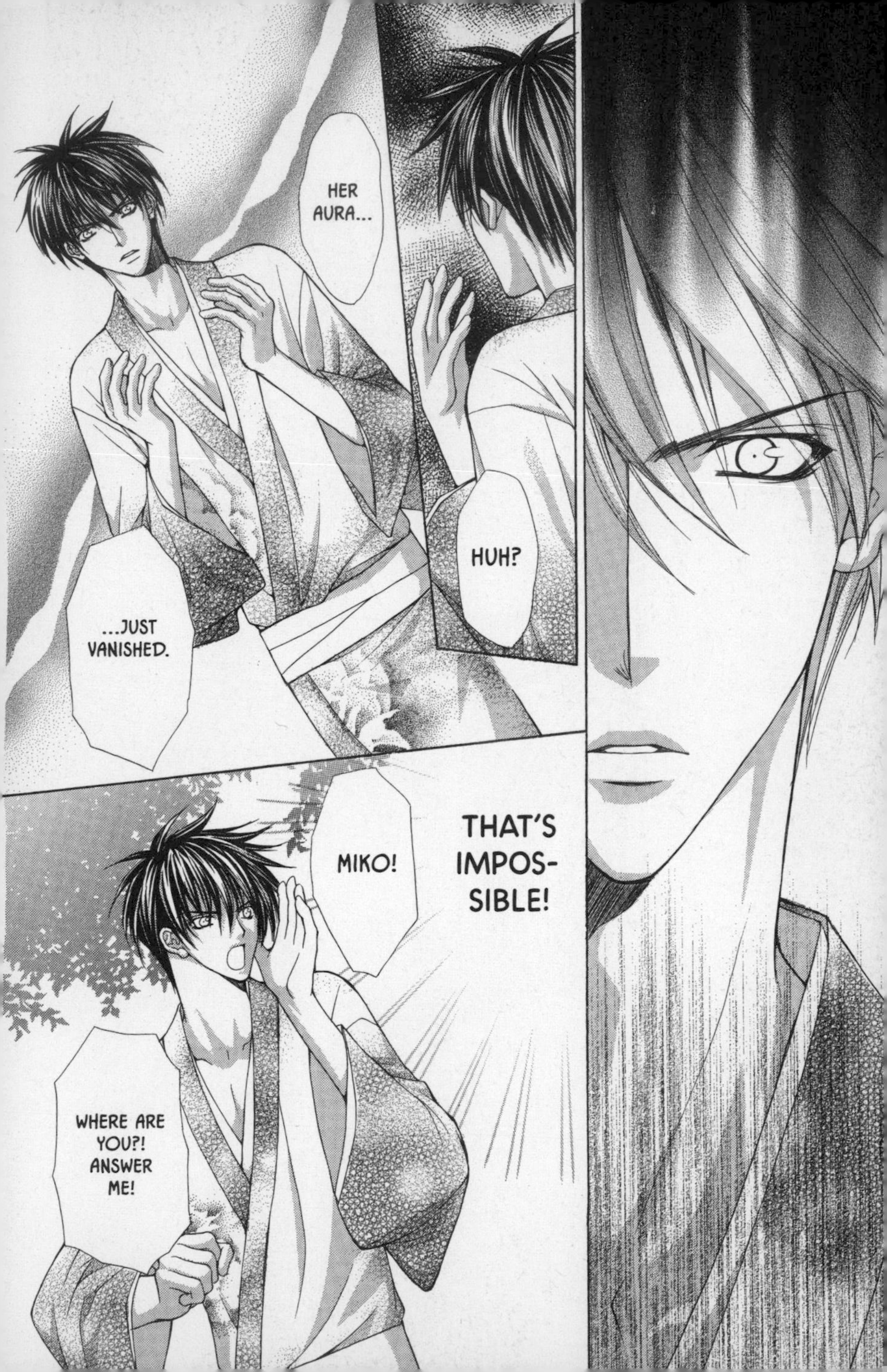
HUH?
HER AURA...
...JUST VANISHED.
THAT'S IMPOS-SIBLE!
MIKO!
WHERE ARE YOU?! ANSWER ME!

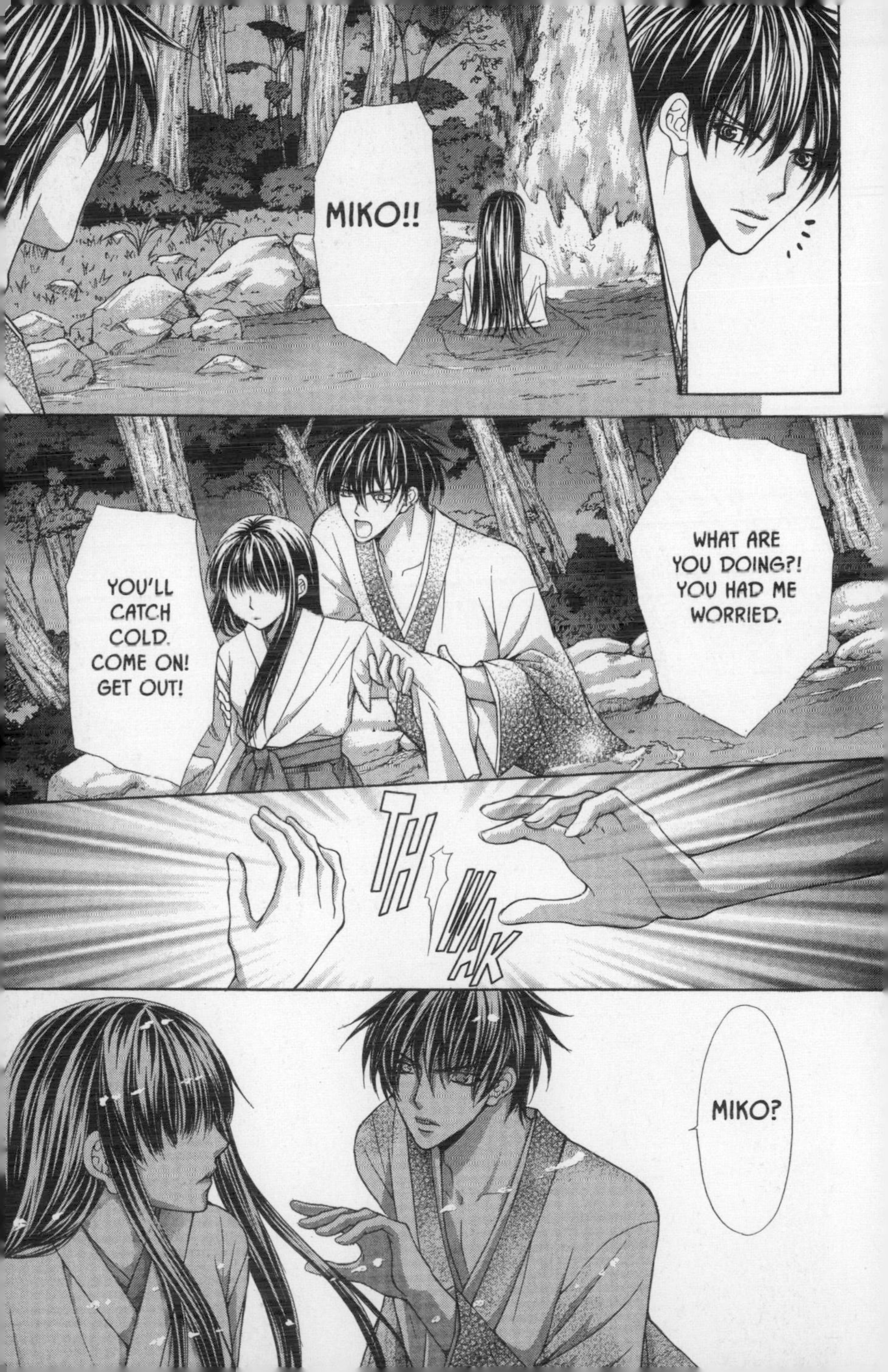
MIKO!!
WHAT ARE YOU DOING?! YOU HAD ME WORRIED.
YOU'LL CATCH COLD. COME ON! GET OUT!
THWAK
MIKO?

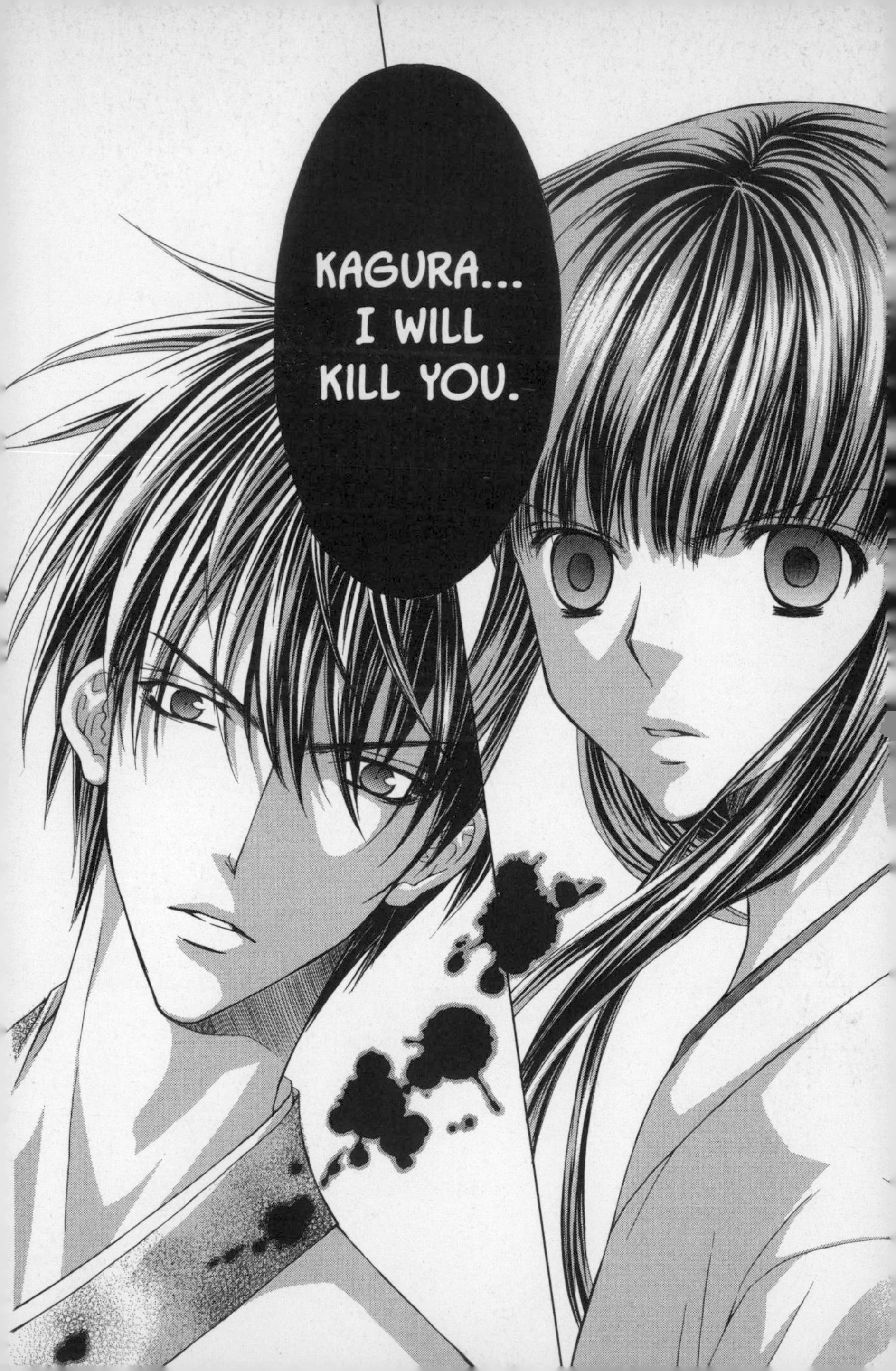
KAGURA... I WILL KILL YOU.

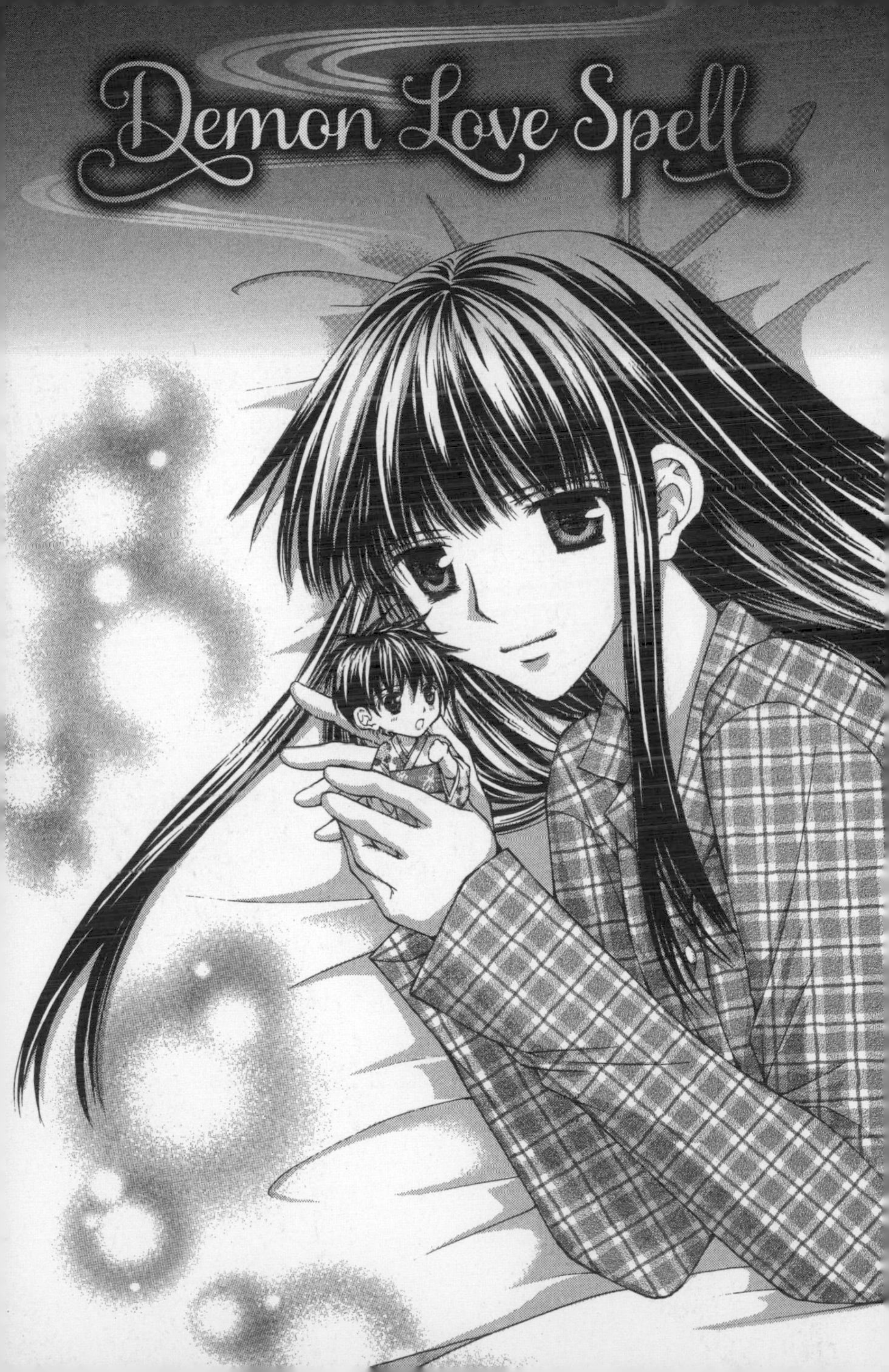
Demon Love Spell

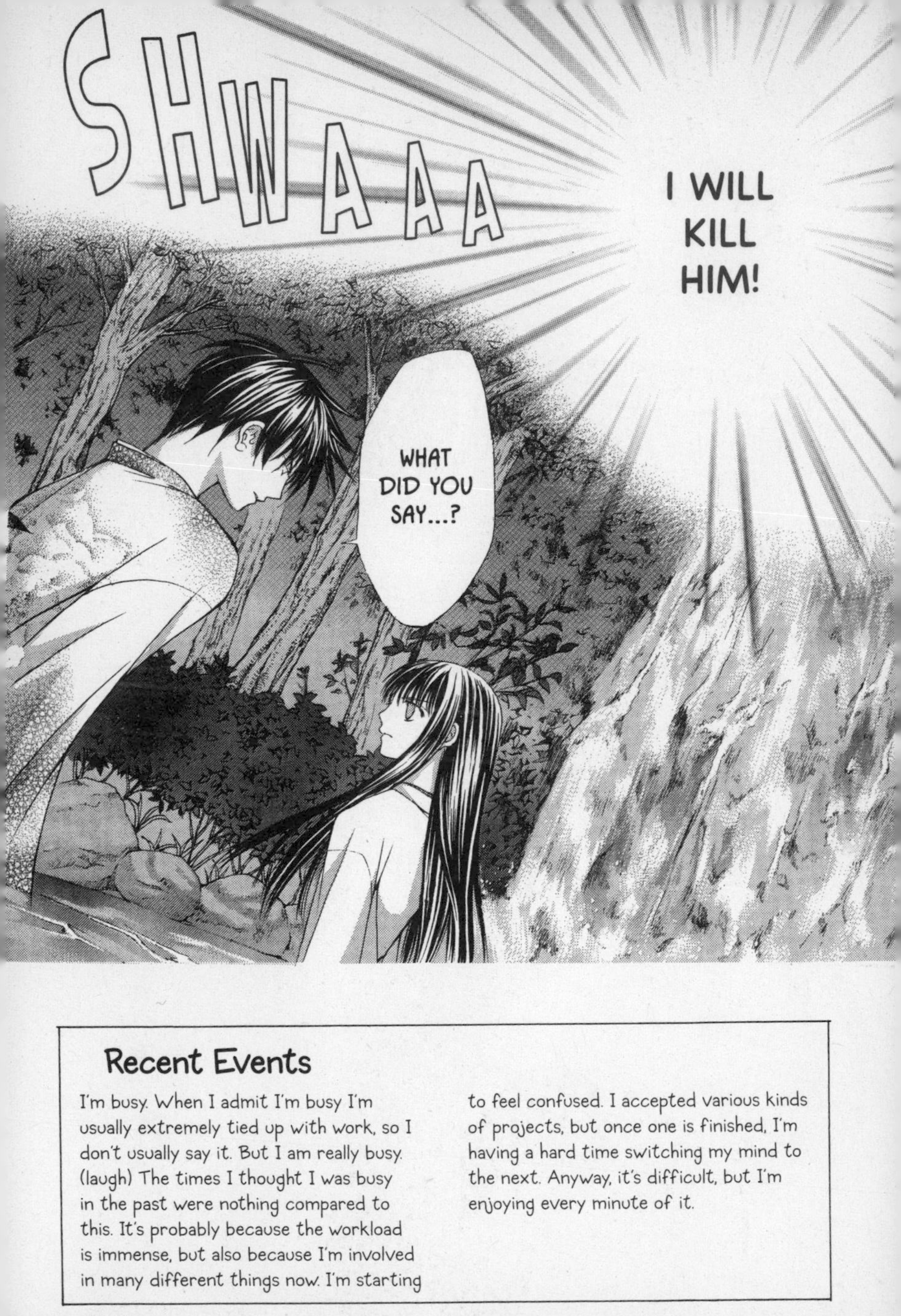
SHWAAA
I WILL KILL HIM!
WHAT DID YOU SAY...?

Recent Events

I'm busy. When I admit I'm busy I'm usually extremely tied up with work, so I don't usually say it. But I am really busy. (laugh) The times I thought I was busy in the past were nothing compared to this. It's probably because the workload is immense, but also because I'm involved in many different things now. I'm starting to feel confused. I accepted various kinds of projects, but once one is finished, I'm having a hard time switching my mind to the next. Anyway, it's difficult, but I'm enjoying every minute of it.

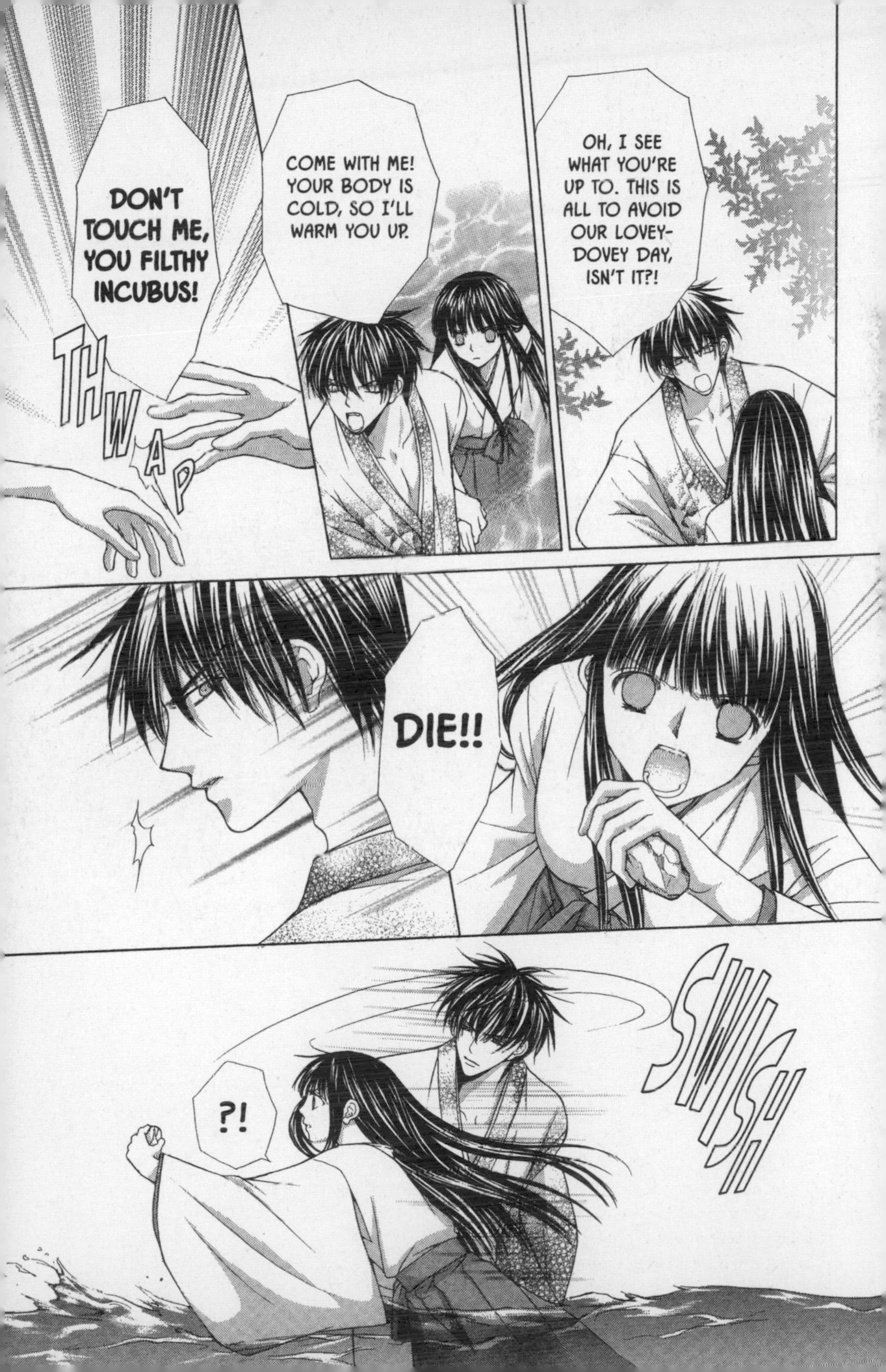
OH, I SEE WHAT YOU'RE UP TO. THIS IS ALL TO AVOID OUR LOVEY-DOVEY DAY, ISN'T IT?!
COME WITH ME! YOUR BODY IS COLD, SO I'LL WARM YOU UP.
DON'T TOUCH ME, YOU FILTHY INCUBUS!
THWAP
DIE!!
SWISH
?!

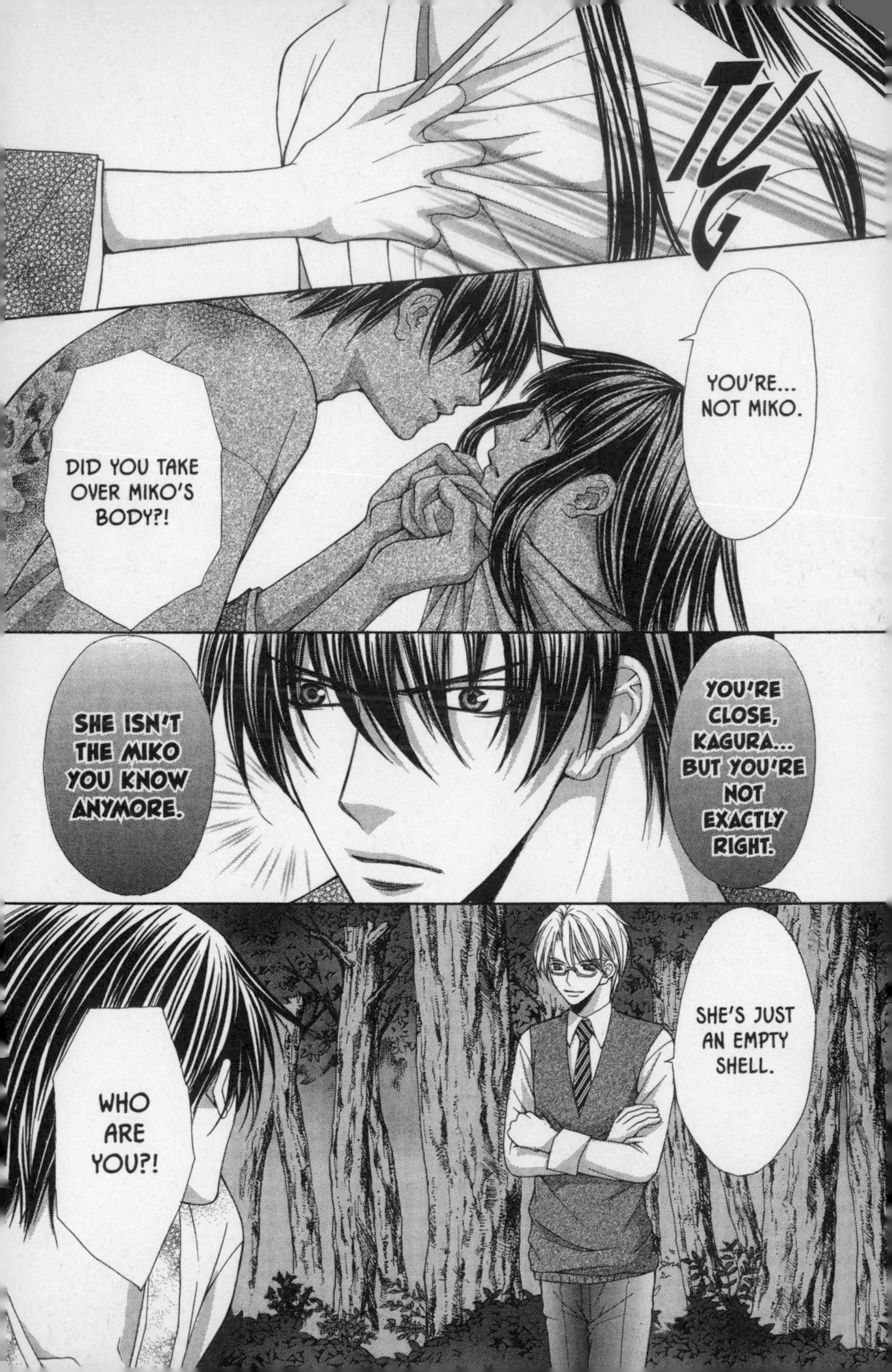
TUG
YOU'RE... NOT MIKO.
DID YOU TAKE OVER MIKO'S BODY?!
YOU'RE CLOSE, KAGURA... BUT YOU'RE NOT EXACTLY RIGHT.
SHE ISN'T THE MIKO YOU KNOW ANYMORE.
SHE'S JUST AN EMPTY SHELL.
WHO ARE YOU?!

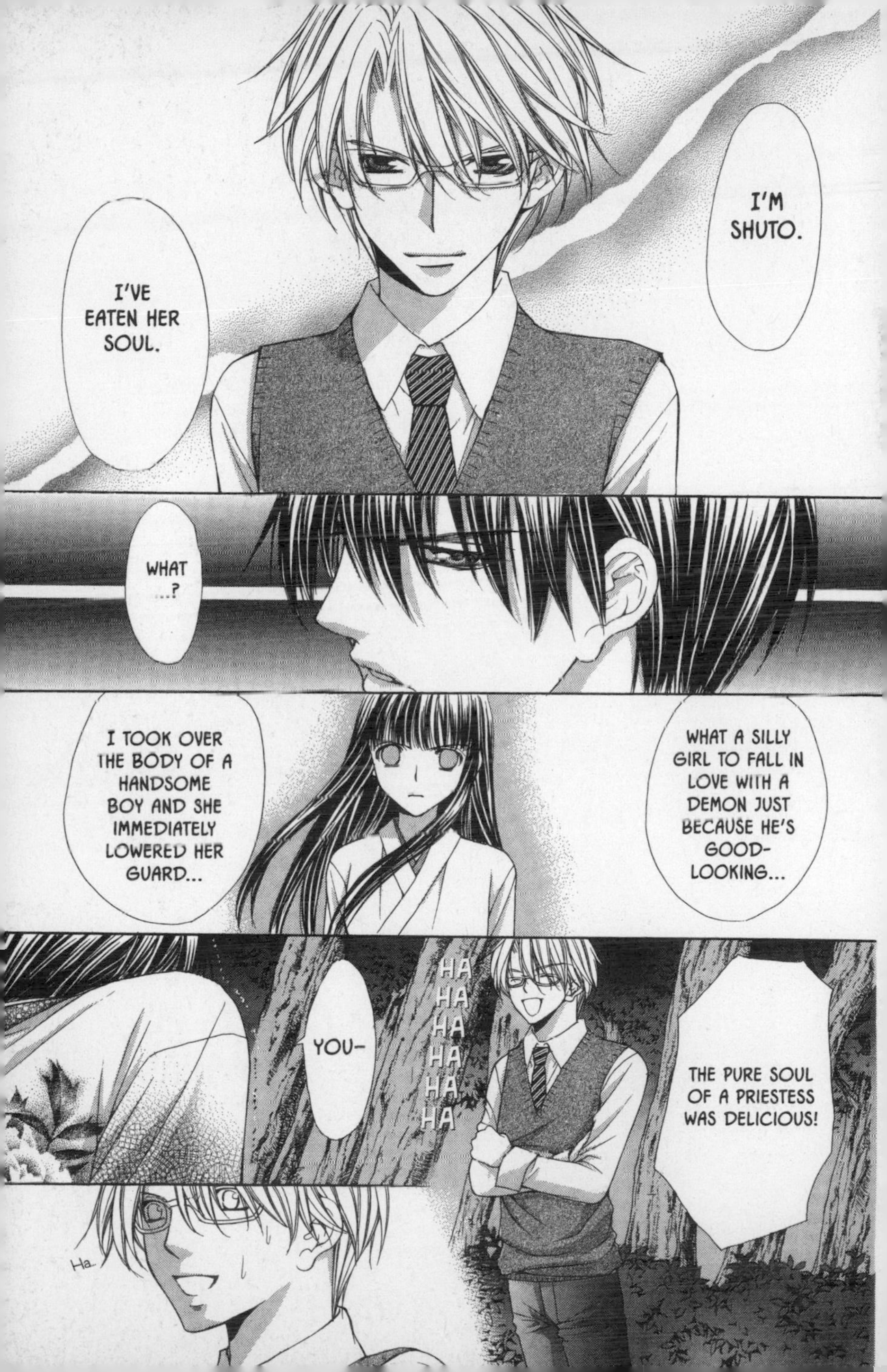
I'M SHUTO.
I'VE EATEN HER SOUL.
WHAT ...?
WHAT A SILLY GIRL TO FALL IN LOVE WITH A DEMON JUST BECAUSE HE'S GOOD-LOOKING...
I TOOK OVER THE BODY OF A HANDSOME BOY AND SHE IMMEDIATELY LOWERED HER GUARD...
THE PURE SOUL OF A PRIESTESS WAS DELICIOUS!
HA HA HA HA HA HA HA
YOU-
Ha..

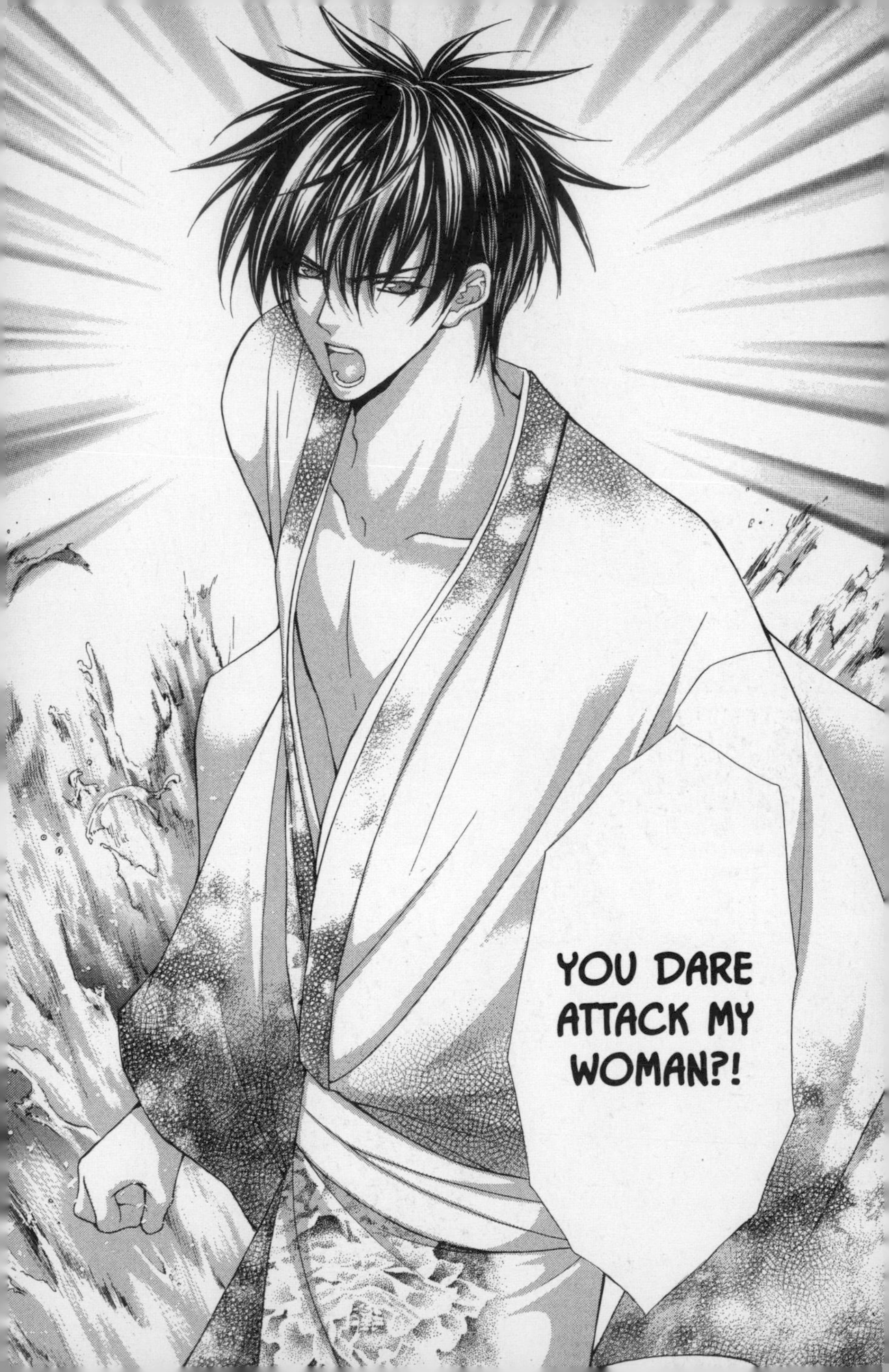
YOU DARE ATTACK MY WOMAN?!

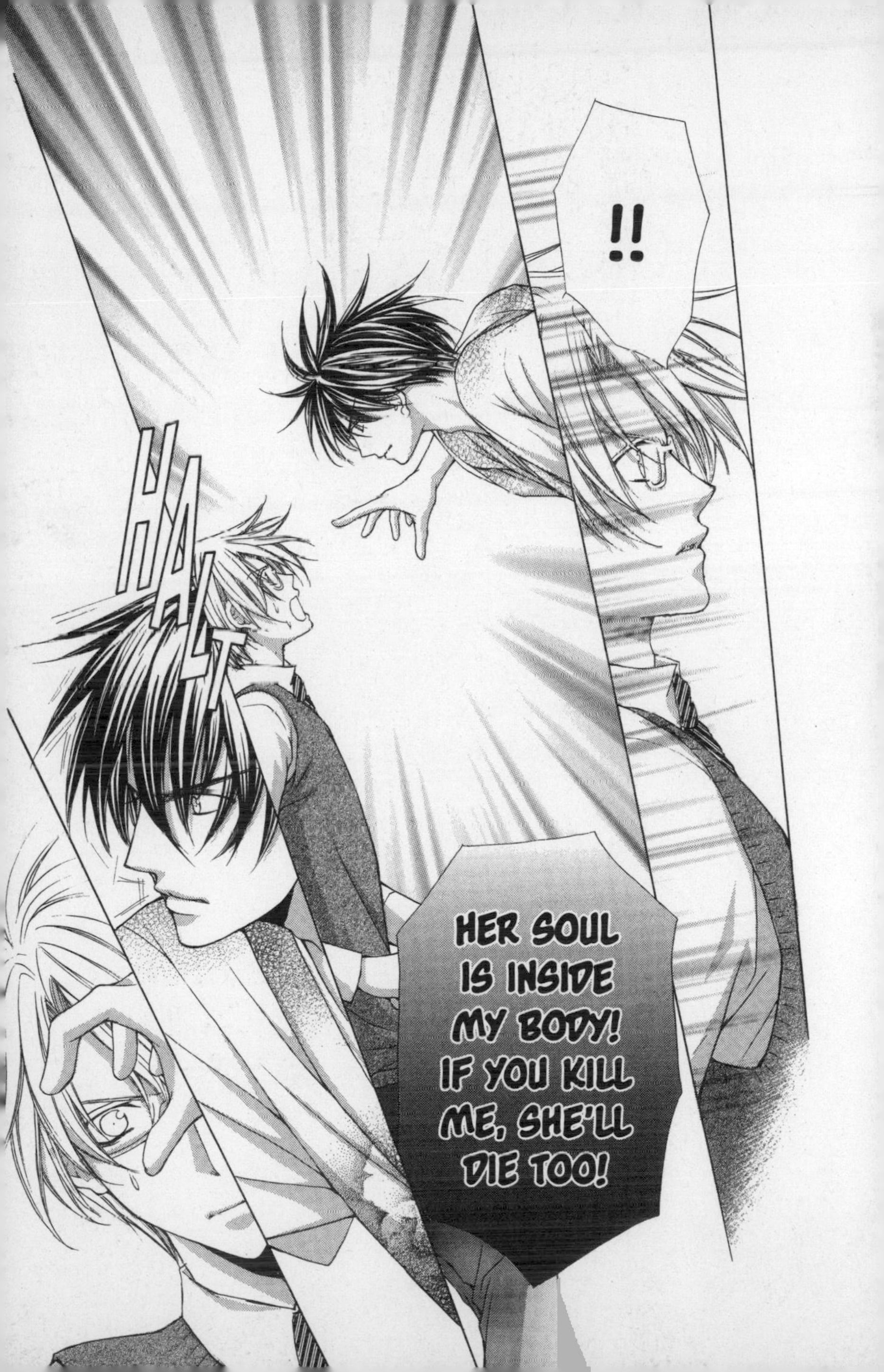
!!
HALT
HER SOUL IS INSIDE MY BODY! IF YOU KILL ME, SHE'LL DIE TOO!

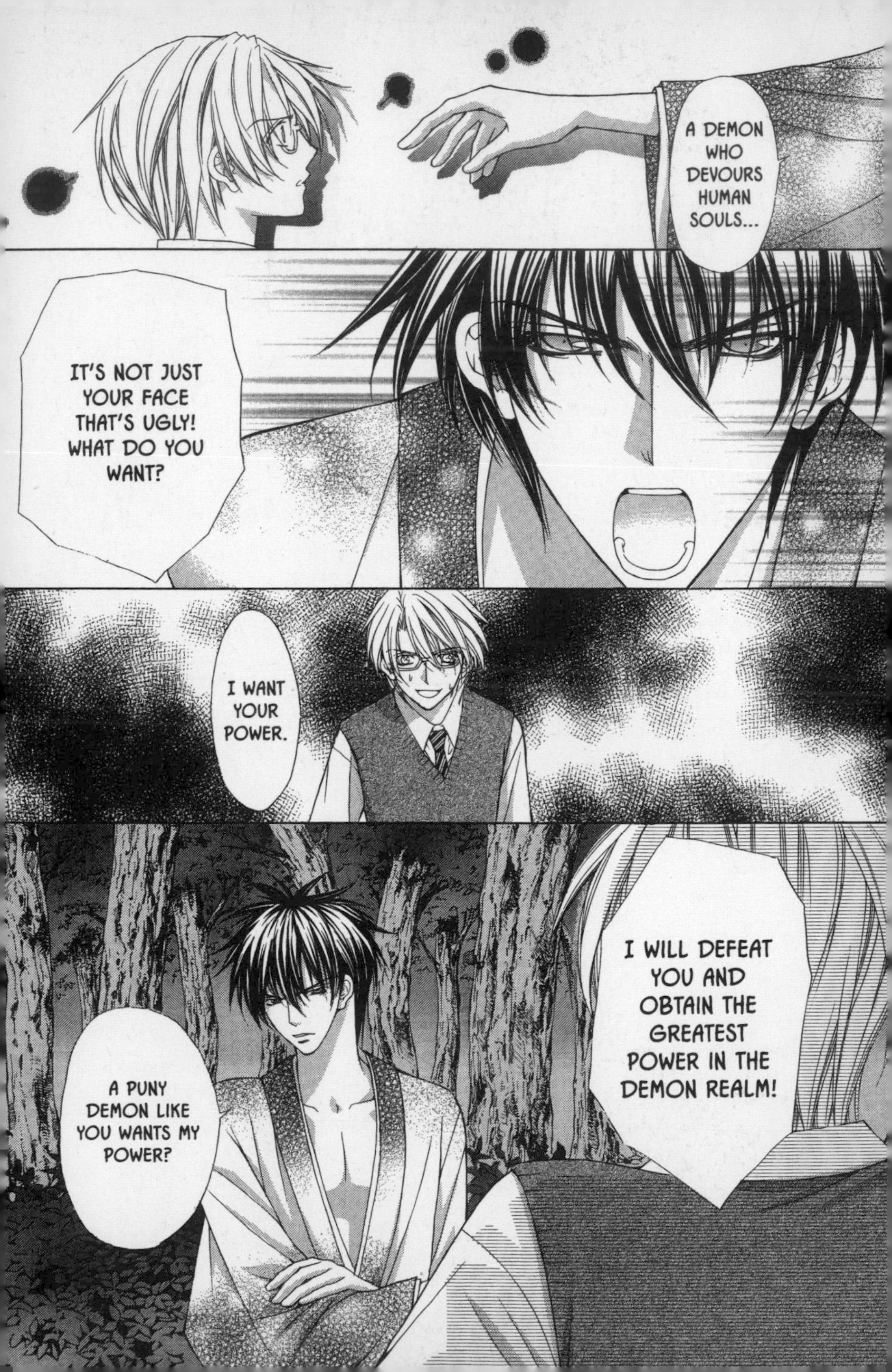
A DEMON WHO DEVOURS HUMAN SOULS...
IT'S NOT JUST YOUR FACE THAT'S UGLY! WHAT DO YOU WANT?
I WANT YOUR POWER.
I WILL DEFEAT YOU AND OBTAIN THE GREATEST POWER IN THE DEMON REALM!
A PUNY DEMON LIKE YOU WANTS MY POWER?

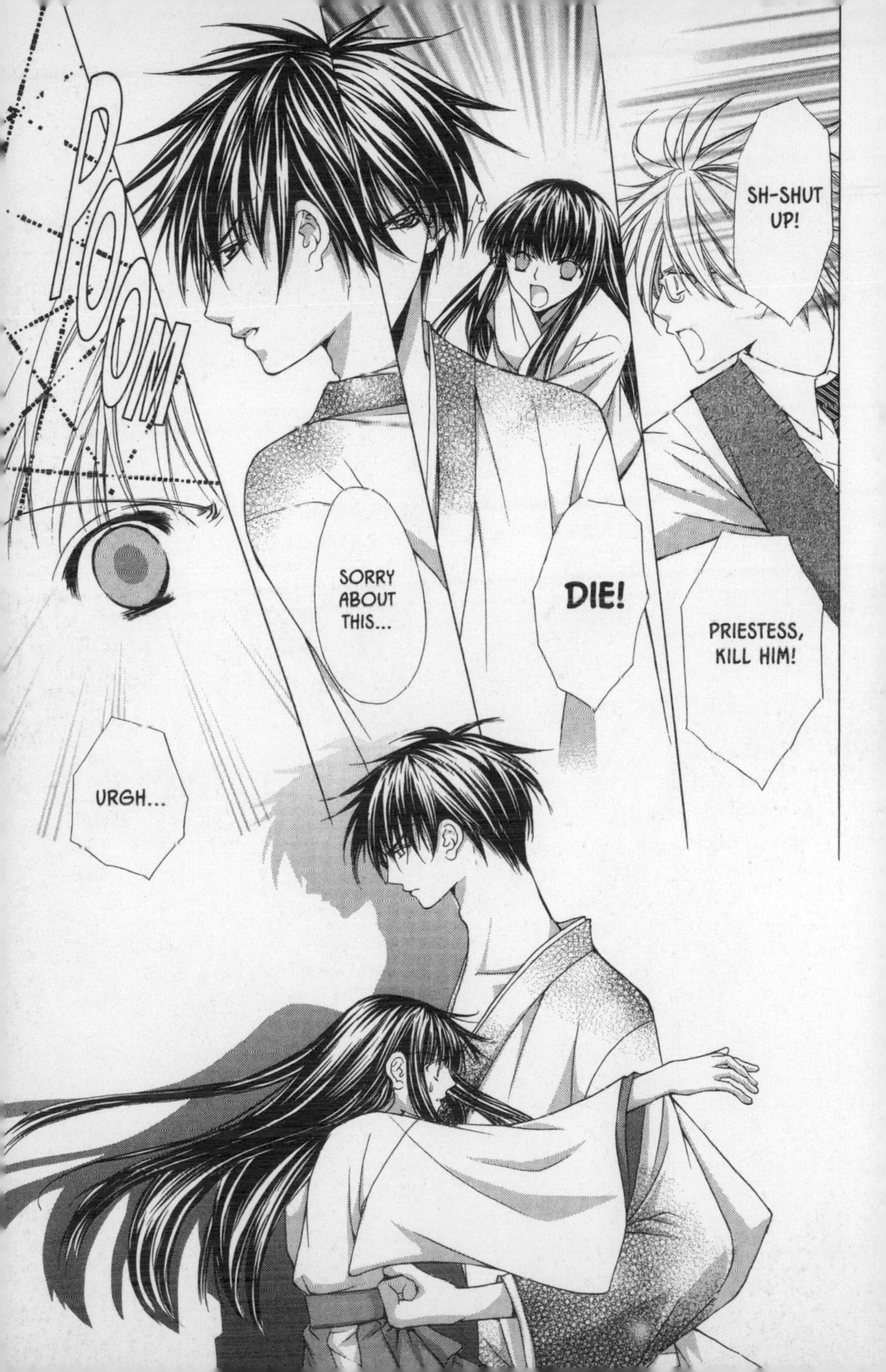
SH-SHUT UP!
PRIESTESS, KILL HIM!
DIE!
SORRY ABOUT THIS...
POOM
URGH...

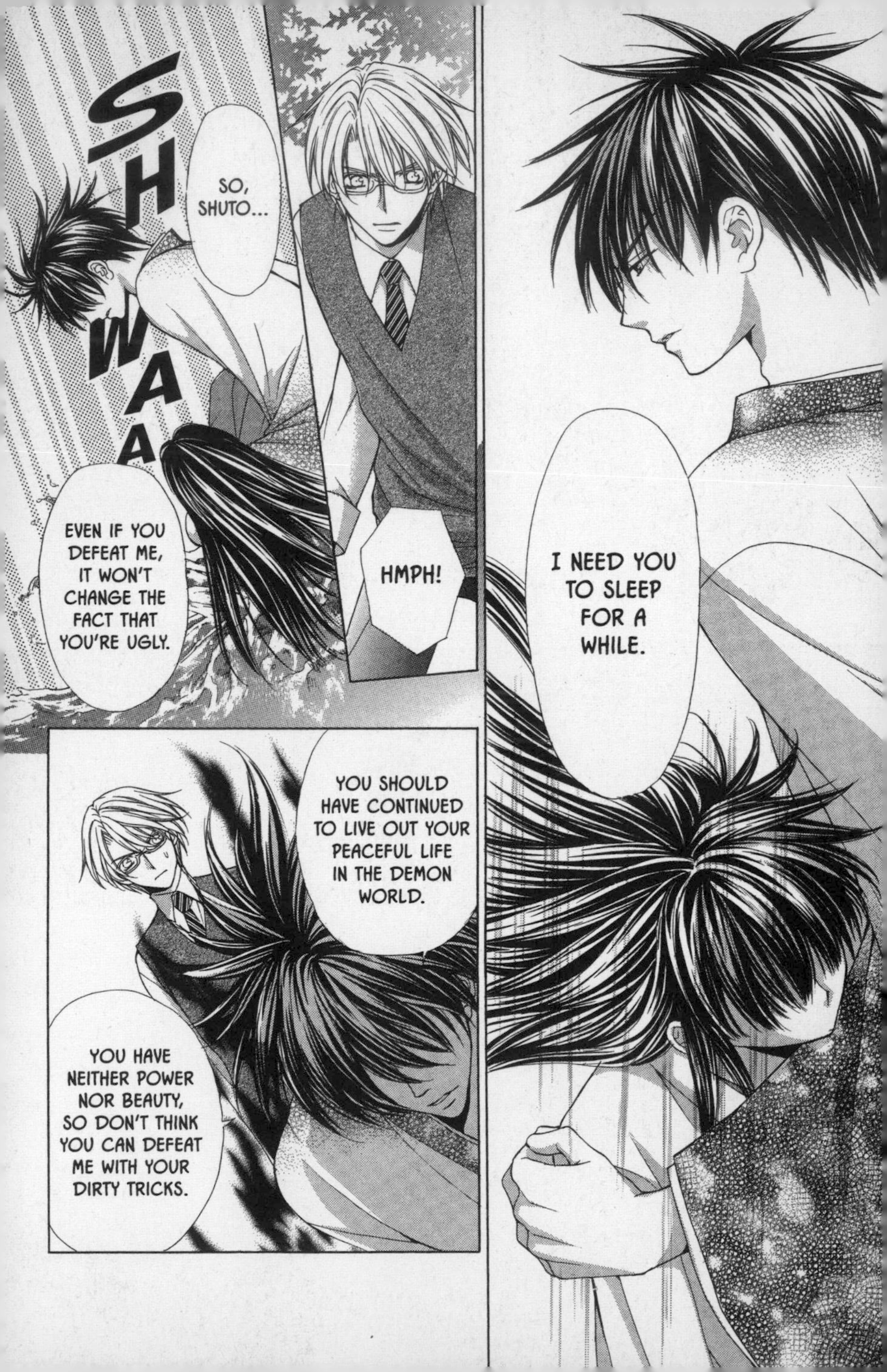
I NEED YOU TO SLEEP FOR A WHILE.
SO, SHUTO...
HMPH!
SHWAAA
EVEN IF YOU DEFEAT ME, IT WON'T CHANGE THE FACT THAT YOU'RE UGLY.
YOU SHOULD HAVE CONTINUED TO LIVE OUT YOUR PEACEFUL LIFE IN THE DEMON WORLD.
YOU HAVE NEITHER POWER NOR BEAUTY, SO DON'T THINK YOU CAN DEFEAT ME WITH YOUR DIRTY TRICKS.

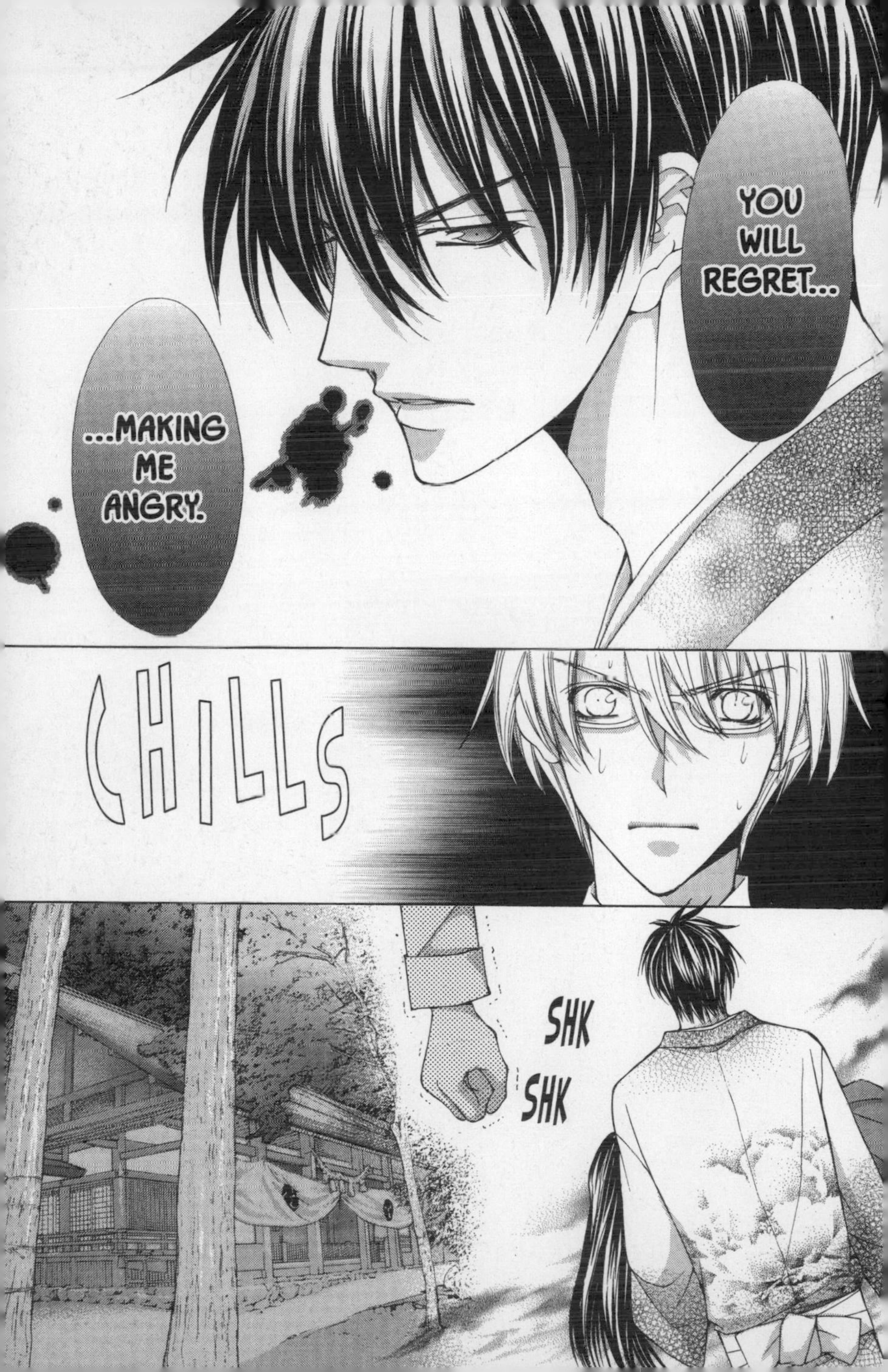
YOU WILL REGRET...
...MAKING ME ANGRY.
CHILLS
SHK
SHK

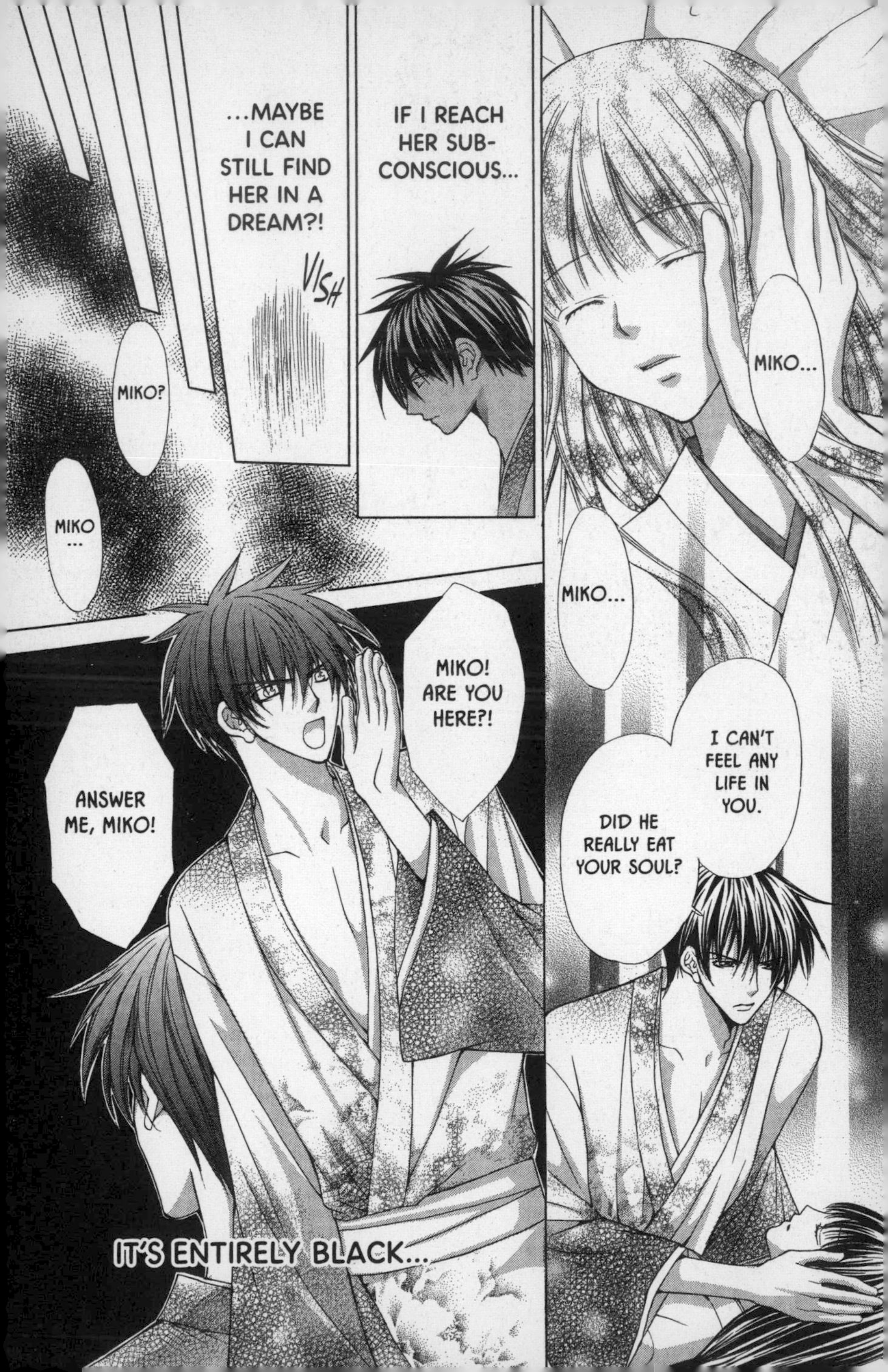
MIKO...
MIKO...
I CAN'T FEEL ANY LIFE IN YOU.
DID HE REALLY EAT YOUR SOUL?
IF I REACH HER SUB-CONSCIOUS...
...MAYBE I CAN STILL FIND HER IN A DREAM?!
VISH
MIKO?
MIKO ...
MIKO! ARE YOU HERE?!
ANSWER ME, MIKO!
IT'S ENTIRELY BLACK...

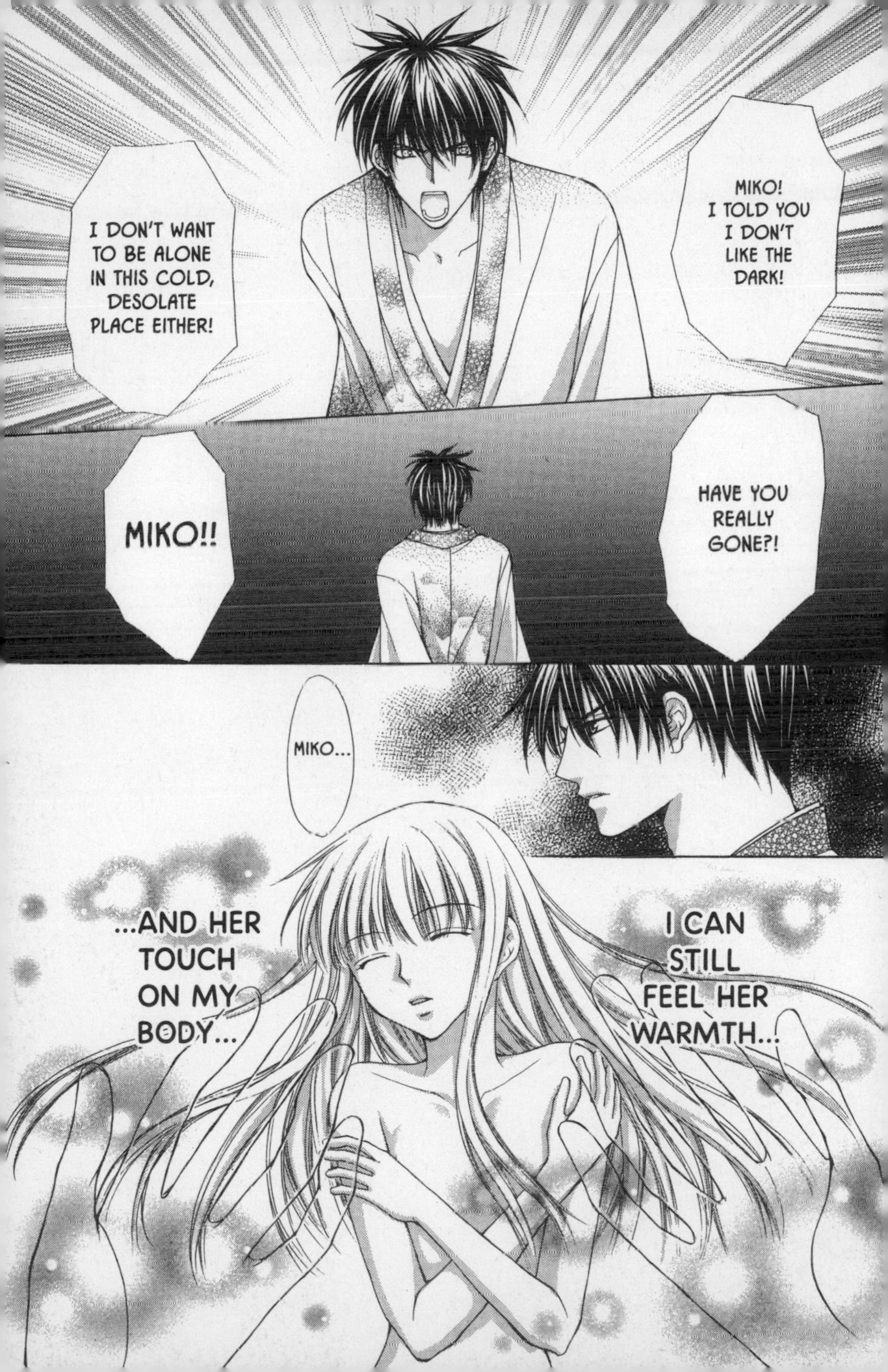
MIKO! I TOLD YOU I DON'T LIKE THE DARK!
I DON'T WANT TO BE ALONE IN THIS COLD, DESOLATE PLACE EITHER!
HAVE YOU REALLY GONE?!
MIKO!!
MIKO...
I CAN STILL FEEL HER WARMTH...
...AND HER TOUCH ON MY BODY...

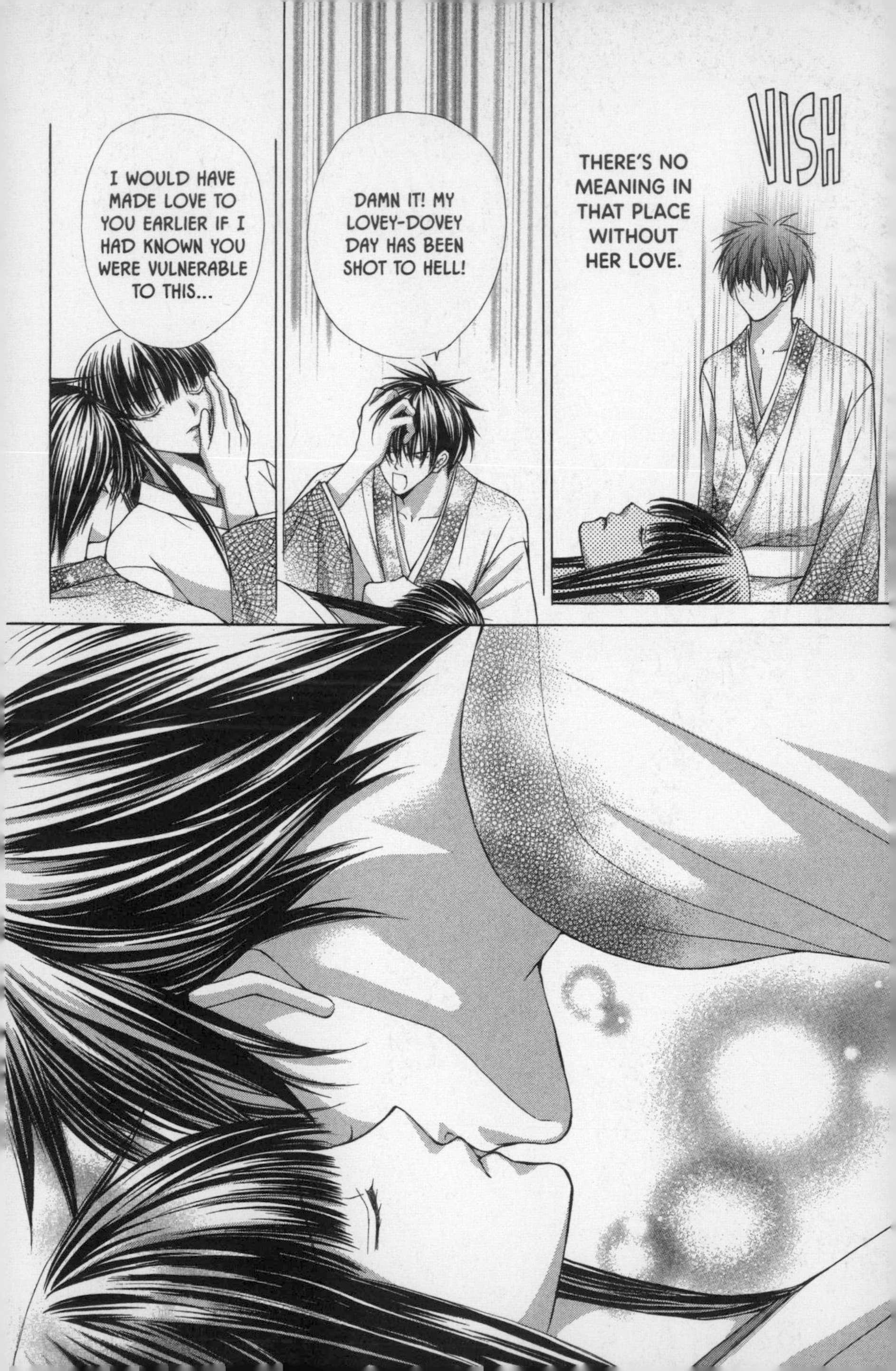
VISH
THERE'S NO MEANING IN THAT PLACE WITHOUT HER LOVE.
DAMN IT! MY LOVEY-DOVEY DAY HAS BEEN SHOT TO HELL!
I WOULD HAVE MADE LOVE TO YOU EARLIER IF I HAD KNOWN YOU WERE VULNERABLE TO THIS...

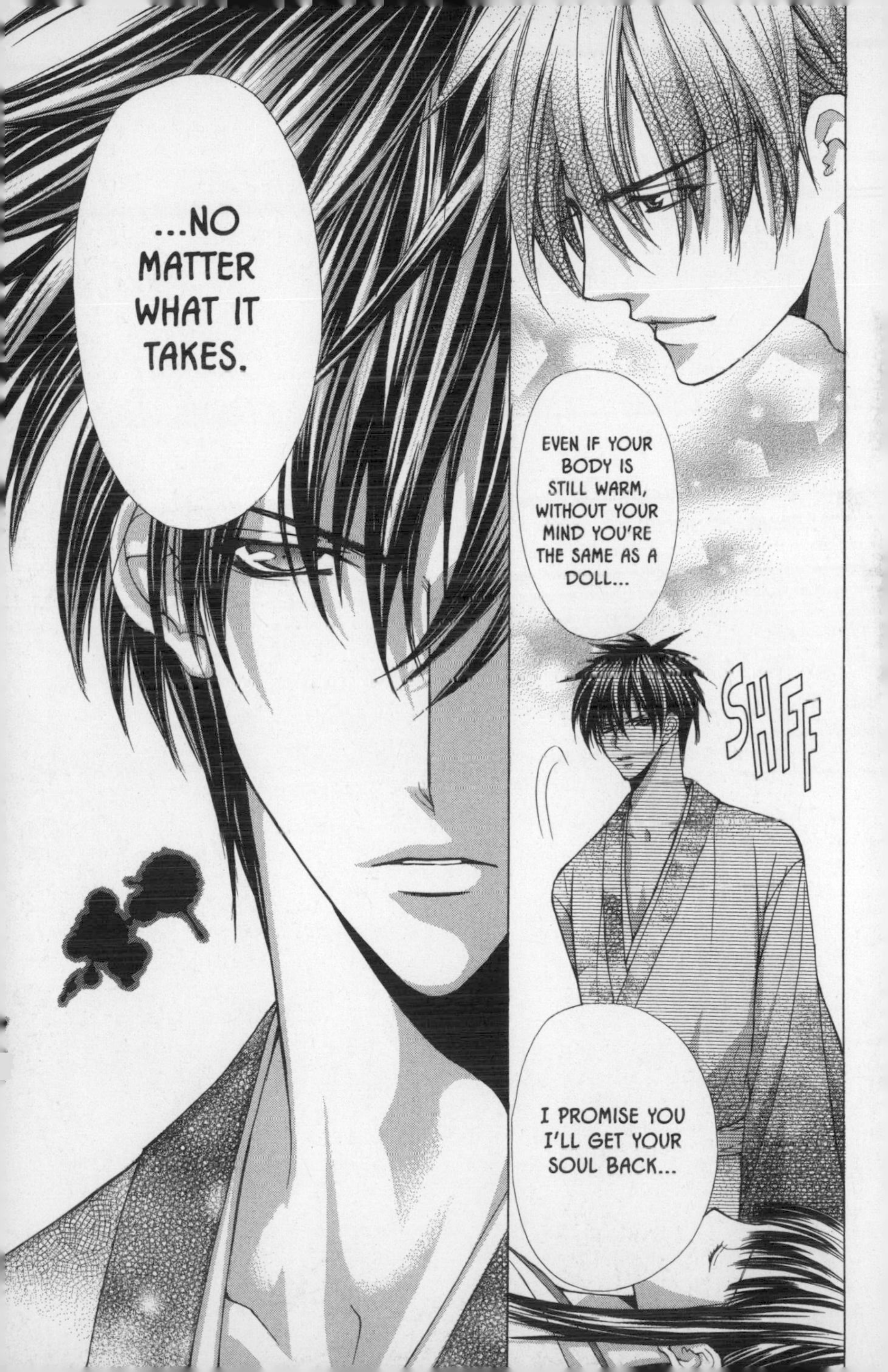
EVEN IF YOUR BODY IS STILL WARM, WITHOUT YOUR MIND YOU'RE THE SAME AS A DOLL...
SHFF
I PROMISE YOU I'LL GET YOUR SOUL BACK...
...NO MATTER WHAT IT TAKES.

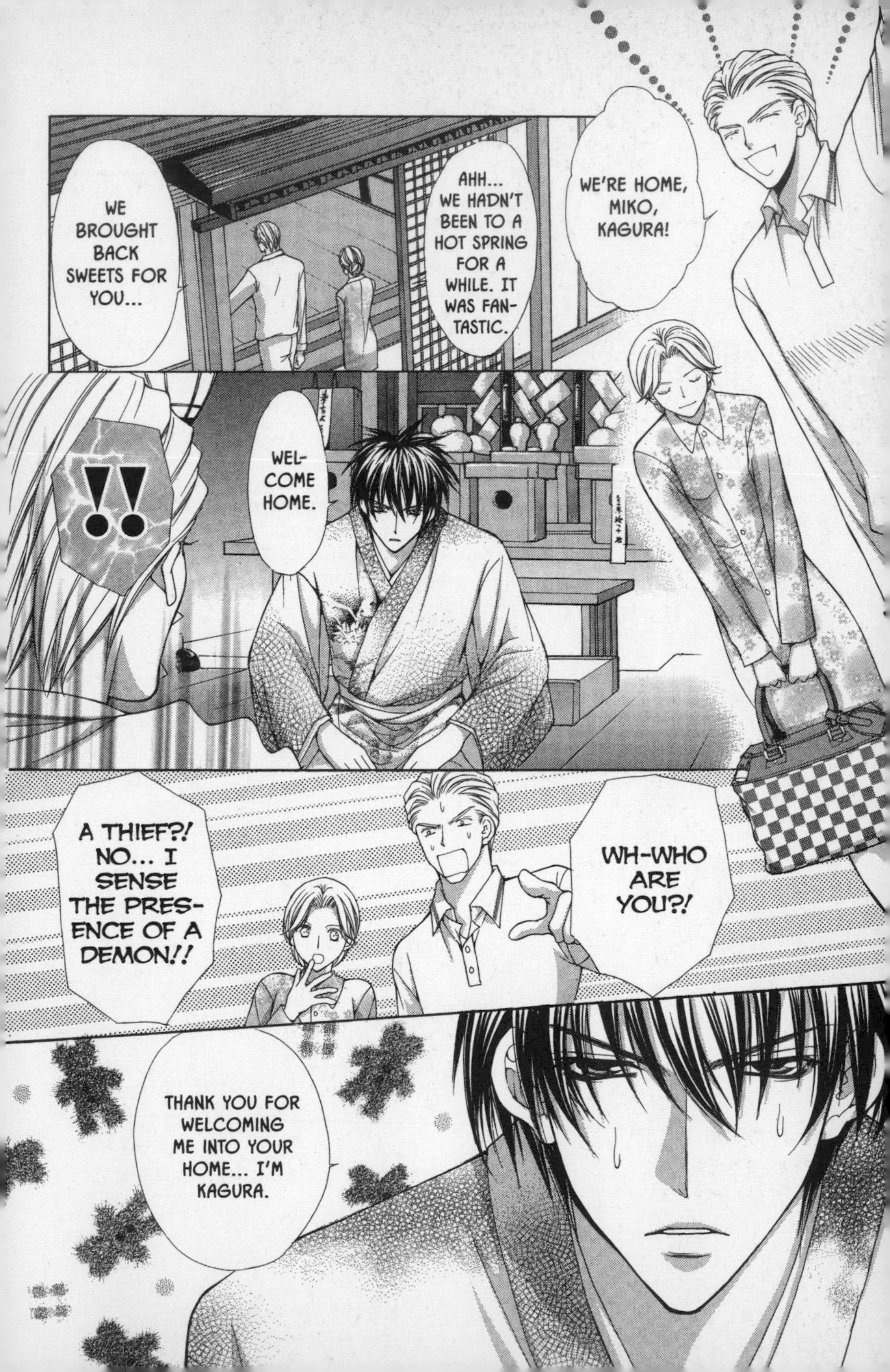
WE'RE HOME, MIKO, KAGURA!
AHH... WE HADN'T BEEN TO A HOT SPRING FOR A WHILE. IT WAS FAN-TASTIC.
WE BROUGHT BACK SWEETS FOR YOU...
WEL-COME HOME.
!!
WH-WHO ARE YOU?!
A THIEF?! NO... I SENSE THE PRES-ENCE OF A DEMON!!
THANK YOU FOR WELCOMING ME INTO YOUR HOME... I'M KAGURA.

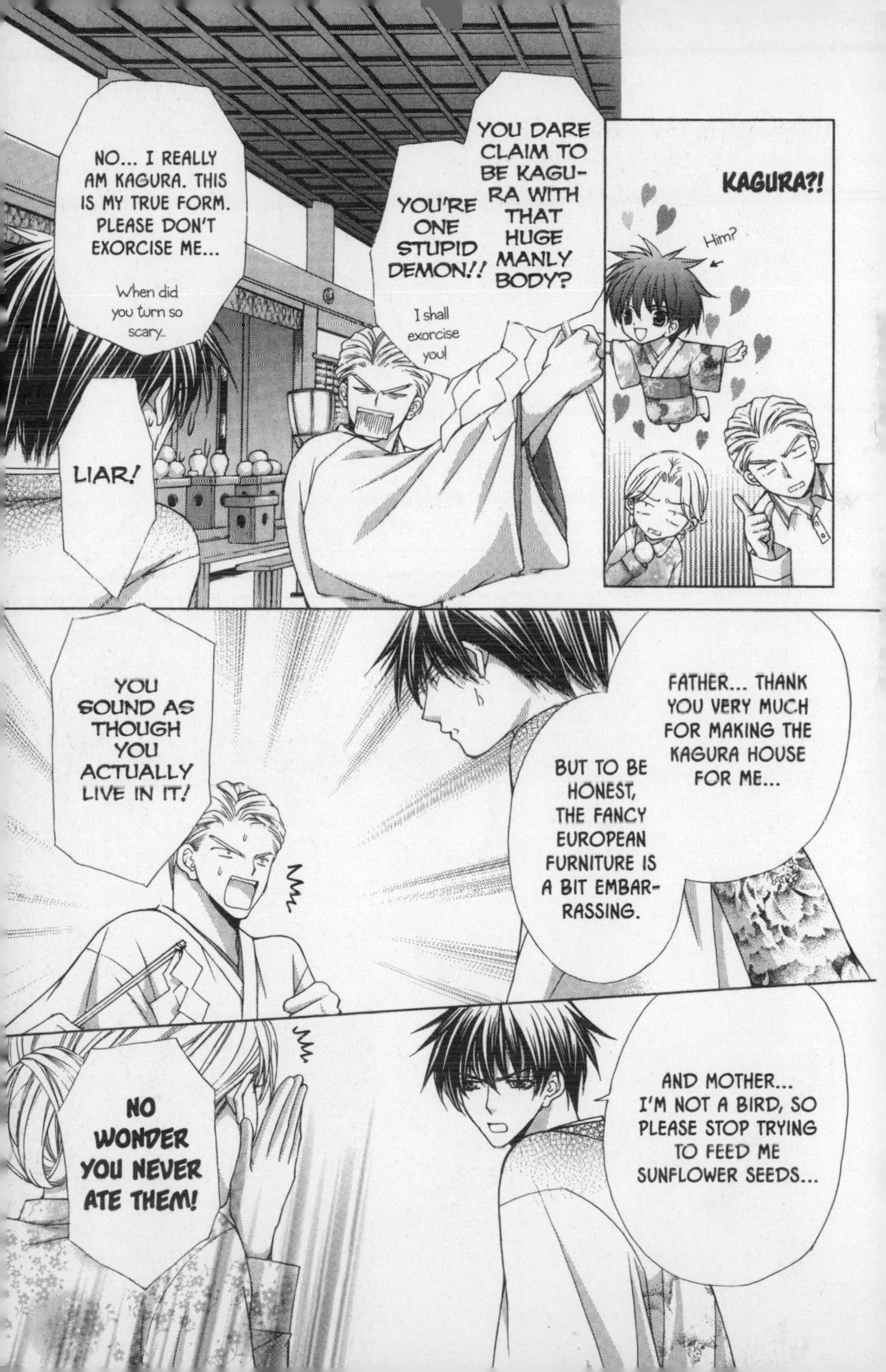
KAGURA?!
Him?
YOU DARE CLAIM TO BE KAGURA WITH THAT HUGE MANLY BODY?
YOU'RE ONE STUPID DEMON!!
I shall exorcise you!
NO... I REALLY AM KAGURA. THIS IS MY TRUE FORM. PLEASE DON'T EXORCISE ME...
When did you turn so scary..
LIAR!
FATHER... THANK YOU VERY MUCH FOR MAKING THE KAGURA HOUSE FOR ME...
BUT TO BE HONEST, THE FANCY EUROPEAN FURNITURE IS A BIT EMBARRASSING.
YOU SOUND AS THOUGH YOU ACTUALLY LIVE IN IT!
AND MOTHER... I'M NOT A BIRD, SO PLEASE STOP TRYING TO FEED ME SUNFLOWER SEEDS...
NO WONDER YOU NEVER ATE THEM!

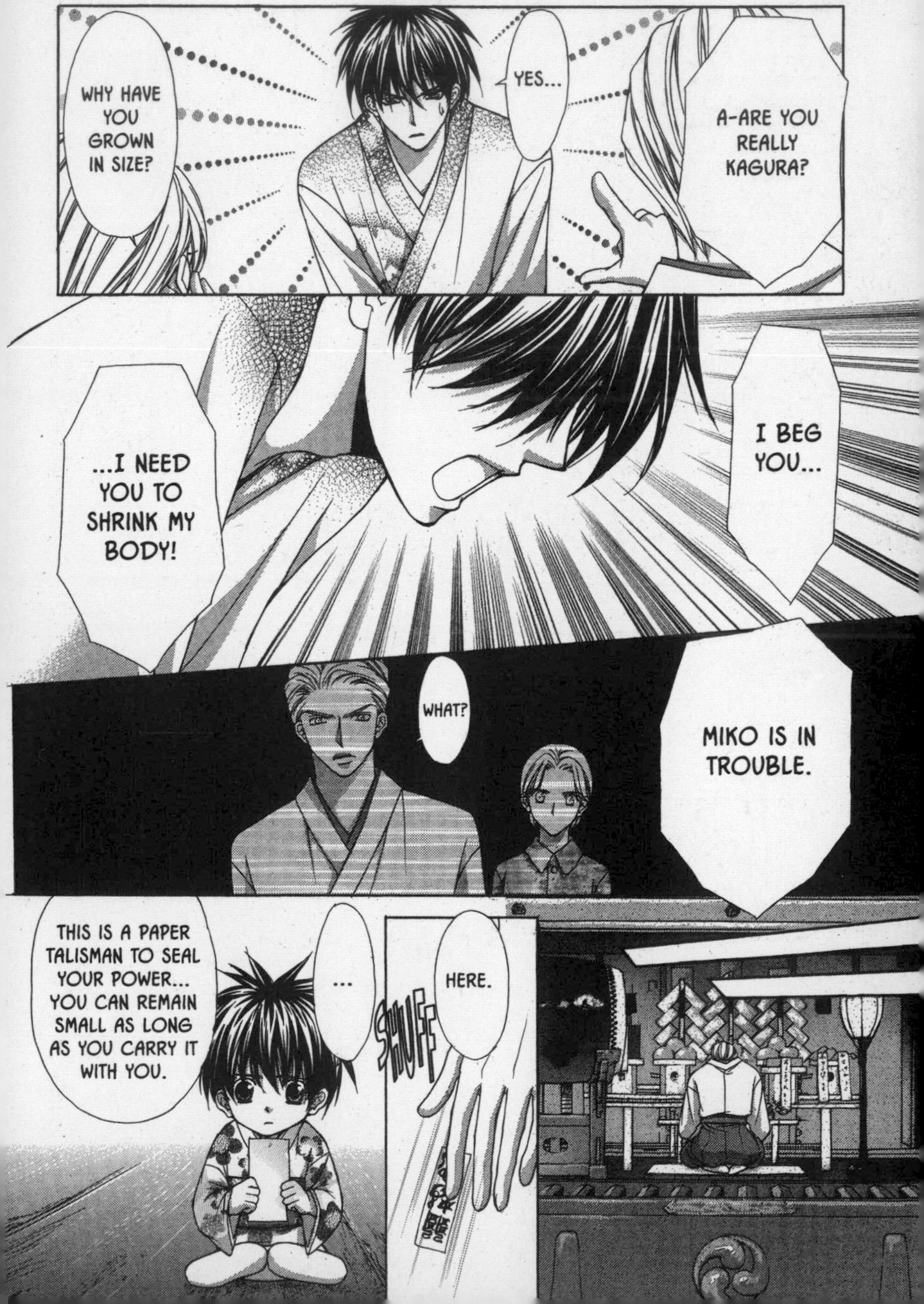
A-ARE YOU REALLY KAGURA?
YES...
WHY HAVE YOU GROWN IN SIZE?
I BEG YOU...
...I NEED YOU TO SHRINK MY BODY!
MIKO IS IN TROUBLE.
WHAT?
HERE.
SHUFF
...
THIS IS A PAPER TALISMAN TO SEAL YOUR POWER... YOU CAN REMAIN SMALL AS LONG AS YOU CARRY IT WITH YOU.

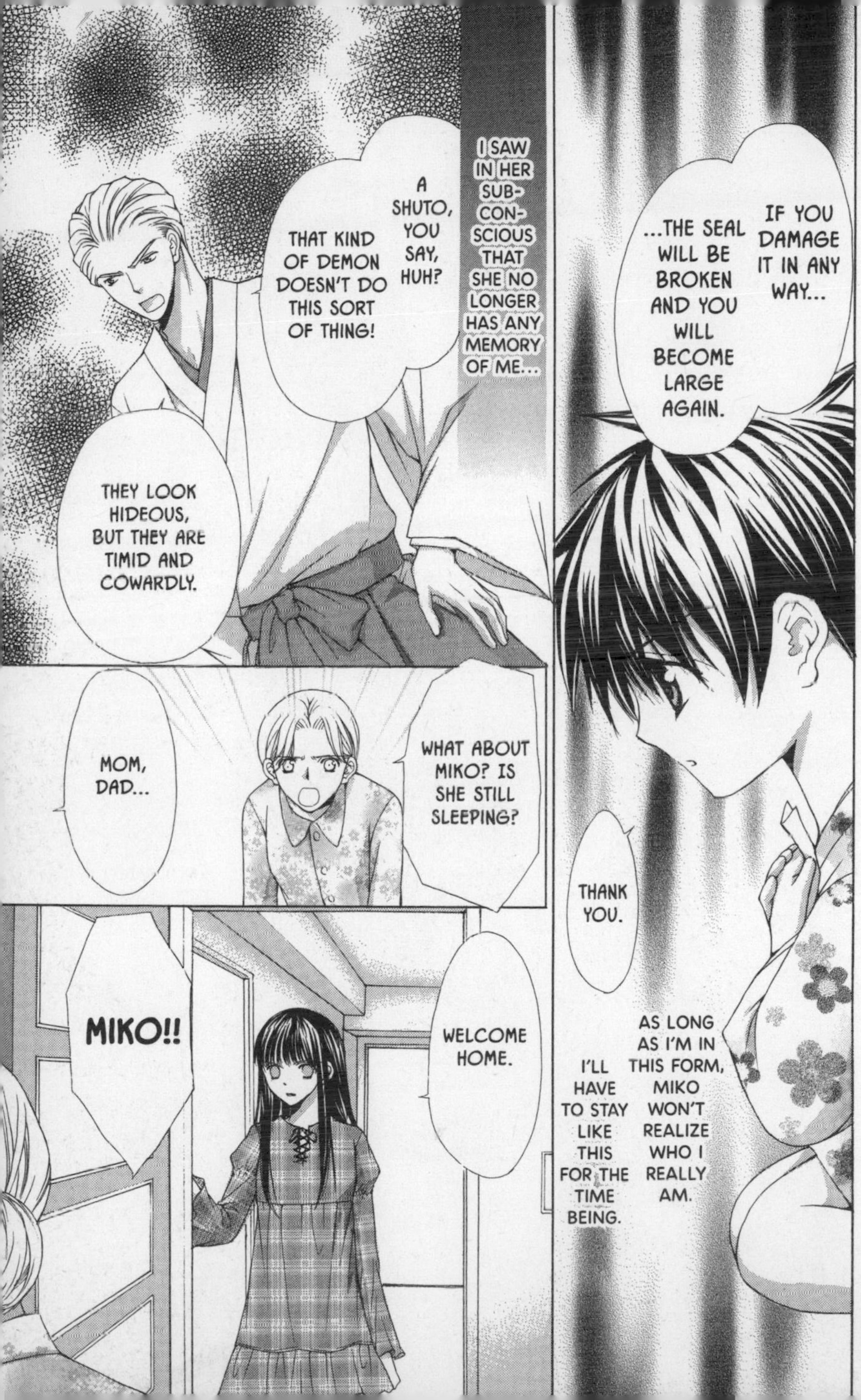
IF YOU DAMAGE IT IN ANY WAY...
...THE SEAL WILL BE BROKEN AND YOU WILL BECOME LARGE AGAIN.
THANK YOU.
AS LONG AS I'M IN THIS FORM, MIKO WON'T REALIZE WHO I REALLY AM.
I'LL HAVE TO STAY LIKE THIS FOR THE TIME BEING.
I SAW IN HER SUB-CONSCIOUS THAT SHE NO LONGER HAS ANY MEMORY OF ME...
A SHUTO, YOU SAY, HUH?
THAT KIND OF DEMON DOESN'T DO THIS SORT OF THING!
THEY LOOK HIDEOUS, BUT THEY ARE TIMID AND COWARDLY.
WHAT ABOUT MIKO? IS SHE STILL SLEEPING?
MOM, DAD...
WELCOME HOME.
MIKO!!

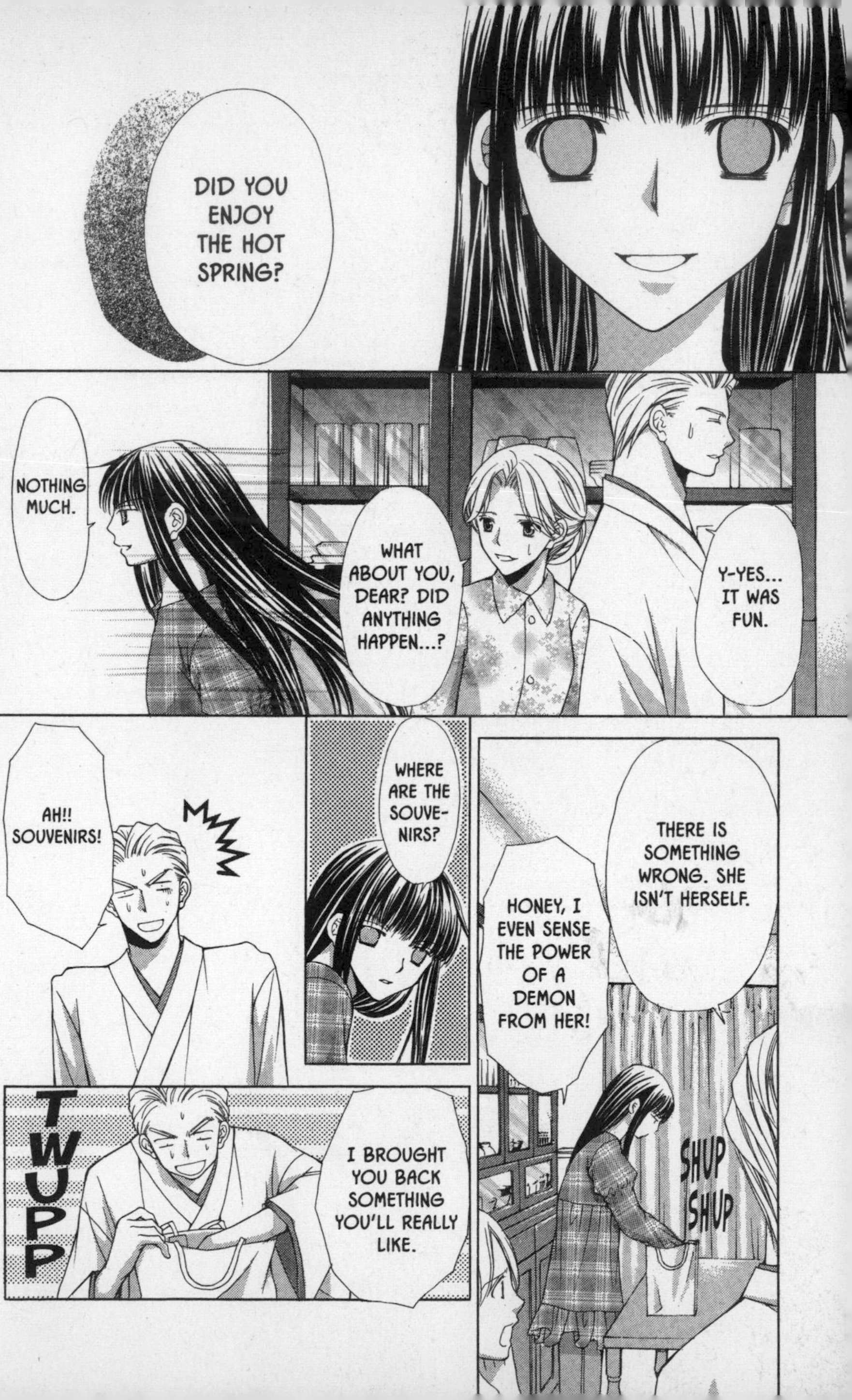
DID YOU ENJOY THE HOT SPRING?
Y-YES... IT WAS FUN.
WHAT ABOUT YOU, DEAR? DID ANYTHING HAPPEN...?
NOTHING MUCH.
THERE IS SOMETHING WRONG. SHE ISN'T HERSELF.
HONEY, I EVEN SENSE THE POWER OF A DEMON FROM HER!
SHUP SHUP
WHERE ARE THE SOUVE-NIRS?
MMM
AH!! SOUVENIRS!
I BROUGHT YOU BACK SOMETHING YOU'LL REALLY LIKE.
TWUPP

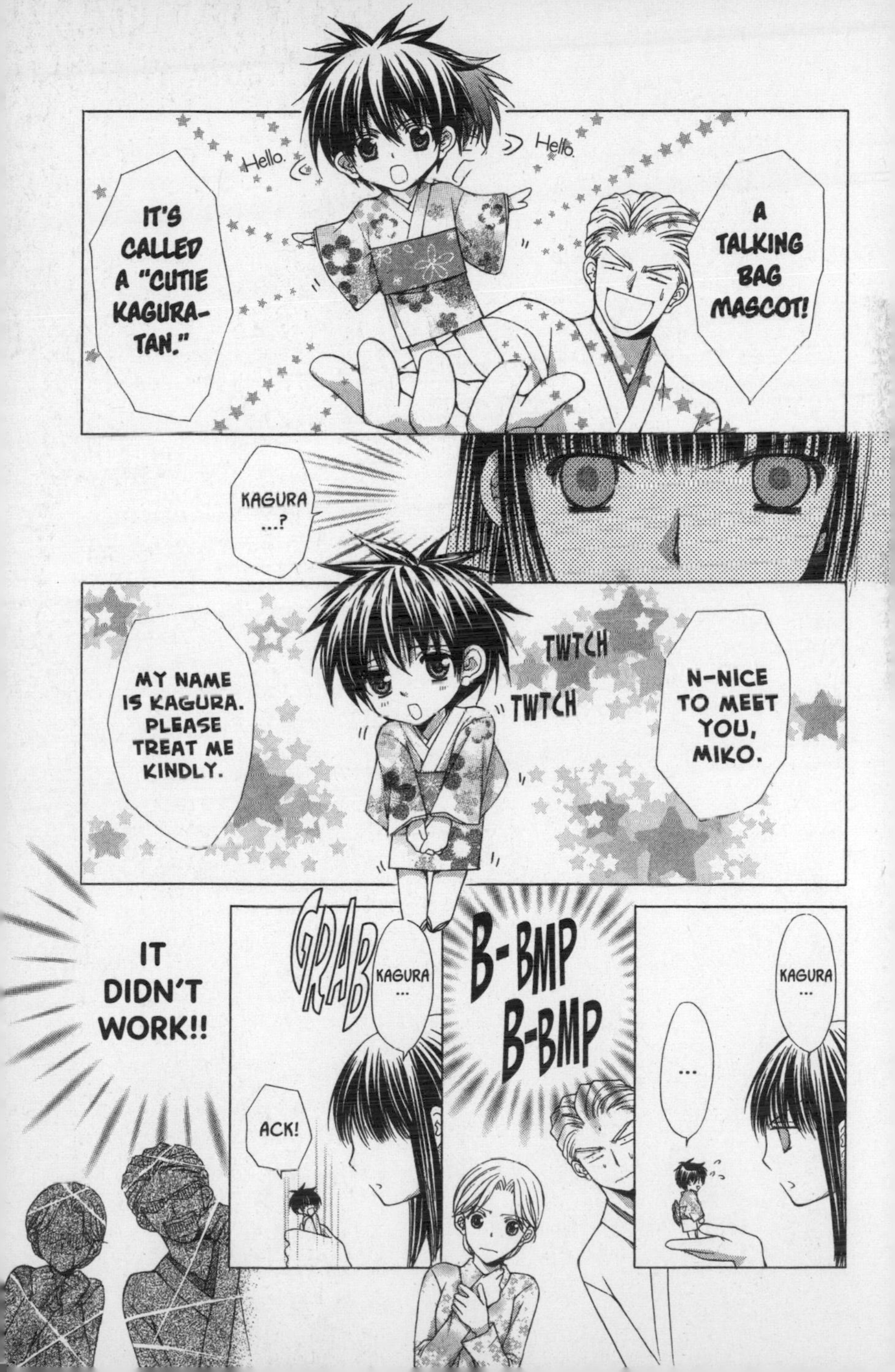
A TALKING BAG MASCOT!
Hello.
Hello.
IT'S CALLED A "CUTIE KAGURA-TAN."
KAGURA ...?
N-NICE TO MEET YOU, MIKO.
TWTCH
TWTCH
MY NAME IS KAGURA. PLEASE TREAT ME KINDLY.
KAGURA ...
...
B-BMP
B-BMP
GRAB
KAGURA ...
ACK!
IT DIDN'T WORK!!

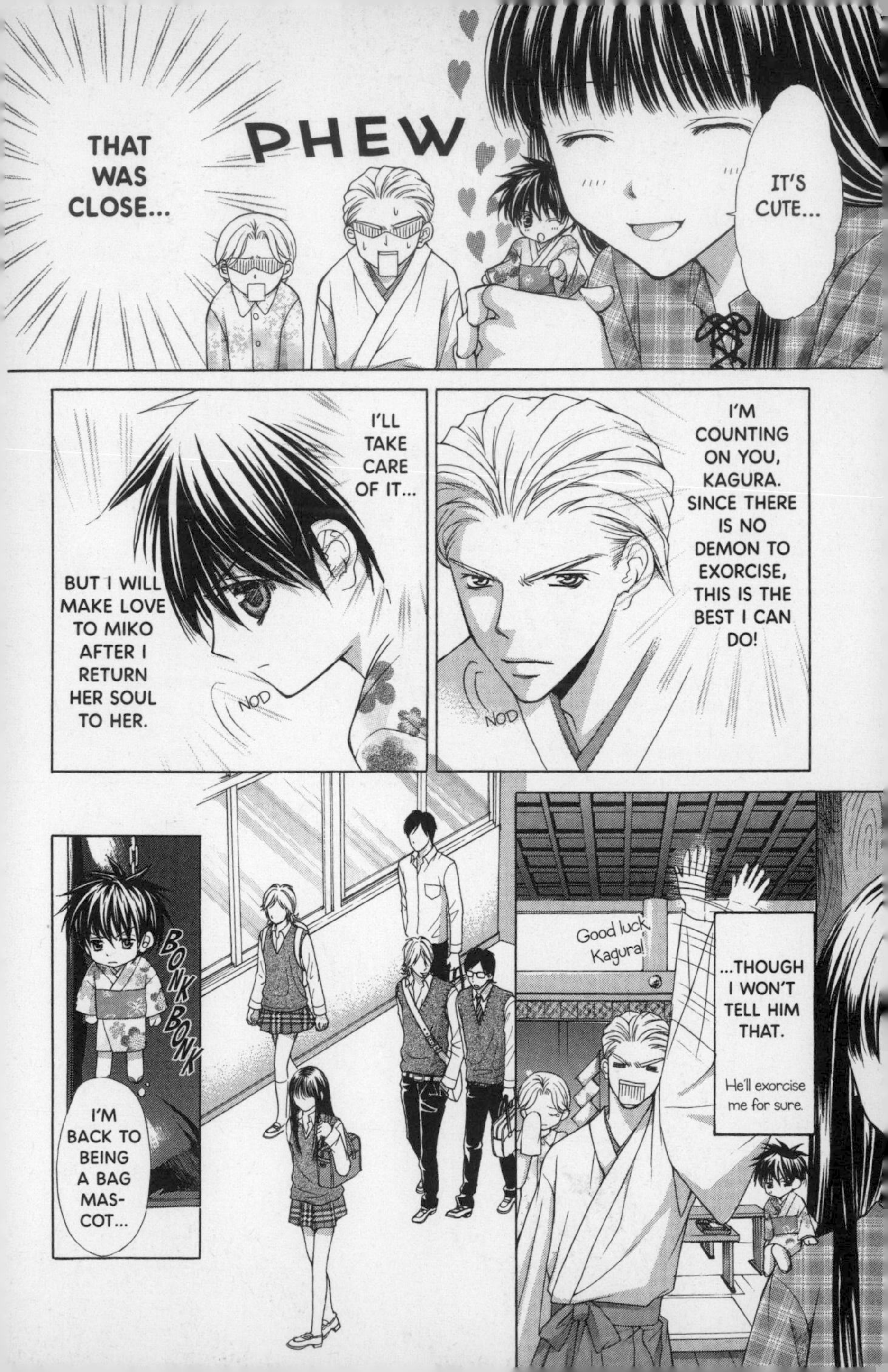
IT'S CUTE...
PHEW
THAT WAS CLOSE...
I'M COUNTING ON YOU, KAGURA. SINCE THERE IS NO DEMON TO EXORCISE, THIS IS THE BEST I CAN DO!
NOD
I'LL TAKE CARE OF IT...
BUT I WILL MAKE LOVE TO MIKO AFTER I RETURN HER SOUL TO HER.
NOD
Good luck, Kagura!
...THOUGH I WON'T TELL HIM THAT.
He'll exorcise me for sure.
BONK BONK
I'M BACK TO BEING A BAG MAS-COT...

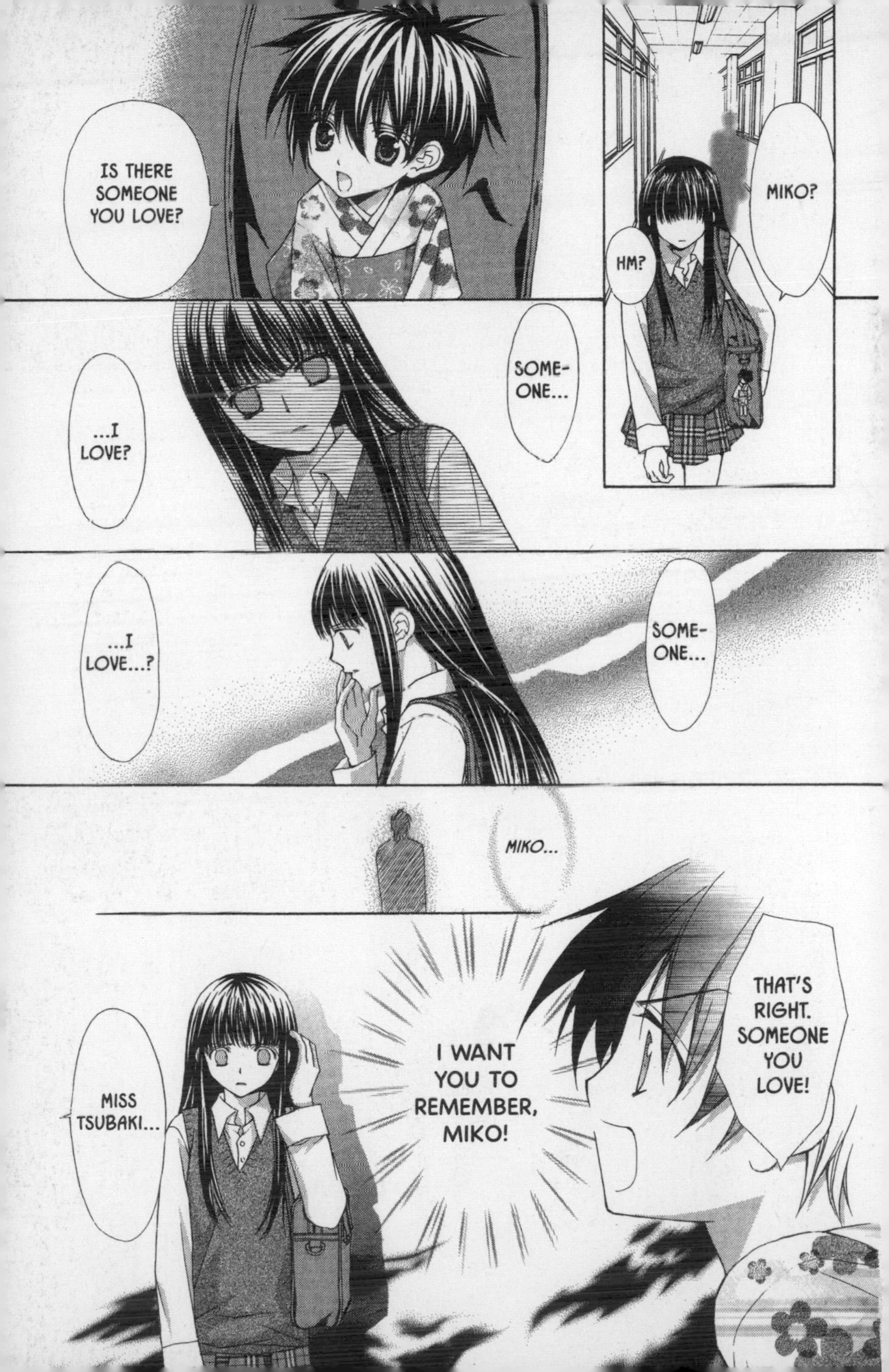
MIKO?
HM?
IS THERE SOMEONE YOU LOVE?
SOME-ONE...
...I LOVE?
SOME-ONE...
...I LOVE...?
MIKO...
THAT'S RIGHT. SOMEONE YOU LOVE!
I WANT YOU TO REMEMBER, MIKO!
MISS TSUBAKI...

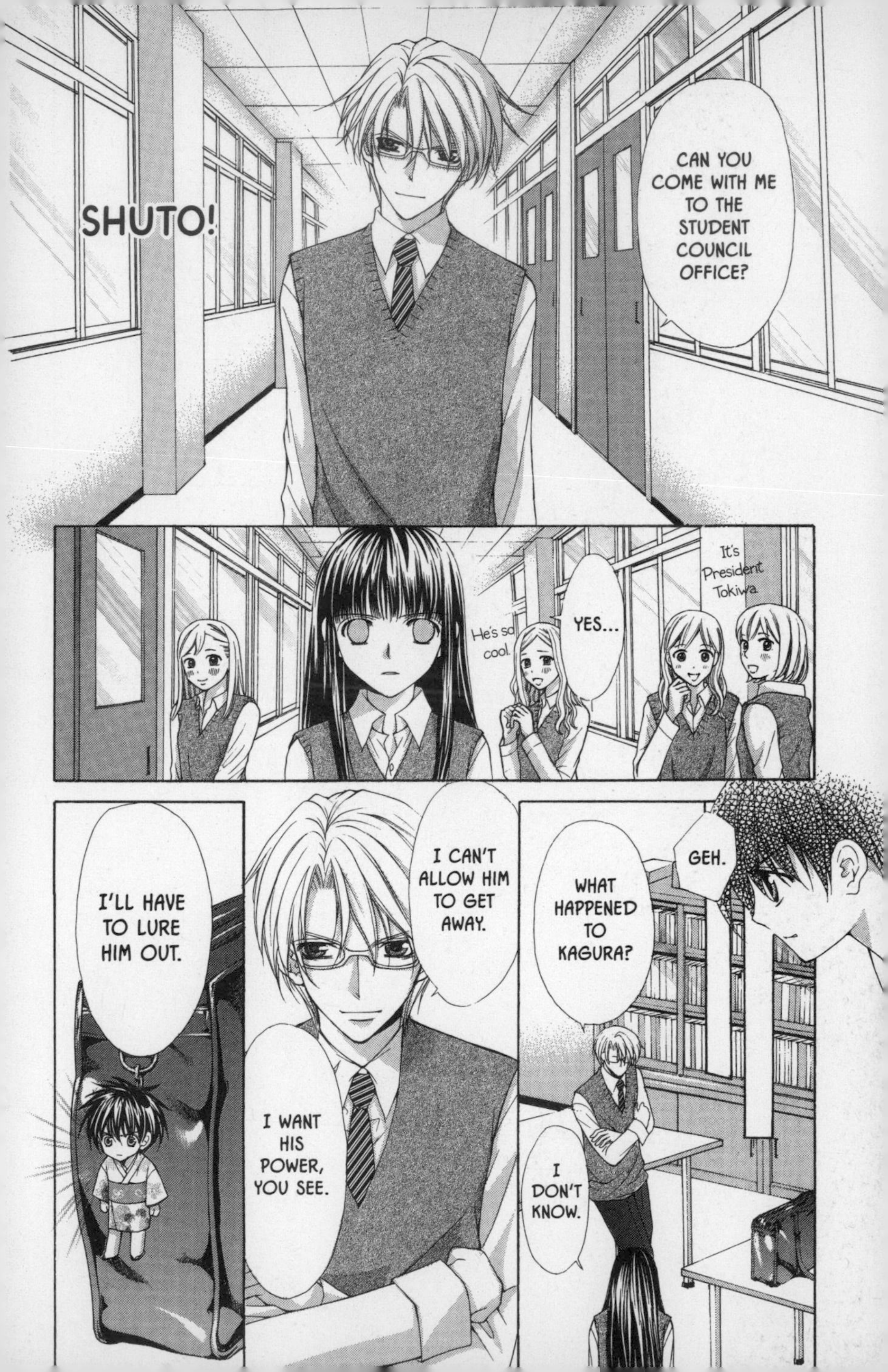
CAN YOU COME WITH ME TO THE STUDENT COUNCIL OFFICE?
SHUTO!
It's President Tokiwa
YES...
He's so cool.
GEH.
WHAT HAPPENED TO KAGURA?
I DON'T KNOW.
I CAN'T ALLOW HIM TO GET AWAY.
I'LL HAVE TO LURE HIM OUT.
I WANT HIS POWER, YOU SEE.

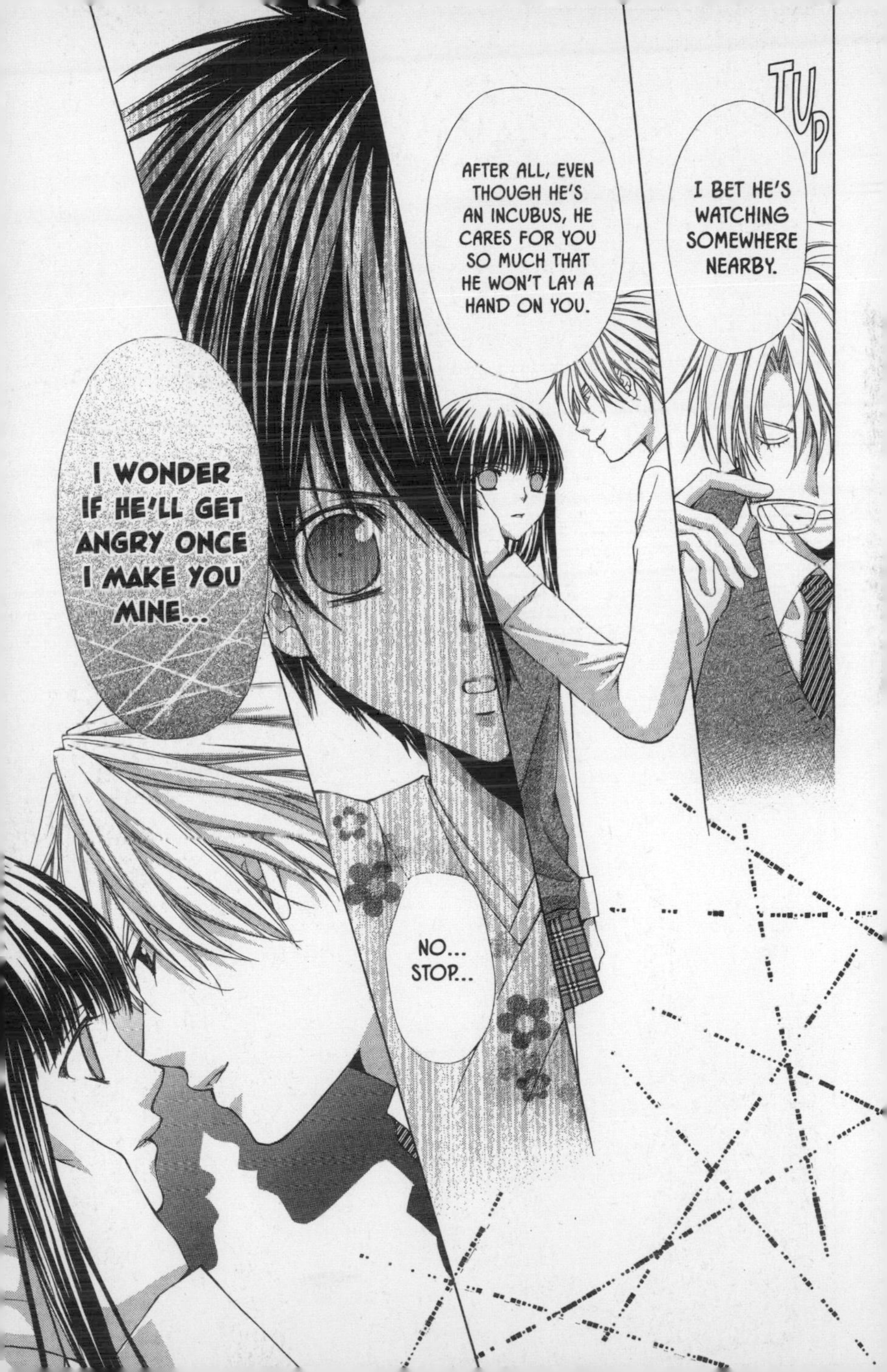
TUP
I BET HE'S WATCHING SOMEWHERE NEARBY.
AFTER ALL, EVEN THOUGH HE'S AN INCUBUS, HE CARES FOR YOU SO MUCH THAT HE WON'T LAY A HAND ON YOU.
I WONDER IF HE'LL GET ANGRY ONCE I MAKE YOU MINE...
NO... STOP...

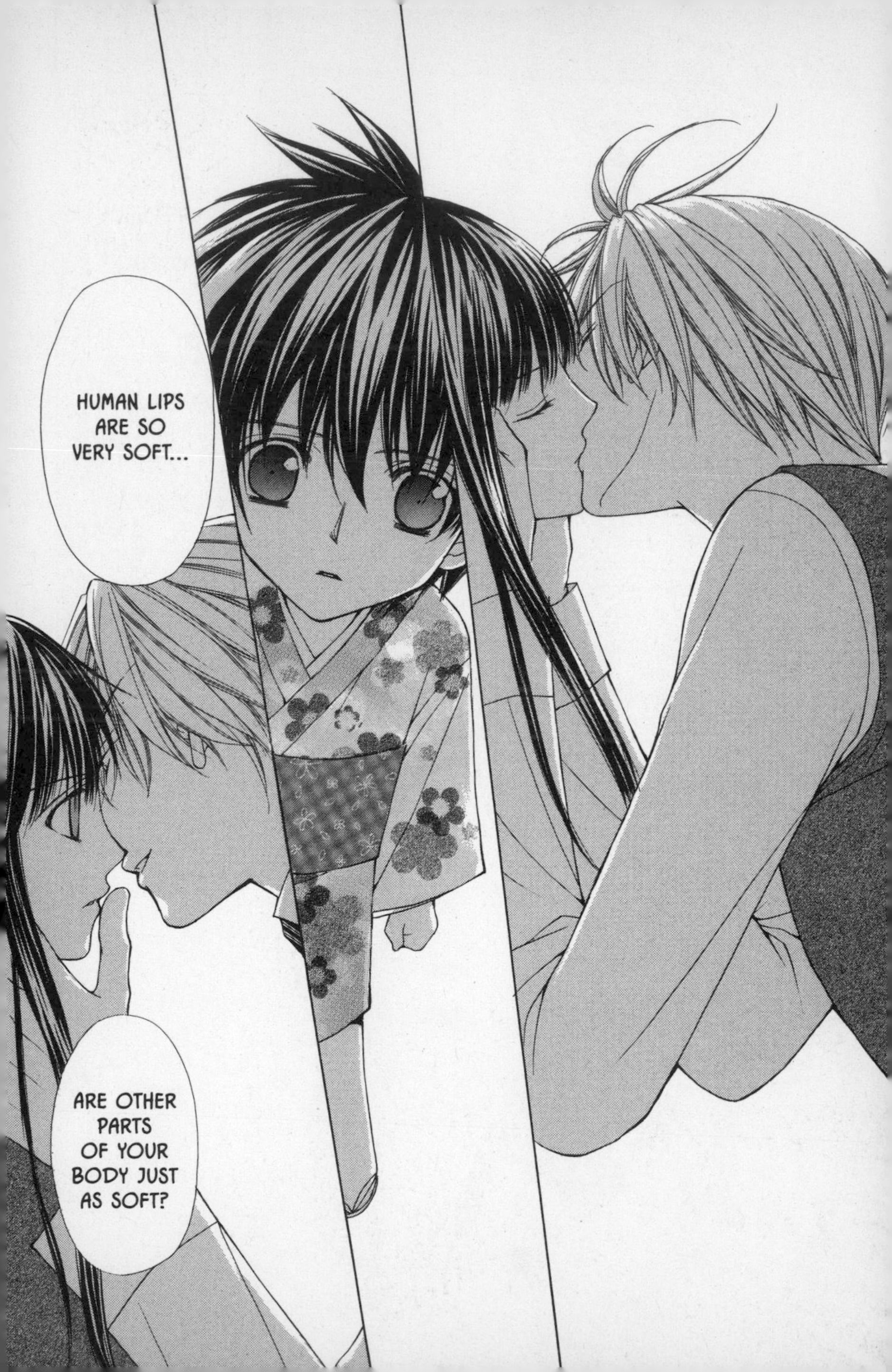
HUMAN LIPS ARE SO VERY SOFT...
ARE OTHER PARTS OF YOUR BODY JUST AS SOFT?

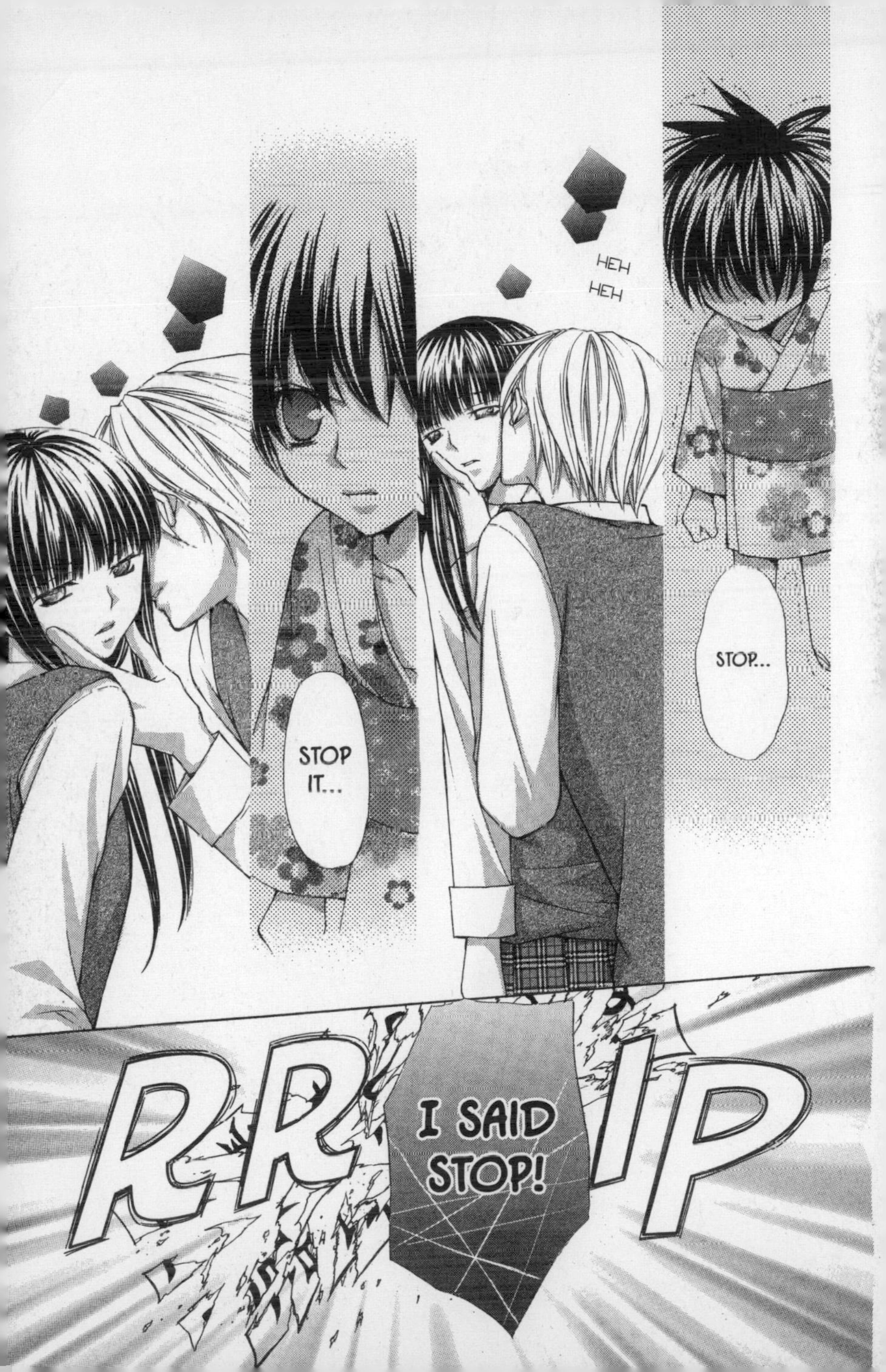
STOP...
HEH
HEH
STOP IT...
RRIP
I SAID STOP!

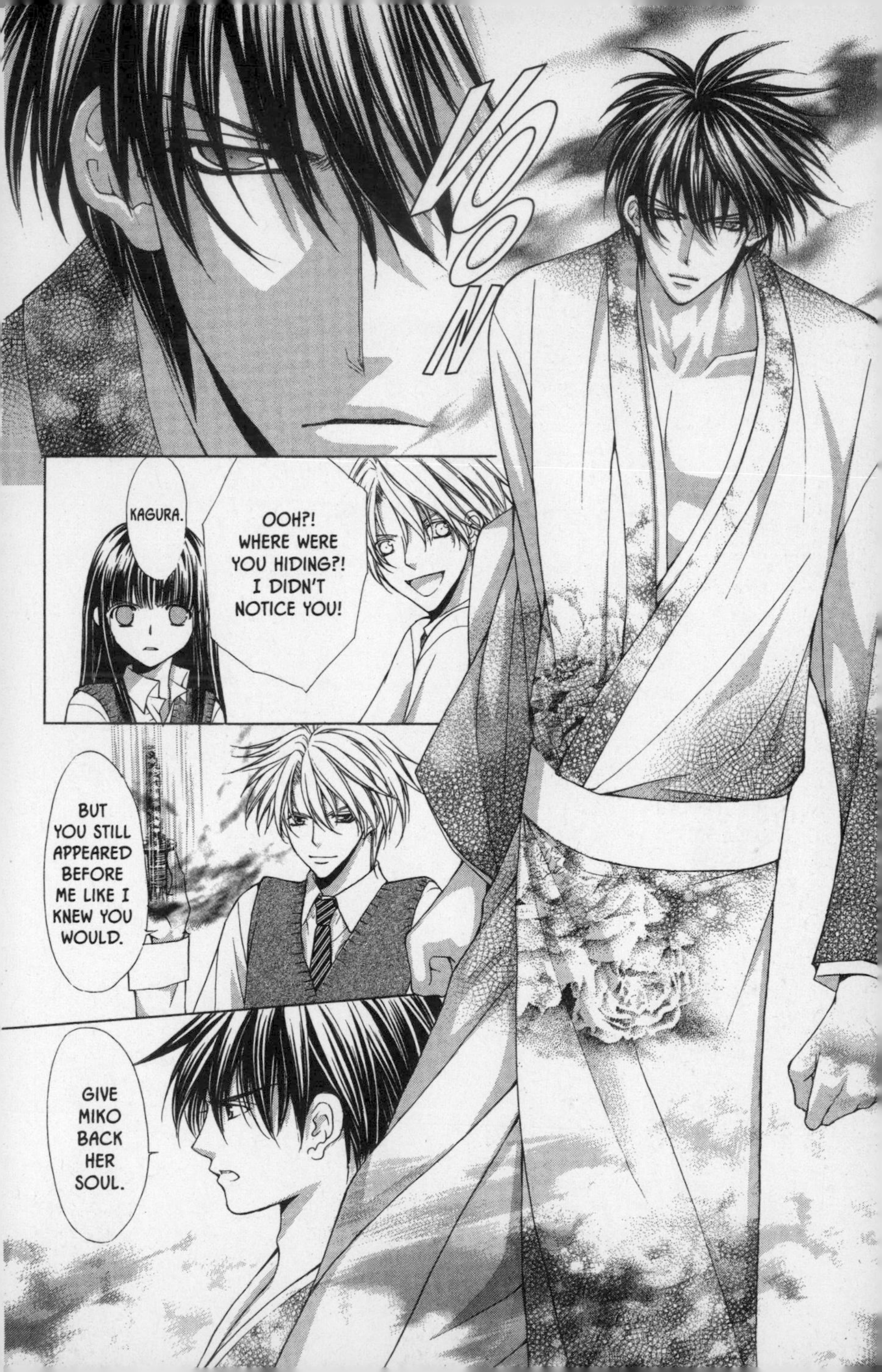
VOOM
KAGURA.
OOH?! WHERE WERE YOU HIDING?! I DIDN'T NOTICE YOU!
BUT YOU STILL APPEARED BEFORE ME LIKE I KNEW YOU WOULD.
GIVE MIKO BACK HER SOUL.

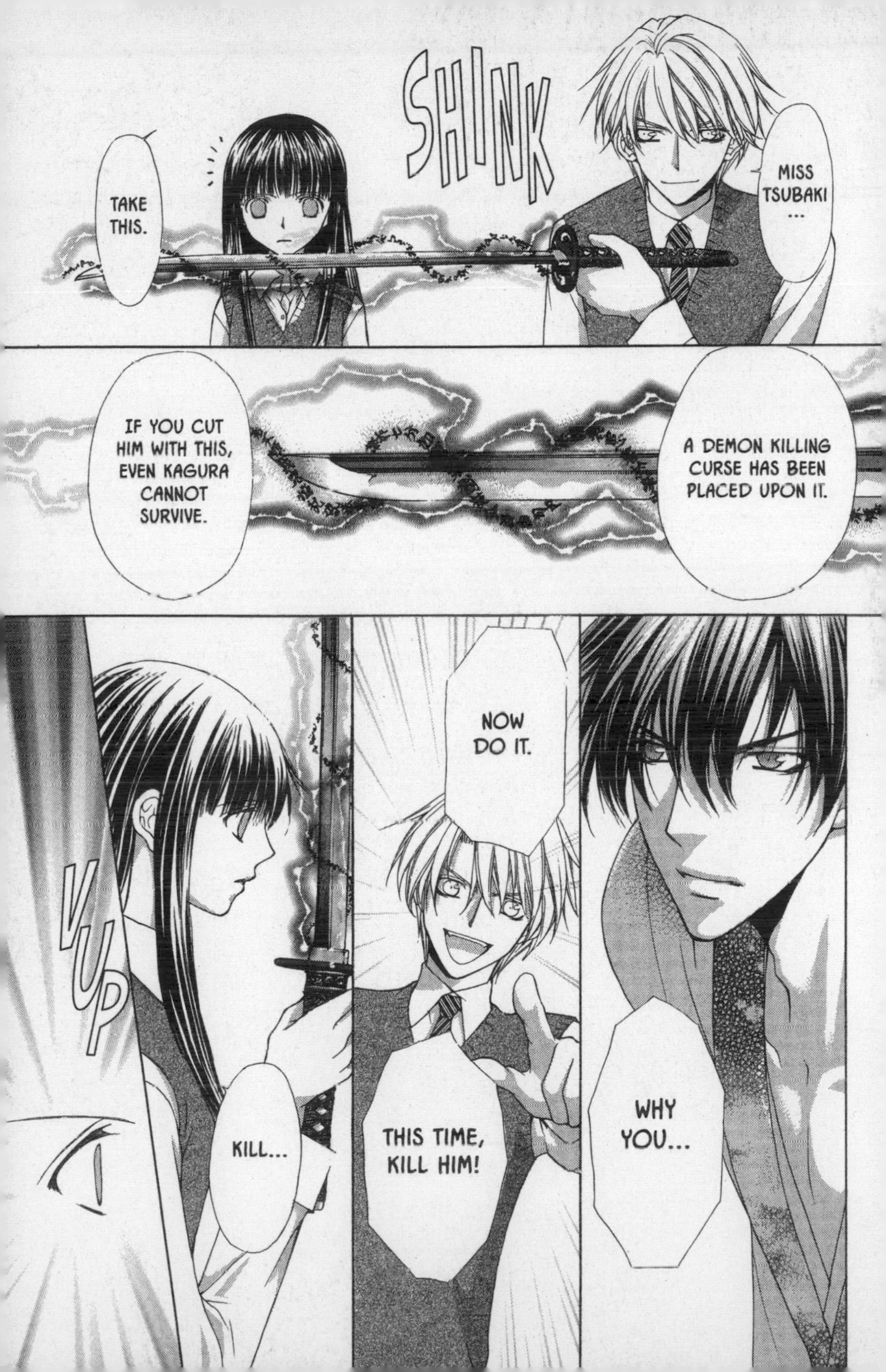
MISS TSUBAKI ...
SHINK
TAKE THIS.
A DEMON KILLING CURSE HAS BEEN PLACED UPON IT.
IF YOU CUT HIM WITH THIS, EVEN KAGURA CANNOT SURVIVE.
WHY YOU...
NOW DO IT.
THIS TIME, KILL HIM!
VUP
KILL...

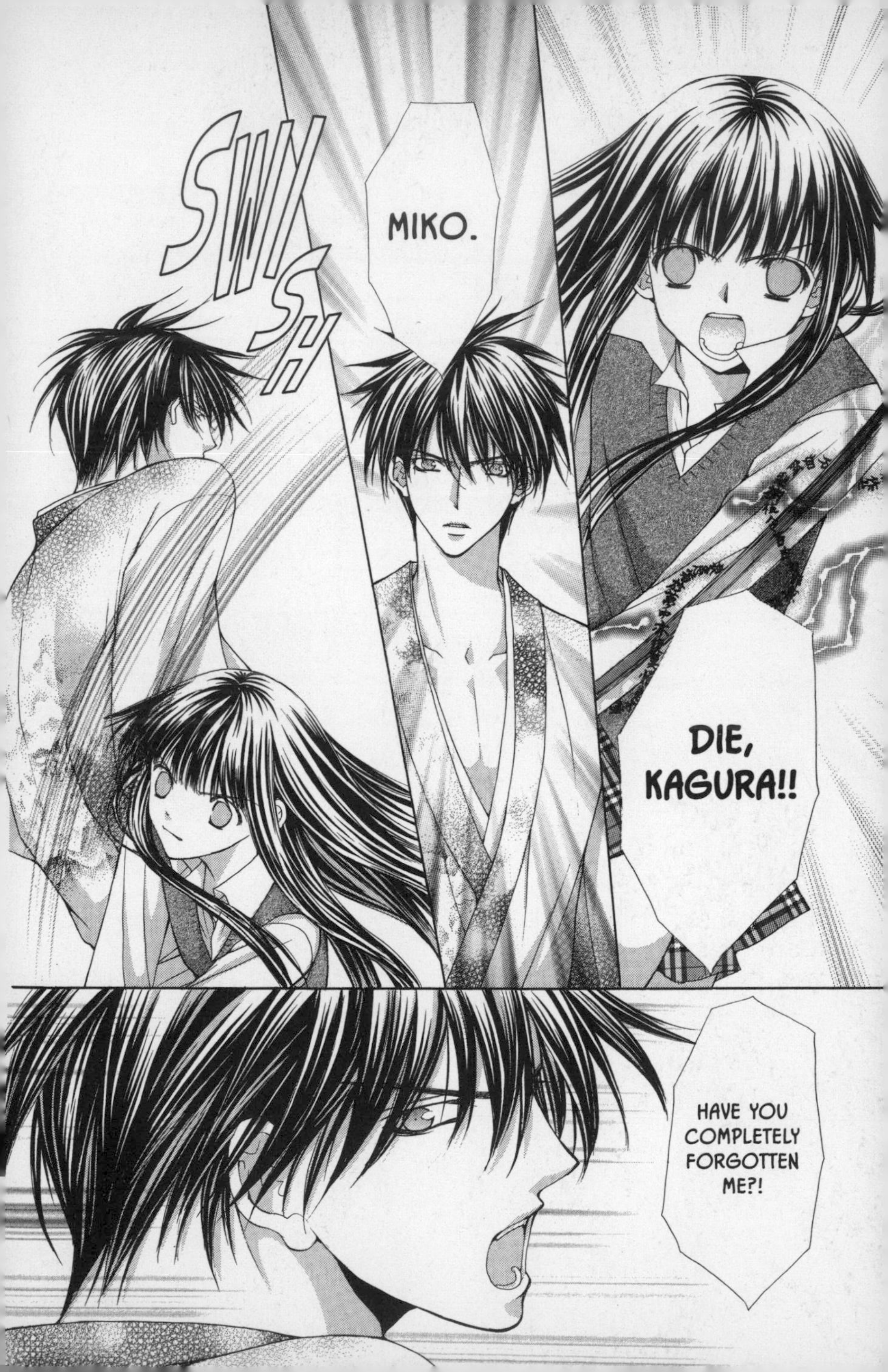
DIE, KAGURA!!
MIKO.
SWISH
HAVE YOU COMPLETELY FORGOTTEN ME?!

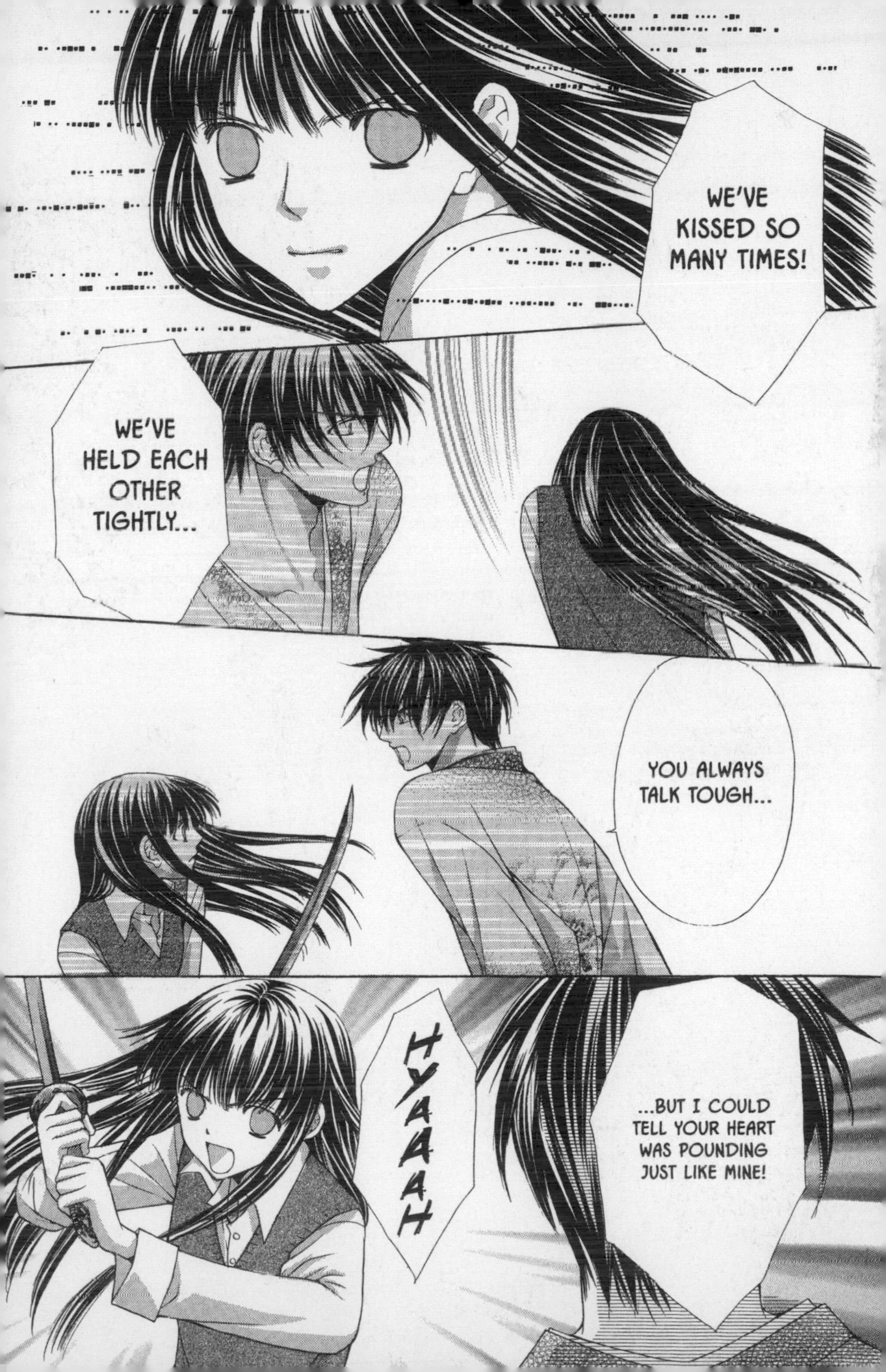
WE'VE KISSED SO MANY TIMES!
WE'VE HELD EACH OTHER TIGHTLY...
YOU ALWAYS TALK TOUGH...
...BUT I COULD TELL YOUR HEART WAS POUNDING JUST LIKE MINE!
HYAAAH

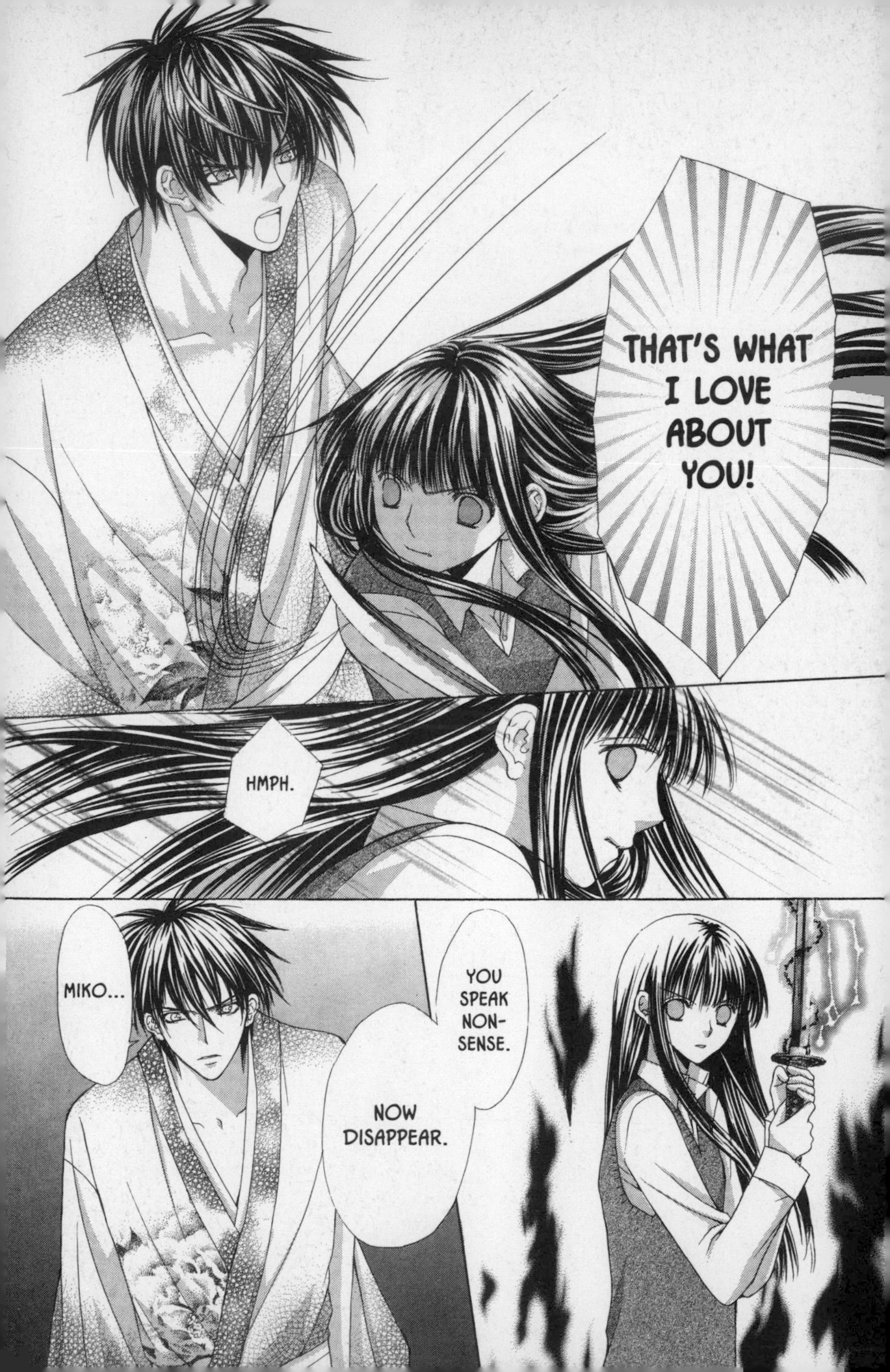
THAT'S WHAT I LOVE ABOUT YOU!
HMPH.
YOU SPEAK NON-SENSE.
NOW DISAPPEAR.
MIKO...

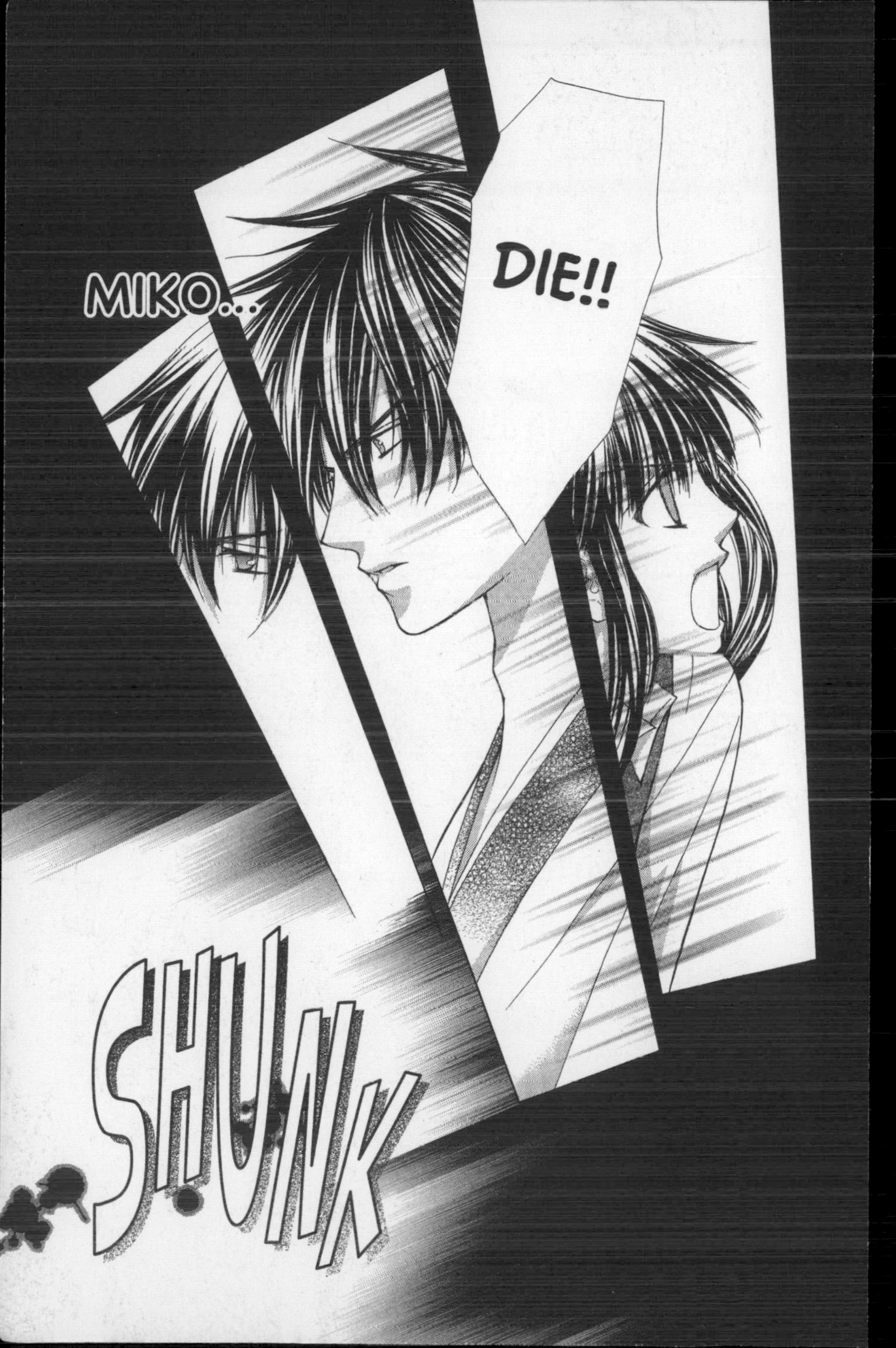
DIE!!
MIKO...
SHUNK

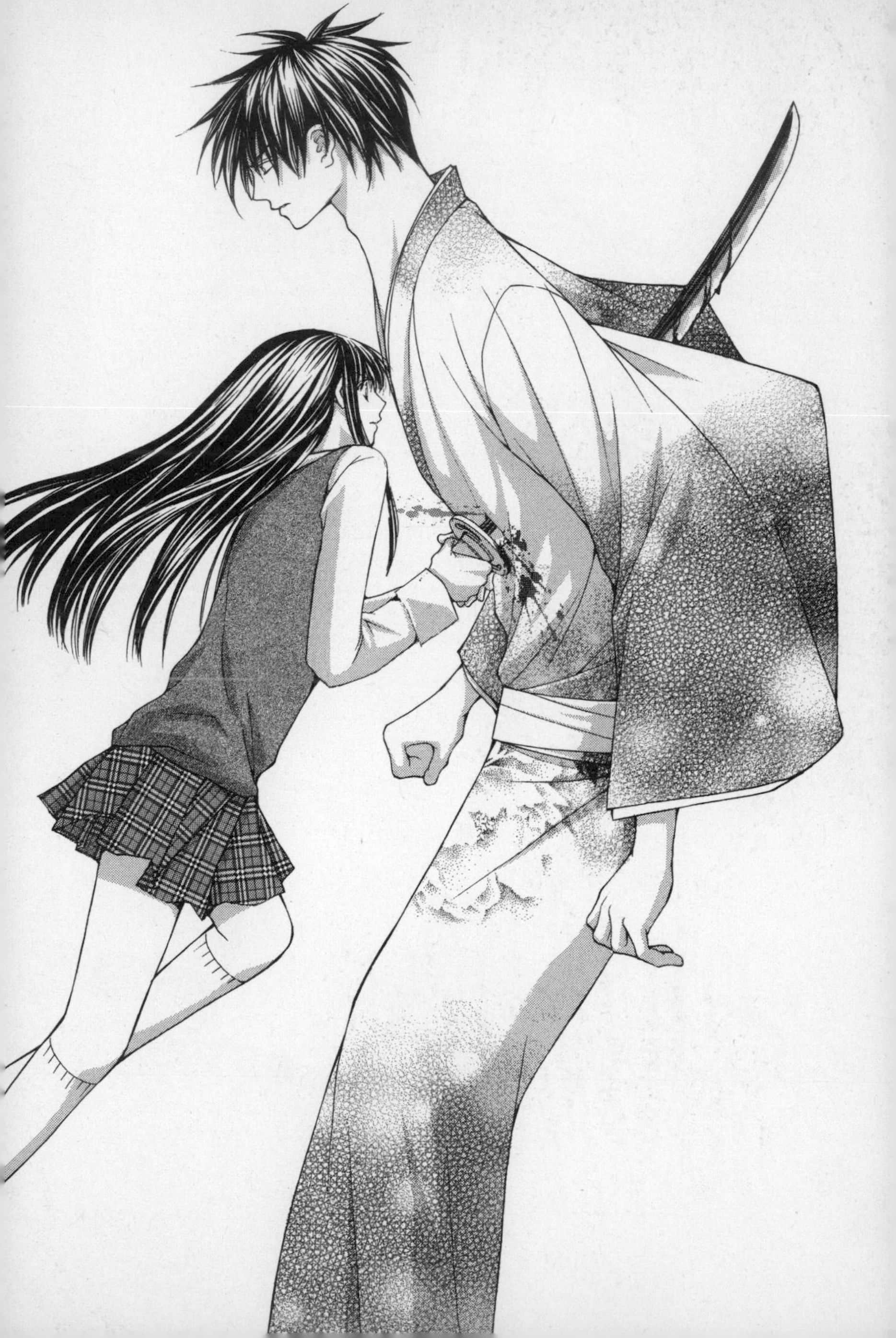

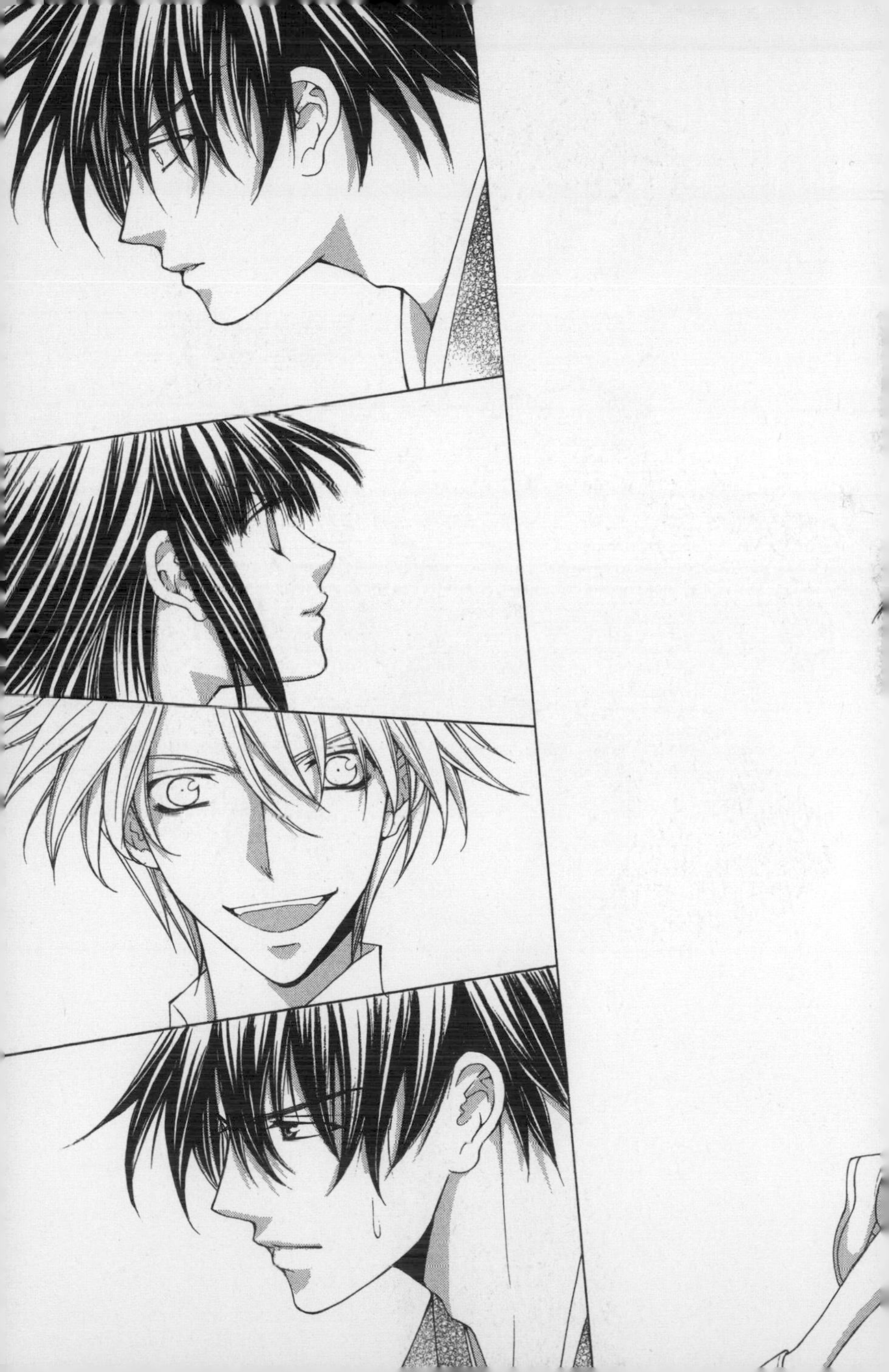

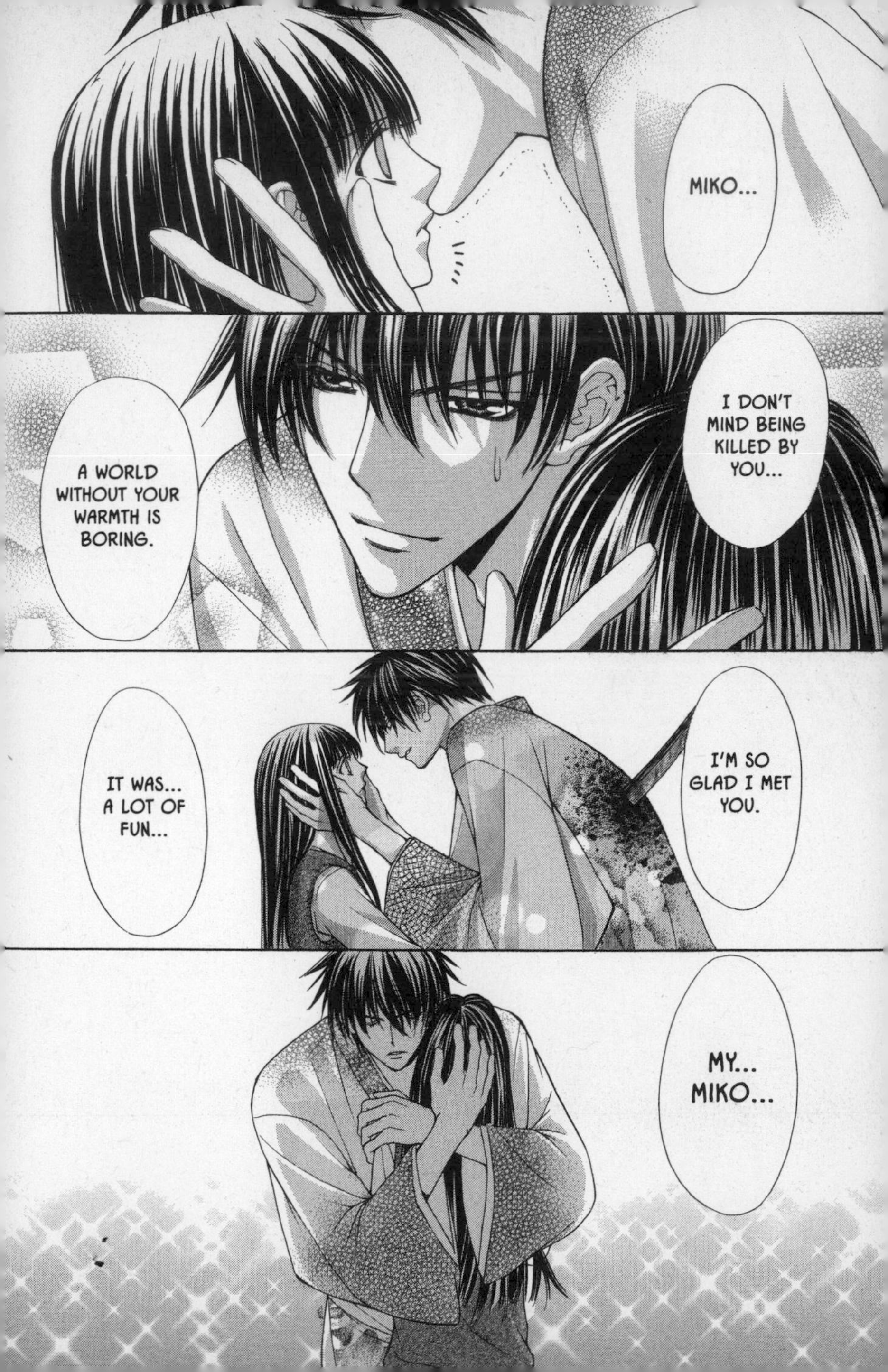
MIKO...
I DON'T MIND BEING KILLED BY YOU...
A WORLD WITHOUT YOUR WARMTH IS BORING.
I'M SO GLAD I MET YOU.
IT WAS... A LOT OF FUN...
MY... MIKO...

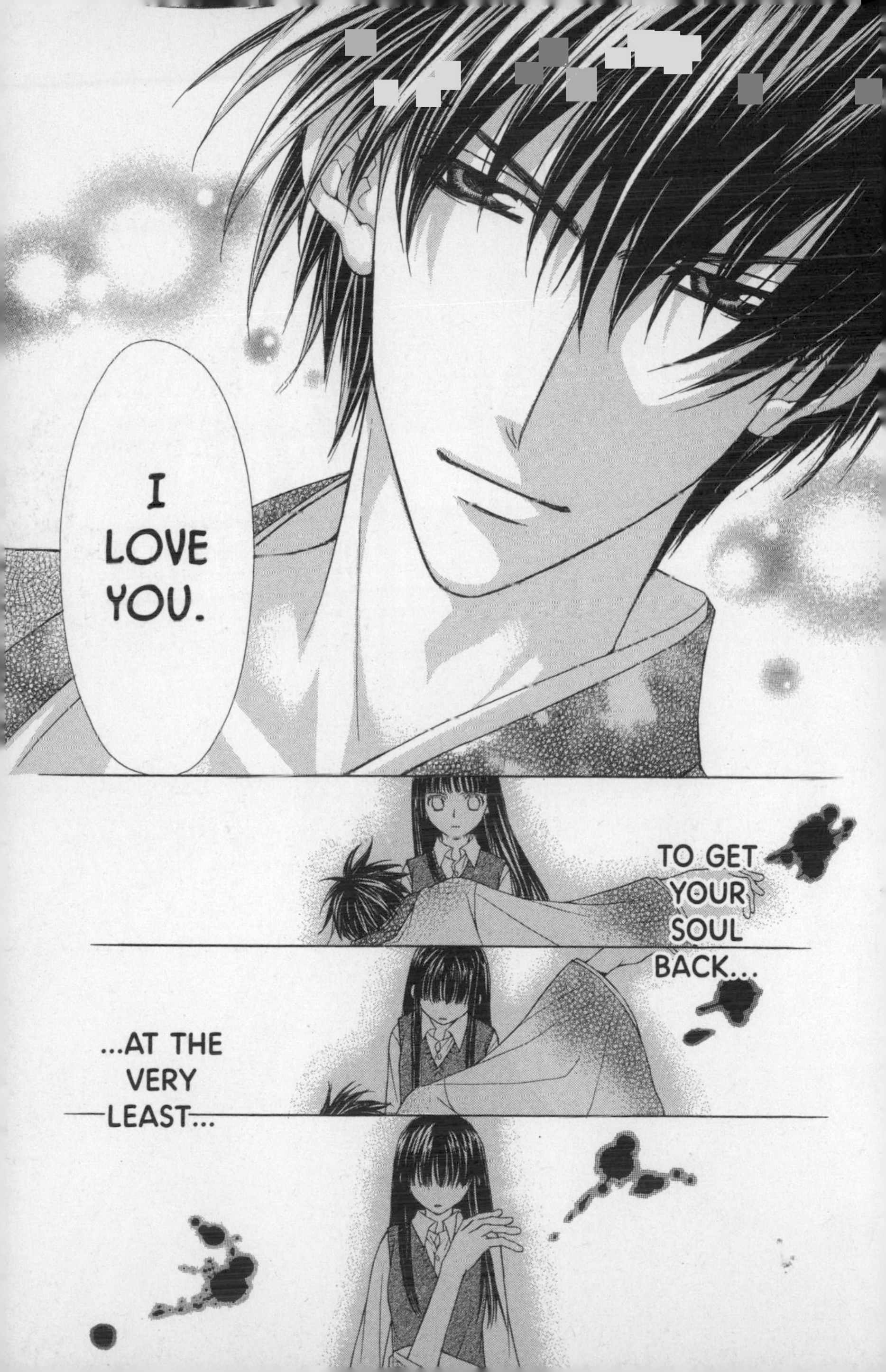
I LOVE YOU.
TO GET YOUR SOUL BACK...
...AT THE VERY LEAST...

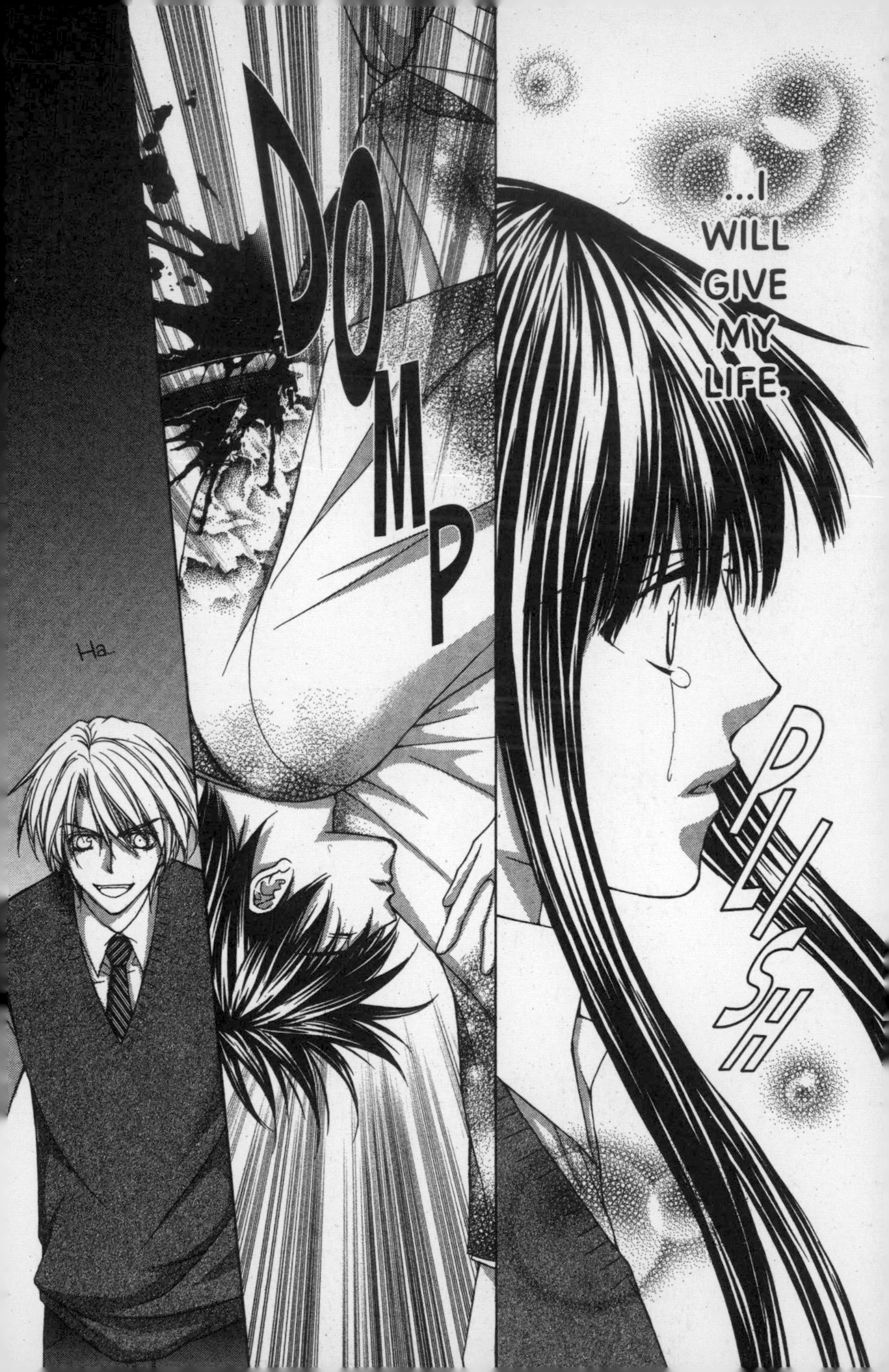
...I WILL GIVE MY LIFE.
PLISH
DOMP
Ha..

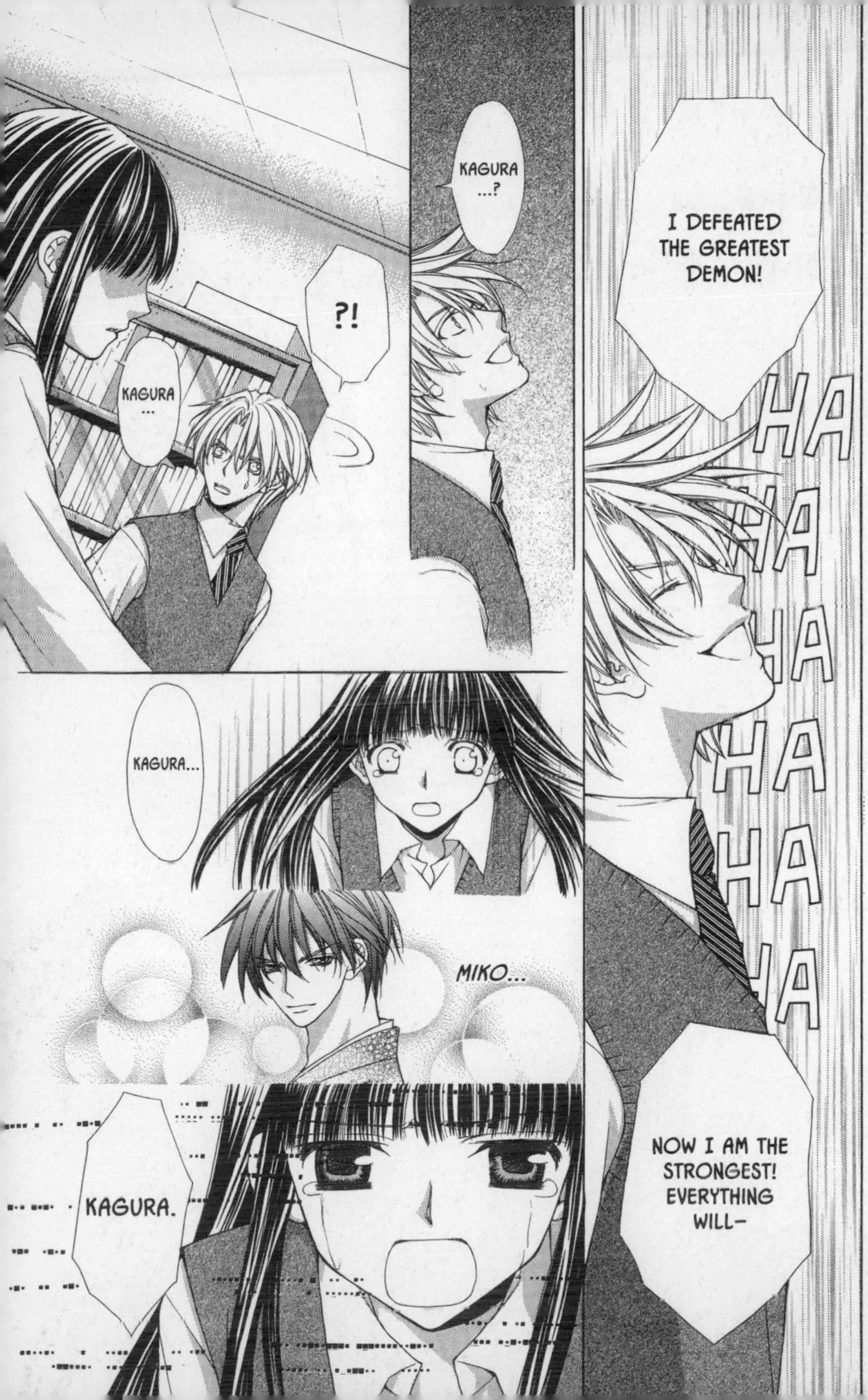

I DEFEATED THE GREATEST DEMON!
HA HA HA HA HA HA HA
NOW I AM THE STRONGEST! EVERYTHING WILL–
KAGURA ...?
?!
KAGURA ...
KAGURA...
MIKO...
KAGURA.

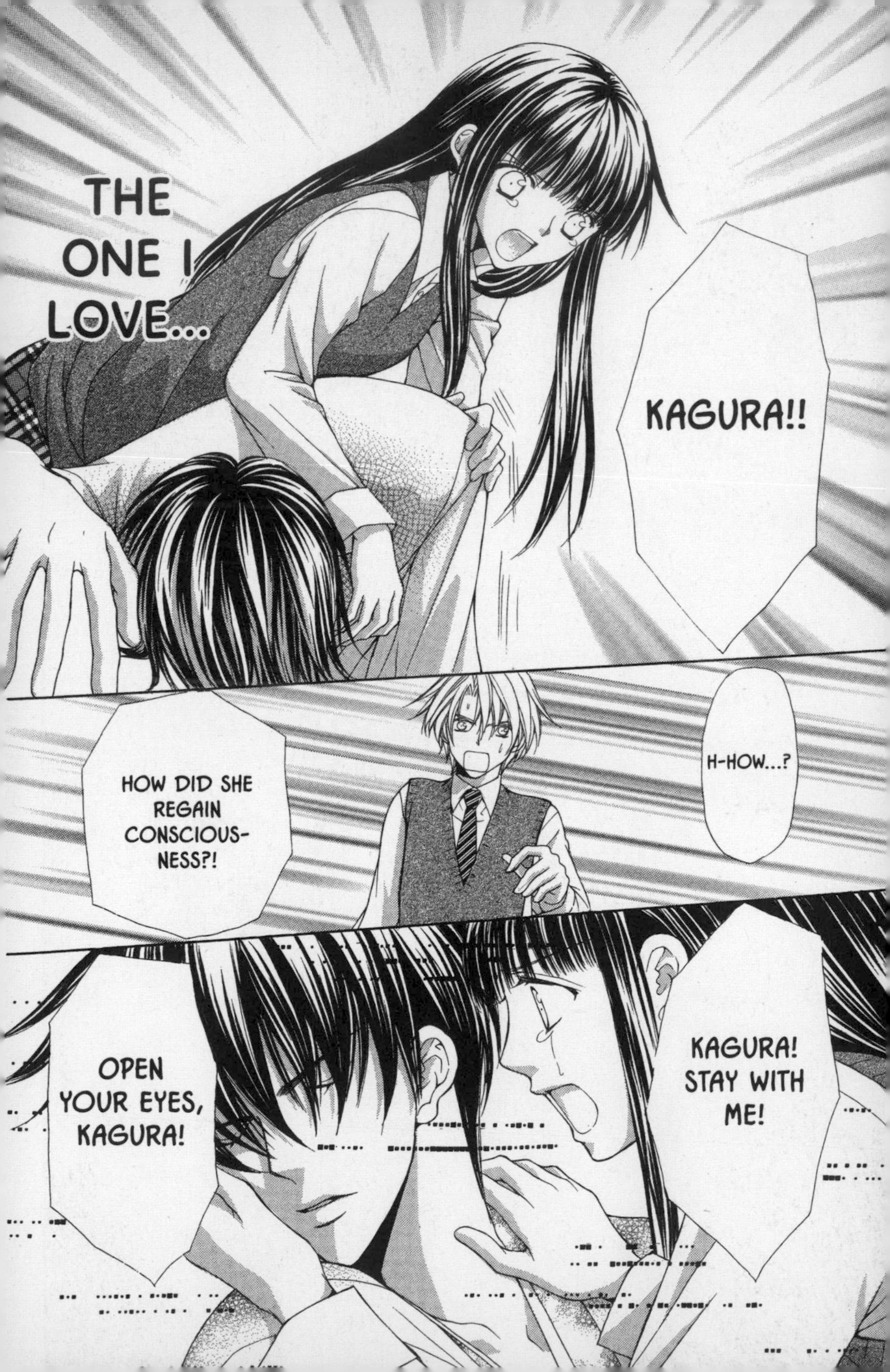
KAGURA!!
THE ONE I LOVE...
H-HOW...?
HOW DID SHE REGAIN CONSCIOUS-NESS?!
KAGURA! STAY WITH ME!
OPEN YOUR EYES, KAGURA!

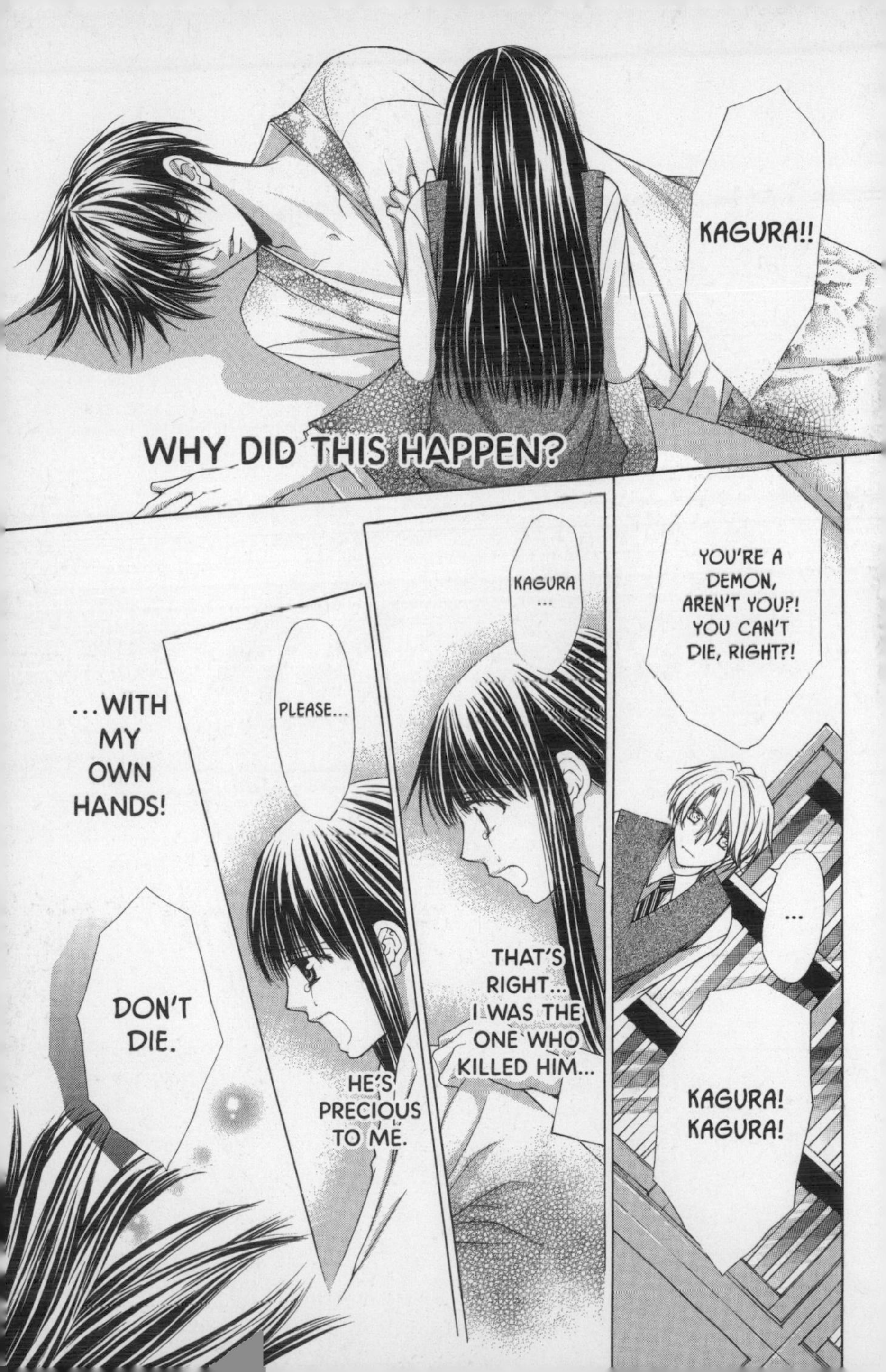
KAGURA!!
WHY DID THIS HAPPEN?
YOU'RE A DEMON, AREN'T YOU?! YOU CAN'T DIE, RIGHT?!
...
KAGURA! KAGURA!
KAGURA ...
THAT'S RIGHT... I WAS THE ONE WHO KILLED HIM...
...WITH MY OWN HANDS!
PLEASE...
HE'S PRECIOUS TO ME.
DON'T DIE.

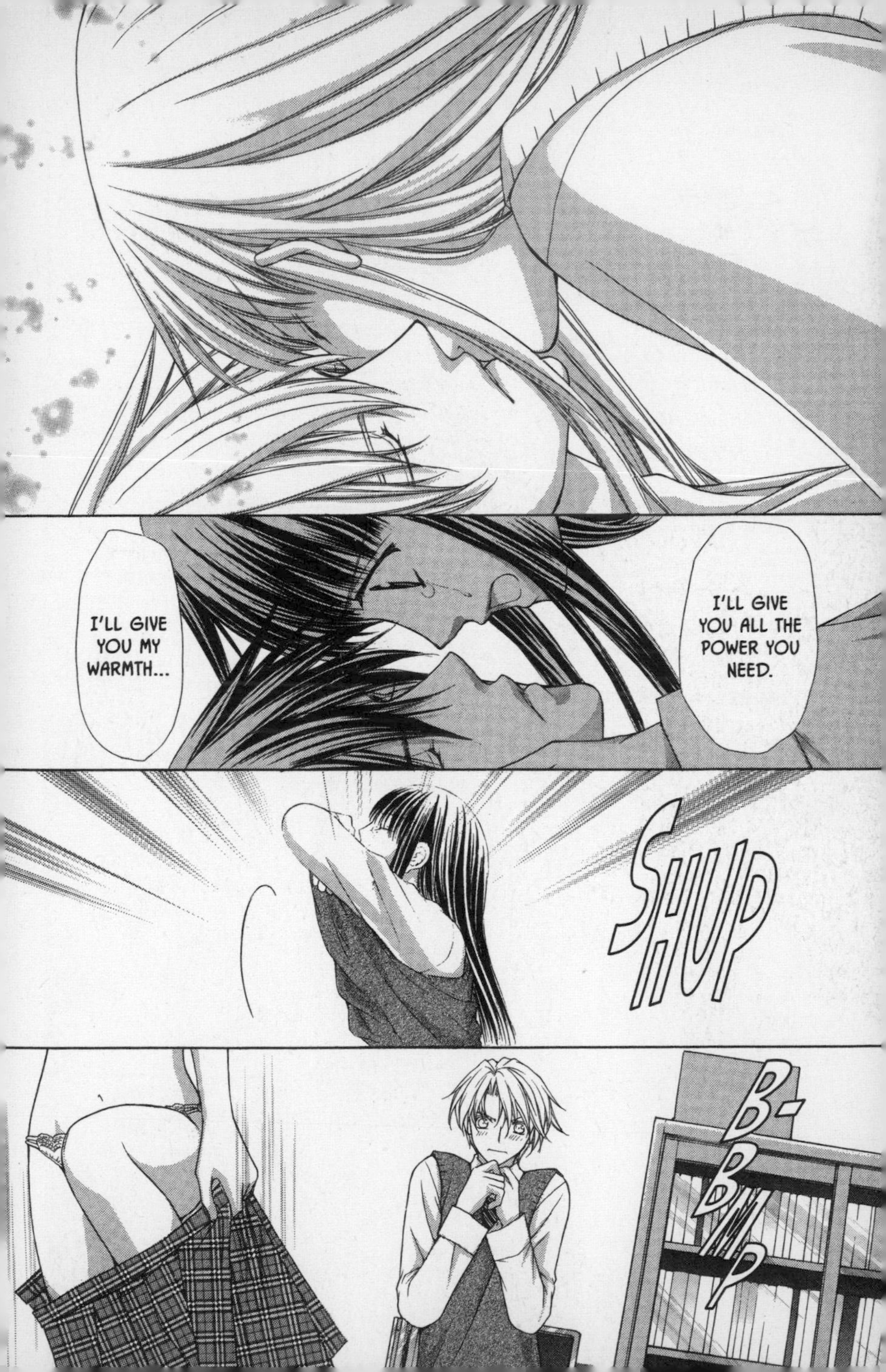
I'LL GIVE YOU ALL THE POWER YOU NEED.
I'LL GIVE YOU MY WARMTH...
SHUP
B-B-BMP

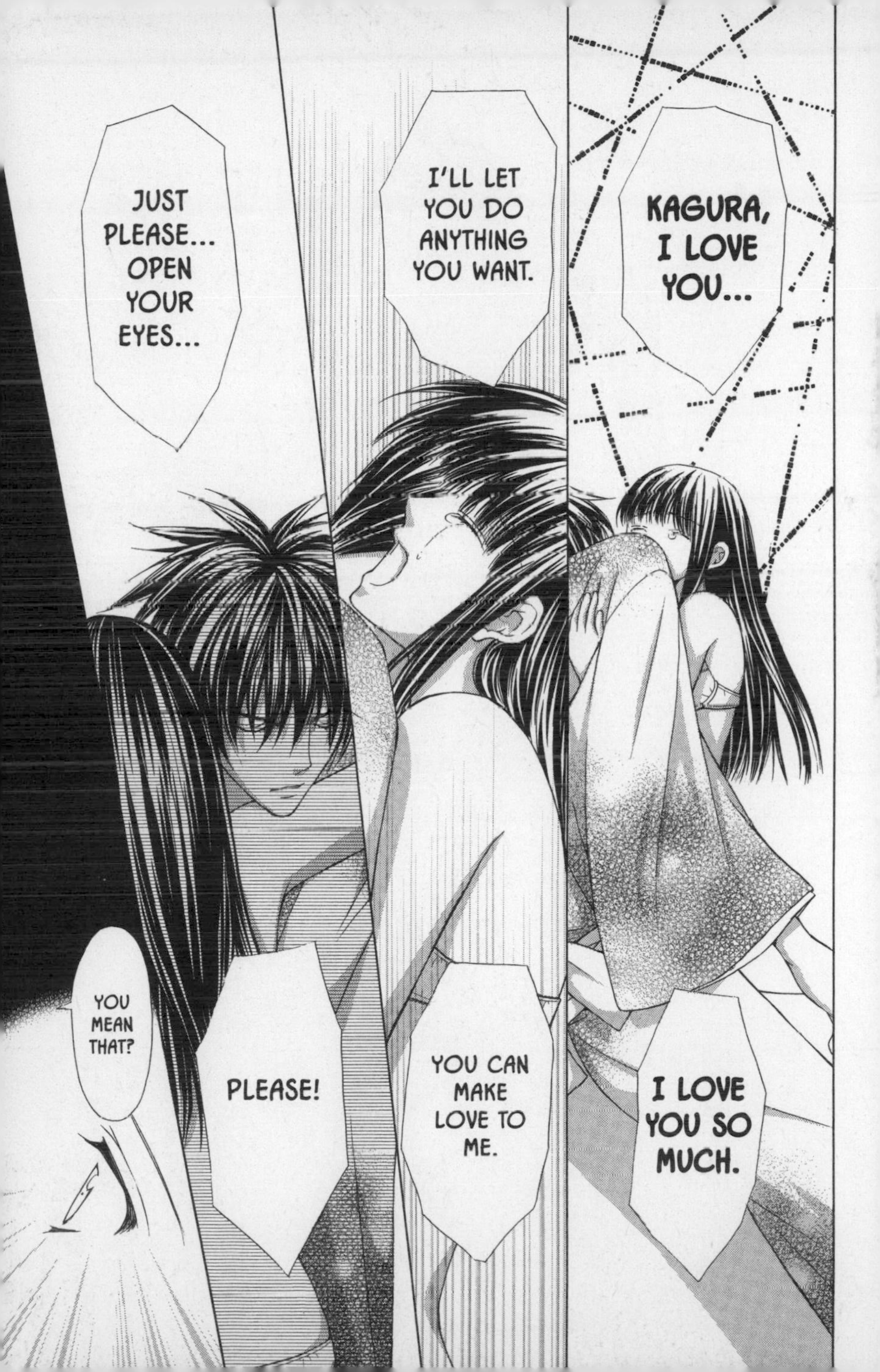
KAGURA, I LOVE YOU...
I LOVE YOU SO MUCH.
I'LL LET YOU DO ANYTHING YOU WANT.
YOU CAN MAKE LOVE TO ME.
JUST PLEASE... OPEN YOUR EYES...
PLEASE!
YOU MEAN THAT?

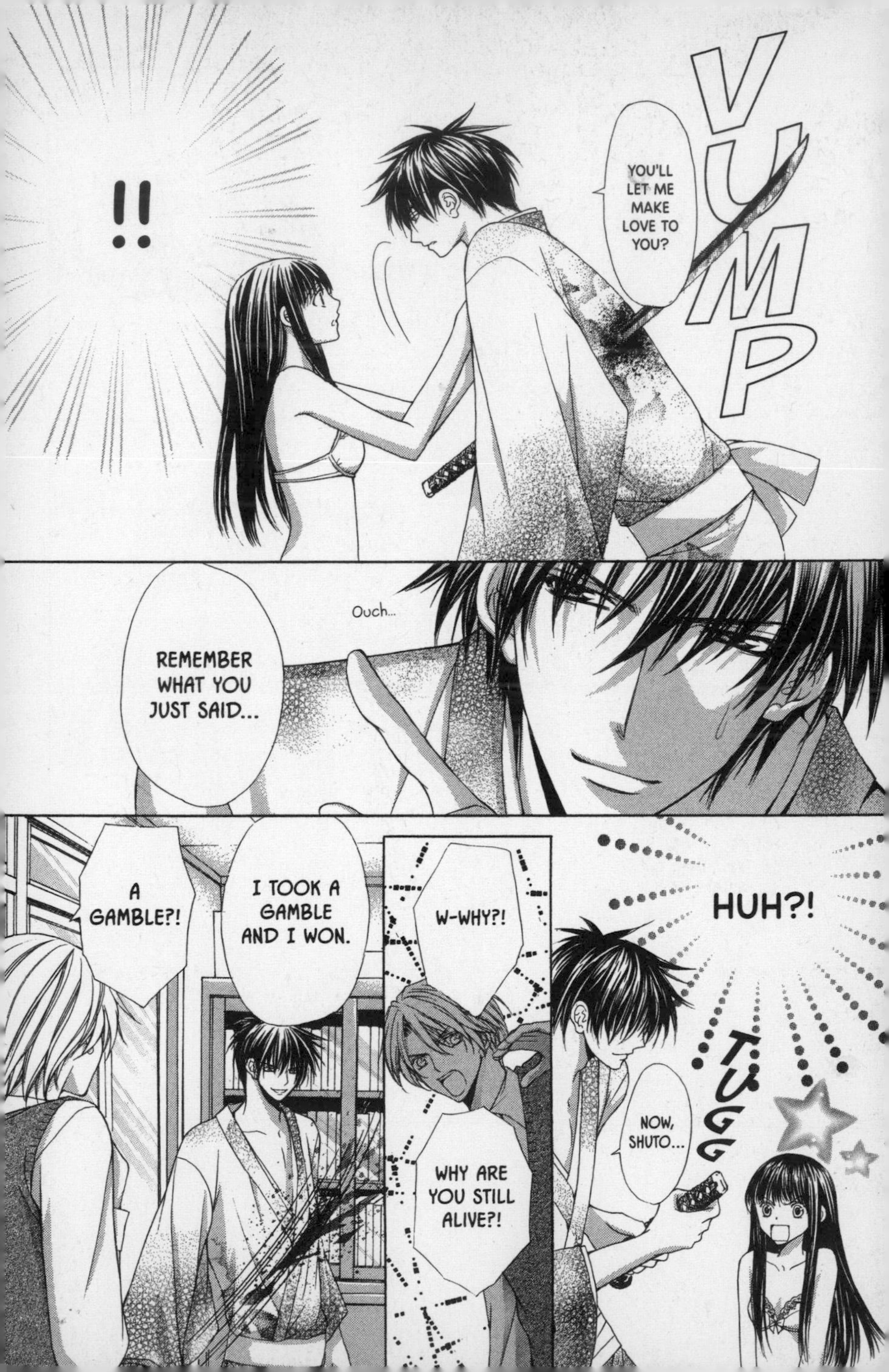
VUMP
YOU'LL LET ME MAKE LOVE TO YOU?
!!
Ouch...
REMEMBER WHAT YOU JUST SAID...
HUH?!
TUGG
NOW, SHUTO...
W-WHY?!
WHY ARE YOU STILL ALIVE?!
I TOOK A GAMBLE AND I WON.
A GAMBLE?!

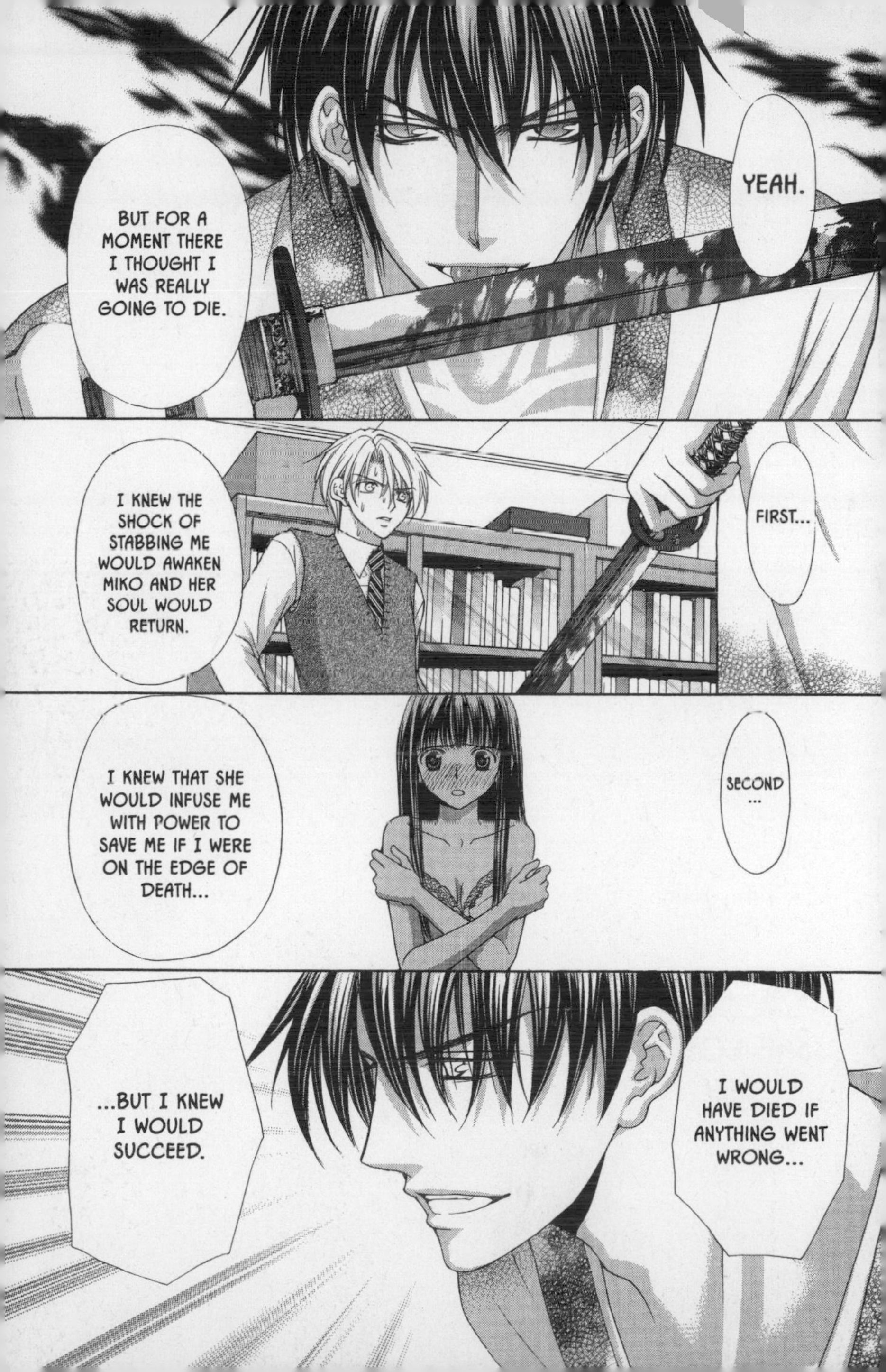
YEAH.
BUT FOR A MOMENT THERE I THOUGHT I WAS REALLY GOING TO DIE.
FIRST...
I KNEW THE SHOCK OF STABBING ME WOULD AWAKEN MIKO AND HER SOUL WOULD RETURN.
SECOND...
I KNEW THAT SHE WOULD INFUSE ME WITH POWER TO SAVE ME IF I WERE ON THE EDGE OF DEATH...
I WOULD HAVE DIED IF ANYTHING WENT WRONG...
...BUT I KNEW I WOULD SUCCEED.

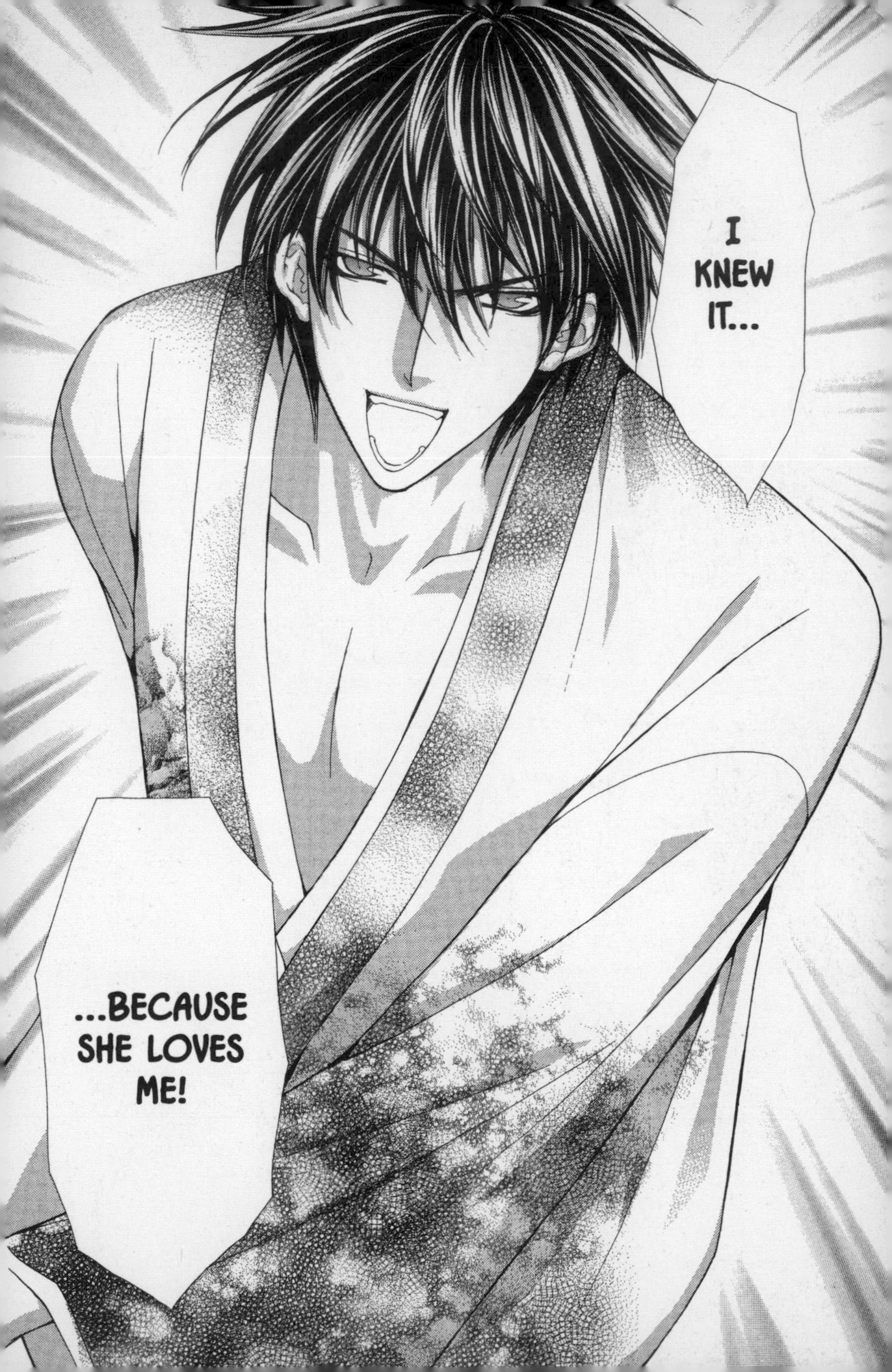
I KNEW IT...
...BECAUSE SHE LOVES ME!

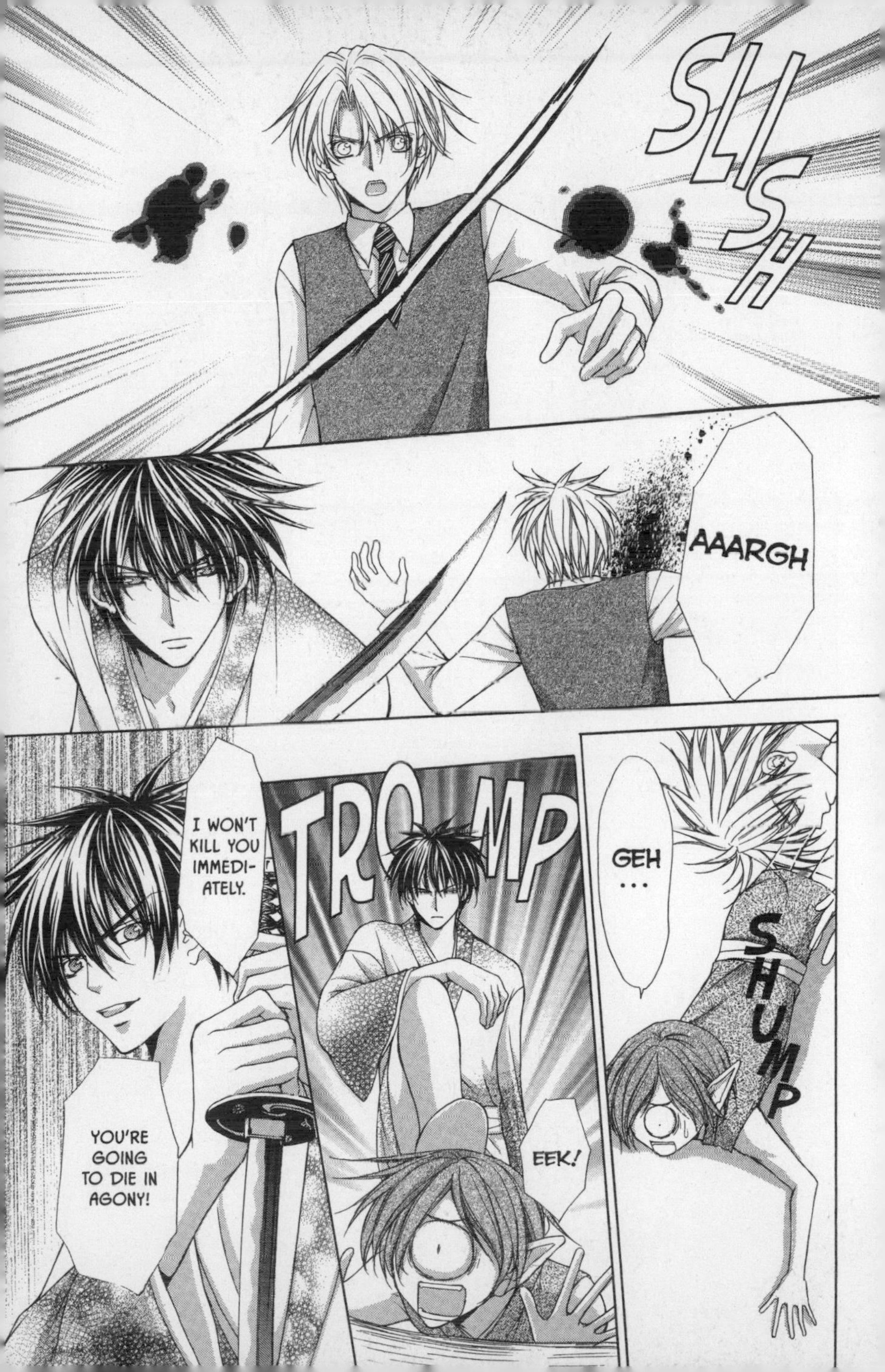
SLISH
AAARGH
GEH...
SHUMP
TROMP
EEK!
I WON'T KILL YOU IMMEDI-ATELY.
YOU'RE GOING TO DIE IN AGONY!

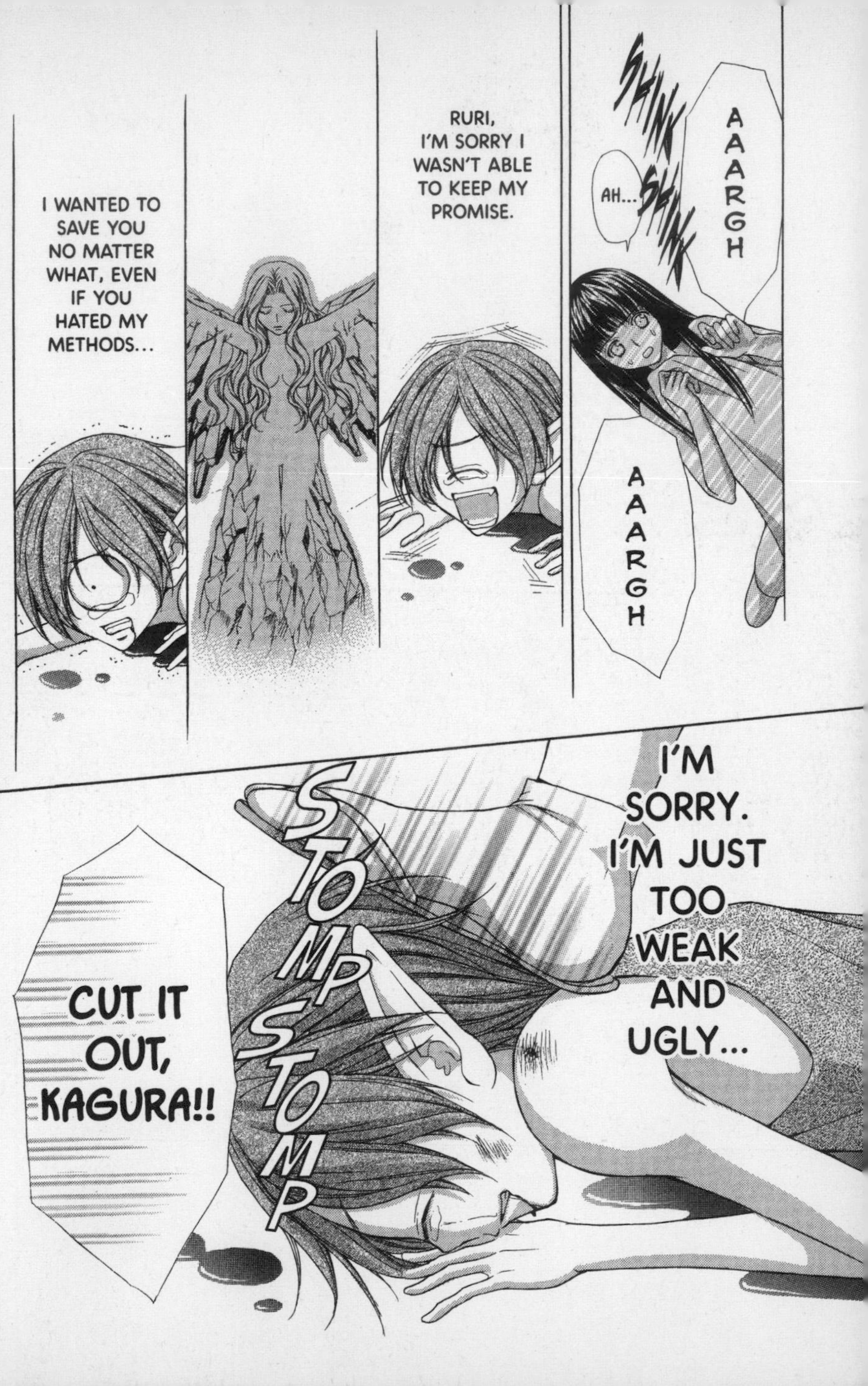
AAARGH
SKINK SKINK
AH...
AAARGH
RURI, I'M SORRY I WASN'T ABLE TO KEEP MY PROMISE.
I WANTED TO SAVE YOU NO MATTER WHAT, EVEN IF YOU HATED MY METHODS...
I'M SORRY. I'M JUST TOO WEAK AND UGLY...
STOMP STOMP
CUT IT OUT, KAGURA!!

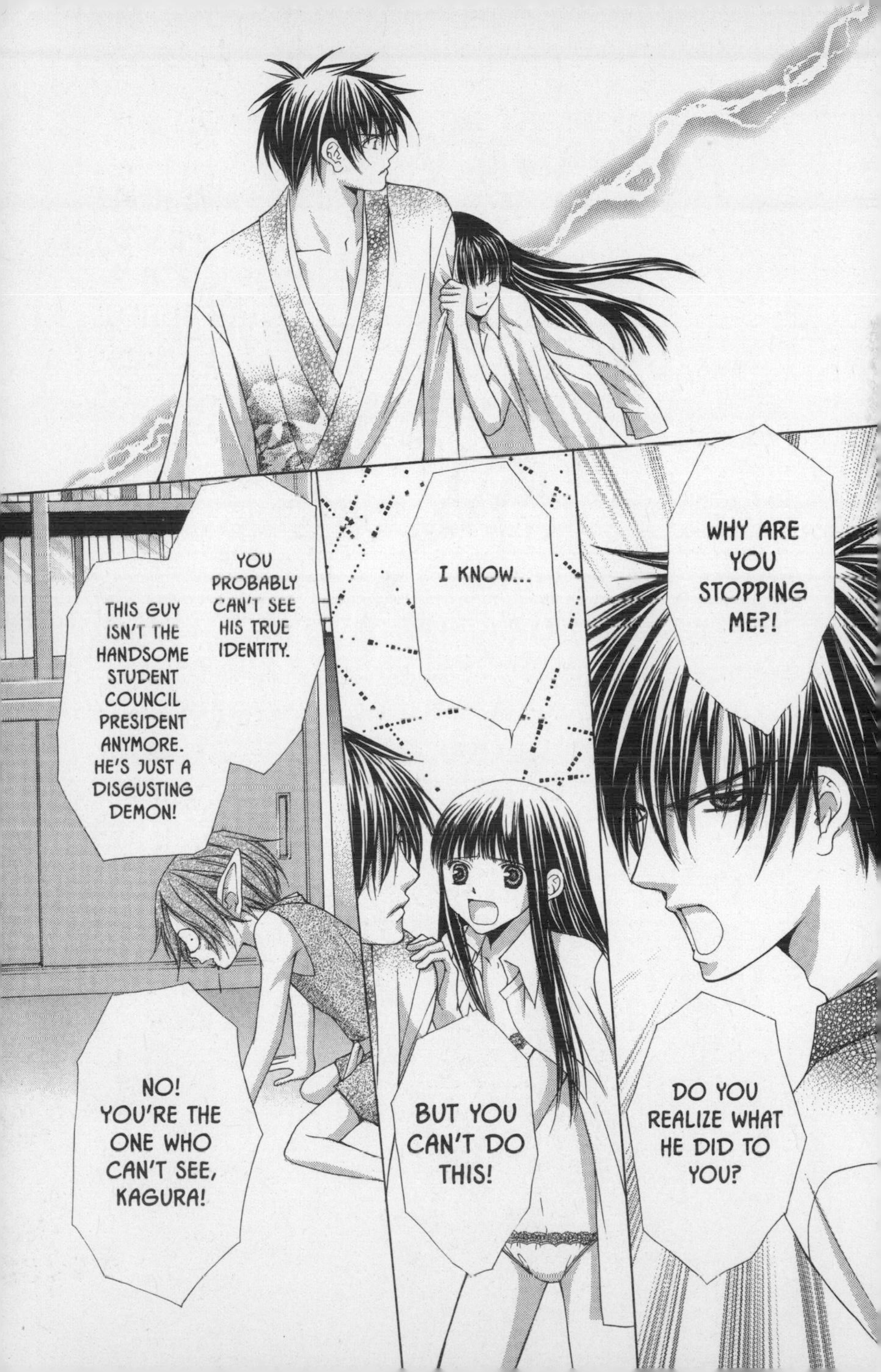
WHY ARE YOU STOPPING ME?!
DO YOU REALIZE WHAT HE DID TO YOU?
I KNOW...
BUT YOU CAN'T DO THIS!
YOU PROBABLY CAN'T SEE HIS TRUE IDENTITY.
THIS GUY ISN'T THE HANDSOME STUDENT COUNCIL PRESIDENT ANYMORE. HE'S JUST A DISGUSTING DEMON!
NO! YOU'RE THE ONE WHO CAN'T SEE, KAGURA!

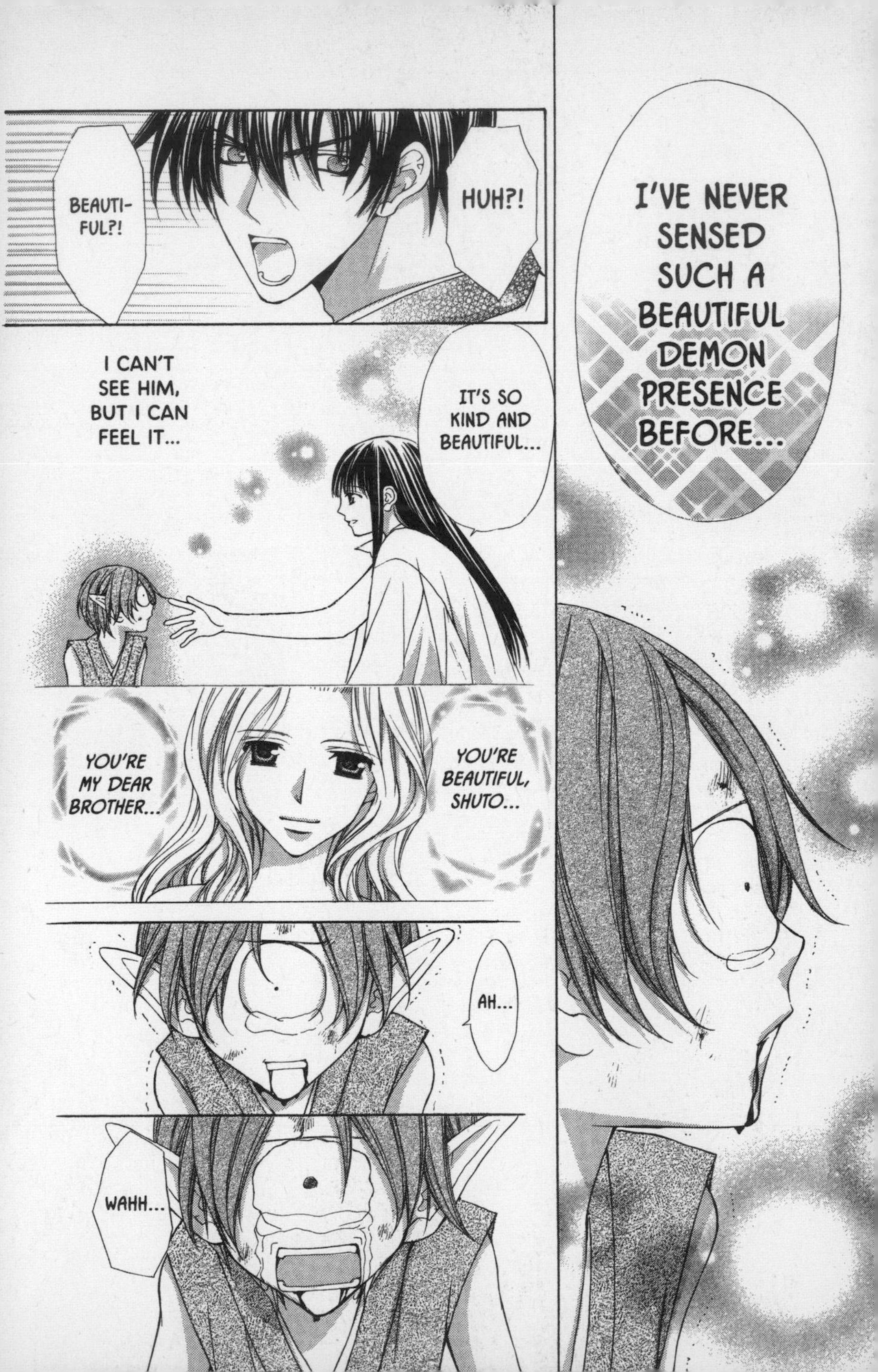
I'VE NEVER SENSED SUCH A BEAUTIFUL DEMON PRESENCE BEFORE...
HUH?!
BEAUTI-FUL?!
IT'S SO KIND AND BEAUTIFUL...
I CAN'T SEE HIM, BUT I CAN FEEL IT...
YOU'RE BEAUTIFUL, SHUTO...
YOU'RE MY DEAR BROTHER...
AH...
WAHH...

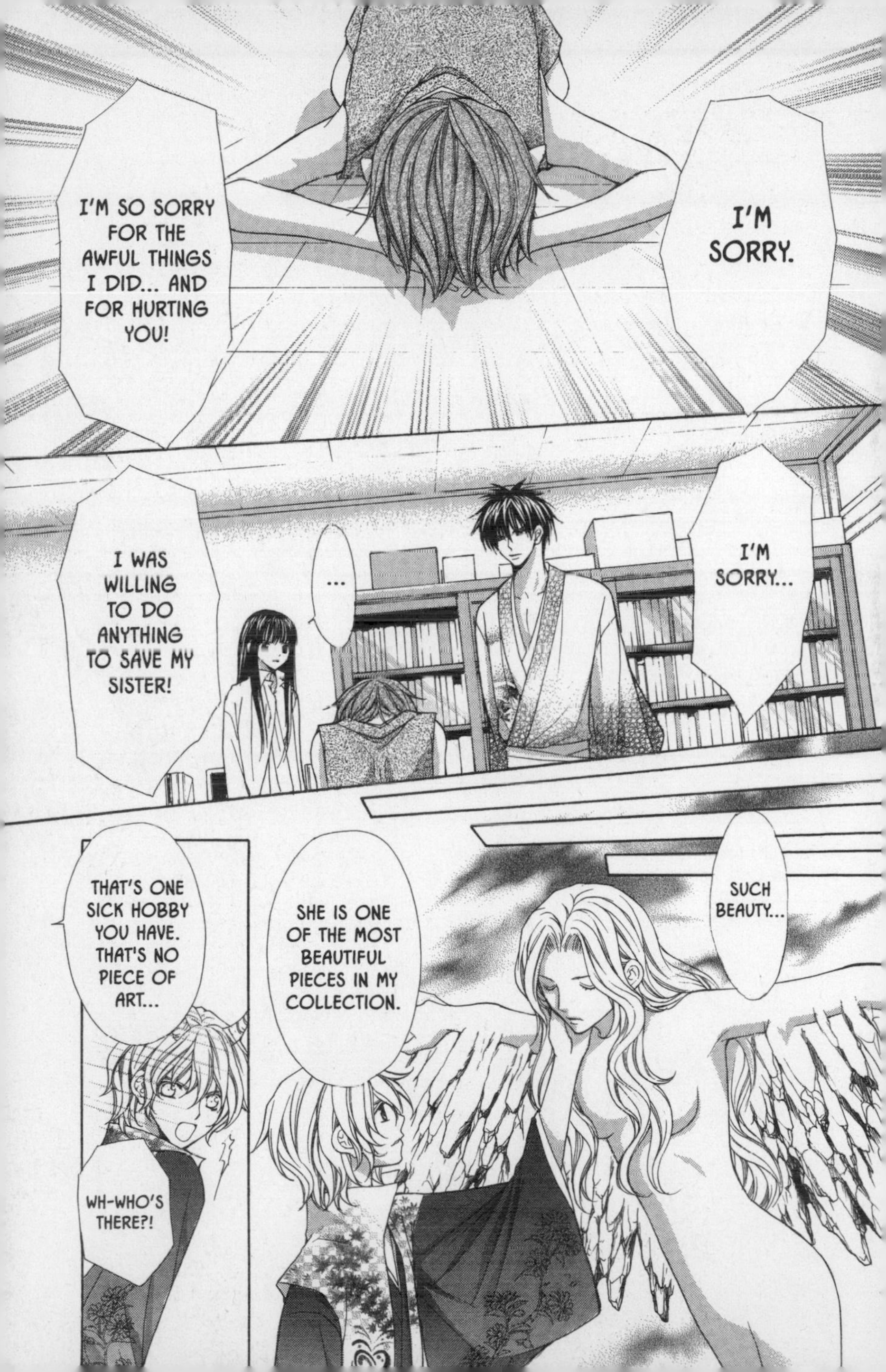
I'M SORRY.
I'M SO SORRY FOR THE AWFUL THINGS I DID... AND FOR HURTING YOU!
I'M SORRY...
...
I WAS WILLING TO DO ANYTHING TO SAVE MY SISTER!
SUCH BEAUTY...
SHE IS ONE OF THE MOST BEAUTIFUL PIECES IN MY COLLECTION.
THAT'S ONE SICK HOBBY YOU HAVE. THAT'S NO PIECE OF ART...
WH-WHO'S THERE?!

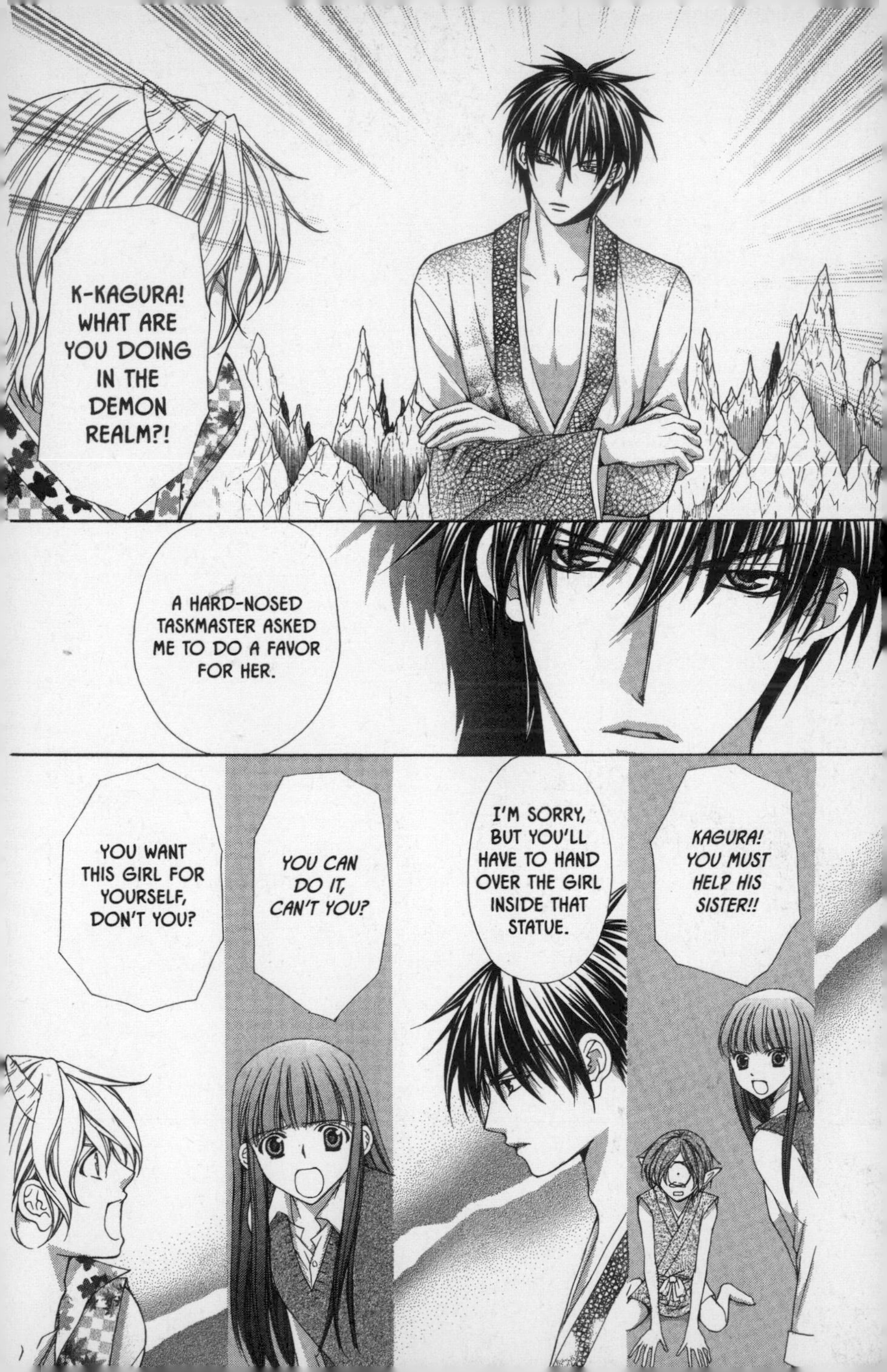
K-KAGURA! WHAT ARE YOU DOING IN THE DEMON REALM?!
A HARD-NOSED TASKMASTER ASKED ME TO DO A FAVOR FOR HER.
KAGURA! YOU MUST HELP HIS SISTER!!
I'M SORRY, BUT YOU'LL HAVE TO HAND OVER THE GIRL INSIDE THAT STATUE.
YOU CAN DO IT, CAN'T YOU?
YOU WANT THIS GIRL FOR YOURSELF, DON'T YOU?

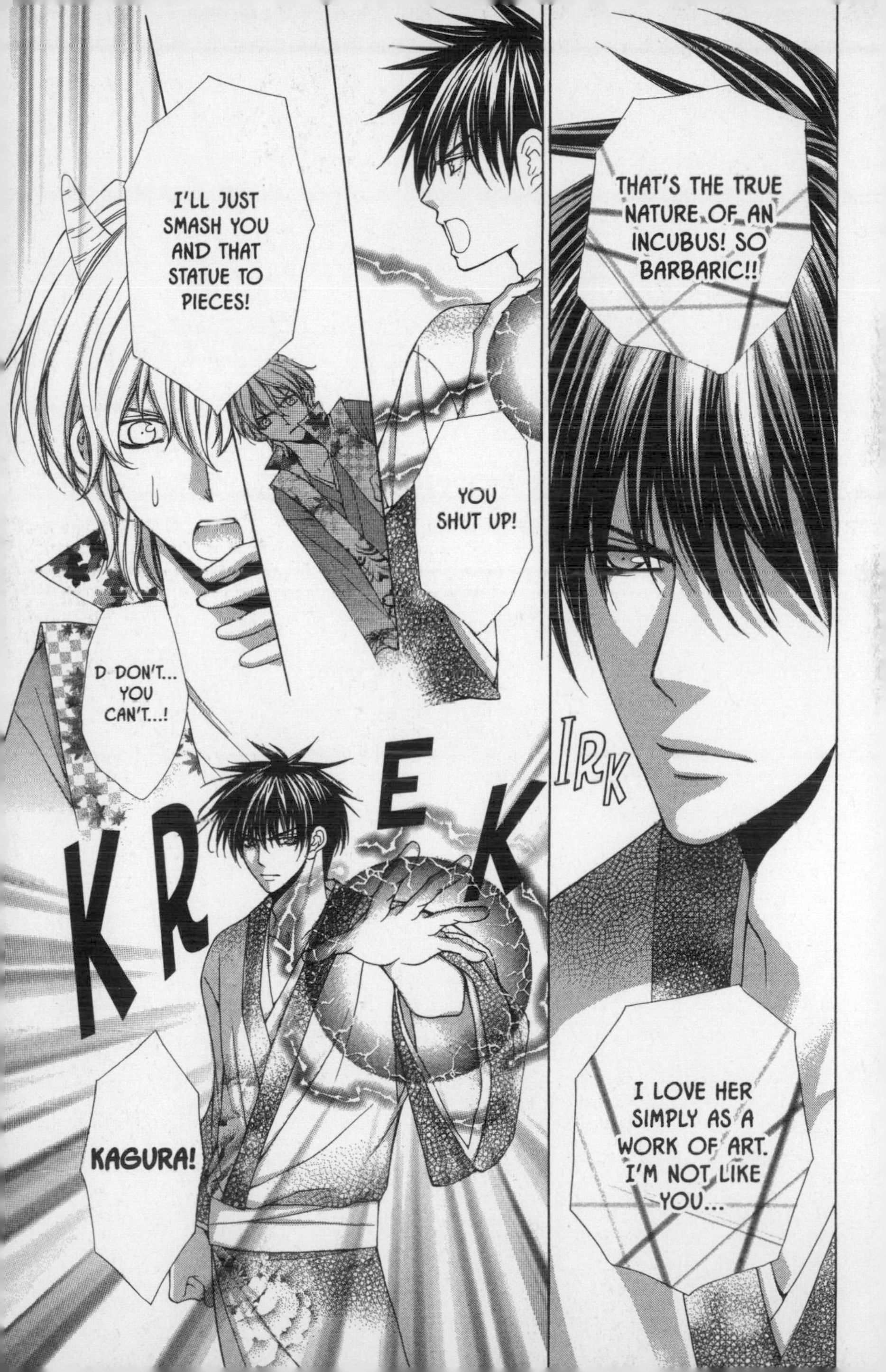

THAT'S THE TRUE NATURE OF AN INCUBUS! SO BARBARIC!!
IRK
I LOVE HER SIMPLY AS A WORK OF ART. I'M NOT LIKE YOU...
YOU SHUT UP!
I'LL JUST SMASH YOU AND THAT STATUE TO PIECES!
D DON'T... YOU CAN'T...!
KREEK
KAGURA!

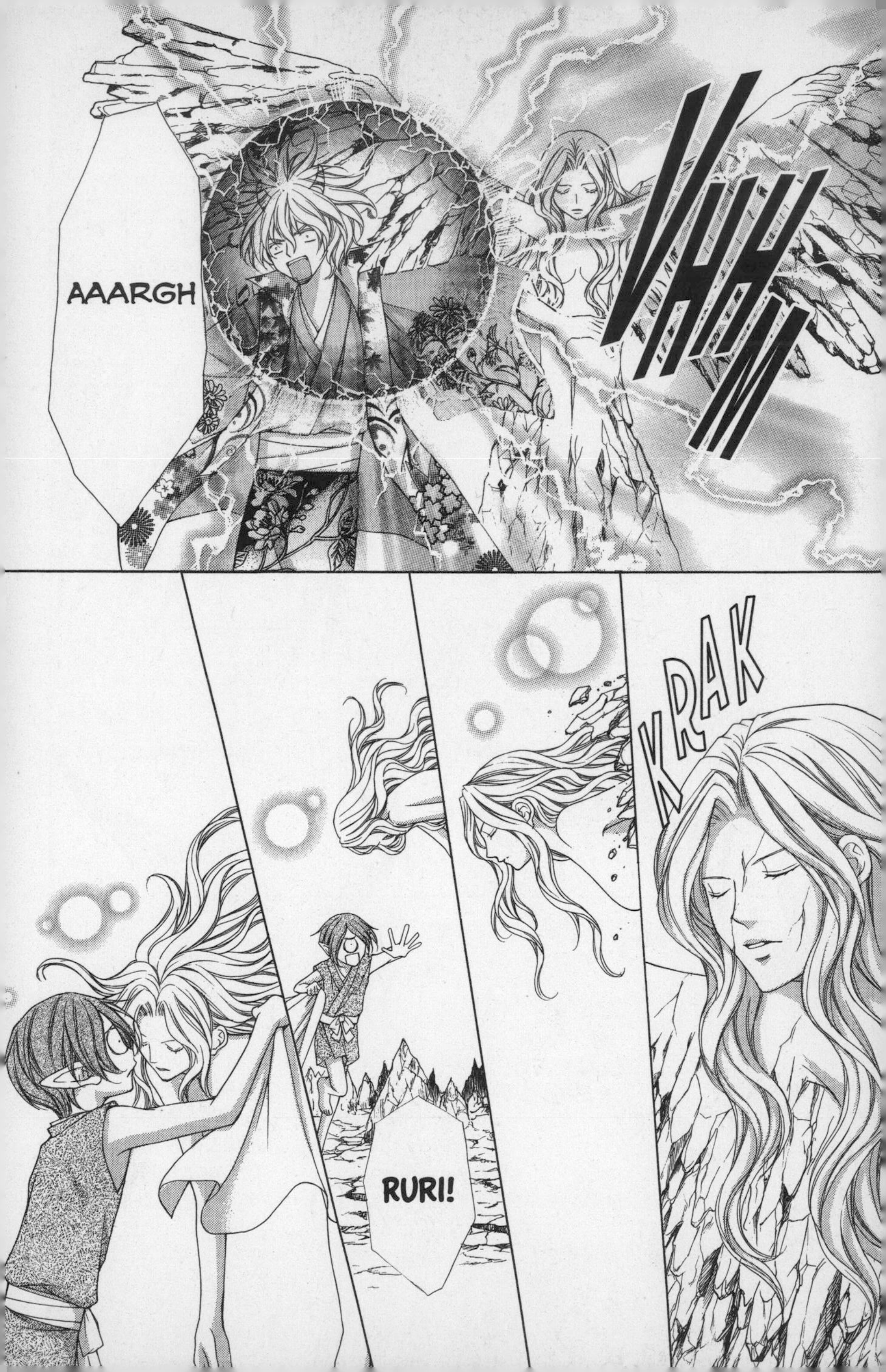
VHHM
AAARGH
KRAK
RURI!

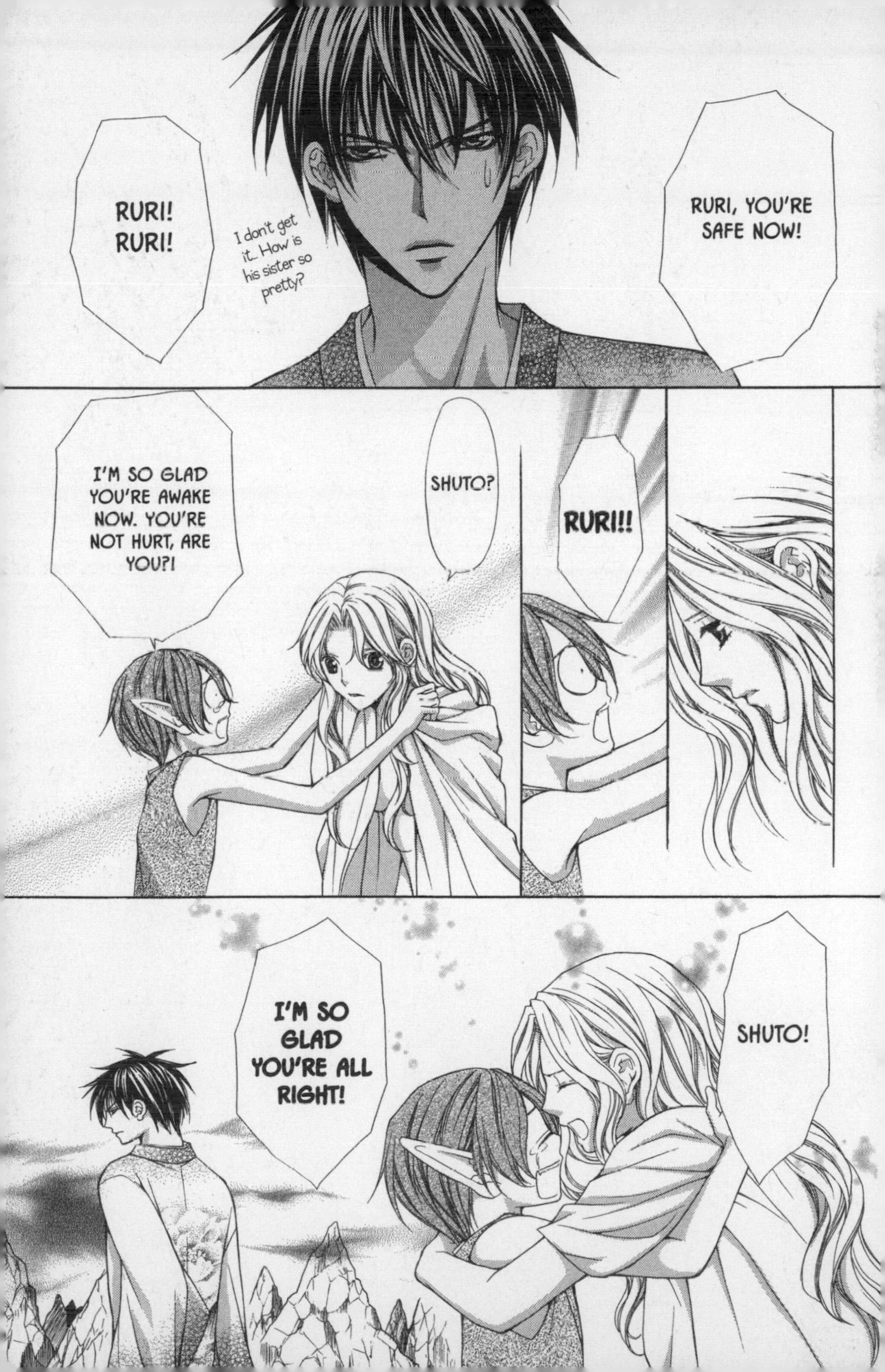
RURI, YOU'RE SAFE NOW!
RURI! RURI!
I don't get it.. How is his sister so pretty?
RURI!!
SHUTO?
I'M SO GLAD YOU'RE AWAKE NOW. YOU'RE NOT HURT, ARE YOU?!
SHUTO!
I'M SO GLAD YOU'RE ALL RIGHT!

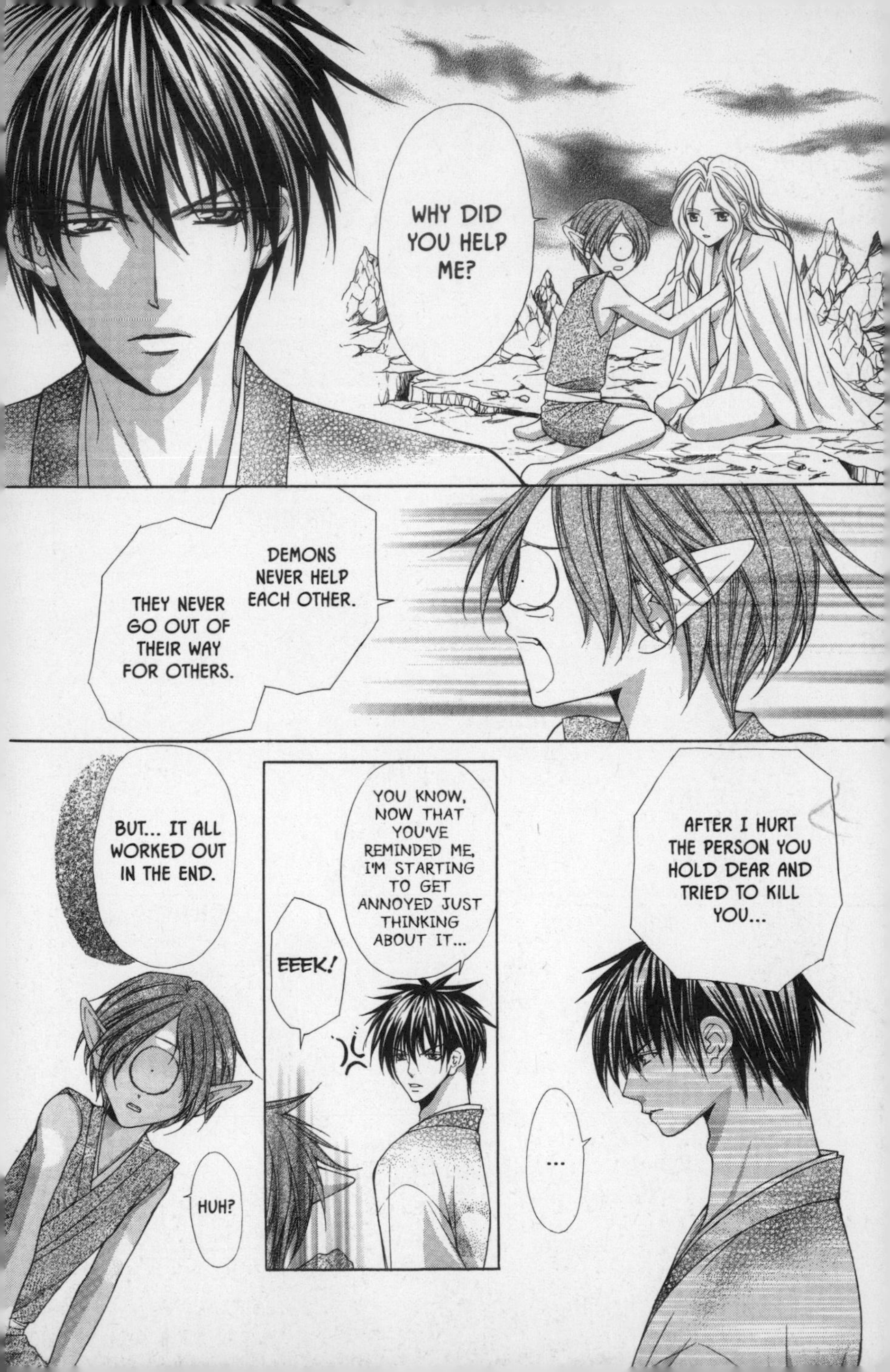
WHY DID YOU HELP ME?
DEMONS NEVER HELP EACH OTHER.
THEY NEVER GO OUT OF THEIR WAY FOR OTHERS.
AFTER I HURT THE PERSON YOU HOLD DEAR AND TRIED TO KILL YOU...
...
YOU KNOW, NOW THAT YOU'VE REMINDED ME, I'M STARTING TO GET ANNOYED JUST THINKING ABOUT IT...
EEEK!
BUT... IT ALL WORKED OUT IN THE END.
HUH?

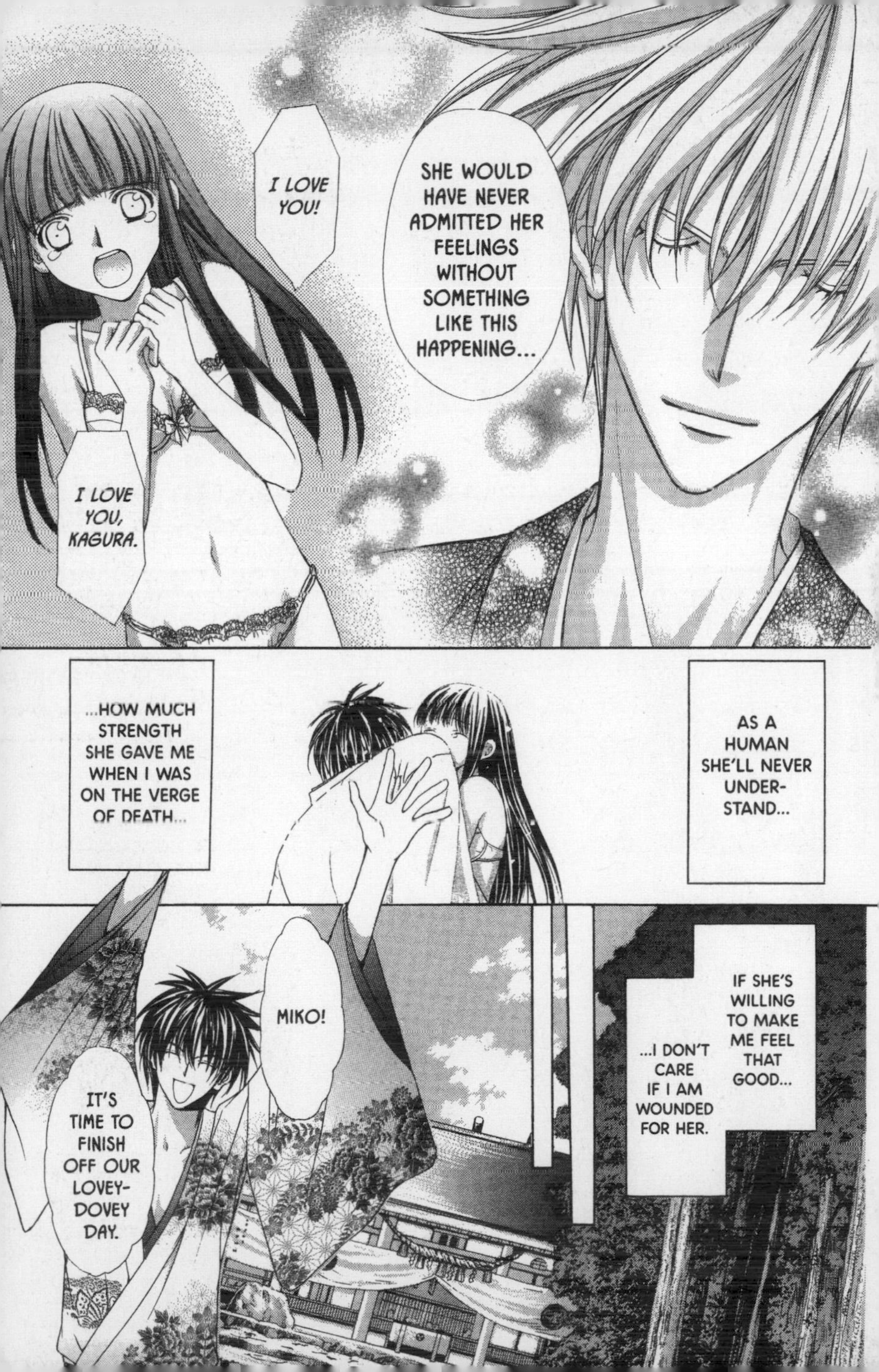
SHE WOULD HAVE NEVER ADMITTED HER FEELINGS WITHOUT SOMETHING LIKE THIS HAPPENING...
I LOVE YOU!
I LOVE YOU, KAGURA.
AS A HUMAN SHE'LL NEVER UNDER-STAND...
...HOW MUCH STRENGTH SHE GAVE ME WHEN I WAS ON THE VERGE OF DEATH...
IF SHE'S WILLING TO MAKE ME FEEL THAT GOOD...
...I DON'T CARE IF I AM WOUNDED FOR HER.
MIKO!
IT'S TIME TO FINISH OFF OUR LOVEY-DOVEY DAY.

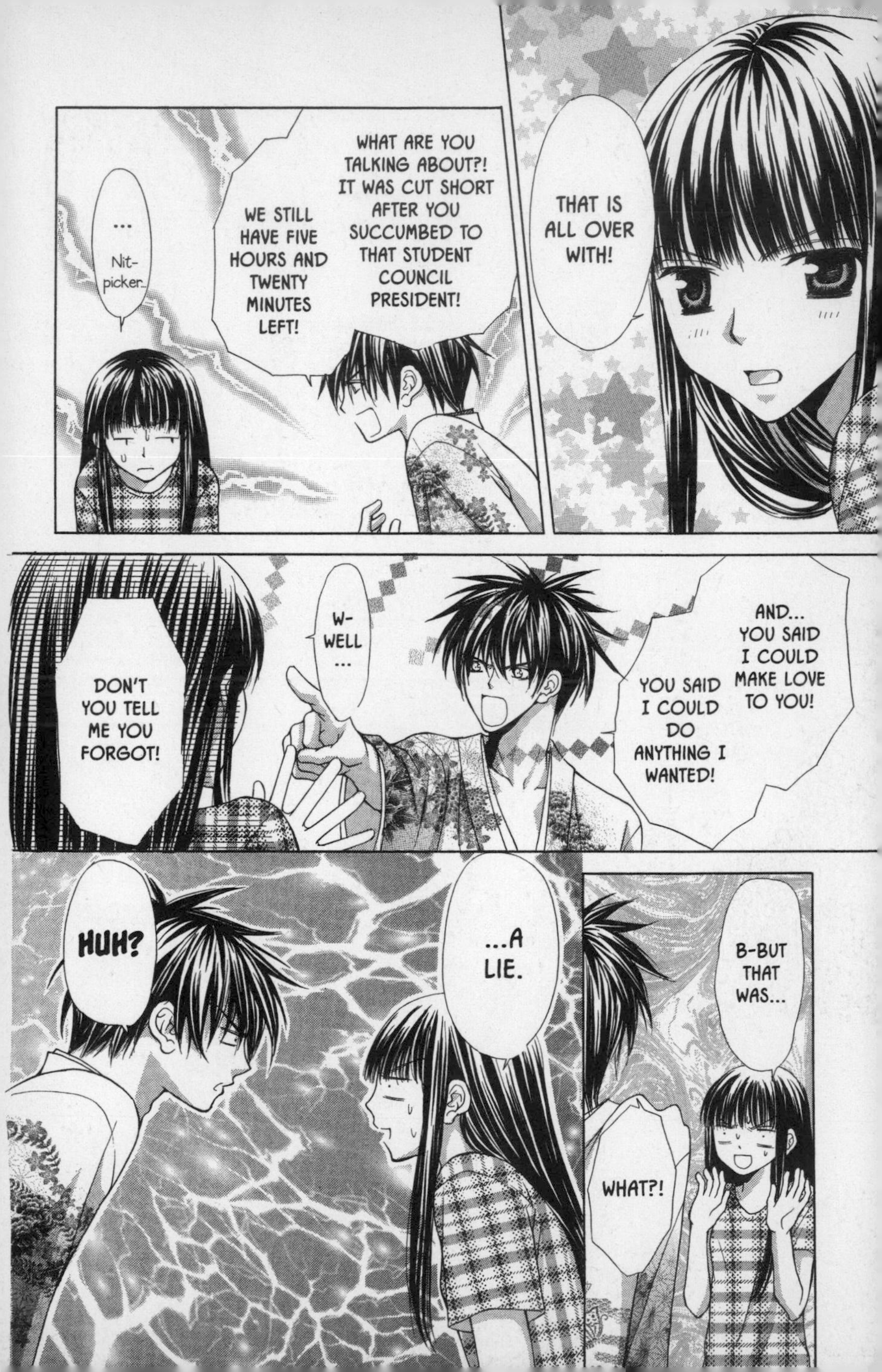
THAT IS ALL OVER WITH!
WHAT ARE YOU TALKING ABOUT?! IT WAS CUT SHORT AFTER YOU SUCCUMBED TO THAT STUDENT COUNCIL PRESIDENT!
WE STILL HAVE FIVE HOURS AND TWENTY MINUTES LEFT!
...
Nit-picker...
AND... YOU SAID I COULD MAKE LOVE TO YOU!
YOU SAID I COULD DO ANYTHING I WANTED!
W-WELL ...
DON'T YOU TELL ME YOU FORGOT!
B-BUT THAT WAS...
WHAT?!
...A LIE.
HUH?

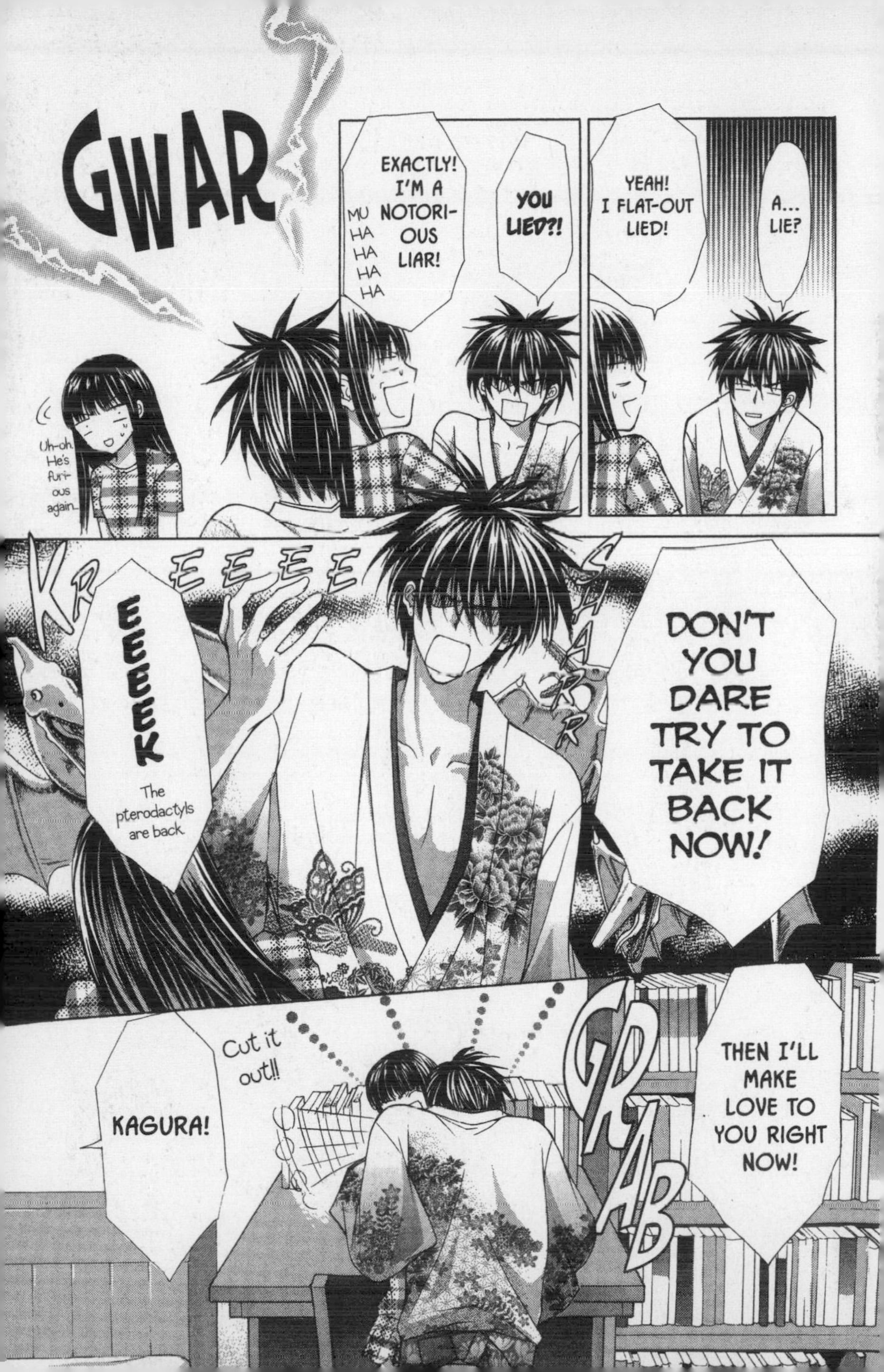
A... LIE?
YEAH! I FLAT-OUT LIED!
YOU LIED?!
EXACTLY! I'M A NOTORIOUS LIAR!
MU HA HA HA HA
GWAR
Uh-oh. He's furious again...
DON'T YOU DARE TRY TO TAKE IT BACK NOW!
SHAARRR
KREEEEE
EEEEEK
The pterodactyls are back.
THEN I'LL MAKE LOVE TO YOU RIGHT NOW!
GRAB
Cut it out!!
KAGURA!

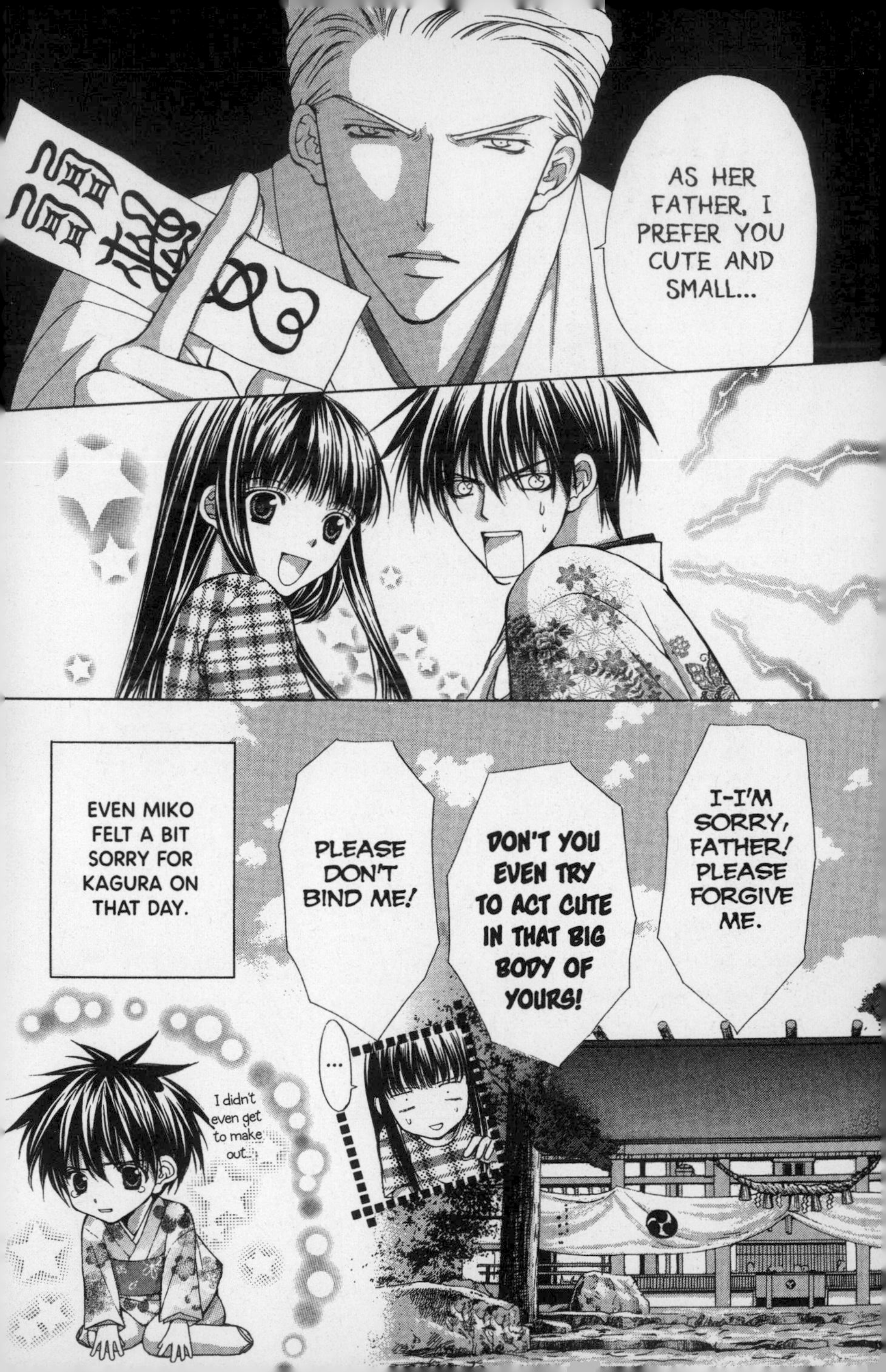
AS HER FATHER, I PREFER YOU CUTE AND SMALL...
I-I'M SORRY, FATHER! PLEASE FORGIVE ME.
DON'T YOU EVEN TRY TO ACT CUTE IN THAT BIG BODY OF YOURS!
PLEASE DON'T BIND ME!
EVEN MIKO FELT A BIT SORRY FOR KAGURA ON THAT DAY.
...
I didn't even get to make out...

About the Fox

This arc started with the idea of doing a story about a beautiful boy with fox ears who dies. In the beginning my editor was all for it, but when I showed the storyboard to him, he started to sympathize with the fox. "How could we stop the fox from dying?" he would ask. So I told him, "He's going to die. That's what I want to draw," to which he replied, "You're an ogre." (laugh)

The reason the fox has no name is because he is not a demon. He's a fox spirit who can transform.

The fox does die in the end, but being someone who loves *kemo-mimi otoko* (boys with cat, fox, or dog ears) more than anything else, I really enjoyed drawing him. I poured all my love into the fox, and it made Kagura look like the bad guy... (laugh)

The fox truly became a character everyone loved. I created this story because I wanted to draw that last page. I hope the fox will continue to have a place in your heart.

My Editor Who Loves Mr. Fox

WHILE TALKING ABOUT THE STORYBOARD
EDITOR
Do you really have to kill the fox?
Yes. That was my idea from the start...
We already talked about that, didn't we?
SHINJO
DEADLINE DAY
Killing off such a kind boy makes you an ogre.
EDITOR
I hate him! I hate Kagura!
...
SHINJO
FINAL SCRIPT COMPLETION PARTY
I'm still shocked about the fox dying. You'll never find such a kind boy. The other editors never thought he would end up dead. I knew about it, so I felt really bad. I understand the story is poignant because he dies in the end, but...
EDITOR
SHINJO
...
You're still talking about it...
NEW EDITOR TRANSITION
EDITOR
I still think about ways how I could have stopped you from killing the fox.
NEW EDITOR
EDITOR
SHINJO

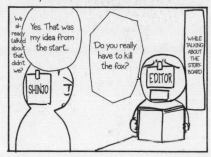

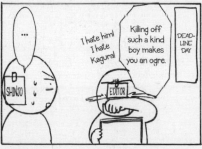

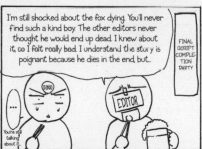

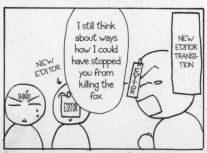

My editor really liked the fox!

About Shuto

This is a story I wanted to do ever since we decided to make *Demon Love Spell* into a series. It's more like a chapter than an entire story, I guess. For some reason I really wanted to draw a scene with Miko being controlled and stabbing Kagura. It was strange because it stayed in my mind. I thought this was about the right time to do it. In some ways, it was a test of Miko's love...or how honest she could be about her feelings. I create my own rules for this series. The series ran in the magazine with 120 pages for the first and second half. And the rule for this series is that little Kagura and big Kagura will appear at least once in each chapter. In other words, you will never see big Kagura continue to appear for all 60 pages. He will always be turned into little Kagura. (laugh) This isn't because little Kagura is more popular, but because I feel that big Kagura cannot exist without little Kagura and vice versa. But that is the difficult part, and I have a hard time creating the storyboard. I started to grow fond of Shuto when I was working on the second half, but since he was the person behind Kagura being stabbed, no one felt the same way I did... (laugh)

The hamster, little Kagura's partner (?) is popular too.

I actually don't have a name yet. I want you to come up with a name for me.

And so, I would like you to think of a name for the hamster. If that name is chosen, it will appear in *Demon Love Spell*!! (Obviously.)

Please send your reviews on to me too!

-Mayu Shinjo

Please!!

Volume 2 of *Demon Love Spell* starts with the second half of the fox story. Both my editor and I ended up empathizing with the fox. And it's so fun and exciting to draw boys with animal ears. I'd love to hear what you think about the story.

—Mayu Shinjo

MAYU SHINJO was born on January 26. She is a prolific writer of shojo manga, including the series *Sensual Phrase* and *Ai Ore!* Her hobbies are cars, shopping and taking baths. Shinjo likes The Prodigy, Nirvana, U2 and Masaharu Fukuyama.

Demon Love Spell

Vol. 2
Shojo Beat Edition

STORY AND ART BY Mayu Shinjo

Translation & Adaptation
Tetsuchiro Miyaki

Touch-up Art & Lettering
Inori Fukuda Trant

Design
Fawn Lau

Editor
Nancy Thistlethwaite

AYAKASHI KOI EMAKI © 2008 by Mayu Shinjo
All rights reserved.
First published in Japan in 2008 by SHUEISHA Inc., Tokyo.
English translation rights arranged by SHUEISHA Inc.

The rights of the author(s) of the work(s) in this publication to be
so identified have been asserted in accordance with the Copyright,
Designs and Patents Act 1988. A CIP catalogue record for this
book is available from the British Library.

Printed in the U.S.A.

Published by VIZ Media, LLC
P.O. Box 77010
San Francisco, CA 94107

10 9 8 7 6 5 4 3 2 1
First printing, March 2013

VIZ
MEDIA
www.viz.com

www.shojobeat.com

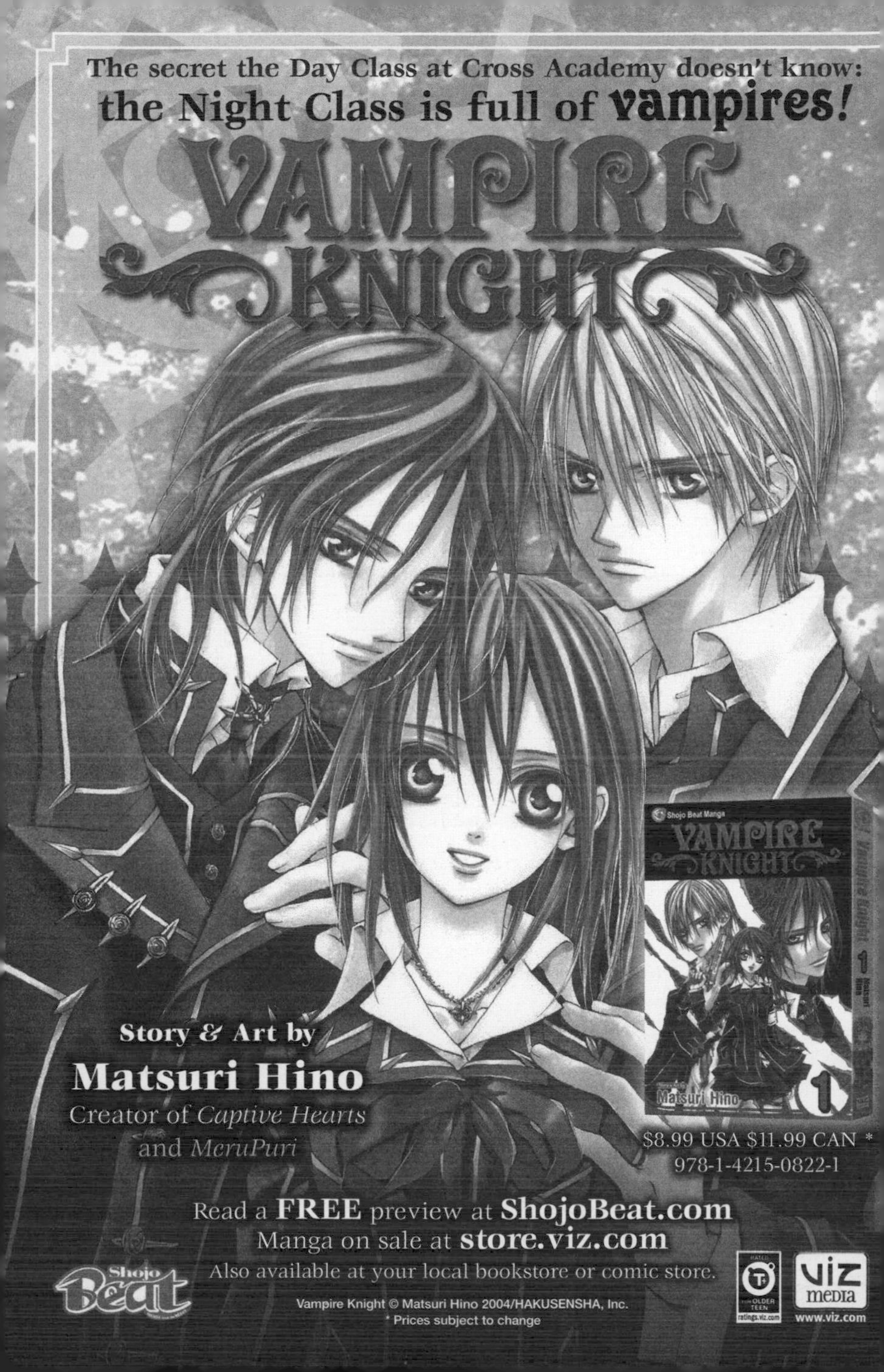
The secret the Day Class at Cross Academy doesn't know:
the Night Class is full of vampires!
VAMPIRE KNIGHT
Shojo Beat Manga
VAMPIRE KNIGHT
Matsuri Hino
1
Story & Art by
Matsuri Hino
Creator of Captive Hearts and MeruPuri
$8.99 USA $11.99 CAN *
978-1-4215-0822-1
Read a FREE preview at ShojoBeat.com
Manga on sale at store.viz.com
Also available at your local bookstore or comic store.
Shojo Beat
Vampire Knight © Matsuri Hino 2004/HAKUSENSHA, Inc.
* Prices subject to change
RATED T FOR OLDER TEEN ratings.viz.com
VIZ MEDIA
www.viz.com

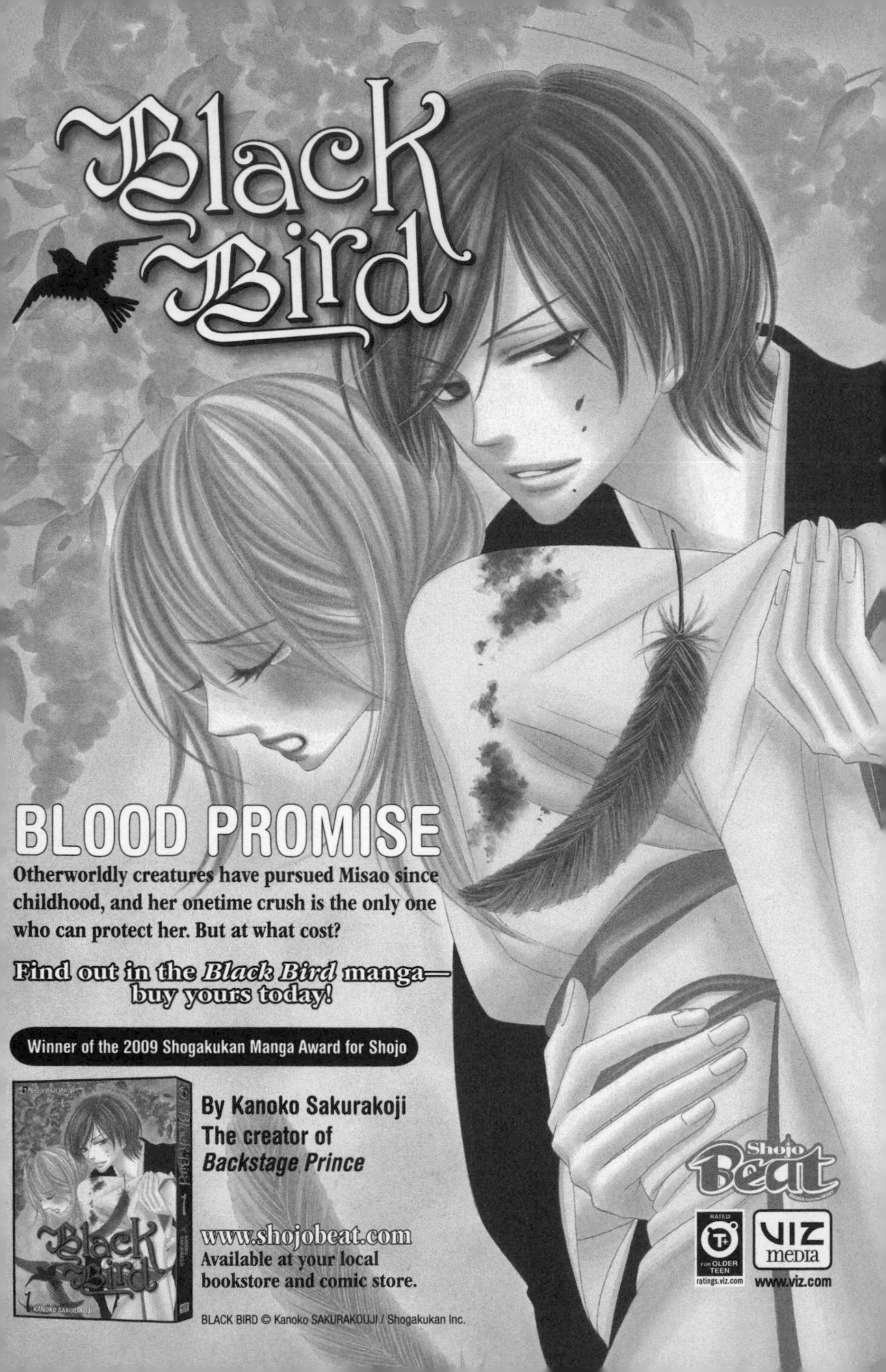
Black Bird
BLOOD PROMISE
Otherworldly creatures have pursued Misao since childhood, and her onetime crush is the only one who can protect her. But at what cost?
Find out in the Black Bird manga—buy yours today!
Winner of the 2009 Shogakukan Manga Award for Shojo
Black Bird
KANOKO SAKURAKOJI
By Kanoko Sakurakoji
The creator of
Backstage Prince
www.shojobeat.com
Available at your local bookstore and comic store.
BLACK BIRD © Kanoko SAKURAKOUJI / Shogakukan Inc.
Shojo Beat
RATED
T+
FOR OLDER TEEN
ratings.viz.com
VIZ media
www.viz.com

You may be reading the wrong way!

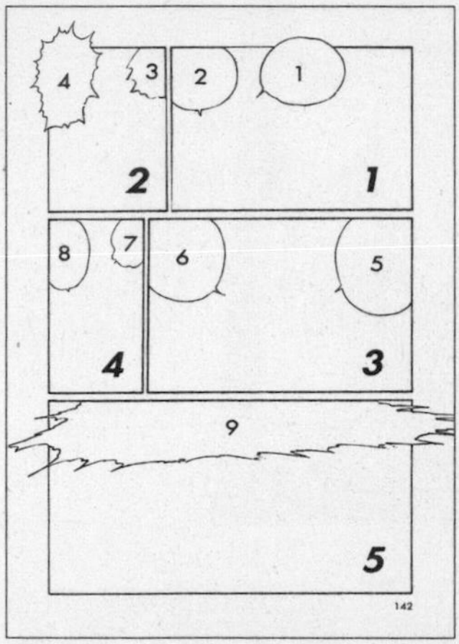
1
2
3
4
1
2
5
6
7
8
3
4
9
5
142

IT'S TRUE: In keeping with the original Japanese comic format, this book reads from right to left—so action, sound effects, and word balloons are completely reversed. This preserves the orientation of the original artwork—plus, it's fun! Check out the diagram shown here to get the hang of things, and then turn to the other side of the book to get started!

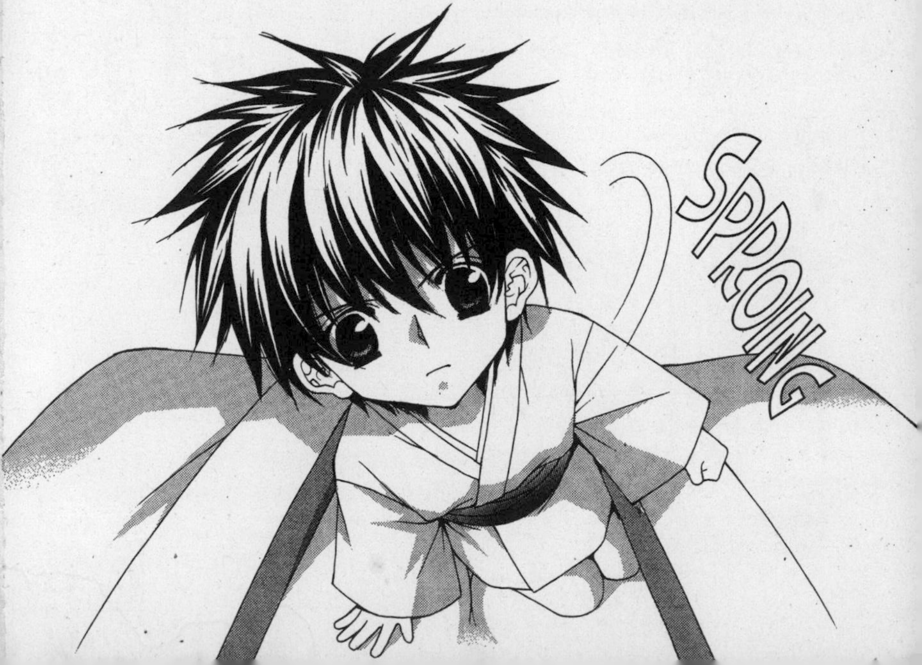
SPROING